HANDGUN

STOPPING

POWER

To our wives, Maryann and Cindy, who patiently tolerated autopsy photos on the dining room table, ordnance gelatin in the refrigerator, and bullets everywhere.

And to the memory of my mother, Rose Marshall.

HANDGUN STOPPING POWER

The Definitive Study

Evan P. Marshall

Edwin J. Sanow

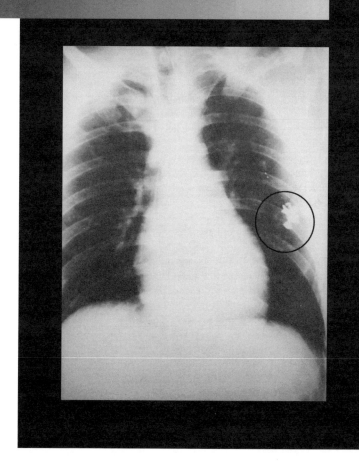

Paladin Press · Boulder, Colorado

Also by Evan P. Marshall and Edwin J. Sanow:

Handgun Stopping Power: The Video
Stopping Power: A Practical Analysis of the Latest Handgun Ammunition
Street Stoppers: The Latest Handgun Stopping Power Street Results

Handgun Stopping Power:
The Definitive Study
by Evan P. Marshall and Edwin J. Sanow

Copyright © 1992 by Evan P. Marshall and Edwin J. Sanow

ISBN 0-87364-653-3
Printed in the United States of America

Photographs by Evan P. Marshall, Edwin J. Sanow, Melissa Marshall,
and Tom Burczynski

Library of Congress Catalog Number: 91-50796

Published by Paladin Press, a division of
Paladin Enterprises, Inc.
Gunbarrel Tech Center
7077 Winchester Circle
Boulder, Colorado 80301 USA
+1.303.443.7250

Direct inquiries and/or orders to the above address.

Visit our Web site at www.paladin-press.com

CONTENTS

FOREWORD

In recent years, the pursuit of the perfect round of handgun ammunition has assumed a status in the police culture and the gun-owning public second only to the search for the Holy Grail! The quest has been every bit as impassioned and, unfortunately, every bit as successful. In magazine articles and press releases alike we are bombarded unremittingly by the siren song of the "magic bullet" salesman and the naive gun writer. They tell us of bad guys being flung into the air or exploding in a shower of sparks after being struck by one of their charmed slugs. Unfortunately, it's all just wishful thinking. There is, it seems, an inexhaustible supply of anecdotal narrative about bullet performance but very little credible data upon which we can really rely. As you will learn shortly, there are no "magic bullets" — there is no free lunch and there is no substitute for marksmanship. That is the central theme of this excellent work.

There is a great deal to know about ammunition, however. Once precision accuracy is achieved, we would like to know that the bullet we've selected will do its job too. Fortunately, there is now a body of credible evidence, which, if studied carefully, will go a long way toward selecting the best possible ammunition for the task at hand.

Beware! There are poor choices. There is ammunition commercially available which will constantly turn in inadequate performance in most defensive situations. It must be avoided. The selection criteria are legion, and it is essential that they be contemplated in the correct order.

My colleagues, Evan Marshall and Ed Sanow, have researched this subject exhaustively. They have gathered information from every source available, not the least of which is their own extensive personal experiences. What you are about to read is the most complete and credible digest of the factual information on this subject that has ever been assembled. It is correctly organized and presented in a dignified but very entertaining way.

You will find that Ev and Ed don't pontificate and don't insult your intelligence by insisting that they are the possessors of the ultimate truth. They know, as I do, that there are still many things that we don't understand about the human body and psyche. They simply lay out the facts before you in as intelligent and logical a way as I have ever read. Ultimate decisions with regard to selection of equipment for yourself or your crew are left up to you.

I have been close friends with Ev and Ed for some time. We have also been colleagues, fellow instructors, and brother police officers for quite some time. They know their business. They are the best of the best, and when they talk, I listen.

John S. Farnam
Boulder, CO

ACKNOWLEDGMENTS

No project of this magnitude could have been completed successfully without the help of a number of people. The persons listed below assisted, supported, and often provided critical analysis of the authors' efforts:

Shep Kelly, Mike Bussard, Alan Newcombe, Bob Kramer, Ron Ives, and Mike Larson of Federal Cartridge Corporation

Dick Dietz, Bill Forson, and Ed Herring III of Remington Arms Company

Don Emde, Henry Halverson, Mike Jordan, Rod Van Wyk, and Johnny Falk of Winchester-Olin Corporation

Massad Ayoob, Lethal Force Institute

John Farnam, Defense Training

Leroy Thompson, CQB (Close Quarters Battle) Training

Colonel Robert Young, USMC

Peter Pi, Cor-Bon Ammunition

John Klein, Sage International

John Meyer, Phil Singleton, and Charlie Sunderlin of Heckler & Koch

Brian Felter, Beretta Arms

Dr. Thomas Mijares, S.W. Texas State University

Dr. Dan Kennedy, University of Detroit

Dr. Carroll Peters, University of Tennessee

Inspector Gerald Solai, Commanding Officer, Special Response Team, Detroit Police Department (Ret)

Jeff Hopkins, Central Florida Criminal Justice Institute

Dr. Joseph Macri, Oakland Community College

Sgt. Dave Spaulding, Montgomery County Sheriff

Cpl. James Horan, Howard County Sheriff

Sgt. Dennis Tueller, Salt Lake City Police

Sgt. Al Kulavitz, Cook County Sheriff

Richard Davis, Second Chance Body Armor

Joe Zambone, MagSafe Ammo

Rob Lewis, Power Plus Ammo

O. Richard Bauman and Thomas Burczynski, Hydra-Shok Corp.

James Patton, (former) Sheriff, Benton County, IN

Boston L. Pritchett, Sheriff, Benton County, IN

C. Kurt Canon, Glaser Safety Slug Inc.

Allan Jones, CCI-Speer/Blount, Inc.

Judy Hamilton, J's Custom Printing

Larry Fletcher, Southwestern Institute of Forensic Sciences

Paul Dougherty, San Mateo Sheriff's Department

Dr. Vincent DiMaio, Medical Examiner, Bexar County, TX

Colonel Martin Fackler, U.S. Army Wound Ballistics Lab

Rob Reiber, Stan Isa, PMC-Eldorado Cartridge

Dr. Daniel Frank, NIJ Law Enforcement Standards Lab

Anthony Gregory, Tactical Training Associates

Dr. John Pless and Dr. Dean Hawley, Marion County, IN, Coroner's Office

Jim Reinholt, Reinholt Firearms

Tony Trezza, Hi-Vel, Inc.

Clarence Reker, Taracorp

Gene Wolberg, San Diego Police Crime Lab

Stan Robinson, Cook County Sheriff's Department

Steve Bowling, Hobart, IN

Dennis Martin, CQB Services (England)

David Scott-Donlin, CQB Training

Gary Weistrand, Kennedy Space Center

John Wiseman, 22nd SAS (retired)

Jan Libourel, *Handguns* magazine (Petersen Publications)

Denny Hansen, *S.W.A.T.* magazine

Virginia Commander and Harry Kane, *Combat Handguns* magazine (Harris Publications)

Emmanuel Kapelsohn, Peregrine Corporation

Sgt. Pete Dordal, former instructor, USMC Scout Sniper School

Capt. Steve Walsh, USMC

Officer Frank Repass, Orlando Police

Warren Buttler, FAA Security

Marcus Wynne, FAA Security

Sid Swanson, Pathcor Corporation

Ken Hackathorn, Marietta, Ohio

Sgts. Roy McGruder, Dale Johnston, Bob Wilson, Bernard Farr, David Pouch, and Officer Paul Dragen of the Detroit Police Department Crime Laboratory

Vince O'Neill, Oklahoma City, OK

Ed Lovette, Williamsburg, VA

Dr. Dennis Tobin, Victoria, Texas

Renee Smeets, Brussels

Col. Rex Applegate

John Jacobs, FLETC

Dr. Ed Hancock, Mesa, AZ

Walt Farr, Los Angeles Sheriff's Dept.

Alex Luvall, Second Deputy Chief, Detroit PD

Sgts. Don Drake, Joe Solomon, and Norm Sieloff, Detroit PD

Joseph Piersante, Dept. of Public Safety, University of Michigan

Dean Speir, Westhampton Beach, NY

Marty Hayes, Seattle, WA

Scott Blacklidge, New Mexico Dept. of Public Safety

Joe Viviano, U.S. Secret Service

Chuck Karwan

In addition, there are individuals whose contributions were extremely valuable but who cannot be identified by name for obvious reasons. They belong to the following organizations, and we want them to know we appreciate the help they gave at great personal risk:

Federal Bureau of Investigation

FBI Hostage Rescue Team

SEAL Team 5

SEAL Team 6

Marine Corps Force Recon

GSG 9

British Royal Marines

Delta Force

Special Boat Squadron

DEA Clandestine Lab Enforcement Teams

Secret Service CAT (Counterassault Team) Team

Illinois State Police

Medical Examiners personnel in a variety of cities throughout the United States and several foreign countries

Harvard Medical School

U.S. Army-Mott Lake

Crane Laboratory

U.S. Army Rangers

Several veterans of Operations URGENT FURY, JUST CAUSE, and DESERT STORM

Defense Intelligence Agency (DIA)

Naval Investigative Service

Maryland State Police

Detroit Homicide

Wayne State University Medical School

Wayne County Morgue

University of California Medical School

Los Angeles PD SWAT

LASO Special Enforcement Bureau

California Highway Patrol

New Jersey State Police

Michigan State Police

Las Vegas Metro PD

Washington, D.C., PD

San Francisco PD

Los Angeles PD Crime Laboratory

Dallas PD

New Orleans PD

Metro Dade SWAT

Atlanta PD

Georgia Bureau of Investigation

Federal Law Enforcement Training Center (FLETC)

U.S. Postal Inspectors

New York PD Emergency Services Unit

Drug Enforcement Administration, Miami

U.S. Border Patrol

Utah Highway Patrol

University of Michigan Medical School

Chicago PD Narcotics

Long Beach PD

Phoenix PD

Alaska Highway Patrol

Pasadena PD

Newark PD

Madison PD

Texas DPS

Seattle PD

St. Louis PD

Oklahoma City PD

Jackson PD

Houston PD

Boston PD

University of Texas Medical School

Metro Dade Homicide

Winston-Salem PD

Austin PD

San Diego PD

Macon PD

State Department Security

INTRODUCTION

The goal of this book is really quite straightforward: to provide readers with reliable information that will assist good guys and gals in choosing handgun ammunition for law enforcement and personal survival use. Attempting to accomplish this goal successfully has been extremely difficult.

For years we have been inundated with theories that have attempted to assist us in choosing proper loads. While the creators of these theories had good intentions, there was generally no correlation between such speculation and how various handgun loads worked in actual shootings. As a twenty-year veteran of the Detroit Police Department, whose assignments included Crime Scene Investigation and Homicide, I discovered several years ago that there were critical differences between how bullets *should* perform according to the various theories and how they *were* performing in actual shootings.

I spent 15 + years collecting data on actual shootings. It was a slow and difficult process that was accomplished only through a significant investment of personal funds and time.

Ed Sanow is well known for his common sense and scientific approach to the study of wound ballistics. Unlike many researchers in the wound ballistic field, Sanow understands both the value and limitations of artificial test mediums. He realizes that test medium results combined with confirmed street results can give us an indicator of how loads will probably work on the street. Ed's commitment to thoroughness and truth has been critical to the success of this study.

There has been, of course, a number of criticisms of this work. Some complain that the sample is too small. There is certainly some validity to this, yet those same people who have been so critical have not been willing to help increase the data base. Other complaints, however, have been either irrelevant or dishonest. Those who attempt to dismiss the relevance of this study by talking about flipping coins and/or mathematical probability are not only begging the question but are silly. We are discussing reality, and mathematical probability and theoretical arguments are often specious at best.

When I sat on the FBI's Wound Ballistic Panel in the fall of 1987, one of its more distinguished members pointed out that virtually everyone on the panel was highly upset because a mere cop had managed to develop the idea of looking at actual shootings to understand how handgun ammunition really worked. It is unfortunate that so many talented people are more concerned about their egos and reputations than with providing answers on this critical subject. Such attitudes have resulted in many folks spending more time criticizing the attempt to use actual shooting data instead of attempting to gain information.

This work is an attempt to provide information based on actual shooting results. The authors have studied all the wound ballistics theories available and found that they offered little, if any, correlation with what was happening on the street.

It is extremely important, however, that readers understand that correct bullet placement is absolutely critical. While the selection of the best load in a particular caliber is important, it doesn't negate the importance of appropriate tactics and enhanced marksmanship skills.

Here, then, are the results of a decade and a half of research into the incredibly complex subject of wound ballistics. It has been a work of love, and it is clear evidence of our concern for the survival of good guys and gals in a dangerous world.

Readers with questions, comments, criticisms, or additional shooting data can contact the authors in care of the publisher.

A Federal .45 Auto 230-grain Hydra-Shok fully expanded in two inches of gelatin. (Photo courtesy of Tom Burczynski.)

The Remington .38 Special +P 95-grain S-JHP shown in this X ray is fully expanded. The light, fast hollowpoint struck at an angle and penetrated cross-torso, incapacitating the officer's attacker.

CHAPTER 1

MECHANISMS OF COLLAPSE

Stopping power is an illusion.

It is important to start a book on handgun stopping power with that in mind. There are no magic bullets. There are no manstopping calibers. There is no such thing as one-shot stopping power.

Everyone reading this book will make more survival-oriented decisions if they expect their bullet to have little, if any, effect on the target. Instead they will fire from behind cover or get behind cover as soon as possible. They will fire numerous times. They will be more precise in their fire. They will keep their gun pointed at the target until they are absolutely sure the action is finished.

Sometimes the bullet will produce the sought after "instant" effect, and the person will collapse in 1 to 2 seconds. However, there is no predictable and reliable medical reason for a person to fall and become "instantly incapacitated." With the exception of a wound to the brain stem, handgun bullets cannot be depended upon to take effect that fast.

Sometimes the bullet will produce no visible effect at all. It may take 30 to 90 seconds or even longer for the person to fall. This generally is far too long for the urgent time frame of most gunfights.

All this assumes reasonable shot placement, i.e., somewhere in the head, neck, or torso. We are not even talking of shots that miss, that are stopped short by an obstacle or soft armor, or that engage an extremity or other less significant part of the body. Overall, even if shot placement is good and vital tissue is damaged, it is reasonable to expect the person to remain mobile, active, and hostile for 10 to 15 seconds after the shot. You must make plans for your survival during that period of time.

Throughout this book, incapacitation will be defined as the inability to perform hostile acts, whether unarmed or armed with a firearm or contact weapon. The shooting victim must be unable to continue hostile acts toward anyone, even if determined to do so. Pain inflicted on the person, even extreme pain, should never be confused with incapacitation. Neither does the simple act of falling to the ground upon bullet impact constitute incapacitation.

Incapacitation has a great deal to do with exactly what tissue in the body was engaged by the bullet. Strangely, it sometimes is not related to the actual severity of the wound. Neither is incapacitation, otherwise known as "stopping power," necessarily related to killing power. A person can receive a lethal injury and remain hostile for a relatively long period of time. Likewise, a person can receive a nonlethal injury and fall to the ground, inert, relatively quickly.

All of these precautionary statements will make more sense when we review what really happens when a bullet meets a man. Why does a person collapse when he is shot? Why does a person *not* collapse when he is shot, even when bullet placement is good? What mechanism of injury does the bullet use to force a collapse?

Let's first look at the medical reasons why a person falls down when shot. These clear and well-accepted reasons include the interruption of oxygen-carrying blood to the brain, the intervention of the bullet with the brain and central nervous system, and the physical breakage of the bones or skeletal support structure.

Yet these reasons explain only a portion of what we see on the street. Other reasons have been offered to fill this gap, to explain what hard medical logic cannot. These include the psychological and psychosomatic reactions to being shot, and the physiological reaction to the body's organs being shoved around by the temporary cavity rather than being hit by the bullet. Admittedly, these explanations are less predictable, less well defined, and less well substantiated.

First, let's look at blood flow. Damage to the vascular system is one of the most destructive things a bullet can do. Ideal damage is caused when a bullet tears a hole in or completely severs a blood vessel. A large hole in the vessel is probably better because severed vessels tend to contract, which, depending on vessel size, reduces or stops bleeding. A bruise to the vessel that becomes a complication later does not count — we are only interested in what happens in the next few seconds, not days.

Blood vessels can be damaged by two means. One is the direct crushing action of the bullet. The larger the caliber, referring to the bullet's expanded diameter, or the greater number of fragments from the bullet, the larger the permanent crush cavity.

Blood vessels can also be damaged by a less direct method. High-energy bullets that produce large temporary cavities can stretch the vessel enough to rupture it. This is pretty rare, and it is unreliable for most parts of the human body. However, if the vessel is trapped by a ligament or by other tissue or if it is at a branching point, the vessel can be broken open just by the violent movement of tissue.

The liver is one place where this occurrence is highly likely. In the liver, dense pulpy tissue surrounds a large number of big veins and arteries. Damage to the liver by a powerful bullet generally produces profuse bleeding. The cranial vault is another place where you can count on the temporary cavity to do real damage. Because the skull is closed and rigid, any expanding stretch cavity will exert all its force on the brain. A large enough stretch cavity will explosively shatter the bones of the skull.

Damaging vessels via the temporary stretch cavity is something we can only expect from the best magnum rounds, close-range shotgun blasts, and high-power rifle loads. With most handgun loads and longer-range shotgun blasts, the stretch from the temporary cavity does not exceed the elastic limits of the tissue, and little damage is done outside the bullet path.

While blood loss, both internal and external, is the most common cause of incapacitation, it is also very time consuming. Police files are full of cases where the person received a lethal injury to the vascular system and still remained active and hostile for a dangerously long period of time.

In central Indiana, a large knife-wielding person advanced on two police officers. The attacker was double tapped with .357 Magnums loaded with 125-grain JHP and 160-grain SWC ammo. The effect was to reduce the charge to a walk. Two more double taps caused the person to pause and sit down. The heart was hit numerous times but the body was slow to respond.

Hostile actions and consciousness are affected by oxygen supply to the brain. Yet even when the blood supply to the brain is totally cut off, a person can still function for 10 seconds or more before collapsing — and few gunshot wounds *totally* cut off the blood supply. *This 10 seconds can be considered a minimum.* With 5 to 8 seconds of vision and neural function to the arms, a lot of return fire can be generated.

A recent case where blood loss was the cause of collapse involved a machete-wielding felon who charged a police officer on a building search. The officer fired twice with a .38 Special from a range of less than 3 feet. One bullet severed the pulmonary artery and the other perforated the heart. With the exception of a shot to the brian, spinal cord, aorta, or carotids, this is just about the best shot placement.

The problem was that the attacker was barely stunned and had enough power to continue the chase into an adjacent room. After a few steps the felon collapsed, yet he still swung the machete at another officer attempting to disarm him. Only a burst of M16 fire from a SWAT team member stopped the attack.

The process of bleeding until the brain can no longer control motor functions is an extremely long one. Yet this is the stopping-power mechanism you are most likely to be depending on. If you do end up depending on blood loss to take out your attacker, you must lower your expectations of how fast your bullet will have its effect. In the above example, the initial volley produced lethal injuries to a major organ and blood vessel, yet a considerable amount of time elapsed and a great deal of physical activity was possible before the injuries took effect.

The fastest and most reliable way to stop a person is to get the bullet into the cranial vault, inside the skull. However this shot has problems, too. While most gunshot wounds to the head produce an instantaneous result, the amount of physical activity possible after the wound can vary widely, depending primarily on the area of the skull penetrated and the power of the bullet.

The cranial vault is the one place in the body where we can get reliable and predictable results *if* high-power or expanding bullets are used. Nearly any rifle or potent handgun bullet striking anywhere inside the upper skull will have an immediate effect. Hydraulic pressure will be generated inside the closed bone structure by a good-sized temporary cavity. This will be equally distributed to both less critical and more critical areas of the brain and will most likely fracture skull bones from the internal pressure.

With lower-velocity (under 1,000 fps) or nonexpanding bullets that do not produce sizable temporary cavities, the result can be very different. The bullet may need to hit the brain stem or lower brain for a reliable result. Numerous cases have been documented where a person had been shot in the head or brain and was physically active for quite some time because a less critical part of the brain was struck with a lower-power load.

Most bullet wounds to the brain involve the upper brain. This is called the cerebrum and it accounts for seven-eighths of the brain. Prolonged survival and various degrees of physical activity are possible with these wounds. It's not necessarily probable but certainly possible. With lower-power loads, therefore, the brain stem or the cerebellum at the center and rear base of the brain should be engaged. These vital areas lie on a plane formed by the two ear canals and the nose.

Lower-power loads have two disadvantages in terms of instantly stopping a person with a shot to the head. First, they need to hit the small brain stem for the same degree of success as higher-power bullets. Second, they are more easily stopped or deflected by the bony vault surrounding the brain. In any event, be aware that the person can be instantly stopped, simply disoriented, or even completely unaffected.

In terms of instant effect, the most insidious kind of bullet performance is when the bullet strikes and fractures a support bone, causing the person to be "knocked down." It is entirely possible for handgun bullets to break a bone in the leg or hip and physically cause the person to fall because the bullet has taken away his column support.

Yet even though he appears to have been "instantly stopped" by the bullet, it is very unlikely that he has been incapacitated. He can still fire a gun or slice with a knife. The only thing he can't do is walk.

Such was the recent case where a felon was shot just below the kneecap with a 9mm Glaser Safety Slug. The physical damage to the joint was enormous — the knee was pulp.

According to the reports, the felon fell instantly. The officer felt that his center torso point of aim took the man down. The fact was that the shot was off. The felon was still very able and willing to fire his shotgun. He was far from being incapacitated even though his reaction to the bullet indicated he was so. *Knocked down* does not mean *knocked out*. The felon was finally taken out with six torso shots from a .38 Special.

There are some ways that skeletal failure could possibly render a felon harmless, though they are not probable. One, he could be knocked unconscious by the fall if it was hard enough or if his head struck an object on the way down. Unlikely, but possible.

Two, the felon could be incapacitated if the bones in the hand or arm using the weapon were shattered. Of course, the other hand could come around to pick up the weapon. His ability to return fire would be limited, but the point is he could return fire.

Third, while collapsing, a sharp broken bone could cut nerves, tendons, muscle bundles, and blood vessels. So could secondary missiles of bone and lead that can be propelled away from the bone by the bullet. This mechanism of stopping power, however, is not skeletal damage — it is blood loss or nerve loss.

A bullet breaking bones is strictly mechanical. Even if you see an instant collapse, it does not mean the attack is stopped, especially if the victim is using a firearm. As a general rule, broken bones cannot be trusted to stop an attack. The wounded person can respond in a lethal way for literally hours. Be cautious about any instant collapse.

Once we leave the mechanisms of blood loss and central nervous system loss, we enter a very dangerous zone of "maybes."

Many theories have been put forth as to why a person will collapse and apparently be incapacitated when the injury was not severe enough to reliably down a person, such as shots that hit mere skin or muscle or that result in organ damage that does not produce excessive blood loss. This includes all gut shots and most shots to the extremities. Let's state for the record that no one writing in professional or popular literature knows for sure what causes people to collapse under these circumstances. Further, these are not reliable or dependable ways to stop an attack.

Some theories are psychological in nature. For example, for all of our lives we have watched people like John Wayne and Don Johnson drop people instantly with pistol fire. The stimulus or cause is the pistol bullet hitting the bad guy. The response or effect is an instantly fallen and inert bad guy. It even happens to good guys now and then.

It has been postulated that through the years of watching this stimulus and response, some people have brainwashed themselves at the subconscious level to fall down and play dead after being hit with a bullet. Hit *anywhere* with a bullet. Sometimes only fired at. There probably is something to this acquired, psychosomatic response.

This is, in essence, modern-day voodoo. We have been conditioned that gunfire kills instantly or at the very least causes people to fall. If the felon is hit and if he has been conditioned to fall, guess what? He will fall, totally incapacitated, and in some cases even *die* from a nonlethal injury, just like a pin in a voodoo doll can really kill.

A case illustrating this point occurred during a robbery attempt at a northern Illinois fast-food restaurant. A big off-duty police officer confronted a robber armed with a .22-caliber rifle. The robber fired his rifle and the officer felt a hot stinging sensation.

The officer yelled, grabbed the sharp pain in his stomach, and fell backward to the ground. As he fell, he returned fire and struck the felon four times. When the officer stood up and searched for his own injuries, he found none. Yet he had felt real pain and was forced to the ground. It can happen to anyone.

Voodoo, better than anything else, may explain why a person shot in the leg with a handgun bullet could fall over and be rendered totally harmless despite the fact that his blood supply, brain activity, nerve connections, and bone and muscle integrity would allow him to remain standing and return fire. However, since this is an acquired mental precondition, it is extremely dangerous to think that all of your opponents will react in a similar manner.

Another mechanism of collapse that has received a lot of attention lately is the effect of the temporary stretch cavity on the central nervous system. Dr. Dennis Tobin, a Victoria, Texas, neurologist, offers this explanation of incapacitating neural shock:

The lower part of the brain stem contains an area called the reticular activating system which controls consciousness. This can be interrupted structurally by trauma, that is, direct bullet contact or cranial pressure resulting from a temporary cavity in the head, or it can be interrupted physiologically by an intense emotional or pain stimulus.

Certain visceral pain receptors such as from an acutely ruptured abdominal organ like the liver, spleen, and kidneys can send pain impulses to the brain stem indicating a severe or overwhelming body injury. This reticular activating system can produce a functional "shutting down" of this system and result in loss of consciousness within 1 to 2 seconds.

This immediate shutdown can occur even from intense emotional fear or severe *perceived* pain. However, it can be lost when the felon is on drugs such as PCP or heroin and explains so many failures to stop.

This concept of neural shock explains many of the variable results we see with shootings. Some people have tremendous mental conditioning or high pain thresholds and therefore may be immune to neural shock. They may also be less susceptible as a result of alcohol or drug effects or a psychotic state. These people go down with only a direct head shot or due to loss of blood.

The abdomen seems to be especially sensitive to visceral or subconscious pain. Same for the kidney areas. This confirms reports from knife fighters, where a stab to the nonvital stomach area seems to have a much greater effect than a stab to the more vital lung or upper chest area. Neural shock also offers a plausible medical reason why a felon will almost instantly collapse when shot in the liver, even though the blood loss from liver damage will normally allow him to continue the attack for another 30 to 90 seconds.

A perfect example of an aggressive person collapsing far sooner than can be explained by blood loss, nerve loss, or bone breakage comes from a police-action shooting in Illinois. This account was documented in the popular press by police researcher and legal expert Massad Ayoob.

An Illinois State Trooper crouched behind his squad car for cover was under fire from a felon firing an autoloading 20-gauge shotgun. Near the end of the firefight, the felon charged the trooper. Before the felon could outflank his cover, the trooper fired and hit the felon with one 9mm bullet.

At that time the Illinois State Police load was a Federal 95-grain dish-nose softpoint with a muzzle velocity of 1,400 fps. The bullet struck the felon in the right mid-torso, disintegrating the liver and dropping the charging, would-be cop killer face forward onto the pavement.

No support bones were broken. No major nerves were severed. The rate of blood loss, even from the vascular liver, would have allowed the felon to easily close the 50-foot gap between himself and the trooper, who he thought was out of ammo. Instead, the felon was nearly instantly forced to the ground by some other mechanism of collapse. That mechanism was the overloading effect of a large and properly placed temporary stretch cavity.

Despite the variables, there are level-headed professional people who firmly believe that this temporary cavity-induced neural shock exists. The effects can be observed, if not always positively explained. They maintain that the inability to completely explain the effect beyond all doubt does not deny its presence. Naturally, the reliability of this mechanism of collapse is something each person must decide for himself.

As you analyze shooting results and bullet performance, keep these mechanisms of collapse in mind. Ask yourself, what good reason did the bullet give for the body to collapse?

Bullet effectiveness can be extremely slow even when the bullet perforates the heart, collapses both lungs, or cuts open the aorta and vena cava. Imagine how slow bullet effectiveness can be if vital organs like these escape its damage. A person can be shot eleven times with a 9mm, as in a recent Texas episode, but if no vital tissue is damaged, the person can remain quite active and aggressive for an astonishing period of time. If the bullet penetrated deep enough and expanded (if it was so designed), it did its part. We cannot logically blame poor stopping power on the bullet or caliber when the real culprit was poor shot placement.

CHAPTER 2

A NEUROLOGIST'S VIEW OF "STOPPING POWER"

Dr. Dennis Tobin is a medical doctor specializing in neurology, the science and medicine of the human nervous system. He is an avid handgunner and rifleman and is well versed in all firearms. He has been affiliated with law enforcement as a reserve deputy sheriff and has put in a lot of time in squad cars. His training and experience give him an insight into the police shooting scenario that is unique among medical doctors. Here is what he has to say on the subject.

• • • • •

Why do bullets sometimes incapacitate victims in 1 to 2 seconds with buckling legs or actual loss of consciousness?

Loss of consciousness can be caused by cardiac standstill, when the heart is instantly ruptured by bullet impact. Yet we know a person may remain conscious for 10 to 12 seconds *after* the heart is destroyed. Why do some people fall immediately after being shot, while others high on PCP or heroin seem impervious to sudden incapacitation and only drop from actual blood loss or a shot to the spine or head? The answer lies in understanding the part of the brain controlling both consciousness and extensor support of the leg muscles.

The brain stem contains an area called the reticular activating system (RAS). The RAS can be affected indirectly by impulses arising elsewhere in the body such as pain sensations from viscera transmitted up-

ward to the brain. Loss of body support with loss of consciousness can occur if certain areas of the brain stem are stimulated by pain impulses, which weakens the leg extensor muscles that support the body. Drugs like PCP and heroin may block the effect of incoming pain impulses in these areas. This explains why felons on PCP must be shot multiple times over a long period of time to cause blackout from insufficient blood volume to the brain (circulatory shock) or from actual head or spinal cord shots.

As a neurologist active in law enforcement, I have attended numerous meetings for police and have seen films of actual shootings. I have spoken with many officers who report that often, after the subject has been hit by 1 or 2 rounds, almost immediately (i.e., less than 2 seconds) his legs buckle and he falls to the ground. He is often, but not always, *unconscious*.

In observing films of actual shootings, I was struck by how often the person would almost instantly lose consciousness and fall to the ground and either remain unconscious or seem to come around after a few seconds. These people were not shot in the head or spinal cord, causing loss of leg function. And yet they fell immediately. I wondered about the neurologic mechanism for this sudden loss of consciousness, as it is at the very heart of what "stopping power" is about.

It is well known neurologically that intense emotional or pain stimulus can affect the part of the brain stem called the vestibulospinal tract, which maintains extensor muscle tone in the legs. Neural stimuli from the body can inhibit this function and cause the legs to buckle. Likewise, the reticular activating system (RAS) in the brain stem receives severe pain stimuli from the trauma, which may, by some mechanism not clear, shut it off and cause the subject to lose conscience in 1 to 2 seconds rather than 10 to 12 seconds, as we might see with a reflexive slowing of the heart. (All pain or emotional stimuli can reflexively slow the heart, as is seen with the common faint, but it takes many seconds.)

The "shock" of the pain perceived by the body can be from the "momentum" of a large-caliber, slow-moving, heavy bullet such as the .45 ACP ball, or from the "temporary cavity effect" on some body tissues from light, high-velocity rounds such as the 9mm JHP. Certainly, sudden rupture of a hollow viscera in the body (liver, spleen, or bowel) might produce an intense pain impulse transmitted to the RAS that would be perceived as "neural shock," with loss of consciousness.

The debate about stopping power (not killing power) centers around how best to induce this neural shock. Few people realize how much this is affected by the mental and emotional state of the offender. This explains many of the nightmare stories of young offenders stoned on PCP, heroin, or crack taking rounds from a .44 Magnum or 12-gauge and yet seemingly not reacting until becoming weak from blood loss.

Conversely, it may also explain why we see officers in their role-playing training scenarios get "shot" and,

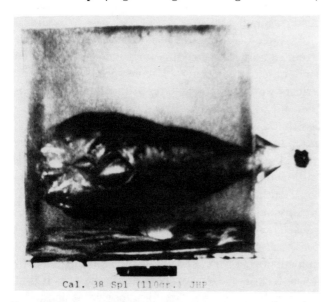

Cal. 38 Spl (110gr.) JHP

It is easy to see the maximum temporary stretch cavity for the Winchester .38 Special +P 110-grain JHP. The dislocation or disruption of tissue sends stress signals to the brain, which can cause a collapse in less than two seconds.

from their own fear and emotional reaction to the event, actually have their legs buckle and even fall because in their mental perceptions, they *have* been shot.

Interestingly, neural shock may explain the exponential effect of multiple hits with a submachine gun or buckshot load. Aside from the increased bullet velocity from submachine guns, two or three sudden hits in a short time may have more effect than multiple single pistol rounds over a longer time. The body receives more "neural shock" from the effects of multiple, near-simultaneous impacts.

All this explains why there is no "100-percent, one-shot stopper, magic bullet," even with rare head shots. It should lend support to the shooting theory to "keep shooting until they are *down* or you are out of bullets," as taught in many academies. Multiple hits *do* count significantly.

I realize these medical concepts may be unfamiliar, but they have a basis in classical neurophysiology and hopefully will aid in the understanding of handgun stopping power. I am sure this will generate debate and controversy and I welcome comment.

W. Dennis Tobin, M.D.
115 Medical Drive, #207
Victoria, TX 77904

• • • • •

Dr. Tobin's comments on visceral pain impulses "overloading" the reticular activating system and the vestibulo/rubrospinal tracts have an implication in gelatin analysis of bullet performance. The greater the *distance* any tissue is displaced and the greater the *amount* of tissue that is disrupted, the more intense the pain signals sent to the consciousness and extensor muscle control areas will be. Thus the larger the temporary stretch cavity, the more likely the central nervous system can be "overloaded" and, all other factors equal, subsequent collapse will occur.

In addition to an intuitive medical explanation for what is actually observed in street shootings, the instantaneous effects of bullet impact are receiving support from the hard-core medical research community. Research performed in Sweden and released at the Fifth Symposium on Wound Ballistics held in Stockholm and later published in the *Journal of Trauma* may explain the sudden loss of consciousness occasionally seen on the street.

Dr. A.M. Goransson supervised the testing on partially drugged hogs. The hogs were wired for blood pressure and breathing rate, as well as with electrocardiograph (ECG) and electroencephalograph (EEG), which monitors brain-wave activity. All these vital signs were monitored well before and well after bullet impact.

The hogs were shot in the hind leg muscle with an unidentified high-energy missile, presumably a 5.56mm NATO ball bullet. Control shots were also fired that did not impact the animals.

In four of the nine pigs, the nonlethal bullet impact caused a pronounced flattening of the EEG lasting 30 seconds or longer. The depression of brain activity occurred at the exact time of impact. Two hogs had the same response but to a lesser degree. The lack of response from three hogs might be explained by too deep a level of anesthesia, according to Goransson.

None of the hogs showed a change in blood pressure or heart activity. Six of the nine experienced a disrup-tion of normal breathing that lasted for up to 45 sec-onds.

Dr. Goransson concluded his findings by stating that the mechanism behind the depressed EEG read-ings is not yet known, nor could the absence of the effect in some animals be fully explained. He called for further studies of the instantaneous effects on the brain from nonlethal injury.

Some people in the wound ballistics field, even doctors, feel that the temporary stretch cavity has no effect on stopping power. They are wrong. The effect may be difficult to describe, but it is real. In fact, as you will read in later chapters, the temporary stretch cavity has an extremely significant place in estimating stopping power, especially with bullet velocities over 1,300 fps.

CHAPTER 3

HATCHER'S THEORY OF RELATIVE STOPPING POWER

Hatcher's Theory of Relative Stopping Power (RSP) has been the Holy Writ of the big-bore handgun carriers for decades. Logically, of course, it's quite attractive. Bigger *must* be better, right? Unfortunately, of course, reality rarely listens to logic.

Julian Hatcher based much of his theory on the Thompson-LaGarde Study, which was seriously flawed. Thompson and LaGarde based their conclusion on the results of shooting live steers and human cadavers. In the latter test, hanging human bodies were shot and the momentum that resulted was measured. The resistance of dead human flesh, of course, differs substantially from that of live human tissue. As a result, any attempt to evaluate penetration and/or tissue damage from dead human flesh is largely invalid.

Shooting fresh cadavers *might* provide some information on bullet expansion and penetration. The Thompson-LaGarde Study, however, was not concerned with that. It was based on the assumption that the momentum of hanging bodies of various weights could somehow be correlated and measured, and that it actually meant something with regard to stopping power. What it actually did was extrapolate questionable data from questionable tests.

The shooting of live steers was also of extremely limited value. First, steers of varying weights and sexes were included in the testing. Second, multiple shots were included. This meant that the study evaluated the effectiveness of two rounds of one load versus three rounds of another. Third, the steers were incapable of understanding what was happening and articulating their concerns, which meant that one could not effectively measure the results of individual shots on the steers. (That statement may sound strange, but some of our best insights into the incapacitating effect of nonlethal gunfire has come from debriefing police officers who were shot and later recovered.) Fourth, steers are much harder to kill than humans, so applying the results of shooting animals to how particular handgun loads would work against humans was a hopeless task. Finally, only a handful of handgun loads were used in the steer tests, and that was hardly a comprehensive evaluation of what was commercially available even at the time.

Hatcher — relying heavily on the data available from Thompson-LaGarde, which as we have seen was of extremely questionable value — assigned factors to various bullet shapes and materials. The obvious result was that, being based on flawed data, Hatcher's factors were of questionable validity at best. As the actual shooting data collected by the authors has shown, for example, .45 ACP full-metal-jacketed rounds produce only adequate results, not the 95-percent stopping-power rate that anecdotal data suggests.

Hatcher's formula to determine Relative Stopping Power is as follows: $RSP = mVoAs/450$ where m is the slug mass in grains, Vo is the impact velocity in feet per second, A is the frontal area of the bullet in square inches, and s is a factor of bullet shape and material.

Hatcher's factors for bullet shape and material are as follows: full-metal-jacket round nose, .90; full-metal-jacket flatpoint, 1.00; lead round nose, 1.00; lead

The Thompson-LaGarde Study involved thirteen steers and a number of cadavers. Hatcher used this data to develop a theory about nonexpanding subsonic bullets. Modern writers have failed to update this theory to include high-speed and expanding/fragmenting bullets.

blunt round nose, 1.05; lead round nose with small flat tip, 1.05; lead flatpoint, 1.10; and lead wadcutter or semiwadcutter, 1.25.

Our .38 Special results from the street, culled from a data base of over a hundred .38 Special lead semiwadcutter shootings, show that there is no significant difference between the round-nose lead load and the lead semiwadcutter, despite the fact that Hatcher tells us there should be a 25-percent difference between these two loads. Obviously, there are some serious holes in his theory.

In our search for the truth, Relative Stopping Power, like all other theories, must be relegated to the trash pile. The subjects of defensive/law enforcement handgun usage and choosing the right ammunition are too critical to bet our lives on mathematical formulas and educated or semieducated guesses. Only actual shooting data provides relevant information for this most serious of decisions.

Julian Hatcher made many valuable contributions to the subject of weaponry and related items, and they cannot be underestimated. His Relative Stopping Power, however, is a hopelessly confused collection of ideas that appeals to prejudice rather than fact. It has not and cannot be supported or validated by fact. Big-bore lovers, however, can take heart in the fact that several of the loads for their favorite calibers have proven to be excellent stoppers in actual shootings.

Relative Stopping Power, like the Justice Department's "computer man" study (see Chapter 4), predicts results that don't jibe with reality. Actual shooting

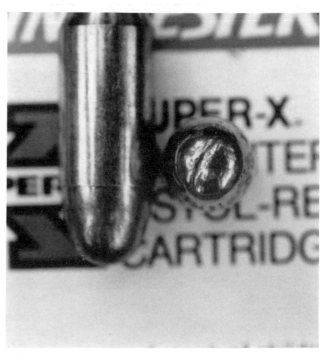

The .45 Auto 230-grain FMJ hardball is the most overrated of all handgun loads. Actual street results show the round to be a marginal stopper at only 61- to 64-percent effective.

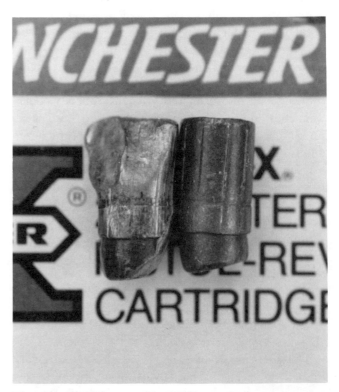

Hatcher's theoretical RSP predicts that the semiwadcutter would be much more effective than a round-nose bullet. The fact is that this .38 Special 158-grain semiwadcutter does not perform any better than a 158-grain lead round nose.

data was available for collection when both these theories were introduced. Spending one's time in the morgue and talking to shooting victims and homicide investigators, however, weren't considered scientific enough. Apparently many "scientists" are afraid to get their hands dirty and face reality. They love to theorize but are extremely reluctant to enter the real world and see what is going on. The hard fact is that nothing provides validated data like actual shootings. Those who work with computer models and arcane mathematical formulas continue to miss the point — if we want to know how handgun ammunition will work against human targets, we *must* look at how it *has* worked against human targets in the past.

Hatcher's Theory of Relative Stopping Power, for all its good intentions, proves virtually nothing. RSP *may* correlate with actual street results with a coefficient of .90; however, this is based *only* on subsonic, nonexpanding designs (see Table 3-1). When modern gun writers try to modify Hatcher's work to include high-speed or expanding bullets (Taylor's Simplified Short Form RSP is shown in Table 3-2), the correlation coefficient crashes from .90 to .64. The National Institute of Justice/Law Enforcement Assistance Administration (NIJ/LEAA) method that these writers condemn and ridicule has an accuracy of .67. A detailed discussion of the correlation coefficient is found in Chapter 17. Suffice to say here that the closer the coefficient is to 1.0, the more accurate the prediction.

Table 3-1

HATCHER'S RELATIVE STOPPING POWER

Caliber	Load	RSP	Actual
.380 Auto	Fed 95-gr. FMJ	16.2	51.25
9mm	W-W 115-gr. FMJ	29.4	60.81
.38 Special (non +P)	Fed 158-gr. RNL	30.8	52.28
.44 Special	W-W 246-gr. RNL	60.6	67.39
.45 Auto	Fed 230-gr. FMJ	60.0	62.65
.45 Colt	W-W 255-gr. RNL	73.6	69.41

Correlation coefficient: .90
Intercept: 47
Slope: .30
Degree of certainty: between 95 and 99 percent

Table 3-2

TAYLOR'S SIMPLIFIED HATCHER RSP

Caliber	Load	Taylor	Actual
.32 Auto	W-W 71-gr. FMJ	4.63	50.00
.380 Auto	Fed 95-gr. FMJ	8.54	51.25
.380 Auto	Fed 90-gr. JHP	8.73	63.82
.38 Special +P	R-P 95-gr. S-JHP	9.98	56.81
.38 Special +P	W-W 110-gr. JHP	11.94	54.21
.38 Special +P	Fed 125-gr. JHP	13.00	68.26
.38 Special (non+P)	Fed 158-gr. RNL	13.02	52.28
9mm	Horn 90-gr. JHP	15.64	64.00
9mm	Fed 115-gr. JHP	17.25	81.10
9mm	W-W 115-gr. FMJ	13.64	60.81
.357 Magnum	Fed 110-gr. JHP	18.84	90.47
.357 Magnum	Fed 125-gr. JHP	21.57	96.05
.357 Magnum	W-W 145-gr. STHP	19.30	83.33
.357 Magnum	R-P 158-gr. S-JHP	16.12	81.48
.41 Magnum	W-W 210-gr. JHP	43.28	82.75
.44 Special	W-W 246-gr. RNL	25.46	67.39
.44 Magnum	Fed 180-gr. JHP	48.50	86.95
.44 Magnum	W-W 210-gr. STHP	49.12	87.87
.44 Magnum	R-P 240-gr. S-JHP	49.50	86.36
.45 Auto	Fed 185-gr. JHP	31.57	84.61
.45 Auto	CCI 200-gr. JHP	31.87	85.48
.45 Auto	W-W 230-gr. FMJ	31.61	64.02
.45 Colt	W-W 255-gr. RNL	34.03	69.41

Correlation coefficient: .64
Intercept: 57
Slope: .66
Degree of certainty: 99.9 percent

CHAPTER 4

RELATIVE INCAPACITATION INDEX

In 1972, the National Institute of Justice (NIJ) funded a project to study the terminal ballistics of common police handgun ammunition. The purpose of the study was to provide law enforcement agencies at all levels with realistic and credible stopping-power predictions so that they could select the best possible personal defense ammo. The results of the study apply to civilian handgunners today, because all of the ammo tested is now available to civilians.

The work got underway in 1973, and by 1975 a full report was available for public inspection. The result was the Relative Incapacitation Index (RII). In 1981, the tests were performed again to include new ammo developments, most significantly the Winchester Silvertip. The results were published in a 1983 report. The tests were conducted again in 1985 to include the new generation of extreme-velocity rounds, including the THV, copper hollowpoints, the new generation of Silvertips, and many late-breaking ammo developments.

The latest results were presented in the 1983 two-volume report: volume 1, NIJ 100-83, entitled "Police Handgun Ammunition: Incapacitation Effects," and volume 2, NIJ 101-83, entitled "Police Handgun Ammunition: Experimental Data."

The tests were cosupervised and the report coauthored by Dr. William J. Bruchey, Jr., representing the Ballistic Research Lab, U.S. Army Armament Research and Development Command, Aberdeen Proving Grounds, Maryland, and Dr. Daniel E. Frank,

representing the Law Enforcement Standards Lab, National Bureau of Standards, Gaithersburg, Maryland. Under the guidance of these men, the RII was developed with input from the U.S. Army Human Engineering Lab, H.P. White Labs, The University of Maryland Shock Trauma Unit, Office of the Surgeon General, the ammunition industry, and numerous other professional sources.

To cover all aspects of stopping power, the NIJ team started with hit probability, or marksmanship. Actual shot placement has a tremendous effect on the overall stopping power of a bullet; in fact, it is the most significant factor. It is also the factor over which we have the least control, so it was important to isolate this variable first.

The hit-probability data used by the researchers came from a stress shooting test given to U.S. Army soldiers by the Human Engineering Lab at Aberdeen Proving Grounds. The soldiers fired the M1911A1 .45 ACP pistol at pop-up targets. They were instructed that the prime purpose was to hit the silhouettes as quickly as possible. The targets appeared randomly at ranges up to 33 yards.

A weighted average of all shot placements at 7 yards was selected. This distribution on a full-size silhouette appears in one of the photos. There were lots of misses and lots of poor shots, just like reality.

Certainly the most controversial and least understood part of the RII was the use of computer modeling to predict stopping power. The "Computer Man" was a complex three-dimensional computer drawing of the human body developed by the U.S. Army. It was divided into horizontal sections 1 inch thick from head to toe. Each of these cross sections was then divided into .2 x .2 x 1-inch segments.

A team of physicians from the University of Maryland Shock Trauma Unit was called on to identify and encode the tissue found in each of the segments. The doctors rated each segment from 0 to 10 according to how much the tissue in that segment would contribute to incapacitating the human body. They were told

to evaluate each tissue segment in every cross-sectional layer with the following scenario in mind:

"The officer is in a situation in which he must use his handgun. The engagement range is within 21 feet. The officer does not have time to wait for the aggression to stop. The felon is in a situation where only an act of violence directed at the officer will save the felon's life or keep him out of jail. The felon is armed with a lethal weapon and is being approached by the officer. The felon begins his attack. The officer is required to deliver an instantly incapacitating injury to the felon. What the officer needs is a weapon and cartridge combination that will render the felon immediately noncombatant."

In this context, each doctor was asked to rank, from no importance to extreme importance, each segment in the computer drawing of the body.

Different parts of the body have different prob-

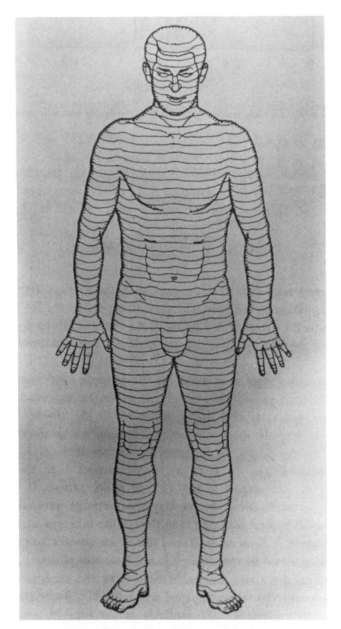

This is the controversial NIJ/LEAA "computer man," a three-dimensional model of the human body developed by the U.S. Army. The computer fired 10,000 bullets at the computer man using the exact hit probability of soldiers firing handguns under stress.

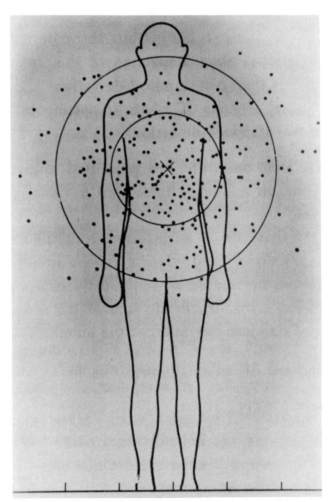

This is the hit probability that was fed into the NIJ/LEAA computer to calculate RII.

abilities of incapacitation. Therefore the brain and spine rated very high, while the limbs rated fairly low. Different parts of the body also have different likelihoods of being hit by the officer. The computer combined the probability of being hit with the effects of that damaged tissue to come up with a Vulnerability Index (VI).

Using the shot-placement and hit-probability data from the soldier, the computer fired 10,000 frontal shots at the computer man and traced the path of each one. The computer missed the target exactly the same weighted-average number of times as the soldiers did in the original stress tests. These were fully weighted as zero.

The computer also connected the same percent as the soldiers did and with the same accuracy the soldiers had. For each bullet that connected, the computer followed it all the way through the body, keeping track of each tissue segment, rated by the Trauma Unit, that the bullet hit.

The Vulnerability Index was compiled for each of the 10,000 bullets, then all of the indices were added together and averaged. The result represented the average vulnerability of the human body combined with the average hit probability in a high-stress scenario, assuming the victim was struck from the front. The amount of vulnerability was listed in half-inch increments of depth into the human anatomy. Two and a half inches of penetration from the front had one index of incapacitation potential, while eight inches of penetration from the front had another index.

The use of computer modeling caused most of the controversy. The use of ballistic gelatin as the tissue simulant caused the rest. The following, reprinted directly from NIJ 100-83, is the reason Bruchey and Frank chose the gelatin they did:

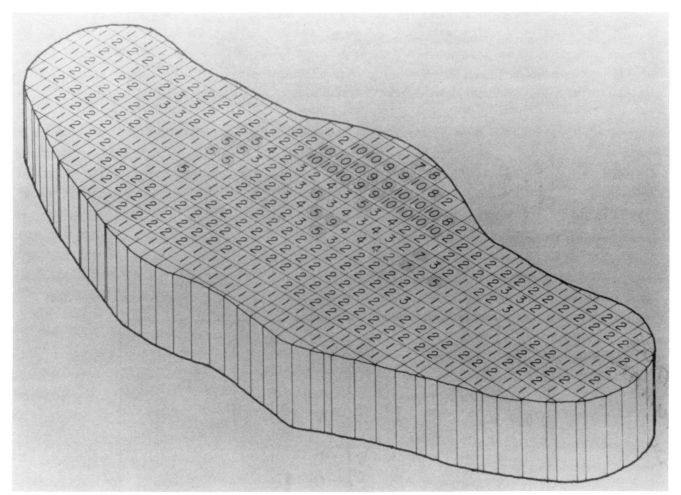

A horizontal section from near the shoulder of the computer man. A team of physicians from the University of Maryland Shock Trauma Unit rated each segment from 1 to 10 based on how damage to that tissue would lead to instant incapacitation.

DiMaio in his article states, "At autopsy, one cannot specifically tell from the extent of the injury if an individual has been shot by a .38 Special 158-gr. round nose lead bullet traveling at 789 ft/s or a 110-gr. Norma hollow point at 1,334 ft/s." This statement leads one to conclude that at handgun bullet velocities, the final wound track shape is fairly constant for all bullet constructions. However, x-ray studies of bullets interacting with animal tissue and high-speed studies of bullets interacting with gelatin targets clearly show that different bullet constructions do have different temporary effects on the target medium. To deal with this situation, a measure of bullet performance, called the Maximum Temporary Cavity (MTC), has been developed.

The Maximum Temporary Cavity, simply defined, is the curve connecting the points of maximum temporary displacement of the target medium around the bullet track. Since the volume of the MTC changes with bullet construction and bullet velocity while the final wound channel may not, the volume of the MTC was chosen to be the measure of bullet performance for this study.

Over the years many different target simulant materials have been proposed and used (animals, clay, soap, sand, wet paper, gelatin, etc.) and different researchers tend to have their own favorites. The usual reasons for choosing a particular simulant are cost, availability, ease of use, and the researcher's familiarity with the material's performance relative to the real world. In this study a tissue simulant meeting the following criteria was sought:

1. The material must provide reproducible results.
2. The material must behave similarly to tissue when struck by a bullet.
3. The material should have a sufficient history so that comparisons to the historical work can be made.

As a result of wound ballistics experiments in the 1940s and 1950s it became well known that trauma such as bone fracture, hemorrhage and nerve damage could occur beyond the permanent wound track of complete tissue maceration. By 1962, when the U.S. Office of the Surgeon General published a treatise on wound ballistics, the kinetic energy mechanism of wounding was accepted to be cavitation. The basic idea is that as the bullet penetrates soft tissue it cuts and tears tissue directly in its path. In addition, the bullet transfers some of its momentum to the neighboring tissue causing an outward radial motion. This outward motion can be thought of as rings of tissue expanding about the bullet path. Often this expansion severely stretches or tears the tissue and trauma results. Experimental evidence has shown that the rate at which bullets transfer momentum to the surrounding tissue as a function of penetration distance is very similar to that observed in gelatin.

Therefore, the material chosen as the tissue simulant for this study was 20-percent gelatin at a temperature between 8 and 10°C (46.4 and 50°F). The choice of 20-percent gelatin as the target material rather than another simulant is based on the following considerations:

1. Similarity between bullet retardation in gelatin and animal tissue.
2. Similarity between the size and shape of the temporary cavity in gelatin and tissue. Figure 8 depicts the results of measuring the temporary cavities produced when a steel sphere impacts the two test media (pig muscle and gelatin) at essentially the same velocity.
3. Similarity between the permanent cavity remaining in tissue and gelatin after the passage of a bullet.
4. Homogeneity/reproducibility of the gelatin response to bullet penetration.
5. The material has been in use since the 1940s for wound ballistics experiments, yielding a reasonable amount of historical data for comparisons.

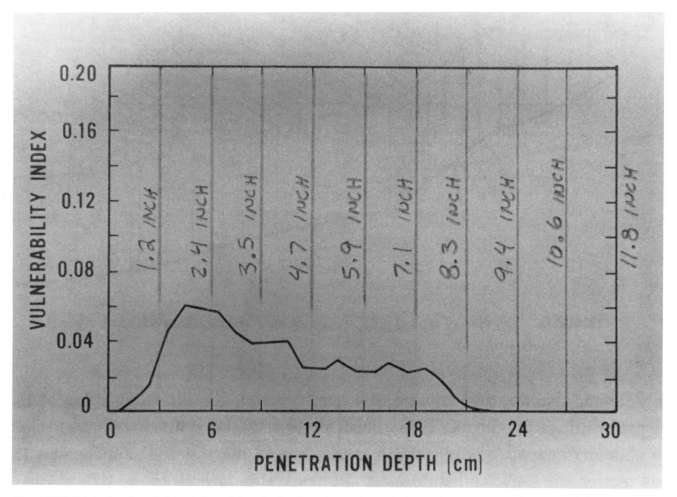

The NIJ/LEAA developed this Vulnerability Index based on a frontal shot. The VI is a combination of the location of the vital tissue in the human body and how likely the shooter is to hit that vital area.

We will discuss in detail the use of gelatin as a wound predictor later in the book. The NIJ team illustrated that the temporary cavity and permanent depth of the bullet in gelatin were similar to excised pig muscle by comparing the wound cavity generated in gelatin versus the wound cavity generated in the pig muscle.

As stated in NIJ 100-83, when the bullet penetrates soft tissue, it cuts and tears tissue directly in its path. It also transfers some of its energy to nearby tissue, resulting in an outwardly expanding air cavity in the wake of the bullet path, called the Temporary Gas Cavity (TGC). This nearby tissue stretches violently and sometimes tears. At its peak, the Temporary Gas Cavity is called the Maximum Temporary Cavity (MTC), which shows the exact form of the energy release. Through the use of X-ray and 10,000-frames-per-second photography, the NIJ team was able to accurately measure the diameter, depth, and overall shape of the Maximum Temporary Cavity. They did this for more than 140 handgun loads and caliber combinations.

The Vulnerability Index is a set of numbers that represents the relative vulnerability of the human body at each depth of penetration from the front. The VI takes into account the detailed construction of the body and the hit probability of trained shooters under stress using weapons of moderate to heavy recoil. The Maximum Temporary Cavity is a set of numbers that indicates tissue stretch in a tissue simulant depending on the caliber, design, and velocity of the particular bullet. The controversial Relative Incapacitation Index is a combination of these two. It ranks each bullet in a defensive context based on shooter capabilities, human anatomy, and bullet characteristics.

To get the RII, the NIJ multiplied the volume of the MTC at a certain depth of penetration times the VI at that penetration. This was done in .4-inch penetration increments for the entire penetration depth. The weighted volumes of the MTC were added together to become the Relative Incapacitation Index. An example of the RII calculation for the Speer .45-

caliber 200-grain JHP bullet at 1,227 fps is shown in Table 4-1. The final results for popular calibers are in Table 4-2.

The general conclusions from NIJ 100-83 and 101-83 are as follows:

1. *Bullet Velocity.* The most important property of a handgun bullet affecting its performance in a target is its velocity. The velocity is important because the size and shape of the MTC depend upon the impact velocity and the total available energy. It is also important because hollowpoint bullets have a minimum opening velocity, which affects the rate of the total energy actually transferred.

2. *Bullet Construction.* The expansion of the bullet depends on the impact velocity and the bullet's construction. Construction includes such things as the presence of hollowpoint cavities; core hardness; whether the bullet is copper, aluminum, or not jacketed; the dimensions and hardness of the jacket; and so on. Hollowpoint bullets begin expanding as low as 705 fps. The expansion of the bullet greatly affects the size and shape of the MTC.

3. *Caliber.* A large-caliber bullet may yield a higher RII at nonexpansion velocities. However, once the velocity reaches levels where expansion is possible, smaller-caliber bullets may outperform larger-caliber bullets.

4. *Bullet Shape.* The bluntness of the nose is only important in that it establishes the initial value for the bullet drag. At velocities too low for expansion to occur, this drag factor is constant and the blunter bullets will have a higher RII. At velocities high enough to cause expansion, the drag factor changes as the bullet expands. Bullets with smaller initial drag factors can expand to outperform bullets with larger initial drag factors.

5. *Point of Aim.* The RII is dependent on the point of aim. For a given amount of shooter stress and accuracy, a point-of-aim level with the armpit produces a better chance of incapacitation than a conventional mid-torso aim point. This higher aim point is especially significant for loads that do not penetrate as deeply or cause as much tissue damage.

The authors of the RII concluded with comments on how much RII is enough to reliably produce instantaneous incapacitation in a typical urban police-action shooting. Loads with RIIs of less than 10 produce low-volume temporary cavities. They maintain that with these loads, the probability of the MTC affecting vital tissue is low, as is the probability of incapacitating a felon in time. The more RII, therefore, the better.

Nonexpanding high-speed bullets can produce good RIIs. Lower-velocity expanding bullets can also produce good RIIs. The problem with nonexpanding high-velocity bullets is overpenetration. For that reason, the NIJ team put a ceiling of 30 on the RII for police use, and it specified that bullets must expand.

Their concluding sentence is as follows: "This study has shown that for handguns in the .38-caliber/9mm to .45-caliber range, a *deforming* projectile driven at a velocity above the minimum expansion velocity *and* an RII between 10 and 30 is a reasonable goal for handgun ammunition for use against normally clad assailants in an urban environment."

Like the RSP, the RII in its present form is seriously flawed.

Some feel that predicting wounding effects by the temporary stretch cavity is an error. They believe that "stretch" is a less reliable and less predictable means of damaging tissue than the "crush" of a permanent cavity. (The significance of the two wound cavities will be discussed in detail in Chapter 15.) The NIJ report, in fact, does not present sufficient evidence that the temporary stretch cavity is a valid wound predictor. The profile of the cavity was plotted over the profile of the computer man, and all tissue affected by the cavity was considered "destroyed."

The NIJ team selected the temporary stretch cavity as a wound predictor based to a large degree on the statements of Vincent J.M. DiMaio, M.D., the Chief Medical Examiner of Bexar County (San Antonio), Texas.

In his book, *Gunshot Wounds*, Dr. DiMaio states, "As to increased wounding, to this day, the author cannot distinguish a wound by a hollowpoint bullet from that by a solid lead bullet of the same caliber until recovery of the actual bullet." This statement deemphasizes the crush advantages of expanding bullets and thus discredits the use of crush as a wound predictor.

On the other hand, in conversations with Dr. DiMaio, he has stated that the temporary stretch cavity from most handgun loads rarely exceeds the elastic limits of most soft tissue. This tends to discredit the use of stretch as a wound predictor. The elastic limit must be exceeded in order for the tissue to be torn and thus genuinely damaged. Stretch alone may not damage tissue.

Dr. DiMaio claims two general exceptions. One is when the highest-velocity magnum loads are involved, which may create a stretch cavity large enough to exceed the elastic limits of most soft tissue. He referred to the .44 Magnum, but this may presumably also include the .357 Magnum and .41 Magnum. He also included contact wounds, where large portions of expanding gas from the load actually enter the body.

(Contact wounds occur when the muzzle is pressed against the skin or the skin is blown back into the muzzle after bullet impact. Either way, the muzzle is sealed to the skin by pressure, forcing the blast inside the body.) This causes tissue stretch often far in excess of what the bullet itself is capable of producing.

The other general exception pertains to the kind of soft tissue encountered. Most soft tissue can withstand more stretch than nonmagnum-velocity bullets can generate. The most notable exception is the liver (and possibly the spleen and kidneys).

With these exceptions in mind, one can start to build a case for the following statement: with a .38 Special, .45 Auto, or 9mm and bullet placement in the upper torso, the RII is based on a flawed assumption. The RII and its stretch mechanism applies only to the best magnum loads or when specific organs in the body are struck.

This statement, however, is too extreme. It is incorrect to ignore the temporary stretch cavity and the effects on the body discussed in Chapter 1, just as it is incorrect to depend totally on the temporary stretch cavity at the exclusion of other wound indicators, notably the diameter of the crush path through the body. Therefore total dependence on the stretch cavity as a basic assumption constitutes a real but minor flaw in the RII.

The major and more dangerous flaw in the RII lies with the Vulnerability Index. This major component of the RII credits or discredits the effect of the bullet by penetration distance. The extent of wounding at 1.6 inches deep was weighted the most favorable. Wounding beyond 8.7 inches was flatly ignored.

The depth of 1.6 inches was the weighted average depth of the most vital organs in the human body shot from the front. This was a combination of how deeply the vital tissue was buried from the front along with how vital the tissue was on a scale from 1 to 10. This included *all* tissue, from skin (rated at 1) to major blood vessels (rated at 7) to the brain (rated at 10). When all these segments were factored together for a grand average, tissue at 1.6 inches was determined to be the most vital. Using the same method, the researchers determined that the human body ended at 8.7 inches.

The gross flaw in this methodology is that the penetration depths were based *only* on frontal shots. According to the Institute of Forensic Sciences in Dallas, Texas, up to 70 percent of officer-involved or police-action shootings are *nonfrontal*. This high percentage of nonfrontal shots has been acknowledged by numerous other law enforcement and forensic professionals, including Dr. Dean Hawley with the Marion County,

Indiana, Medical Examiner's Office, and Dr. Dan Frank, coauthor of the RII report.

In law enforcement, especially with a partner system, the partner not under attack is as likely or even more likely to fire than the partner under attack. At 90 degrees from one another, the partner not under attack has a better field of vision, can detect a forward movement or movement of the hands more easily, and is cooler and under less stress. The nonthreatened partner, who shoots more frequently, will be delivering a transverse shot, not a frontal shot. Now, instead of 6 to 8 inches of penetration being acceptable, the bullet needs to penetrate 12 to 15 inches. The same deep penetration is needed against a crouched or prone assailant, a felon seated in a car, a shooter seeking cover and exposing only nonvital parts, or a person who shoots with his body at a quarter angle.

So common is the nonfrontal shot in law enforcement that, according to Dr. Frank, the National Institute of Justice plans to "reshoot" the RII computer man. This shooting will be at 45, 90, and 180 degrees from the front. Presumably, bullet performance for all angles will be factored together to get one rating. Yet regardless of the factoring procedure, those tests will show that a bullet needs to penetrate significantly deeper than the RII currently shows in order to be street realistic.

As it stands now, the RII is incomplete. It is workable as far as it goes, but it does not go far enough. Certain top-rated expanding loads with RIIs between the recommended 10 and 30 have produced street failures, even with reasonable shot placement. One example is the Winchester 95-grain STHP Silvertip in .38 Special + P. This load has an RII of 18.0, yet has had a less than effective street record due to poor penetration. On the other hand, the best load in the caliber based on street results, the 158-grain lead SWC-HP, has an RII of 17.2. The reasonably well-performing Winchester 110-grain + P + JHP, the Q4070 "Treasury load," has an RII of 17.9.

The issue of overpenetration was addressed by the NIJ authors in their concluding remarks. However, penetration per se was not a part of the RII analysis. Specifically, adequate penetration under most law enforcement scenarios was not a part of the RII calculation. As a result, bullets that produced large stretch cavities were given top RII ratings even though the penetration they produced could be too shallow for common police shooting scenarios.

Another example of reported street failure is the 110-grain JHP in .357 Magnum. The number of incidents of failure from this more powerful round is lower, but it is nonetheless documented. This round produces an RII of 29.9, very near the maximum recommended by the NIJ authors, yet the street failures were based on insufficient penetration despite reasonable bullet placement.

Revision of the RII to include shots from the front quarter, side, rear quarter, and rear are essential to make it realistic for the street. Loads with ratings be-

tween the recommended RII of 10 and 30 have under-penetrated and produced dangerous failures. Until the Vulnerability Index is recalculated, the conclusions of the RII are suspect. Unfortunately, at the time of writing, the NIJ has no definite plans or allocated funds to perform this necessary recalculation.

Table 4-1

SAMPLE CALCULATION FOR RII *

Speer .45 Auto 200-grain JHP @ 1,227 fps

Penetration Depth (cm)	Vulnerability Index (VI)	Cavity Radius r (cm)	r^2 x VI
1	0.0061	4.3	0.113
2	0.0169	5.1	0.440
3	0.0477	5.8	1.604
4	0.0608	6.0	2.189
5	0.0588	6.3	2.333
6	0.0564	6.4	2.309
7	0.0458	6.2	1.761
8	0.0388	6.1	1.444
9	0.0401	5.6	1.257
10	0.0405	5.4	1.181
11	0.0248	5.0	0.621
12	0.0238	4.4	0.460
13	0.0292	4.0	0.467
14	0.0231	3.1	0.222
15	0.0227	2.4	0.131
16	0.0273	2.3	0.144
17	0.0230	2.2	0.111
18	0.0247	1.8	0.080
19	0.0196	1.3	0.033
20	0.0074	1.1	0.009
21	0.0014	0.8	0.001
22	0.0003	0.6	0.000
			16.910

RII equals 16.910 times pi (3.1416)
RII equals 53.1

*reprinted from NIJ 101-83

Table 4-2

RELATIVE INCAPACITATION INDEX

Cartridge	Bullet Weight (grains)	Bullet Type	Manufacturer	RII	Actual
.380 Auto	85	STHP	Winchester	13.4	54.23
.38 Spl. +P	95	S-JHP	Remington	28.9	56.81
.38 Spl. +P	125	S-JHP	Remington	23.2	65.11
.38 Spl. +P+	110	JHP	Q4070, Winchester	17.9	68.75
.38 Spl. +P	158	SWC-HP	Winchester	17.2	72.78
.38 Spl. +P	158	RNL	Federal	8.6	52.28
9mm	115	JHP	Remington	28.2	76.42
9mm	115	STHP	Winchester	27.5	79.14
9mm	115	FMJ	Winchester	10.3	60.81
.45 Auto	185	STHP	Winchester	25.5	80.32
.45 Auto	185	JHP	Remington	18.0	78.57
.45 Auto	230	FMJ	Remington	4.3	60.72
.44 Spl.	246	RNL	Remington	6.3	67.39
.357 Magnum	125	S-JHP	Remington	40.8	93.96
.357 Magnum	110	JHP	Winchester	29.9	85.29
.357 Magnum	158	JSP	Federal	25.6	72.41
.357 Magnum	158	SWC	Remington	17.3	67.60
.41 Magnum	210	JSP	Remington	51.6	80.00
.41 Magnum	210	SWC	Remington	6.2	76.08
.44 Magnum	240	S-JHP	Remington	47.3	86.36
.44 Magnum	240	SWC	Winchester	33.4	81.81

Correlation coefficient: .67
Intercept: 59
Slope: .58
Degree of Certainty: 99.9 percent

CHAPTER 5

SOUTHWESTERN INSTITUTE OF FORENSIC SCIENCES METHODOLOGY

Two police officers stopped a man for suspicious activity. They approached and asked him for identification. The subject reached into his right front pocket slowly and deliberately, just as he would to get his wallet. Instead, he pulled out a .25 ACP auto pistol. The subject fired one time, striking one of the officers in the knee.

The other officer drew his Colt Python .357 Magnum 4-inch service revolver. His load was the 1,295-fps Winchester .357 Magnum 110-grain JHP, producing 400 foot-pounds of energy. He fired six times at the offender. As the offender turned to flee, the fifth or sixth bullet fired from the Python struck him under his right arm. (The officer felt that shooting with one hand and trying to assist his wounded fellow officer with the other had resulted in all misses.)

The subject showed no reaction to the bullet impact whatsoever. He turned his back on the officers and walked away. The officer dumped his empty cases, loaded two or three magnum rounds in the cylinder, and ran after the offender. When the officer caught up with him, he grabbed the man and placed the Python at the base of his skull, all the while yelling for him to stop.

Having second thoughts about how this particular bullet placement may look to the Shooting Review Board, he ordered the man to turn around and pointed the gun at his nose. The offender, who the officer thought was not shot at all, rolled his eyes back in his head and fainted. The elapsed time from bullet impact to collapse was between 20 and 30 seconds.

A single 110-grain .357 Magnum JHP had entered the upper chest cavity from the side, struck a rib, perforated the right lung, and came to rest in the heart. Significantly, the bullet lodged in the heart muscle without penetrating it or causing a leak. The bullet had fully expanded and fragmented. The recovered weight was a typical 65 grains.

By all accounts, this failure of stopping power was the fault of the ammo.

The .357 Magnum 110-grain JHP has an RII of 29.9, right at the top of the recommended RII range of 10 to 30. The round produces a large-diameter stretch cavity that, according to NIJ/LEAA, occurs at an ideal depth of penetration. Yet it clearly failed to perform in this incident. This was a point clearly made by the officer involved to those who recommended and approved the round.

This profound failure from a top-rated RII round caused quite a stir in the Dallas area law enforcement community. The Southwestern Institute of Forensic Sciences (SIFS) had originally recommended the load based in part on NIJ/LEAA recommendations that were confirmed by gelatin tests conducted at the Institute.

The Institute originally had performed "energy deposit" tests on a variety of calibers and loads. The tests involved blocks of 20-percent gelatin at 10°C measuring 5.5 inches long. The entrance velocity into and the exit velocity out of the blocks were measured.

Velocity loss in the gelatin was converted into energy loss (also called energy transfer or energy deposit).

For each load in a caliber, the energy loss was expressed as a decimal. This represented exit energy divided by entrance energy. For example, the Federal .357 Magnum 125-grain JHP had an impact velocity of 1,311 fps and an exit velocity of 515 fps. Converting both figures to energy, that load had a rating of .84.

The rating is best described as an energy distribution factor. Specifically, 84 percent of the bullet's energy is transferred in the first 5.5 inches of gelatin. If the bullet did not exit, it received a rating of 1.00. This is, in fact, the rating for shallow-penetrating loads and rapid-energy-transfer loads that do not exit the Institute's 5.5-inch block.

The length of the gelatin block was arbitrarily chosen, and the selection of 20-percent gelatin was based on the findings of the NIJ/LEAA. Naturally, the amount of energy transferred to a block is entirely dependent upon the block length and gelatin ratio.

Using this energy-deposit method, the Institute assigned the same relative results to various loads, as in the NIJ/LEAA study. Ammo recommendations to area police agencies were made based on these relative results. Loads with ratings closer to 1.00 were rated superior to loads further from 1.00. Then the house of cards collapsed in the wake of the .357 Magnum 110-grain JHP failure.

The problem was that high-energy-transfer slugs often lacked the necessary penetration for the type of shots required in a law enforcement scenario. As mentioned, in police-action shootings, up to 70 percent of the shots can be nonfrontal. Many involve intermediate, energy-absorbing targets, which are obstructions that come between the firearm and the intended target, such as glass, metal, wood, or an upper arm (the torso is always the assumed final target).

By basing its energy-transfer data on such short blocks of gelatin, the Institute had adopted the "frontal only" assumption made by NIJ/LEAA. Unfortunately, this assumption is still widely held as valid.

While it may seem obvious to include total penetration in any evaluation of ammo, it is obvious only by hindsight. It was *not* obvious in the late 1970s in the wake of the prestigious NIJ/LEAA report, which ignored assured penetration. Yet unlike the NIJ/LEAA, and to its credit, immediately after the 110-grain JHP failure the Institute reacted to revise its ammo recommendations and develop a better method of predicting ammo performance.

Like going back to the basics or back to the drawing board, the Institute went back to the street. It researched its gunfighting records to find loads that were generally acceptable and unacceptable on the street. These shooting successes and failures were analyzed for things in common.

This is the wound profile of a .357 Magnum 110-grain JHP. This load typically penetrates 11 to 12 inches of tissue. When one of these hollowpoints did not penetrate far enough, the SIFS began a bold new study of stopping power.

Until this review, the failures blended in with all the other failures and no one incident stood out. A closer look revealed a whole group of failures with two things in common: they involved light, fast-expanding bullets and either heavily muscled or fat people, or involved shot placement at an angle that placed otherwise shallow organs quite deep in the body. The common thread was lack of penetration.

In these cases, bullet expansion from the light and fast JHP loads was very good to excellent. The recovered bullets generally were only 50 to 70 percent of their original weight. This rapid expansion and fragmentation gave excellent results as measured by NIJ/LEAA — but NIJ/LEAA did not measure or set standards for minimum penetration. Against heavily muscled, extra big, or extra fat people, or with other shots requiring deep penetration, these light JHP bullets underpenetrated. They transferred energy too soon, leaving too little energy for deep-enough penetration.

The Institute reviewed the gelatin performance of rounds that produced street successes. It discovered that successful bullets distributed their energy much later. The street failures produced early, basketball-shaped stretch cavities typical of light, fragmenting bullets. The street successes produced late, football-shaped stretch cavities typical of medium and heavy expanding bullets. The more moderate rates of energy transfer resulted in deeper penetration.

Using street successes as a benchmark, the Institute was able to identify a minimum and maximum energy-distribution factor. Rounds with factors less than the minimum were deemed likely to perforate the target and become a bystander hazard and civil liability. Rounds with factors greater than the maximum were likely to underpenetrate in a police-action shooting scenario.

The minimum factor based on street experience was .75 — the slug should transfer 75 percent of its energy in 5.5 inches of 20-percent gelatin at 10°. The maximum factor was .90 — the slug must not transfer more than 90 percent of its energy in that much gelatin.

Examples of ideal, under- and overpenetration can be found in all common police calibers. Using the

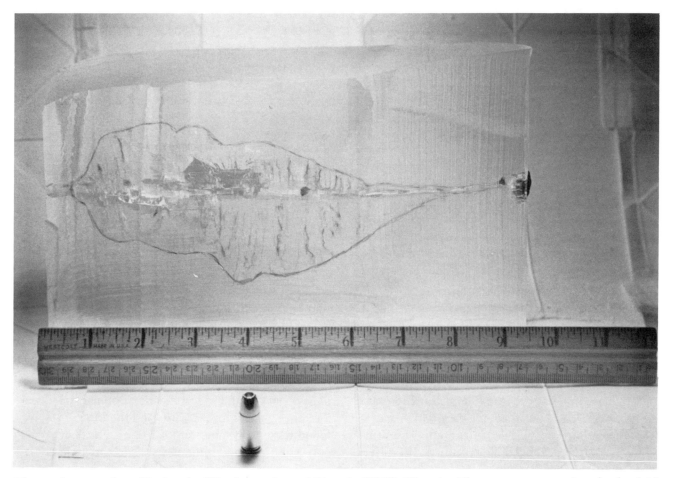

This is the wound profile for the Winchester 9mm 115-grain STHP Silvertip. The average penetration depth of 10 inches is enough to produce 79-percent one-shot stops. That is better than all 147-grain hollowpoints and all hardball loads, all of which penetrate deeper.

Table 5-1

SOUTHWESTERN INSTITUTE OF FORENSIC SCIENCES
DALLAS COUNTY FORENSIC LABORATORY
(select loads)

Caliber, Make and Description	Striking Velocity	Striking Energy	Exit Velocity	Exit Energy	Energy Transfer	Efficiency Factor	Street Actual
.38 Special Fed 158-gr. RNL	743 fps	194 ft-lb	575 fps	117 ft-lb	77 ft-lb	.39	52.2
.38 Special Fed 158-gr. SWC	816 fps	233 ft-lb	642 fps	145 ft-lb	89 ft-lb	.38	52.9
.38 Special W-W 158-gr. SWC-HP (+P)	908 fps	289 ft-lb	359 fps	45 ft-lb	244 ft-lb	.84	72.8
.38 Special W-W 110-gr. JHP (+P+) (Q4070)	1126 fps	310 ft-lb	375 fps	35 ft-lb	275 ft-lb	.88	68.8
.38 Special Fed 125-gr. JHP (+P)	906 fps	228 ft-lb	202 fps	13 ft-lb	215 ft-lb	.94	68.3
9mm W-W 115-gr. FMJ	1131 fps	327 ft-lb	928 fps	220 ft-lb	107 ft-lb	.32	60.8
9mm R-P 115-gr. JHP	1183 fps	358 ft-lb	504 fps	69 ft-lb	289 ft-lb	.80	76.4
9mm Fed 115-gr. JHP	1126 fps	324 ft-lb	310 fps	23 ft-lb	301 ft-lb	.92	81.1
9mm W-W 115-gr. STHP	1224 fps	382 ft-lb	220 fps	13 ft-lb	370 ft-lb	.96	79.1
.357 Magnum R-P 158-gr. SWC	1191 fps	498 ft-lb	972 fps	332 ft-lb	166 ft-lb	.33	67.6
.357 Magnum R-P 158-gr. JHP	1170 fps	481 ft-lb	559 fps	111 ft-lb	370 ft-lb	.76	81.5
.357 Magnum Fed 125-gr. JHP	1311 fps	477 ft-lb	515 fps	74 ft-lb	403 ft-lb	.84	96.1
.357 Magnum W-W 145-gr. STHP	1256 fps	509 ft-lb	421 fps	56 ft-lb	452 ft-lb	.88	83.3
.357 Magnum Fed 110-gr. JHP	1337 fps	437 ft-lb	421 fps	44 ft-lb	394 ft-lb	.90	90.5
.41 Magnum R-P 210-gr. JSP	1259 fps	739 ft-lb	722 fps	241 ft-lb	498 ft-lb	.67	80.0
.41 Magnum W-W 210-gr. JHP	1228 fps	704 ft-lb	427 fps	85 ft-lb	618 ft-lb	.87	82.7
.44 Magnum W-W 240-gr. SWC	1263 fps	850 ft-lb	633 fps	214 ft-lb	636 ft-lb	.74	81.8
.44 Magnum R-P 240-gr. JHP	1221 fps	795 ft-lb	537 fps	155 ft-lb	639 ft-lb	.80	86.4
.45 Auto Fed 230-gr. FMJ	837 fps	358 ft-lb	691 fps	244 ft-lb	114 ft-lb	.31	62.7
.45 Auto R-P 185-gr. JHP	914 fps	343 ft-lb	403 fps	71 ft-lb	272 ft-lb	.79	78.6
.45 Auto CCI 200-gr. JHP	931 fps	385 ft-lb	314 fps	44 ft-lb	341 ft-lb	.88	85.5
.45 Auto W-W 185-gr. STHP	941 fps	364 ft-lb	152 fps	10 ft-lb	353 ft-lb	.97	80.3

NOTE: The Energy Distribution factor (efficiency) is not a *direct* estimate of stopping power. An effective load must transfer at least 200 foot-pounds of energy in this test and have an efficiency of more than .75 but less than .90. The correlation coefficient, excluding loads over .90 efficiency, is .81, giving excellent predictions of reality.

.357 Magnum for example, the Remington 158-grain lead semiwadcutter has an energy-distribution factor of .33, indicating probable overpenetration. The Winchester 110-grain jacketed hollowpoint, the load that started the closer review, has an energy-distribution factor of .97, indicating probable underpenetration. The Federal, Winchester, and Remington 125-grain jacketed hollowpoints have energy-distribution factors of between .84 and .86, indicating optimal street performance — and, in fact, we (and the Institute) have found these to be the top loads for the caliber.

In addition to a minimum and maximum "rate" of energy transfer, the Institute established a minimum "amount" of energy transfer. The power floor was concluded to be 200 foot-pounds of energy transferred to the 5.5-inch block. In other words, besides transferring between 75 to 90 percent of their energy, bullets also had to transfer at least 200 foot-pounds.

The .38 Special 148-grain mid-range wadcutter has a factor of .78, which is inside the acceptable range. However, the total energy transferred is only 144 foot-pounds, which is below the minimum amount of energy needed to be effective.

So according to the Institute, calibers and loads with a generally successful street record transfer between 75 and 90 percent of their energy and at least 200 foot-pounds of energy to the gelatin block. Unlike the NIJ/LEAA before them, the Institute's gelatin re-sults are credible because the gelatin performance standards were set from street-successful rounds. This totally avoids the controversial issues of energy theory, momentum theory, underpenetration, and overpenetration. Instead, its predictions are based on what has previously worked in actual lethal encounters.

Simply put, the Southwestern Institute of Forensic Sciences found what a generally successful round looked like in gelatin. If a new or proposed round looked like that, it too would probably be generally successful. In predicting stopping power, that is state of the art.

CHAPTER 6

FEDERAL BUREAU OF INVESTIGATION METHODOLOGY

On April 11, 1986, at 10:40 A.M., FBI agents in Miami, Florida, stopped a car containing two men suspected of armed robbery. The shootout that followed has gone down in history as equaling the infamous Newhall, California massacre of four California Highway Patrolmen.

Two FBI agents were conducting a surveillance when they spotted the dark Monte Carlo they had been seeking. After calling several backup units, the agents forced the car to stop. Two subjects emerged from the vehicle with multiple weapons, most notably a Ruger Mini-14, which fires the 5.56mm NATO cartridge.

William Matix was a 34-year-old white male, 5′ 11″, 180 pounds. Michael Platt was a 32-year-old white male, 5′ 10′, 210 pounds. Five minutes and 144 rounds of gunfire later, the two subjects were dead. Matix was hit six times with combinations of 9mm 115-grain STHP Silvertip and .38 Special +P 158-grain SWC-HP bullets. Platt was struck twelve times with the same kinds of ammo. Significantly, the toxicology report on both felons revealed *no* drugs of any kind in their blood.

Tragically, Matix and Platt killed two FBI agents and wounded five others during the firefight. America's confidence in its most elite law enforcement agency had been shattered. This incident would have far-reaching effects on tactical training and weapon, caliber, and ammo selection.

Later testimony on the Miami shootout revealed that Platt was able to fire the Mini-14 even after taking a 9mm bullet in the chest. Officers were killed or wounded *after* Platt had taken this hit, so this one failure, if it was that, was critical. For quite some time, the FBI lost sight of the numerous tactical errors and horrible marksmanship demonstrated during this shootout. Even though over 100 rounds of ammo were fired, they focused on the one 9mm Silvertip bullet as a scapegoat despite the excellent police record it had up to that point (and still has today).

Indeed, according to autopsy, one wound was a penetrating gunshot through the biceps muscle of the right arm and into the lower lobe of the right lung. This 9mm Silvertip did expand as designed — the medical examiner described it as "markedly deformed." Many believe that had this bullet penetrated just a little deeper it would have struck the heart. These same people fail to realize that simply penetrating the heart still allows full physical activity for up to 90 seconds after the impact.

This wound must not be confused with a second chest wound. This 9mm Silvertip penetrated the triceps muscle of the right arm and also struck the chest. However, the bullet path only went through skin tissue and muscle. This "markedly deformed" bullet ended up near the shoulder blade without striking any internal organs.

On September 15, 1987, the FBI sponsored a Wound Ballistics Workshop at their academy in Quantico, Virginia. In attendance were Robert Adkins,

The Remington .45 Auto 185-grain JHP was the hero of the FBI Wound Ballistics Workshop. Most of the panelists liked its moderate expansion and deep penetration.

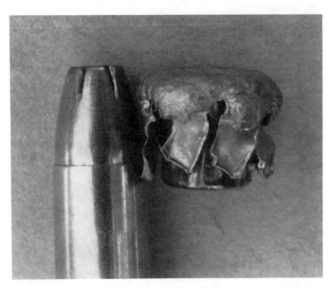

This Winchester 9mm 147-grain OSM was fired from a Glock 17 and expanded to the typical .58 caliber. It failed to stop a knife-wielding psycho who wounded an officer before a second OSM fired into the attacker's head ended the incident.

Southwestern Institute of Forensic Sciences; Dr. Vincent DiMaio, Chief Medical Examiner, Bexar County, Texas; Dr. Martin Fackler, Army Wound Ballistics Lab; Stan Goddard, Battelle Columbus Labs; Dr. Douglas Lindsey, University of Arizona; Sgt. Evan Marshall, Detroit Police Department; Dr. Carroll Peters, University of Tennessee; and Dr. O'Brien Smith, University of Tennessee.

The official summary of their findings makes an excellent commentary on where the black art of handgun stopping power was in 1987. The following is that summary, taken directly and without edit, from the published report:

WOUNDING — Except for hits to the central nervous system (CNS), reliable and reproducible instant incapacitation is not possible with any handgun bullet. Whether incapacitation occurs depends entirely upon the physical, emotional, psychological, and mental state of the individual, including the presence or absence of narcotics, alcohol, or adrenalin. Even if the heart is destroyed, the individual still has enough oxygen in the brain for full and complete voluntary action for 10 to 15 seconds.

Temporary cavitation caused by a handgun round has no wounding effect. Kinetic energy deposit has no wounding effect. Organs will only be damaged by handgun bullets if they are hit by that bullet. Therefore, bullets must be capable of penetrating deeply enough to pass through the organs to be effective. The experts condemned the use of the well-known Relative Incapacitation Index (RII) as a viable method for the comparison of bullets inasmuch as the RII measurements are based on temporary cavitation and do not reflect actual wound results.

Given equal penetration, a bigger bullet will disrupt more tissue and hopefully cause greater bleeding. Barring a CNS hit, incapacitation can only be forced by blood loss, and that takes time as well as sufficient penetraion to hit major blood vessels through intervening musculature, fat, clothing, arms, etc. Any bullet that will not reliably penetrate a minimum of 10 to 12 inches of soft tissue is inadequate. Penetration is a function of bullet mass and design, not velocity. The feared hazards of overpenetration are greatly exaggerated except in the possible case of full-metal-jacketed (FMJ) ammunition.

9mm VERSUS .45 — The single most important factor in assessing the effectiveness of any caliber is penetration. If the bullet will not penetrate at least 10 to 12 inches of soft tissue, it is dangerously inadequate. Given equal penetration, a larger bullet will disrupt more tissue and could hasten blood loss; however, the experts could not say that the damage caused by the larger .45 caliber was significantly more than that of the 9mm. Barring the FMJ ammunition in both calibers, there are no currently available 9mm hollowpoints that are adequate. If they ex-

The Hydra-Shok design makes the best of a bad situation in the 9mm 147-grain load. In forty-nine shootings, this load was 71-percent effective.

The Winchester 9mm 147-grain OSM was designed for maximum accuracy from carbine weapons in military roles. It is *not* suitable for maximum stopping power from handguns in a police or defensive role.

pand, they do not penetrate enough. If they do not expand, they perform like FMJ ammunition.

A new 9mm round, the 147-grain, subsonic ammunitin developed for the Department of Defense, may be the answer for 9mm pistols. Preliminary testing of this round reflects excellent penetration, expansion, and accuracy. In .45 caliber, the hollowpoint ammunition tested ranged in penetration from marginally adequate to acceptable. Three of the eight experts recommend the .45 over the current 9mm rounds with the exception of the 147-grain, subsonic round, which they recommend for further testing and evaluation. Four of the eight advised that there was no difference in the wounding effects of either caliber given adequate penetration. One of the eight recommended the 9mm based upon future military research and development that will occur in the years to come and which will improve the caliber in terms of ballistic efficiency. Such improvements are conservatively ten or more years away. Because incapacitation cannot be predicted, the Agent should keep on shooting as long as the individual poses a threat. The shooter should not assume that one or two hits will incapacitate or stop the threat. For this reason, several of the experts opted for increased magazine capacity.

While expansion is desirable, no bullet should be selected if it must expand in order to perform properly. The perception of the Agents using the weapons can be an overwhelming factor. If the Agent believes in the reliability and effectiveness

of the weapon and the ammunition, then he/she tends to shoot better with that weapon.

One immediately notices the dramatic pendulum swing on the topic of penetration. Indeed, "adquate penetration" was the catch phrase of the late 1980s. In the early and mid-1970s, the NIJ/LEAA considered penetration beyond 8.7 inches as wasted. The depth of 1.6 inches was given the most significance (see Chapter 4).

In the late 1970s and early 1980s, the penetration pendulum moved to the moderate and controlled range of 9 to 10 inches of tissue. The Southwestern Institute of Forensic Science wanted bullets exiting a 5.5-inch block of 20-percent gelatin with 10 to 25 percent of its energy left (see Chapter 5).

The authors of this book feel that the new penetration requirements that allow or encourage penetration as deep as 16 to 18 inches of tissue are a dangerous overreaction. The 9mm Silvertip has an excellent street record. The single instance of underpenetration in the FBI/Miami shootout is not grounds for withdrawal from service.

But this was exactly what happened. The FBI pulled the 115-grain 9mm Silvertip from the field. As an interim load and until a more suitable replacement was found, the 147-grain Olin Super Match hollowpoint was issued in April 1988. This round overpenetrates too much in soft tissue for a police scenario, just like the 158-grain .357 Magnum hollowpoint.

The FBI got what it asked for; namely, expert opinion and a lot of it. The Bureau sent out the message that it wanted deeper penetration, and most of the

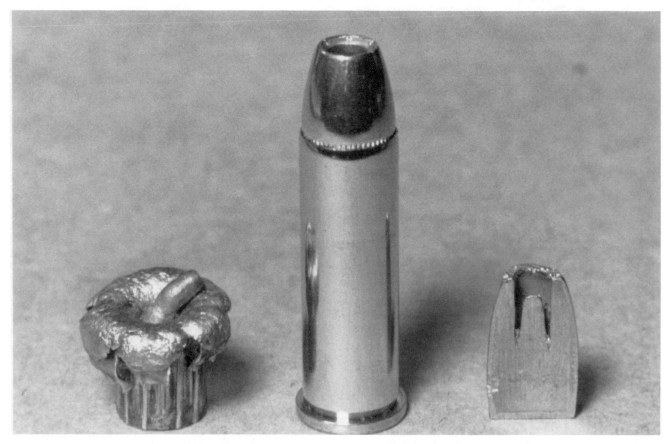

The Federal .38 Special +P 147-grain Hydra-Shok is shown recovered from bare gelatin. This load has been adopted by the FBI to replace the 158-grain SWC-LHP.

experts on the panel were more than willing to give that. Pay no mind to the facts: the OSM was intended not for police work but for special operations work that included the use of suppressed handguns and submachine guns. Supersonic ammunition cannot be effectively silenced because of the sonic "crack" of the bullet.

The 9mm 147-grain JHP OSM works perfectly when used as it was designed to be used. But it could not be a worse round for police use, according to actual police shooting results. Compare the 9mm 115-grain STHP Silvertip with the 9mm 147-grain OSM hollow-point in Table 8-4.

Based on vocal endorsements by a few members of the panel, the FBI dropped the Silvertip and adopted the OSM. Yet the FBI evidently learned its lesson about listening to experts who are too far removed from the streets and courts and set out to do its own ammo tests in late 1988. The pressure to "do something" in the wake of the 1986 tragedy was off. Now it had time to go back and do it the right way. It still held to some basic dogmatic assumptions pushed on it by some of the experts. However, the ammo tests themselves were extremely good. *Other police departments should adopt these test procedures.*

TEST ONE: BARE GELATIN

The gelatin block was bare and shot at a range of 10 feet measured from the muzzle to the front of the block. This test correlated FBI results with those being obtained by other researchers, few of whom shot into anything other than bare gelatin. It was common to obtain the greatest expansion in this test. Rounds that did not meet the standards against bare gelatin tended to be unreliable in the more practical test that followed.

TEST TWO: HEAVY CLOTHING

The gelatin block was covered with four layers of clothing: one layer of cotton T-shirt material (48 threads per inch); one layer of cotton shirt material (80 threads per inch); a 10-ounce down comforter in a cambric shell cover (232 threads per inch); and one layer of 13-ounce cotton denim (50 threads per inch). This simulated typical cold weather wear. The block was shot at 10 feet, measured from the muzzle to the front of the block.

TEST THREE: STEEL

Two pieces of 20-gauge, hot-rolled steel with a galvanized finish were set 3 inches apart. The steel was in 6-inch squares. The gelatin block was covered with light clothing and placed 18 inches behind the rearmost piece of steel. The shot was made at a distance of 10 feet measured from the muzzle to the front of the first piece of steel. Light clothing was defined as one layer of the above-described cotton T-shirt material and one layer of the above-described cotton shirt material (used in all subsequent tests).

The steel used was the heaviest gauge commonly found in automobile doors. This test simulated the weakest part of a car door — an area or areas where the heaviest obstacle is nothing more than two pieces of 20-gauge steel. Unfortunately, there is no way of telling exactly where those spots are from car to car.

TEST FOUR: WALLBOARD

Two pieces of .5-inch standard gypsum board were set 3.5 inches apart. The pieces were 6 inches square. The gelatin block was covered with light clothing and set 18 inches behind the rearmost piece of gypsum. The shot was made at 10 feet, measured from the muzzle to the front surface of the first piece of gypsum. This test simulated a typical interior building wall.

TEST FIVE: PLYWOOD

One piece of .75-inch AA fir plywood was shot through. The piece was 6 inches square. The gelatin block was covered with light clothing and set 18 inches behind the rear surface of the plywood. The shot was made at 10 feet, measured from the muzzle to the front surface of the plywood. This test simulated the resistance of typical wooden doors or construction timbers.

TEST SIX: AUTOMOBILE GLASS

One piece of A.S.I. .25-inch laminated automobile safety glass measuring 15 x 18 inches was set at 45-degree angle. The weapon's line of bore was offset 15 degrees to the side, resulting in a compound angle of impact for the bullet upon the glass. The gelatin block was covered with light clothing and set 18 inches behind the glass. The shot was made at 10 feet, measured from the muzzle to the center of the glass pane. This test, with its two angles, simulated a shot taken at the driver of a car from the left front quarter of the vehicle.

TEST SEVEN: LIGHT CLOTHING AT 20 YARDS

The gelatin block was covered with light clothing and shot at a range of 20 yards, measured from the muzzle of the weapon to the front of the block. This test assessed the effects of increased range and, consequently, decreased velocity.

TEST EIGHT: AUTOMOBILE GLASS AT 20 YARDS

This event repeated Test Six but at a range of 20 yards, measured from the muzzle to the front of the glass, and without the 15-degree offset. The shot was

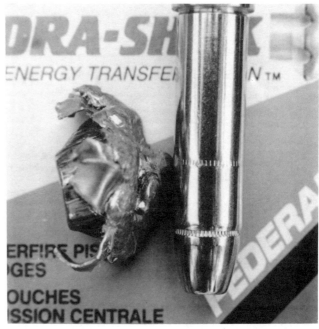

The FBI replaced the 158-grain SWC-LHP in .38 Special +P with this Federal 147-grain Hydra-Shok. The Hydra-Shok has the same wound ballistics and slightly better penetration against vehicles.

made from straight in front of the glass, simulating a shot at the driver of a car bearing down on the shooter.

In addition to the above described series of tests, each cartridge was tested for velocity and accuracy. Twenty rounds in 10-shot groups were fired through a test barrel (a rifled barrel bolted solidly to a test fixture) and the velocity of each measured. The velocities were averaged and the results reported with extreme spreads, maximums and minimums, and the standard deviations. Twenty rounds were then fired through the service weapon used in the penetration tests and the velocities measured and reported the same way. All groups were fired at 25 yards. They were measured from center to center of the two most widely spaced holes, and the results were averaged and reported.

It is important to note here that the test barrel results demonstrate the ammunition's potential independent of the various weapon factors that can influence ammunition performance. Test barrel results are the purest measure of ammunition capability for accuracy and velocity. Repeating these tests with a service weapon measures how well the cartridge/weapon combination can realize that potential and is a significant factor to be considered.

In each test, the depth of penetration into the gelatin and the diameter of the recovered bullet was measured. The summarized results included the average penetration from all eight tests, the number of bullets

As a contrast to the poor performance that all 147-grain bullets have in 9mm, the 147-grain Hydra-Shok works extremely well in the .38 Special +P. This one ended a holdup.

that penetrated *less* than 12 inches, the average expansion, and the average permanent crush cavity volume factored for a maximum of 18 inches of penetration. This is all extremely valuable information that should be studied before making a load selection.

The FBI results also included some hocus-pocus things like wound "efficiency" and wound "value." These carry excess baggage called "assumptions." As a result, the FBI wound "value" has absolutely no relevance to the street. It is just so much number crunching (see Table 6-2).

When the "wound value" (W) is compared to actual street results, we do *not* see that as W increases, the bullet becomes more reliable. The three 9mm results are perfect examples of this. In this caliber, W tells us exactly nothing. Nor do we see that a round with twice the W value has twice the incapacitation potential. The .38 Special 158-grain SWC-HP has a W of .42 and an actual effectiveness of 69 percent. The .357 Magnum 158-grain JSP has a W of 1.86. That is 4.5 times the .38 Special load, yet the actual effectiveness is only 3 percentage points greater.

With a confidence factor of 90 percent, the FBI W value has a correlation coefficient with actual results of .53. That is the *worst* correlation of any method ever offered to predict effectiveness. It is only slightly more reliable than throwing darts. As a statement of fact, our weather is predicted with better reliability than the W value predicts stopping power.

The basic FBI methodology involves calculating the permanent crush cavity after shooting through a variety of obstacles. *When restricted to just that,* this methodology is excellent, especially for ammo below 1,300 fps.

The FBI clouds the issue with factoring in the percent of times a bullet does not reach the arbitrary minimum of 12 inches, regardless of the obstacle. If this method must be used, at the very least ammo that penetrates more than 18 inches must be equally penalized with ammo that penetrates less than 12 inches. This is for two reasons. We, as cops, cannot lose sight of the hazards of overpenetrating bullets. Furthermore, beyond a certain minimum, ammo that penetrates deeper produces less stopping power. More on this in Chapter 17.

Table 6-1

FBI AMMO BEFORE 1986 MIAMI SHOOTOUT

Ammo	Effectiveness
.38 Special +P 158-grain SWC-HP	69.7%
9mm 115-grain STHP Silvertip	79.1%

FBI AMMO AFTER 1986 MIAMI SHOOTOUT

Ammo	Effectiveness
.38 Special +P 147-grain JHP Hydra-Shok	69% (est)
9mm 147-grain JHP Hydra-Shok	71.4%
10mm 180-grain JHP medium velocity	78% (est)
.45 Auto 230-grain JHP Hydra Shok	88.4%

"est" is an estimate based on predictive formulas from actual street results found in Chapter 17. The .38 Special results are averages of the 2-inch and 4-inch results for W-W ammo.

1. "Date Tested" is important because manufacturers frequently change aspects of their ammunition without notice, and without labeling changes. Some changes in bullet design or powder charge, for example, can have significant effects on that round's performance.

2. "Caliber" is the diameter of the unfired projectile in inches (in).

3. "Velocity" is the average velocity of 20 rounds fired through the indicated "Weapon Used," expressed in feet per second (fps).

4. "KE" is the kinetic energy of the projectile expressed in foot/pounds (ft/lb). It is calculated by the formula

$$\frac{Bw \, (Vo)^2}{450,400} \qquad \text{where}$$

Bw=Bullet weight in grains.
Vo=Velocity of the bullet in fps.

450,400 is a constant for converting weight in grains times velocity squared into foot/pounds. Note that rounds with the highest KE are seldom the best performers.

5. "Pen" is the average penetration in inches of all 40 shots fired through the FBI Ammunition Test, (eight test events, five shots fired in each event). The complete test represents the obstacles and situations commonly found in FBI shootings.

The resultant measured performance of the ammunition is an indicator of how well it can be expected to perform in general FBI use. Analysis of ammunition performance in FBI shooting incidents is used to cross-check and validate the Ammunition Test results.

The FBI minimum standard for penetration is 12 inches. A round that meets or exceeds that minimum in all test events will be more successful and effective over a variety of shooting incidents than one that meets the standards in only five or six test events. The closer the "Pen" figure approaches 18 inches, the better the round has performed.

6. "Exp" is the average expansion in inches for all 40 shots in the FBI Ammunition Test. The expansion of each individual shot is measured by averaging its greatest diameter with its smallest diameter. Expansion can vary widely depending on the test event. For example, in test events 4 and 5, few rounds expand at all. Test event 1 commonly yields the greatest expansion recorded.

Expansion is important in that it increases the size of the wound inflicted. Given penetration in excess of 12 inches, the only means of increasing the effectiveness of the wound is by increasing its size. On the other hand, expansion can limit penetration unacceptably.

Ammunition that achieves the best balance between these two factors will provide the best results within each caliber.

7. "Adj Vol" is the average 18-inch volumetric figure in cubic inches for all 40 shots. Volume is calculated for each individual test shot with the formula

$$(\pi) \, (R^2) \, (P) \qquad \text{where}$$

π=3.1416
R=1/2 the expansion of the bullet.
P=penetration in inches up to a maximum of 18.

Penetration in excess of 18 inches is ignored. It represents no practical benefit in FBI usage. The resultant figure, in cubic inches, is a measure of the bullet's *potential* to disrupt tissue. The larger the Adj Vol figure, the more severe the wound the bullet can inflict.

8. "Rds <12" is the number of shots out of the 40 test shots in which the round did not meet or exceed the 12-inch minimum penetration standard.

9. "Sr" is the Success Rate in meeting or exceeding the 12-inch minimum penetration standard through the forty-shot FBI Ammunition Test.

10. "T" is the average of two 10-shot groups fired from a test barrel in a Ransom Rest at a range of 25 yards. Each group is measured from center to center of the two most widely separated holes.

11. "G" is the average of two 10-shot groups fired from the actual "Weapon Used" in a Ransom Rest at a range of 25 yards. Each group is measured from center to center of the two most widely separated shots.

12. "P" is the percent the average penetration "Pen" is greater or less than the 12-inch minimum standard.

13. "E" is the percent the expansion "Exp" is greater or less than the specific bullet's original, unfired diameter, which is listed in the "Caliber" column.

14. "Vc" is a comparison of the "Adj Vol" to the minimum acceptable *for that caliber*. The minimum acceptable volume for the caliber is calculated by using the same formula

$$(\pi)\ (R2)\ (P) \qquad\qquad where$$

$(\pi)=3.1416$
$R=1/2$ "Caliber"
$P=12$ inches

The resultant volume figure assumes an unexpanded bullet of that caliber penetrating 12 inches. It is the minimum acceptable for that caliber. Vc is the percent which the "Adj Vol" is greater or less than that minimum.
Vc is useful for comparing tissue disruption potentials *within a given caliber*. For example, of two .45 rounds, if one has a Vc twice that of the other, it has twice the tissue disruption potential, all else being equal.

15. "V" is the percent the "Adj Vol" is greater or less than the minimum standard volume regardless of caliber. The minimum standard volume is defined as an unexpanded .38 bullet (caliber .357 inches) penetrating 12 inches. That figure is 1.20 cubic inches.
"V" is useful for comparing tissue disruption potentials of different caliber bullets relative to a standard, all else being equal. A bullet with V=240% has twice the relative tissue disruption *potential* of a different caliber bullet with V=114%.

16. "P+V" is the sum of the values "P" and "V" with those values expressed as percentiles, i.e., 94% = 0.94. The result is a measure of *potential* wounding effectiveness suitable for comparison *across calibers*.

17. "We" is the Wound Efficiency. It is an index of how efficiently the bullet creates the wounds it does. The formula is

$$We=[(Vt-Vmin)/Vmin]/0.5 \qquad where$$

Vt=Adj Vol obtained in test
Vmin=volume of an unexpanded projectile of that caliber penetrating 12 inches. Vmin for
    various calibers is as follows

.45-	1.93
10mm-	1.51
.38/.357-	1.20
9mm-	1.19

The value 0.5 is the ratio of Vmax (an unexpanded projectile in that caliber penetrating 18 inches)
minus Vmin, over Vmin.

"We" of about 3.0 is indicative of an optimum combination of penetration and expansion. Less
than 3.0 denotes inefficent combinations of expansion and/or penetration. "We" above 3.0 indicates
excessive penetration and expansion, usually at the cost of high pressure and recoil. *"We" has no value for
comparing across calibers.*

18. "A" is an expression of accuracy potential and its practical realization in the actual weapon used. It
is calculated by the formula

$$A=[(G-T)/Sr]+T \qquad \text{where}$$

G=Average weapon group.
T=Average test barrel group.
Sr=Success Rate.

This formula accounts for accuracy potential and accuracy realized from the specific weapon used,
modified by the measured Success Rate.

The modifier Sr adjusts the accuracy quotient by the important factor of practical utility. An
unsuccessful round that is highly accurate is far less desirable than an adequately accurate, highly successful
round. The lower the value of A, the better the round has realized its accuracy potential *in that specific
weapon*. "A" of 4.0 or less is desirable.

19. "W" is the index of actual wounding effectiveness, not potential, as measured by the FBI
Ammunition Test results. It is obtained by the formula

$$W=[(P+Vc)(Sr)]+[(V-Vc)(E)]$$
$$\text{where}$$

P=percentile average penetration "Pen" is greater or less than 12".
V=percentile "AdjVol" is more or less than the defined minimum of a
    .357 caliber bullet penetrating 12".
Vc=percentile "adjVol" is more or less than the caliber minimum Vmin.
Sr=Success Rate.
E=percentile "Exp" is more or less than the bullet's unfired diameter.

"W" is the critical value for comparative purposes. As W increases, the more effective and reliable the
wound that round will inflict.

Given identically located hits, a round with twice the W value should have twice the potential for
incapacitating the subject.

From "Ammunition Tests," January 1990, Firearms Training Unit, FBI Academy, U.S. Dept. of Justice.

Table 6-2

FBI WOUND VALUE VS. ACTUAL RESULTS

	FBI	Actual
.38 Special +P W-W 158-gr. SWC-HP	.42	69.72
.38 Speical +P R-P 158-gr. SWC-HP	.72	67.39
.357 Magnum W-W 145-gr. Silvertip	1.56	83.33
.357 Magnum W-W 158-gr. JSP	1.86	72.41
9mm W-W 115-gr. Silvertip	.41	79.14
9mm W-W 147-gr. JHP OSM	.68	68.54
9mm Fed 147-gr. Hydra-Shok	1.65	71.42
.45 Auto W-W 185-gr. Silvertip	1.01	80.32
.45 Auto Fed 230-gr. Hydra-Shok	2.49	88.37
.45 Auto Rem 185-gr. JHP	1.94	78.57

Correlation coefficient: .53
Intercept: 69
Slope: 4.5
Degree of certainty: 90 percent

CHAPTER 7

INTRODUCTION TO RESULTS FROM THE STREET

Readers need to understand that what follows is not some arcane mathematical formula or complex computer designed to predict what handgun loads *might* do in actual shootings. Instead, it is the result of over a decade of research on the results of actual shootings.

While traveling across the country on magazine assignments, I developed a number of sources who were willing to report on shootings in their areas. Furthermore, I met with emergency room physicians in all parts of the country to gain their insights into the degree of actual incapacitation suffered by gunshot victims. Whenever possible, I also attended autopsies in various cities across the country.

Later, while assigned to the Homicide Section of the Detroit Police Department, I took advantage of the opportunities present there. Attending over 400 autopsies provided insight that proved invaluable in dispelling the hype and myth about handgun bullet performance. The result is the most detailed study of handgun bullet performance to be published to date.

CRITERIA

The results of "stops" that are included in this study are of little value without also informing the reader of the criteria used. Readers need to understand that detailed, reliable information on shootings is *extremely difficult to obtain*. For every fifty shootings that I heard about, I might obtain enough data in ten to include in this study. I avoided the temptation to use the broad data base available in Detroit as an exclusive source. This was done because geographical and other

factors present in Detroit might not be reflected across the country.

The criteria used to determine whether a shooting was defined as a stop or a failure are as follows:

1. Only torso shots were used. I didn't think it was a fair indication of any round's stopping power to include shootings where the victim was hit in the hand and continued to pursue his antisocial activities, and then log this as a failure.

2. Multiple hits were also discarded. Again, I didn't consider it a true indication of any round's performance to include instances where the victim took three hollowpoints in the chest and collapsed. How could we include these along with cases where one round was effective? If I included multiple hits, then this study could legitimately be attacked on the grounds that multiple hits are not a reliable indicator as to any round's stopping power.

3. A stop is defined as follows: if the victim was assaulting someone, he collapsed without being able to fire another shot or strike another blow. If he was fleeing, he collapsed within 10 feet.

4. In order to include a shooting in this study, I insisted on either having or at least being able to review some of the following: police reports, evidence technician reports, statements by the victim (if he survived), homicide reports, autopsy results, and photos. Whenever possible, I also talked to the emergency room doctors and attending physicians.

5. Recovered bullets were either personally

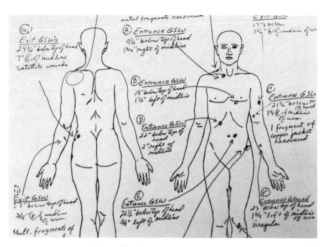

Evan Marshall attended over 400 autopsies in an attempt to understand bullet performance.

Police shooting reports provide useful information. Hundreds of reports like this have been used to collect shooting data.

ternally, this passes through soft tissue and muscle of the right neck, transects the right jugular vein and common carotid artery, passes through the tongue to the anterior lower surface of the tongue where a deformed, copper jacketed, medium caliber bullet is recovered. This is marked with the decedent's initials and the date and placed into an evidence envelope.

3. There is an irregular graze wound and associated lacerations on the right side of the posterior scalp. The major component of this wound begins 2" right of the midline and 4" below the top of the head, is up to ¼" wide and extends 1-3/4" inferiorly and anteriorly toward the right ear. There is a central area of abrasion in the main part of the wound and a 1" long perpendicular laceration extending posteriorly from the inferior portion of the main wound. A 3/8" long superficial laceration lies approximately 1" anterior to the medial aspect of the main wound. ¼" posterior to the posterior end of the major wound is a perpendicular, 3/4" laceration. Deep to this laceration, there is a depressed skull fracture and four bullet fragments are recovered in the soft tissue. There is no penetration of the skull. There is focal subarachnoid hemorrhage deep to the fracture. The recovered fragments are placed into an evidence envelope.

4. On the point of the right shoulder, 5½" right of the midline, is an irregular, 3/4" antero-posterior by ¼" graze wound with a ¼" diameter area of ecchymosis at the anterior end. This corresponds to rips in the shirt and T-shirt.

5. There is an irregular puncture wound in the right upper back, 10" below the top of the head and 2-3/4" right of the midline. This is an irregular, 1/8" diameter area of ecchymosis with a central 1/16" defect. Foreign bodies are not detected within this wound.

No evidence of close range fire is seen around any of the above wounds.

Autopsy reports are vital to the study of wound ballistics. Evidence technician reports are also helpful.

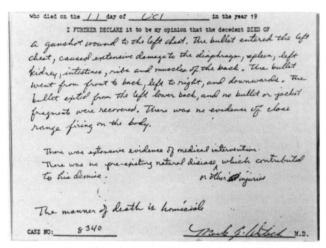

Autopsies hold the key to understanding bullet performance in human beings.

examined or photographed by me, or I was provided with photographs of the bullets. Interestingly enough, there were several stops where hollowpoints did not expand, reenforcing the fact that bullet placement is the key.

6. A minimum of five shootings were required before a handgun load was included in this study. Fortunately, in most instances I was able to obtain much more than that, and the actual number of shootings using each load (at the time of publication) is listed.

MISCONCEPTIONS

When this study was first reported in depth (in the premier issue of *Peterson's Handguns*), I received an incredible amount of mail — in excess of 100 letters! Over 90 percent were favorable, while the remaining 10 percent generally were critical of the fact that I was relying on too small a sample or had failed to include multiple hits.

What these critical readers failed to understand is the extreme difficulty in obtaining reliable and detailed

data. On two separate occasions, I undertook transcontinental flights at my own expense because medical examiners in large West Coast cities had promised to let me review their files. When I arrived, however, the permission was withdrawn without explanation.

Other readers failed to realize that that in the statement, "detailed information on at least five shootings had to be available before a load would be included in this study," the key words were "at least." Fortunately, the publication of the article in *Peterson's Handguns* opened a floodgate of detailed information that allowed me to rely on a much broader data base. Interestingly enough, the added data changed only some of the shooting results.

It should be understood that prior to initiating this study, I was a dyed-in-the-wool fan of the .45 ACP. My devotion to the big-bore, moderate-velocity, full-metal-jacketed slug was based on what I had considered credible sources. I was to find to my extreme disappointment, however, that such dogmatic statements were actually based on rumor, innuendo, and "sea stories." The .45 ACP is a good load that offers good, though not spectacular, stopping power in the real world. It is not, however, the Sword Excalibur, and the sooner we realize that and concentrate on bullet placement, the safer we all will be.

While I'll freely admit to all sorts of personal bias, none of it is contained here. Shootings are included not only from Detroit, but also from San Francisco, Washington, D.C., Miami, Los Angeles, and New York. Shootings from Europe and Asia were also included. Remember, this study has only one goal: to provide accurate data to good guys and gals so that they can survive lethal confrontations.

CHAPTER 8

ACTUAL STREET RESULTS FOR ALL CALIBERS

This chapter covers actual street results for common calibers and loads issued to or carried by police officers. Many of these weapons and loads apply to civilian home defense scenarios as well. The results are based on police-action shooting reports, officer and medical examiner interviews, and even press videotapes of actual shootings. The dialogue and narrative were taken directly from these sources (primarily police reports), or, in some cases, were paraphrased from numerous accounts.

The recommendations and results in this chapter take into account a reasonable probability of striking an intermediate target and a reasonable probability of a lower abdominal or transverse shot. All of these scenarios call for deeper penetration and a more moderate energy release than loads for backup or concealed carry weapons provide.

These street results are the heart and soul of this book on handgun stopping power. Predictions based on Relative Stopping Power, Relative Incapacitation Index, and even advanced energy-loss and power-floor methodologies fade in comparison to what really happens when a bullet meets a man.

.32 ACP

Frankly, I had no intention of including any caliber smaller than the .380 ACP, but I kept stumbling across cases where Winchester's excellent Silvertip jacketed hollowpoint was used. The darn thing always seems to expand in soft tissue; at least I haven't been able to find an instance where it has failed to do so. Re-

member, one of the most important reasons for talking to attending physicians is to determine the wound track and whether or not bone was struck.

Street Results: .32 ACP

An undercover narc, he routinely carried three guns: a cocked-and-locked Government .45, a S&W Model 469, and a Seecamp .32 auto. His fellow team members poked good-natured fun at him, but it had no impact on the size of his personal arsenal.

Going into a high-rise luxury apartment complex on a bitterly cold February night, he had $87,000 in cash in a beat-up brown bag to buy dope. A meeting had been set up with three Colombians to purchase a sample delivery of cocaine, with a tentative arrangement to purchase large quantities on a regular basis. Streetwise, the officer was not wired but the bag was.

He was admitted to the apartment, quickly frisked, and his .45 and 9mm taken from him. He began to protest this lack of good faith when one of the Colombians told him, "We're going to throw you out the damn window so who cares about good faith!" The officer suddenly pushed the one doper out of the way and dove for the bathroom. Jumping into the bathtub for cover, he jerked the Seecamp from the small of his back, where it had been held by an Ace bandage. The bathroom door flew open and a shotgun-armed man appeared. The officer fired four rounds and ducked down. He then heard the front door forced open and a volley of shots fired in the other room.

The autopsy of the officer's attacker determined that

Table 8-1

.32 AUTO ACTUAL RESULTS

	Total Shootings	One-Shot Stops	Percentage	Muzzle Velocity
1. W-W 60-gr. STHP	61	36	59.01	816 fps
2. W-W 71-gr. FMJ	96	48	50.00	784 fps

one Silvertip .32 ACP slug had entered the heart, piercing the left ventricle and causing his death. The recovered diameter of the slug was .410 of an inch and the recovered weight was 46 grains.

• • • • •

A West Coast party store owner had been involved in one prior shooting where he had relied on full-metal-jacketed ammunition in his Walther PP. In that instance the holdup man took 5 rounds and still managed to wound the owner's 15-year-old son while making his escape.

The store owner went to his local gun shop to buy some better ammunition and came home with two boxes of Winchester .32 ACP Silvertip.

The next weekend he drove up the coast to a deserted beach and test fired his new ammunition. He returned to his store and cleaned the pistol. He had just reloaded it and stuck it in an inside-the-pants holster when he heard a shot from the store. Drawing

his pistol, he came through the back door and saw his cashier on the floor bleeding. A white male was standing over him holding a pistol. The owner fired four times at the holdup man. The felon turned toward the entrance, took five steps, and collapsed.

The autopsy indicated that one of the four rounds had hit the bad guy. It had entered the left armpit, piercing the vena cava and causing severe bleeding and death. The recovered slug weighed 41 grains and had a diameter of .53 caliber. A coroner's inquest cleared the store owner in the shooting, but he was arrested and convicted for being in possession of an unregistered pistol!

• • • • •

A southern cop was stopped by an elderly lady who wanted to give him a pistol that had belonged to her deceased husband. The pistol was a Manhurin .32 in mint condition. Reluctant to accept a gift, he offered

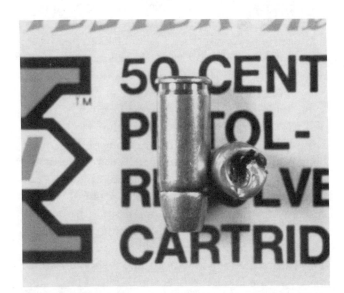

This .32 Auto 60-grain Silvertip was recovered from a dope dealer. The aluminum-jacketed bullet deformed slightly.

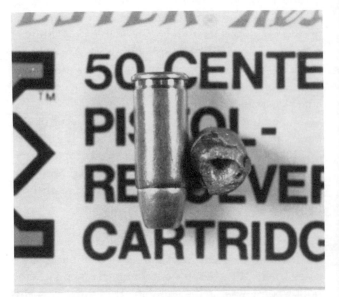

This .32 Auto 60-grain Silvertip stopped a felony in progress. The Silvertip is superior to FMJ hardball.

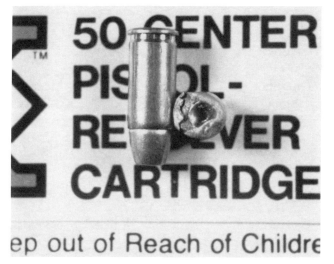

This .32 Auto 60-grain Silvertip ended a domestic dispute. The Silvertip performs well in this inadequate caliber.

to take the weapon if the woman would accept $50 for it. She agreed, and the officer loaded it with Silvertip and carried it as a second gun.

Working the graveyard shift in January, one of his responsibilities was to check the local lovers lane. He noticed a car parked with the motor running. There was a lot of movement inside the car, but he attributed it to the romantic enthusiasm of youth. When he pulled the driver's side door open to warn its occupants that they had better get dressed and go home, the driver shot him in the face! The sexual activity inside the car was not between consenting adults — it was a rape!

The officer fell on his back and was only semiconscious as one of the two rapists pulled his .357 from his holster. The men started to leave, when one of them said, "Let's kill him!" Terrorized by this remark, the officer pulled the .32 from his waistband and opened fire. The first round hit one of the bad guys in the stomach, and he dropped to his knees screaming, "Bob, Bob, he killed me!" The second felon jumped in the police car and ran over the officer's left leg as he escaped, breaking it. The officer crawled to the first felon, handcuffed him, and sent the rape victim for help.

At the hospital, the officer was found to have a small-caliber wound in his forehead. It was determined that the round had ridden along the outside of the skull and exited over the left ear, causing minor though painful damage. The bad guy had been hit in the stomach, losing a large portion of his large intestine. After a lengthy hospital stay he was convicted of rape and attempted murder. The slug was recovered 2 inches from the spine, weighed 47 grains, and had a recovered diameter of .50 caliber.

• • • • •

She was a white female in her sixties who worked in a self-serve gas station in a large urban center. Worried about a series of holdup/murders of gas station attendants, she went to a sporting goods store and bought a used Browning auto in .32 ACP. The clerk at the shop had convinced her that Silvertip was the round she should rely on.

Two weeks later, she saw a man stagger into the gas station and collapse by the pumps. Fearing that he was injured, she left her secured office to check on him. As she bent over him, she found herself looking down the wrong end of a sawed-off shotgun. He forced her back into the office and took the cash bag that was under the counter. He pointed the shotgun at her face and said, "You know what happens now, bitch!"

A car pulled into the station and while the bad guy was distracted, the woman dove for her purse. Seeing the movement, he discharged the shotgun, missing her. Grabbing her pistol, she fired twice. The holdup man collapsed dead. One of her two rounds had taken effect, entering the left side of the chest and traveling on into the heart, inflicting a fatal wound. The recovered slug weighed 39 grains and had a diameter of .59 caliber.

• • • • •

A retired cop, his wife good-naturedly kidded him about the pistol he carried. After all, they had left a crime-ridden East Coast urban center for a small, rural, western town.

Thirty-one years as a big-city cop, however, had left him with a lingering feeling that there were punks everywhere. Firm in this conviction, he carried his Walther .32 wherever he went.

He was leaving the neighborhood market after buying some groceries when he noticed two long-haired punks harassing one of his neighbors. He went over and told them somewhat impolitely to leave her alone. The bigger of the two turned with an open knife and said, "Buzz off, you old fart!"

The retired cop's response was not what the two miscreants expected. He carefully laid his bag of groceries down, produced his pistol from the small of his back, and told the knife-wielding suspect to drop it and put his hands up. The punk laughed and said, "You better put that popgun down, Pop, before I cut you long, wide, and deep!"

The retired officer fired. The punk went down with

Table 8-2

.380 AUTO ACTUAL RESULTS

	Total Shootings	One-Shot Stops	Percentage	Muzzle Velocity
1. Fed 90-gr. JHP	94	60	63.82	1,003 fps
2. PPS 54-gr. BHP (MPP)	14	8	57.14	1,142 fps
3. W-W 85-gr. STHP	59	32	54.23	985 fps
4. R-P 88-gr. JHP	31	17	54.84	1,001 fps
5. CCI 88-gr. JHP	30	16	53.33	933 fps
6. Horn 90-gr. JHP	19	10	52.63	985 fps
7. Fed 95-gr. FMJ	80	41	51.25	929 fps

a round in the throat. His partner bent down to pick up the knife and was shot in the top of the head before he could accomplish his task. He was dead when he hit the ground, and the first felon died on the way to the hospital.

The slug recovered from the throat weighed 45 grains and had a diameter of .38 caliber.

.380 ACP

The .380 ACP was generally ignored as a serious choice for defensive purposes until Lee Jurras burst on the scene with the Super Vel line of ammunition. Jurras reasoned that the best approach to handgun stopping power was to radically lighten the bullet weight, make it as fragile as possible, and drive it at a substantially increased velocity.

While the .38 Special was the greatest beneficiary of this approach, the .380 also won. Super Vel's offering in this caliber was an 88-grain jacketed hollowpoint that averaged 1,022 fps from my prewar Walther PP. In actual shootings, the SV .380 JHP load rarely expanded evenly. Generally, it would peel down one side, making a sort of "half-mushroom" shape. Only when it hit heavy bone would it provide the shape we all hope for from our hollowpoints.

Currently, of course, Super Vel is out of production. Today we can choose between hollowpoint offerings from Winchester, Federal, Remington, CCI, and Hornady. Of the current commercially available rounds, the Federal 90-grain JHP has proven to be the best performer.

The .380 is a favorite of undercover narcs, off-duty officers, and civilians who like a small pistol for defensive or second-gun purposes. Of all the current .380s, I like the SIG P230 the best and carry it as a backup to my 9mm.

Street Results: .380 ACP Federal 90-grain JHP

He had run the neighborhood bakery for thirty years, watching his neighborhood change from a quiet residential area to a drug-infested hell hole. The first black in the area, he had worked hard to quiet his neighbors' fears and concerns.

His days were now filled with concern over the future of his family, business, and neighborhood. The door to his bakery, which used to stand ajar, was now locked with a buzzer system to allow entry. In the pocket of his clean white apron was a SIG P230 .380 pistol loaded with Federal hollowpoints.

He looked up to see a teenaged girl that he had known for years standing at the door. He buzzed her in and she was quickly joined by two young men her age. He asked her what she wanted, but one of the men shoved a gun in his face and said, "What we want, man, is all your money." Years before he had decided that no punk would ever take the money or property for which he had worked so hard. Turning toward the cash register, he pulled his pistol and opened fire. The gun-toting thug went to his knees and attempted to grab the counter before he died. The second thug started to grab the first one's pistol when the store owner pointed his .380 at him and said, "Boy, don't be any dumber than you have so far!" He held the young man at gunpoint until officers arrived.

The autopsy showed that the Federal JHP had penetrated the heart and lodged in the spine, with a recovered diameter of .57 caliber and a weight of 71 grains.

• • • • •

She didn't know what had prompted her to sign up for a defensive handgun course. She lived in an upper middle class community whose most serious crime the previous year had been a burglary of an appliance store. While completing the course, she had the opportunity to fire several hundguns and had decided that

The Federal 90-grain JHP is the top load in the .380 Auto caliber. This Federal bullet abruptly halted a burglar's career.

The .380 Auto MPP designed by Ed Sanow has the second best street record in the caliber. At 1,150 fps, this brass hollowpoint always expands and sometimes fragments.

a Walther PPK .380 was the weapon she wanted to own.

Since her state had no law specifically prohibiting the carrying of loaded weapons in a vehicle, she carried the PPK in the glove compartment of her car. Her husband smiled at his gun-toting wife and never mentioned what he thought was a mild case of paranoia.

Almost three years later they were returning from a golf banquet. They had pulled into their driveway when she noticed the side door ajar. She approached the house. Looking into the garage she saw something that caused her to stop. Her teenaged daughter's skirt was lying next to their subcompact car. She ran back to her car, grabbed the gun from the glove compartment, and told her husband to run across the street and call the police.

Returning to the house, she kicked off her high heels before entering and slowly opened the door. She searched the ground floor without incident and started up the carpeted stairs. As she reached the top, she realized there was a light on in her daughter's room. Stopping to the side of the door, she heard the sounds of obvious sexual activity.

Pushing the door open slightly, she saw the sight that is every mother's nightmare. Two teenaged boys held her nude daughter on the bed while a third was raping her. She opened the door and ordered the rapists to freeze. Their response was sudden and violent as they stopped their assault and rushed her. They were on top of her before she could open fire. As she felt herself loosing control of the weapon, she pulled the

trigger. She felt one of the youths slump against her and then fall to the floor. The others backed off, and remembering what her instructor had told her about the problems inherent in trying to hold multiple suspects, she told them to get out. As they escaped down the stairs, they ran right into the police.

The wounded attacker was taken to a local hospital, where surgery saved his life but did not maintain his mobility. He served his prison sentence confined to a wheelchair. The recovered slug had a diameter of .45 caliber and weighed 67 grains.

• • • • •

An off-duty officer, she carried a Walther PPK .380 auto stuck in the waistband of her jeans. She had planned to get her car washed but realized she was running late for work. She tried to stretch a yellow light and found herself involved in an accident. Exiting her vehicle, she was in the process of opening up her wallet to retrieve her license when she became aware of an angry voice.

Looking up, she observed a tall well-dressed white male shaking his fist at her. As she tried to calm him down, he struck her suddenly, knocking her down. She then realized he was pulling his leg back to kick her in the head. She drew her pistol and identified herself as a police officer. Laughing, he kicked her on the side of the head. She groggily pointed the gun at him and fired two shots. He sat down next to her, said, "You stupid bitch," vomited blood all over her, and died.

The slug had gone through both lungs and the heart. Recovered under the skin on the far side, it weighed 80 grains and had a recovered diameter of .56 caliber.

• • • • •

He drove a delivery truck for a local firm. Because much of his route took him through high-crime neighborhoods, he carried a SIG P 230 .380 in an inside-the-pants holster. While he had never had any problems, he didn't believe in taking chances.

He had finished working his eight-hour shift and was pulling into the loading dock when the dispatcher informed him that his relief had called in sick and he would have to work a double shift. Swearing softly, he reloaded his truck and left to deliver the contents.

It was almost 10 P.M. before he had a chance to eat. Pulling into a fast-food restaurant, he went inside to pick up his order. He was returning to his truck when he noticed the interior light was on. Placing his food on the ground, he drew his pistol and walked around to the other side quietly.

He had just turned the corner when he was struck on the shoulder by a pipe. Looking up, he saw a man leaning halfway out of the truck. The man swung again and this time the driver ducked. Finally remembering the pistol, he took aim and fired six times. In spite of the close range, only one round impacted on its intended target, but that was enough. The round entered the felon's chest, pierced the heart, and was found against the spine at the autopsy. Its recovered weight was 59 grains and it had a diameter of .56 caliber.

Street Results: .380 Auto 85-grain STHP Silvertip

He had stopped for gas and was filling his tank when a car full of teenagers pulled in. He ignored their noise and mischief until they backed into his car. Yelling at them to watch what they were doing, he suddenly found himself confronted by six highly irritated young men who were threatening to do him several different types of injury.

Going to one knee, he quickly produced a .380 auto from an ankle holster and told them to back off. All of them did except one, who produced a balisong knife and commented that a pop gun was no match for the martial arts. The adult then produced his badge, identified himself as a police officer, and ordered him to halt. The teenager just laughed and made a remark about slicing some bacon.

The teenager took two more steps before the officer fired. The young man went to both knees and pitched forward on his face. He was conveyed to a local hospital, where emergency surgery saved his life. The recovered Federal hollowpoint had a diameter of .48 caliber and a weight of 66 grains.

This .380 Auto CCI 88-grain JHP expands differently depending on what tissue is hit. These two slugs are typical of the performance in this caliber.

• • • • •

He was an undercover narc and had been trying to set up a large cocaine buy with some Colombians who were students at a nearby university. The buy was to take place in one of the college dorms and the officer told me later, "Evan, I got really sloppy. I thought because the buy was going down in a college dorm that the risk was minimal." He was wrong — almost dead wrong!

He had no sooner entered the room with $45,000 in marked money when one of the dealers put a S&W .44 Magnum to his head and relieved him of his cash. The officer stood with his hands raised while the two bad guys carried on a conversation in their native tongue. At its conclusion, one of them produced a pair of handcuffs and secured the narc with his hands behind his back. Searching him, they found a cocked and locked Government Model Colt stuck in his waistband over his right hip. What they missed was a SIG P230 .380 auto in a Milt Sparks Summer Special riding in the middle of his back.

More conversation ensued between the two dopers, and when the officer saw one of them pick up a pillow and walk toward him, he knew it was now or never. Turning sideways, he pulled his .380 and, moving as far as he could while handcuffed, opened fire.

One Colombian went down, blood spreading over his crotch. The second one jumped out of the second-floor window with the bag of money. He eluded the officer's backup and was running across the interstate

This .380 Auto CCI 88-grain JHP expanded extremely well for this caliber. Many .380 Auto JHP bullets do not expand at all.

when he was struck by a passing motorist. Both felons were brought to the hospital, where the one suffering a gunshot wound that had pierced his liver died. The slug was recovered from his clothing; its recovered weight was 72 grains and its diameter was .62 caliber.

The other felon recovered to stand trial for armed robbery and attempted murder. He was convicted, given probation, and returned to Colombia.

• • • • •

A distinguished looking, well-dressed black male in his forties, he was driving through an inner-city neighborhood in his new Corvette when a tire blew. He pulled to the curb, removed his suit coat, and proceeded with the task of replacing the tire. He was a doctor who had served the inner city since his graduation from an Ivy League medical school. His compassion and concern for the residents of his hometown were tempered by a realization that there were a lot of genuinely nasty people out there. That's why the pants leg of his $600 suit concealed a stainless Walther PPK in an ankle holster. He had taken a class from me just four months before, and while declining to carry anything more powerful, he had switched from ball to Silvertip.

He was just finishing switching tires when he felt the presence of others. He looked up and saw three young black teenagers standing there. His years of urban life told him that these three were trouble. They commented on what a nice car he had. The doctor thanked them and was in the process of placing the

flat tire in the trunk when one of them picked up the tire iron and suggested he give them his car keys and wallet. My friend's response was short, pithy, and impolite.

As the three advanced on him, he took a couple of steps backward, went to one knee, and drew his pistol. The thug with the tire iron continued to advance, saying "Come on, brother, I know you won't hurt me. Put the gun down." As the bad guy got closer, the doctor double tapped his Walther. The first round caught the thug in the lung, while the second missed. The bad guy turned, took three steps, swore, and died. His partners made good their escape.

The autopsy determined that the round, traversing from left to right, pierced both lungs and the heart. Recovered from the right lung, it weighed 79 grains and had a recovered daimeter of .57 caliber.

• • • • •

She was a nurse who worked the midnight shift in the only trauma center in the rural county she lived in. Engaged to a state trooper, she had taken the .380 auto he offered her for protection, laughed, and put it in the glove box of her Datsun. She told me from her hospital bed that she thought he was slightly paranoid. After all, she didn't live in New York City.

One steamy July morning she crawled into her car after a hectic midnight shift, turned on the air conditioning, and struggled to stay awake as she made the twenty-five minute drive home. Almost there, she saw a man standing next to a car with the hood raised. Normally she would not have stopped, but she saw the clerical collar. As she got closer, she saw a rosary and Bible on the roof of the car and relaxed. A devout Catholic, she was more than willing to assist a priest.

She was to live to regret her decision, for the man was an imposter. An ex-con, he had been sent to prison six times for rape. In each instance, he had used the priestly garb to perpetrate the crime.

She asked him if she could be of assistance, and he replied that he would deeply appreciate a ride to the nearest gas station. They had barely gone two miles when her passenger said, "This will be just fine." Puzzled, she turned and saw the knife. He told her in very blunt terms of the various sexual perversions he expected her to perform.

As he began to force her to comply, she remembered the pistol. Grabbing the glove box door, she pulled it open, removed the pistol, and shot him in the chest. Unfortunately, she only fired one shot. Smiling, he grabbed the gun from her and continued with his sexual assault. When he was done, he dragged her to a nearby stand of trees and shot her once in the head, leaving her for dead.

A few hours later, a member of the state police who knew both the victim and her boyfriend spotted her car parked on a country road. The officer stopped to say hello when a bloody man holding a pistol got out. The officer's survival training took over and he put three rounds of .357 ammo into his attacker. He was calling for an ambulance when he heard someone moaning in the woods. He found the nurse holding her head.

The rapist died at the scene while the nurse was conveyed to the very hospital where she worked. After a long hospital stay and extensive psychological counseling, she recovered. Today she continues to work at the same hospital, although she drags one leg slightly as a result of her wound. The nurses she works with would be shocked to know she carries a S&W Model 469 9mm in her purse.

• • • • •

He stood in line at the grocery store with a cart of items. He looked no different from any of the other men in the Midwest suburban community. Unlike the stock brokers and businessmen surrounding him, however, he was a federal agent.

He was bringing his checkbook balance up to date when he realized that everyone had stopped talking. Looking up, he saw the reason. Two white males in their twenties were pushing the store manager into his office. They had no sooner disappeared when he heard the gunshot. They reappeared shortly, dragging the body of the manager. Dropping him at the feet of the black cashier, the taller of the two said, "Nigger, the same thing will happen to you unless we get all the money."

Realizing that these two had already shown a predilection for violence, the agent prepared to take action before anyone else was killed. As the two holdup men watched the cashier, the agent pulled his Colt .380 and opened fire. His first round hit one of the bad guys in the ear, killing him instantly. The second felon turned to run and the agent's fifth round hit him in the back, severing his spine. He was dead when he hit the ground.

The autopsy results showed that the slug to the head caused massive brain damage and had a recovered weight of 51 grains and a diameter of .67 caliber. The round recovered from the spine had broken into three pieces, with a total recovered weight of 60 grains.

• • • • •

The officer was tired. After working the midnight shift, he had spent most of the day in court testifying in a robbery case. Now, at 6 P.M., he was finally on his way home to get a few hours' sleep before going to work.

He stopped to pick up his mail in the lobby of his apartment building. When a male voice asked him what time it was, he glanced up from his watch to find himself looking down the muzzle of a Walther .380 auto.

Suddenly the fatigue was gone, replaced with a sinking feeling that he had really screwed up. He handed the gunman his wallet, car keys, and money clip from his pocket. The felon told him to turn around and not to move for five minutes. The officer breathed an almost audible sigh of relief when the gun was shoved against his back and fired. The officer collapsed to the floor and started to draw his own weapon. He had the weapon partway out of its holster when he realized that he couldn't feel his legs.

He lay in the hallway until the police responded. He was conveyed to a local hospital, where he was immediately rushed into surgery. While the doctors were able to save his life, they were unable to repair the spinal cord damage. Today the officer is confined to a wheelchair. The recovered slug, a Silvertip hollowpoint, weighed 52 grains and had a recovered diameter of .67 caliber. The holdup man was never caught.

This Remington .38 Special +P 95-grain S-JHP was fired from a 4-inch revolver into a professional wrestler. This is perfect expansion.

.38 SPECIAL

Gelatin results factored for intermediate targets and tranverse shots predict the most effective load in .38 Special +P to be the 158-grain lead semiwadcutter hollowpoint. This is the so-called "Chicago PD" and "FBI" load. The SWC-HP expands reliably from .57 to .61 caliber and penetrates from 9.5 to 11 inches of soft tissue. When gelatin results are analyzed properly, i.e., with the police officer and probable police scenarios in mind, the 158-grain SWC-HP is the load with the most promise.

Loads from all major manufacturers perform the same. The 158-grain SWC-HP loads from Remington, Winchester, Federal, CCI-Speer and others are nearly identical in the volume and shape of the crush and stretch cavities and in the average depth of penetration. Typical muzzle velocities are 865 to 915 fps, with a muzzle energy of 260 to 290 foot-pounds.

A reasonable alternative to the 158-grain SWC-HP is the 125-grain jacketed hollowpoint. Typical muzzle velocities vary widely depending on the manufacturer, from 900 to 1,100 fps. Muzzle energy ranges from 225 to 335 foot-pounds.

The reliability of expansion in tissue for 125-grain JHP loads is not as assured as the 158-grain SWC-HP. Jacketed hollowpoints need a greater impact velocity than lead hollowpoints to produce the same degree of expansion. In gelatin, however, the 125-grain JHP expands reliably from .55 to .67 caliber.

If these 125-grain JHPs have a fault, it is this irregular and unpredictable expansion. If they expand to .65 caliber, the energy transfer can be too rapid and the slug can fall victim to both intermediate targets and transverse shots. If they do not expand or only expand to .40 caliber, the penetration can be excessive and the wound cavities small. Overall, the 125-grain JHP can produce the ideal wounding effects of the 158-grain SWC-HP, but not as reliably nor predictably.

The Federal 125-grain JHP load produces the most moderate rate of reliable expansion and the deepest penetration for an expanding bullet. The Winchester 125-grain Silvertip expands to and holds the largest caliber. The Remington expands early to produce secondary fragments. All gelatin factors considered, the Federal, using Sierra-style bullets, expands and retains a .55- to .65-caliber mushroom and is predicted to be the top 125-grain JHP duty load in .38 Special +P.

The rest of the loads for the .38 Special either expand too rapidly and are defeated by intermediate targets or deep transverse shots, or they do not reliably expand and produce smallish crush and stretch cavities. The loads that expand rapidly to produce large but shallow cavities are cited in the next chapter as some of the very best loads out of short-barreled guns. The loads that do not expand cannot be recommended as top performers in any scenario.

Examples of the rapidly expanding but possibly shal-

Table 8-3

.38 SPECIAL, +P AND +P+ ACTUAL RESULTS

	Total Shootings	One-Shot Stops	Percentage	Muzzle Velocity
1. W-W 158-gr. LHP +P	169	123	72.78	992 fps
2. Fed 158-gr. LHP +P	163	116	71.16	971 fps
3. Rem 158-gr. LHP +P	97	67	69.07	926 fps
4. W-W 110-gr. JHP +P+ (Q4070)	16	11	68.75	1,126 fps
5. Fed 125-gr. JHP +P	167	114	68.26	991 fps
6. Rem 125-gr. S-JHP +P	86	56	65.11	929 fps
7. CCI 125-gr. JHP +P	41	26	63.41	988 fps
8. W-W 125-gr. JHP +P	44	27	61.36	942 fps
9. Fed 125-gr. JSP +P	93	54	58.06	963 fps
10. R-P 95-gr. S-JHP +P	132	75	56.81	1,128 fps
11. W-W 110-gr. JHP +P	83	45	54.21	1,003 fps
12. Fed 158-gr. SWC (not +P)	174	92	52.87	767 fps
13. Fed 158-gr. RNL (not +P)	306	160	52.28	704 fps

low-penetrating loads are the Winchester and Federal 110-grain JHP + P + loads. These, especially the Winchester Q4070, are the so-called "Treasury" loads. The Remington 95-grain JHP + P and the Winchester 95-grain STHP + P fall in the same class. These loads produce muzzle velocities between 1,030 and 1,190 fps. They expand with extreme reliability to well over .60 caliber, frequently fragmenting and occasionally producing secondary missiles. However, the penetration depth only ranges from 8.25 to 8.75 inches in ballistic gelatin.

Loads of this nature topped the RII evaluation with their large and shallow stretch cavities. That fallacy in predicting stopping power in a police-duty scenario was previously discussed. A better analysis of the same results indicates a fatal sensitivity to intermediate targets and cross-torso bullet placements.

The gelatin results further predict that 125-grain jacketed softpoint bullets in .38 Special + P will not reliably expand beyond .40 caliber unless they hit bone. Even at aggressive muzzle velocities between 1,000 and 1,050 fps, the wound cavities are small and the chances of perforation are large. The same relatively substandard results are predicted for 158-grain jacketed hollowpoint, 158-grain lead semiwadcutter, 158- and 200-grain round-nose lead, and 150- and 130-grain jacketed round-nose bullets.

* * * * *

Long the traditional police caliber, the .38 Special round got a real boost from the genius of Lee Jurras. Jurras decided that since a change of caliber by police agencies generally was too expensive, the best approach was to upgrade the ammunition. He reduced the bullet weight from 158 grains to 110, hollow pointed the bullet, and made it rather fragile with a thin jacket and dead-soft lead core.

The round produced an honest 1,100 + fps from a 4-inch-barreled service revolver and expanded well in soft tissue. Producing in excess of 1,000 fps from the .38 snub, expansion was iffy in this barrel length.

Shortly after the introduction of Super Vel, the other ammunition manufacturers were forced to follow suit. Today, of course, we have a bewildering variety of "high-performance" offerings in this caliber.

Despite all the high-velocity, light bullet weight hoopla, in actual shootouts the best performer in this caliber has been the 158-grain lead hollowpoint + P as offered by Federal, Winchester, and Remington. They have produced virtually identical results. Producing a velocity of approximately 830 fps from a 2-inch barrel, they still expand in soft tissue without hitting bone.

Street Results: Winchester 158-grain SWC-LHP + P

The owner of a 24-hour gas station on a lonely stretch of the interstate, he had asked his brother-in-law, the cop, for recommendations on a gun for self-protection. He had recommended a 4-inch barreled S&W Model 64 and had given him a box of his depart-

The Remington .38 Special +P 125-grain S-JHP is issued by the Los Angeles Police Department. This load produces 65-percent one-shot stops.

The top .38 Special +P load is this Winchester 158-grain SWC-LHP. It even deforms reliably from 2-inch barrels, making it the top load for a snub-nosed revolver.

ment-issue ammunition, Winchester's 158-grain lead +P hollowpoints.

Eight months later, he was in the process of doing some paperwork in the back office when he heard a scream and gunshots. Pulling the revolver from the drawer, he entered the retail area. He saw his clerk face down on the floor, with blood spreading from his head. Looking to his right, he saw three teenaged boys with guns. Bringing his gun to eye level, he fired quickly at all three. One collapsed and the other two dropped their guns and dragged the first toward the door. The owner fired again, and they dropped him and fled.

The holdup man was rushed to the hospital, where he expired in emergency surgery. The slug was recovered from his back. It weighed 128 grains and had a recovered diameter of .63 caliber.

• • • • •

He was a rookie federal agent on his first raid and he could hardly contain his excitement. Their warrant was for the arrest of a major drug dealer and even though he was assigned to an outer perimeter position, he looked forward to the opportunity with enthusiasm.

His job was to guard a secondary garage that contained a rather well-used Ford pickup. Other more experienced agents covered the garage containing two BMWs and a Rolls Royce.

Armed with a 4-inch-barreled S&W Model 19 .357 Magnum loaded with his agency's Winchester 158-grain lead +P hollowpoints, he crouched down behind a barbeque in a dark corner and waited. The other agents had been very specific — even if he heard gunfire he was to maintain his position unless ordered to move over the radio.

He heard the sound of the battering rams on the front and back doors, accompanied by the shouts of "Federal agents — search warrant" several times. This was followed by silence for about five seconds before gunfire erupted. Following instructions, he held his position until he heard full-automatic fire. Realizing that none of the raiding party had brought this type of weapon, he ran to the window and pulled back quickly as he saw a male with an Uzi running toward his hiding place.

Returning to his spot behind the barbeque, he locked his Model 19 in a two-handed position and waited. Seconds later, the suspect entered the garage, opened the door of the truck, and, reaching under the seat, came up with a fragmentation grenade. Realizing the danger to himself and the other members of the raiding party, the agent fired four rounds from his re-

volver. To his horror, the dope man spun and started to point the Uzi at him before collapsing.

The suspect was rushed to the hospital, where he recovered and stood trial for drug charges and attempted murder. One of the four rounds struck him in the back just to the right of the spine. It nicked the heart and was found inside his shirt after exiting his chest. The recovered slug weighed 131 grains and had a diameter of .52 caliber.

• • • • •

She was a private investigator with a firm that had a contract with a government agency. Investigating a case of theft of computer equipment, she carried a licensed S&W Model 60 5-shot revolver loaded with W-W lead hollowpoints. She didn't really believe that the target of the investigation would prove to be a problem, but the warehouse where she suspected the stolen merchandise was located was in a bad part of town.

She was parked in a nondescript van down the street from the building. Her surveillance post was in the back of the vehicle, where she used both still photograph and video equipment to record the comings and goings of various individuals. She had been in position for just over an hour when she thought she heard a noise at the front of the van. Dismissing it as nerves, she turned back to the task at hand when she heard the van door open.

The soft 158-grain SWC-LHP works well in living tissue. These .38 Special +P bullets expand to the .60-caliber recovered diameter shown in this photo and sometimes to greater diameters.

This Federal .38 Special +P 158-grain lead hollowpoint saved a federal agent's life. This slug shows nearly classic .65-caliber expansion.

The Remington .38 Special +P 158-grain SWC-LHP has the largest diameter and deepest hollowpoint cavity in this style. It has 69-percent one-shot stops.

Grabbing her Model 60 from her purse, she turned toward the curtain separating the back from the driver's compartment. As the curtain pulled to one side, she saw two black males looking at her. She ordered them to freeze, but they laughed at her. One said, "Bitch, I ain't scared of you or your pop gun. We gonna take this van and your white ass." As the one subject lunged toward her, she fired five times and jumped out of the rear of the van. Running a full block, she stopped to reload her pistol. She called 911 from a pay phone and waited for responding officers. Putting her snubbie back in her purse, she flagged down a responding police car and informed them of the shooting in the van.

The officers approached the van cautiously, peeked inside, and then unceremoniously dumped two bodies on the ground. The autopsy determined that one thug had been hit three times, while the other had taken one round in the upper chest. That single shot had severed the aorta and he had bled to death. The bullet was recovered just under the skin by the left nipple and had a weight of 129 grains and a diameter of .45 caliber.

• • • • •

A big-city cop assigned to his department's Tactical Unit, he took the streets very seriously. A left-handed Bianchi basketweave thumb-break holster carried a S&W Model 57 .41 Magnum revolver loaded with heavy handloads featuring a Sierra 170-grain jacketed hollow-cavity bullet on top of a robust charge of Hercules No. 2400 powder.

His uniform shirt concealed a Second Chance vest, while his right rear pants pocket concealed a S&W Model 38 Airweight Bodyguard loaded with W-W 158-grain lead hollowpoints. His partner was similarly equipped, and both officers had well-deserved reputations for being street smart.

A teletype had been read off at roll call about the fatal shooting of a police officer. One of the suspects wanted was a prostitute with an unusual nickname. The officers checked with an informant who told them that a whore that used that street name was working the near east side. The officers drove over to the location and were told by another prostitute that the woman they were looking for was up in the dope house buying some heroin.

The officers called for another Tac Unit to cover the back and went inside. They found her and were in the process of leaving when a male interrupted them and wanted to know why they were harassing her. They told him it was none of his business. The officers attempted to leave when the fight broke out. One officer was able to put out a call for help on his radio while his partner was holding off the bad guy. Both were then assaulted by several individuals.

The officer armed with the .41 Magnum felt a tugging on his holster and heard one of the combatants yell, "Let's get his gun and kill him like the other pig!" Losing control of his weapon, the officer pulled his snub and yelled at everyone to freeze. His command went unheeded, however, and he saw his .41 Magnum being swung toward him. Without thinking, he shoved his snub into the armed suspect's stomach and pulled the trigger. His face was only inches away from the man he shot, and the officer watched the life disappear from the man's eyes. The bad guy had no sooner collapsed when help rushed into the room.

The slug had severed the bad guy's spine; its recovered weight was 107 grains and its diameter was .42 caliber. The prosecutor ruled it a justifiable homicide, but the officer got an official reprimand for nonapproved ammunition and a citation for capturing the cop killer!

• • • • •

A cop in the rural southwest, he had grown content with his lot in life. Permanently assigned to the afternoon shift, he did home remodeling during the day. The quiet that generally existed during his shift allowed him to work on current and future job planning.

It was just after 9 P.M. when he received his first run of the evening, a shots-fired report. He cursed under his breath, thinking it probably was just another hunter getting ready for deer season. As he pulled into the driveway of the farm where the shots had been heard, he saw something lying next to a pickup. Turning on the high beams, he saw it was the body of a woman. He immediately got on the radio and told the dispatcher that he had a person shot and needed an ambulance and backup.

The dispatcher responded with the information that the nearest backup was fifteen minutes away. Glancing at the empty shotgun rack, he remembered his sarcastic remark about the "hot dogs" who carried shotguns on patrol.

Grabbing his flashlight, he exited his vehicle and drew his S&W Model 10 .38 Special revolver. He approached the body quickly and determined that the woman was alive but suffering a gunshot wound to her back. He noticed that the front door was open and that blood was smeared on the knob. He heard voices inside and entered quietly. Approaching the kitchen, he noticed more blood on the walls. Scattered about on the floor were the bodies of young children, all of them obviously dead. He heard the voices again and realized they were coming from the enclosed back porch.

Getting closer, he heard a young female voice say, "Daddy, please don't hurt me." A deeper, older male voice responded, "You bitch, you're the cause of all this. I'm going to blow your head off!" Turning the corner, the officer yelled, "Police! Freeze!" The farmer's only response was to grin and shoot his daughter. Seeing the shotgun being swung in his direction, the

officer emptied his .38 at his attacker. The farmer grunted, stumbled, and fell to one knee. The officer backpedaled into the next room attempting to reload from his pouches. The farmer followed him into the room, raised the shotgun, and yelling "goodbye cop," fired. The load of birdshot struck the officer in the right side and he fell against the wall.

The farmer ran outside and the officer heard his vehicle being backed out of the yard. He was able to crawl to the phone and tell the operator where he was and that he had been shot before he collapsed.

The farmer was stopped by a state police unit several hours later and was fatally shot when he pointed his shotgun at the trooper. The autopsy found that all six .38 hollowpoints had hit their intended target. All had expanded without hitting bone, with their recovered diameters ranging from .45 to .56 caliber, and weights ranging from 112 to 129 grains. The officer recovered from his wounds and still patrols the same rural area today.

• • • • •

He was an undercover narc working in one of the eastern seaboard's toughest cities. He had been working a major cocaine case that involved a number of Arab and Colombian drug dealers. It had taken him eighteen months to get close enough to these major dealers so they would sell him drugs. The bag in the trunk of his new Chevy contained $800,000 and had a homing device built into its lining. His backup consisted of twelve officers, including five SWAT members with MP5 submachine guns.

Not content to depend on backup, however, the narc was armed to the teeth. Under a blanket was a mini-Uzi, while on his person were three handguns: a SIG P226 loaded with Glaser Safety Slugs, a Glock loaded with THV, and a Taurus .38 snubbie loaded with W-W 158-grain lead hollowpoints in the small of his back.

The meeting was set for 4 A.M. in the parking lot behind a church. As he pulled in, he noticed a battered red pickup truck parked next to a Chevy Suburban. He exited his vehicle, popped the trunk, and removed the money while the occupants of the other vehicles exited theirs.

The narc placed his bag on the hood of the pickup and unzipped it, showing the dealers the cash. The Colombian smiled at him and said, "I'm sorry, but we can't sell you the cane. We still want your money," and shoved a Browning Hi-Power into the officer's face. Raising his hands as high as possible, the narc

This Federal .38 Special +P 158-grain LHP is not a picture-perfect mushroom, but it saved a narcotics officer's life. This load ranks second overall in the caliber.

This Remington .38 Special +P 125-grain S-JHP expanded to 1 1/2 calibers (.54) and ended a holdup.

hoped his backup was in position and that they hadn't forgotten to turn on the night scope.

He was quickly searched, and both the SIG and Glock were discovered. The leader turned to one of the others holding a MAC-10 with attached suppressor and said, "Take this creep into the bushes and kill him." As the narc was shoved toward the nearby field, all hell broke loose. The parking lot was suddenly illuminated by high-intensity lights and a bullhorn-amplified voice said, "Police! Drop your weapons." The dope man with the undercover officer started to turn toward the sound, and the officer made his move. Pulling his snub, he jammed it against the bad guy's sternum and pulled the trigger. Not waiting to see the results, he ran like hell toward his backup. Friendly hands pulled him to the ground as the firefight commenced .

When it was over, three dope men lay dead, including the one shot by the narc. One SWAT officer took a grazing wound to the head, and his vest had absorbed three 9mm JHPs.

The autopsy results indicated that the lead hollowpoint had pierced the heart and severed the spine. The slug was recovered from the dead man's clothing and weighed 69 grains, with a recovered diameter of .39 caliber.

Street Results: Federal 125-grain JHP +P

He was a 70-year-old black man who lived in one of the roughest neighborhoods in the city. Surviving on Social Security and without any family, he was forced to remain in what had become an urban battlefield. He lived in the downstairs half of a two-family flat. His upstairs neighbors had moved the day

before, finally fed up with the dope dealers and thieves.

He was awakened by noises upstairs. Knowing that his neighbors had taken all their possessions and fearing the presence of thugs, he put on his pants and grabbed his .38 snub loaded with Federal 125-grain JHP +P ammo. Halfway up the stairs he was confronted by four black teenagers carrying the windows they had pried out of the moldings.

He ordered them to halt and when they laughed at him, he fired, striking one in the face. They quickly dropped their contraband and fled with their wounded comrade in the lead.

Street smart but law abiding, he returned to his flat to get dressed. Lacking a phone, he was planning to drive to the nearby precinct to report the crime and shooting. As he was looking for his car keys, he again heard noise upstairs and thought, "My God, they've come back to kill me." Grabbing his gun, he jerked open the door and pulled the trigger as he rounded the corner. He saw too late that the person on the stairs was a uniformed police officer.

The round struck the officer just below the heart. He was rushed to the hospital but died in surgery. The recovered weight of the slug was 108 grains and its diameter was .58 caliber. The citizen was charged with and convicted of manslaughter, while the B&E man who had been shot in the face was never found.

• • • • •

A deputy with a California Sheriff's department, he carried a privately owned S&W Model 66 with a 6-

The Federal .38 Special +P 125-grain JHP ranks fifth overall in the caliber.

This Federal .38 Special +P 125-grain JHP was used by an off-duty federal agent to stop a holdup. It was effective even with moderate expansion.

inch barrel. The magnum, however, was loaded with department-specified .38 Special 125-grain +P JHPs. He and several other deputies had lobbied hard for magnum ammo without success.

It was approaching lunchtime when he realized that he would have to cash a check before heading for his favorite restaurant. He pulled into a small shopping center that had a branch of his bank. Unable to find a parking spot directly in front of the bank, he pulled up in front of a nearby computer store. He was walking toward the bank when a woman came running up to him. "Officer, there's a man in the fabric store with a gun. He said he's going to kill his wife!"

The deputy quickly removed the radio he carried on his belt and called for help. Drawing his revolver, he edged up to the store. He removed his hat, peeked inside, and saw a male holding a gun on an obviously frightened female. The deputy, who would have been content to hold his position until backup arrived, was forced into action by the sound of a gunshot from inside. Moving to the door, he noticed the female lying on the floor and that the white male was now pointing the gun at a black male. The deputy entered the store and yelled, "Sheriff's Department — freeze!"

Instead of complying, the gunman started to turn toward the deputy. Not waiting to see what he intended, the deputy fired twice. The first round skimmed across the gunman's chest, barely scratching him, while the second entered his chest and spun him around. He collapsed to the floor and said, "Don't shoot me again. I quit."

The gunman was rushed to the hospital, where he survived to stand trial for the murder of his wife. The recovered slug weighed 104 grains and had a diameter of .56 caliber.

• • • • •

He was a western cop who moonlighted as a bartender in a local bar. Because he was a realist, he carried his .38 snub in his waistband concealed by his bar apron.

It was almost closing time when they entered: two white males who did not fit in with the clientele in this country-and-western bar. One approached the bar and ordered a beer while the other stood near the restroom door. When the bartender placed the beer on the counter, the man produced a sawed-off rifle and announced a holdup. The second man produced a pistol and ordered all the customers on the floor.

The bartender turned to open the cash register and drew his .38 snub. As he turned, he grabbed the rifle, deflecting its aim, and shot its wielder twice in the chest. Letting go of the rifle, he fired two shots at the second holdup man, who dropped his pistol and put his hands up. The off-duty officer was turning to check on the first holdup man when he was struck in the throat. He tried to bring his gun up but he collapsed dead. He had taken a .22 LR round fired by the first holdup man. His killer ran outside, where he collapsed and died.

Both slugs recovered from the holdup man had ex-

Table 8-4

9 MM +P AND +P+ ACTUAL RESULTS

	Total Shootings	One-Shot Stops	Percentage	Muzzle Velocity
1. Fed 115-gr. JHP +P+ (9BP-LE)	56	50	89.28	1,304 fps
2. W-W 115-gr. JHP +P+ (Q4174)	51	45	88.23	1,299 fps
3. R-P 115-gr. JHP +P+	15	13	86.66	1,283 fps
4. Geco 86-gr. BHP (BAT)	85	70	82.35	1,493 fps
5. Fed 124-gr. LHP-Nyclad	106	87	82.07	1,101 fps
6. Fed 124-gr. Hydra-Shok +P+	22	18	81.81	1,264 fps
7. Fed 115-gr. JHP	127	103	81.10	1,177 fps
8. W-W 115-gr. STHP	211	167	79.14	1,204 fps
9. R-P 115-gr. JHP	106	81	76.42	1,163 fps
10. Fed 147-gr. JHP	16	12	75.00	985 fps
11. Fed 124-gr. Hydra-Shok	21	16	76.19	1,118 fps
12. CCI 115-gr. JHP	71	51	71.80	1,145 fps
13. Fed 147-gr. Hydra-Shok	49	35	71.42	988 fps
14. W-W 147-gr. JHP (OSM, Type L)	89	61	68.54	987 fps
15. Horn 90-gr. JHP	25	16	64.00	1,305 fps
16. Horn 115-gr. JHP	32	20	62.50	1,126 fps
17. W-W 115-gr. FMJ	148	90	60.81	1,149 fps

panded to over .52 caliber and weighed 101 and 104 grains respectively.

9MM PARABELLUM

Ballistic gelatin results clearly predict the 115-grain jacketed hollowpoint to be the top load in 9mm. From 4-inch auto pistols, the muzzle velocity ranges from 1,125 to 1,225 fps for conventional-pressure loads, producing from 325 to 380 foot-pounds of muzzle energy. The restricted +P+ Q load made by Winchester for the Illinois State Police has a muzzle velocity of 1,275 to 1,300 fps and an energy level of 430 foot-pounds.

The ideal revolver bullet has to expand reliably in soft tissue and penetrate deeply enough for most shooting scenarios. The ideal auto pistol bullet is held to even more stringent standards — it must expand and penetrate, but above all it also must feed reliably into the chamber and cycle the weapon fully out of, and back into, battery.

Based both on a large cross-section of weapons and on gelatin tests, the top 9mm loads, in order of feed reliability, are: Remington 115-grain JHP, Federal 115-grain JHP, and Winchester 115-grain STHP Silvertip.

As a fairly bold statement, the Remington 115-grain load will feed and cycle in any weapon that will feed and cycle FMJ hardball. This feed reliability comes from a very rounded ogive and a very narrow hollowpoint cavity opening. It gives the bullet almost the exact profile as ball.

The Remington load expands in gelatin with perhaps 60-percent reliability. When it does expand, the recovered mushroom measures between .57 and .59 caliber, and the overall penetration is roughly 11.5 inches. This fills our expectations of any bullet totally.

Occasionally, the 115-grain Remington JHP will not expand in gelatin. The results are small hardball-type stretch and crush cavities and a large hardball-type probability of target perforation. Many other JHP loads produce greater wound cavities than the 115-grain Remington, but no other hollowpoint produces greater reliability in as many different kinds of weapons.

Significantly, in 1987, Federal once again changed the bullet profile of its 9BP load. Until recently, the bullet had a pronounced semiwadcutter profile with a large hollowpoint opening. This load, with a cylinder-shaped hollowpoint cavity and cut serrations, produced the greatest wound ballistics of any 115-grain JHP load. It expanded to between .70 and .76 caliber and penetrated 10 inches. However, the large cavity and blunt ogive caused feed problems in some autos.

The new Federal 9BP has a round-nose ogive quite similar to the Remington 115-grain JHP. This load expands with better reliability and to a greater degree

This is the wound profile of the Federal 9mm 115-grain JHP. Long before +P+ pressures were available, this load produced excellent stopping power. It still has one of the best reputations among street cops.

than the Remington. The hollowpoint cavities on the Remington and Federal loads are exactly the same dimensions. The Remington has the jacket extending into the cavity while the Federal has the jacket just up to the cavity with lead exposed on the very tip. The Federal jacket is serrated more aggressively.

As a result, the Federal expands with 80- to 90-percent reliability. The expanded mushroom measures between .60 and .65 caliber and the slug penetrates 11 inches. Again, reliability with the new 9BP load is excellent, nearly the same as the Remington 115-grain JHP and ball.

The latest-generation 115-grain STHP silvertip produces the largest wound cavities of any current standard-velocity 9mm jacketed hollowpoint. The Silvertip also feeds reliably in the majority of auto pistols. For those pistols, this is the top 9mm round. Those with access to the 9mm +P+ STHP ammo have an even better load. The +P+ STHP produces essentially the same wounds as the dominating .357 Magnum 125-grain JHP.

This top-level wounding potential, however, is a direct result of a more aggressive hollowpoint design, which can produce reliability problems in some weapons. Most weapons are fully compatible with the Silvertip but some are not (or are not in an unmodified condition).

STHP Silvertip discussed in this book is the third and latest design. The original 9mm Silvertip had an aluminum-manganese alloy jacket, similar to the Silvertip in .380 Auto, .38 Special, and .45 Auto. This jacket was nonserrated. It had far more than its share of weapon and stopping-power problems.

The current Silvertip uses a nickel-plated, copper-zinc jacket like the .357 Magnum. The jacket is heavily serrated in what can best be described as a crease-fold method. The serrations weaken the jacket in three places per serration and also stress-rise the lead core under each serration.

The 9mm Silvertip expands reliably in gelatin to between .65 and .69 caliber. Penetration in gelatin varies from 9 to 10 inches. The penetration from the +P+ load is more ideal at 11 to 12 inches with the same degree of expansion.

The Speer-Lawman and Hornady 115-grain JHP loads produce the same wound cavities and penetration distances as the 115-grain STHP. However, all these loads have blunt ogives and large hollowpoint cavity openings, which can reduce their feed reliability in some weapons to below acceptable levels.

The only other 9mm loads that pass the requirements for feeding, expansion, and adequate penetration are the 95- and 100-grain jacketed softpoints. These loads have muzzle velocities around 1,300 fps

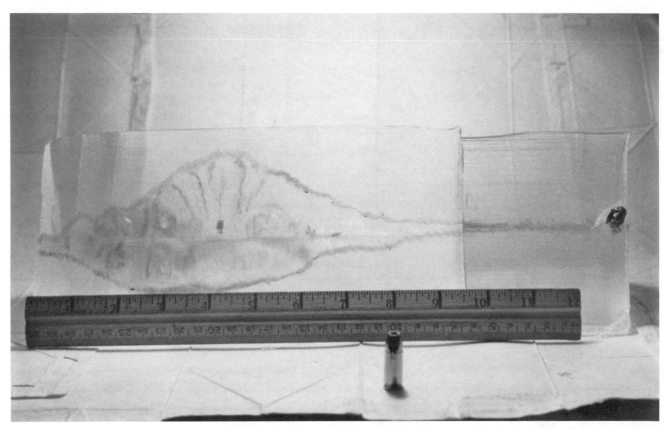

This is the wound profile in ordnance gelatin for the 9mm 115-grain JHP +P+. It transfers more than 400 foot-pounds of energy, similar to a lightweight .357 Magnum hollowpoint.

This Federal 9mm 9BP-LE was developed for the Illinois State Police. This was the first of the higher-pressure 9mm loads and has proven to be the most effective in the caliber.

An expanded Federal 115-grain JHP +P slug recovered from ordnance gelatin. The 9BPLE is the load of the United States Border Patrol.

and energy levels between 350 and 375 foot-pounds. They expand reliably in gelatin to between .45 and .55 caliber and penetrate to 12 inches. The stretch cavities are almost as large in diameter but shorter in length compared to 115-grain JHP loads. The 95- and 100-grain JSP crush cavities are significantly smaller than 115-grain JHP crush cavities. These loads are acceptably tolerant of intermediate targets and transverse torso shots. Striking bone only helps these loads.

The two other kinds of 9mm loads produce much less than ideal bullet performance. The 90- and 100-grain jacketed hollowpoints produce large but extremely shallow wounds and shallow amounts of total penetration. The shallow penetration from these loads is very likely to be defeated by intermediate targets and long cross-torso shots.

The 115-, 123-, and 124-grain FMJ ball loads and the 125-grain jacketed softpoint loads do not expand in gelatin. They produce small stretch and crush cavities and excessive amounts of penetration, which nearly always perforate the target.

* * * * *

Nine millimeter was little known in law enforcement circles until the Illinois State Police and Salt Lake City Police Department adopted the S&W Model 39. Most departments, however, looked at such use as an aberration, and it was not until the Model 59 arrived upon the scene that the 9mm began to receive serious consideration.

The use of high-capacity pistols in this caliber by bad guys increased the interest and demand for this semiauto pistol by police. The U.S. military's change to 9mm was the final straw. Today, of course, it is the overwhelming choice of departments switching to other calibers or handguns.

Super Vel introduced high-performance loads in 9mm, but the stubby 90-grain JHP was not a reliable feeder in the original Model 39s. Eventually, as 9mm guns became popular, Winchester gave us the Silvertip and Federal and Remington gave us comparable loads.

Winchester's 115-grain Silvertip received a bad rap from various gun "experts" after the Miami FBI shootout. Contrary to rumors, the bad guy was struck by two Silvertips, not thirteen. One struck him in the thoracic cavity, and the other in the arm. The first hit was a nonsurvivable wound, while the second one blew out the brachial artery and was potentially fatal. Both rounds did what they were designed to do: expand in soft tissue. The argument that the agents would have survived if they had been equipped with .45 ACP is nonsense.

Street Results: Federal 9mm 115-grain +P+ JHP

The officer looked at his watch. It was almost the end of a busy midnight shift. He had spent the entire

The first of the 9mm +P+ loads is still one of the best. The Winchester 115-grain Q4174 expands well and produces instant stops 88 percent of the time.

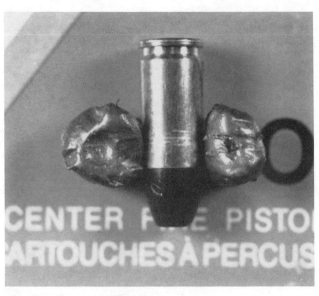

The Federal 124-grain Nyclad LHP has the best street record of all available standard-pressure 9mm loads. This is the street-wise choice for shooters moving to a bullet heavier than the 115-grain JHP.

night answering an endless stream of minor runs. He had just pulled in for what he hoped would be an eye-opening cup of coffee at a local restaurant when the dispatcher called his number and sent him to "see the man, unknown complaint." Cursing under his breath, he drove to the neighborhood where the complainant lived. As he turned the corner onto the street in question, he saw something on a front lawn. Turning on the spotlight, he realized that the "something" was a young boy.

He exited his vehicle, approached the boy, and saw a gunshot wound in his back. He realized the boy was dead after checking for a pulse. He removed his radio from his belt and called for backup and a supervisor. Drawing his Beretta 92F, he approached the front door of the premises. It was then that he observed it was partially open. Listening carefully for any movement inside, he turned to see three additional police units arrive on the scene.

He quickly sent one officer to the rear and entered the premises with the other three officers. Their search took them into the back bedroom, where they found two more bodies: a woman and a little girl. The officers heard movement in the kitchen and entered to find a man sitting at the table with a Browning Hi-Power next to his left hand.

The officer quickly ordered him to freeze. The man looked up, smiled, and reached for the Browning. The officer fired three shots from his Beretta pistol. Two rounds missed while the third entered just above the left nipple. The man got up, took one step, dropped

the gun, and collapsed. He was rushed to the hospital where he survived emergency surgery. He was later tried and convicted of the murder of his wife and two children. The recovered slug weighed 90 grains and had a diameter of .72 caliber.

● ● ● ● ●

She was a private investigator engaged to a city holdup-squad detective. Worried about her safety, he had bought her an H&K P7M8 pistol and loaded it with Federal 115-grain +P+ JHP loads. She was working a case with a large department store chain — cashiers were suspected of pilfering from the cash registers. She had spent several days "shopping" in the store and had observed the methods used. She then followed one of the cashiers to a location in the poorer section of town and watched her enter what was obviously a crack house.

Parked down the street waiting for the cashier to return to her vehicle, she was interrupted suddenly by a man knocking at her passenger window. Suddenly he smashed her car window and attempted to open the door. Pulling her gun, she ordered him away. The man smiled and said, "Bitch, you ain't tough enough!" She placed the front sight in the middle of his chest and pulled the trigger. The man fell half in and half out of the car.

Responding officers rushed him to the hospital, where he expired in the emergency room. The bullet had entered the sternum and lodged in his spinal column. It weighed 94 grains and had a diameter of .67 caliber.

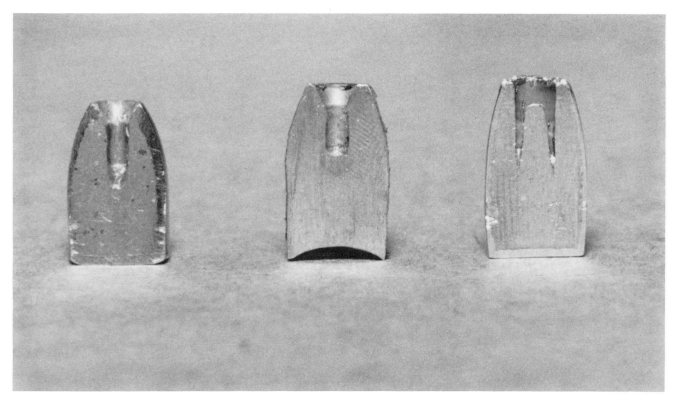

The 9mm 115-grain JHP +P+ (left) has a standard copper-alloy jacket and hollowpoint cavity. The 124-grain LHP Nyclad (center) has a thin nylon jacket and soft lead core. The 147-grain JHP Hydra-Shok (right) has a swaged center post.

• • • • •

A European government agent, he carried a Glock 19 in the course of his official duties as driver and bodyguard. He had dropped the government leader off at his home and was headed for his own residence when he observed a motor scooter behind him in traffic. Despite the fact that it was a warm spring day, both its riders had heavy jackets on.

Looking for a way to get out of rush hour traffic, he observed the scooter make the same three right-hand turns he had. When he was caught at a red light, he pulled his Glock and held it down below the car window. As the scooter pulled almost even with his car, he saw the rider reach under his coat. Quickly throwing his car into reverse, he swerved and struck the scooter.

As the riders were knocked to the ground, the agent exited the passenger side of the vehicle and took cover. They regained their feet, pulled handguns, and opened fire. The agent returned fire and one bad guy collapsed immediately. The second fired additional shots and the agent was shot in the head. Crawling to the rear of his vehicle, he reloaded his Glock and attempted to wipe the blood out of his eyes. Coming around the back of his vehicle, he saw the second bad guy and shot him in the back.

All three were conveyed to a local hospital. One bad guy was DOA while the other lingered in intensive care before expiring. The agent lost his left eye and retired from active duty. The recovered slugs weighed 101 and 93 grains and had diameters of .61 and .67 calibers.

The Federal 9mm Nyclad LHP expands with extreme reliability and has always produced adequate penetration. This load has an actual street effectiveness of 82 percent.

This is the wound profile in ordnance gelatin for the 9mm 124-grain LHP Nyclad. This load produces a more moderate stretch cavity that works best against intermediate targets like car doors and upper arms.

The Federal 124-grain LHP Nyclad is shown as an expanded slug recovered from ordnance gelatin. This load expands more reliably and to larger diameters than any other standard-pressure hollowpoint and produces the largest permanent crush cavity in the caliber.

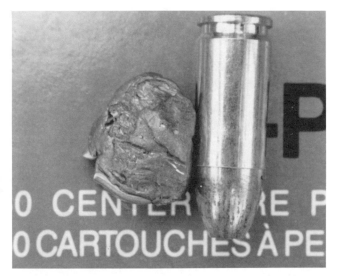

The Federal 115-grain JHP was the top choice in 9mm until just recently. The 9BP is still an excellent police and defensive round.

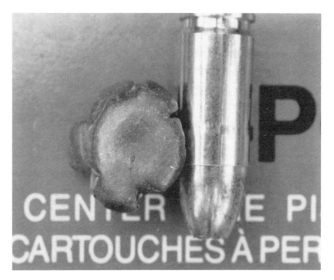

This Federal 115-grain JHP was used in a SWAT shooting. One shot fatally stopped a dope dealer armed with a submachine gun.

• • • • •

A rural deputy sheriff, he belonged to a department that gave its members considerable latitude in the weapons and ammunition they could carry. Because his backup was often 5 to 10 minutes away, he decided on a large-capacity SIG 9mm loaded with Federal's new 9BPLE load.

He was halfway through a relatively quiet day shift when he received a run to the lockup to perform a Breathalyzer test. He pulled into the driveway and called the dispatcher on the radio to open the overhead door. When he failed to get a response he called again. Failing to get an answer a second time, he exited his cruiser and entered the sheriff's office. He stepped behind the counter wondering where everyone was when he saw the blood.

Pulling his SIG, he followed a blood trail toward the squad room. There he saw a deputy lying face down in the corner. Quickly checking him, he saw that the wounded deputy was breathing. He found the rest of the building deserted. He called the paramedics for the downed officer and then called for additional officers to the station. Upon their arrival, he started to search the immediate area for the missing personnel.

A citizen flagged him down and told him that she had seen the sheriff and two other deputies chasing a man toward the railroad tracks. The deputy soon found the other officers and they informed him that the drunk driver had grabbed an officer's gun, shot him with it, and escaped. The bad guy had last been seen down by the railroad tracks.

Several hours later, the officers were unable to find the escaped prisoner. The day shift officers were ordered off duty and the search was taken over by the afternoon shift and state troopers. Tired and frustrated, our SIG-carrying deputy returned to the station, changed his clothes, and headed for home.

He was almost home when he heard an excited state trooper come on the air over the police scanner and put out the information that he had just exchanged shots with the suspect at a local gas station. Responding to the scene, the deputy exited his privately owned vehicle with his SIG in hand. Running to the rear of the station, he suddenly was shot at by an elderly white male dressed in a business suit. The officer fired 11 rounds at his attacker. The man turned, took two steps, and collapsed. He was brought to a hospital some 60 miles away, where he expired. A single Federal +P+ JHP had entered his stomach, causing massive internal bleeding. It weighed 104 grains and had a recovered diameter of .65 caliber.

Street Results: Federal 115-grain JHP

A big-city SWAT cop, he was playing catch with his son when his beeper went off. A call to his command indicated they were being called out to deal with a hostage situation in a liquor store. It took him 15 minutes of red light and siren to get to the rendezvous point. Upon his arrival, he put on his jumpsuit, vest, and boots, and removed his assigned weaponry from the trunk — a Heckler & Koch P7 pistol and H&K Model 33 select-fire-rifle.

The team leader assigned him as a scout and the officer approached the scene to gather intelligence. He was able to reach a position some 15 meters from the front of the liquor store. Concealed in a Dumpster, he was able to pass on intelligence and information to the site commander.

Several hours later, the gunman appeared in the

doorway with a hostage. The sniper broadcast that he did not have a clear shot, and the team leader contacted the scout to see if he had a shot. When the scout responded that he did, the team leader informed him that the hostage negotiator was convinced that the gunman was going to kill the hostages and that the incident had to be terminated immediately.

Realizing that there were other hostages behind the gunman, the officer put his assault rifle down and drew his 9mm pistol. Aiming carefully, he fired twice. The gunman spun to the ground and other team members rushed in to arrest him.

The gunman was rushed to a nearby hospital, where he was successfully operated on. One round had entered his right chest and was recovered 2 inches left of his spinal column just under the skin. The second round missed. The recovered slug weighed 96 grains and had a diameter of .67 caliber.

• • • • •

He was the manager of a chain of movie theaters in a large urban center with the responsibility of making night deposits. After being robbed and shot on a previous occasion, he had traded his .38 snub-nosed revolver for a S&W Model 669 9mm.

It was almost 3 A.M. before he finished his book work and grabbed the money bag. Driving the eleven blocks to the bank, he had his mind on getting home and working on the old sports car he was restoring.

He pulled his Cadillac in next to the bank. Grabbing the money bag, he opened the door and turned to face a large blue-steel revolver in the hand of a young male. "Give me the money, old man!" As our citizen did so he began to get mad — he was tired of being ripped off. As the young man turned to run away, he pulled his Model 669 and emptied it at the fleeing felon. The bad guy jerked, spun, and fell. The citizen got on his car phone and called the cops.

The holdup man was conveyed to a local hospital, where he was DOA. He was only hit one time out of fourteen, but that one round killed him. The recovered slug weighed 89 grains and its recovered diameter was .70 caliber. Unfortunately, the thug was only 13 years old and his gun was a toy. Under state law, the citizen had no right to shoot at a fleeing felon. He was tried and convicted of manslaughter. The dead boy's family sued him and collected $750,000!

• • • • •

The officer was reluctant about going out on patrol. He had just returned to work after being involved in

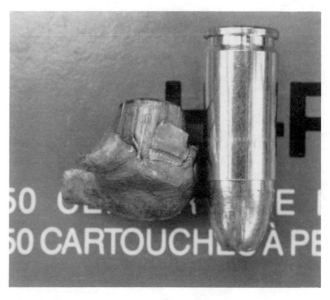

The Federal 115-grain JHP works extremely well in actual shootings. This load produces 81-percent one-shot stops.

a controversial shooting. His partner had been killed and although he had killed the perpetrator, both the press and several members of his department had argued that if he had fired sooner, his partner would be alive.

He asked the watch commander if he could work a one-man unit for awhile (one-man units in his department were primarily report or routine service units). It had been a refreshingly boring shift of accident and theft reports until a half-hour before its end. Driving by a local jeweler's, he realized the customary lights in selected parts of the store were not on. He pulled into the alley and drove up to an overhead door. His interest changed from curiosity to genuine concern when he noticed it was slightly open. Calling for a backup, he drew his 9mm and took cover behind a telephone pole.

Hidden from view, he watched with increasing anxiety as the door began to inch its way upward. The door was approximately 3 feet above the ground when two white males ducked under it. They started to turn to their right and saw the police unit. The officer yelled, "Police, freeze!" and all hell broke loose. One individual swung what was later found to be an Uzi carbine converted to full-auto at him and opened fire. Realizing that he had to act quickly before he was outflanked and killed, the officer shot the Uzi-armed thug three times. Turning his attention to the second bad guy, he felt a burning sensation and realized he had been shot (with a full-power Remington 240-grain .44 Mag JHP!). Praying that his vest had done its job, he fired five rounds at the second felon. His second

The Winchester 9mm 115-grain Silvertip is far superior in actual shootings to every single 147-grain load. The Silvertip is effective 79 percent of the time.

attacker ran a few feet before collapsing. When responding officers arrived, they found their brother officer with his shirt off and looking at his vest, gently probing the beginnings of a large bruise above his left nipple.

Both thugs were DOA at a local hospital. The second thug had died from one Federal JHP to the heart. The recovered slug was resting against the spine and weighed 89 grains, with a recovered diameter of .71 caliber.

• • • • •

A clinical psychologist in one of this country's most antigun urban centers, he shared none of his colleagues' irrational views of the human condition. Raised in the slums of Cleveland, he knew there were a lot of total SOBs out there.

Under the expensive three-piece suits he wore was a Milt Sparks Summer Special holding a Devel chopped-and-channeled Model 59. Loaded with Federal JHP ammo, it gave him a measure of reassurance as he traveled through the urban jungle he practiced in.

He was ushering out his last patient for the day when his wife called asking him to stop and pick up a cheesecake for dessert. Their favorite source for this item was in what could be charitably called a run-down neighborhood. Despite its location, there was a steady stream of customers who were willing to take the risks involved to purchase what some considered the best cheesecake in the country.

He placed his order with the clerk, paid for it, and waited while she boxed it up. Exiting the store, he

turned toward his car and immediately sensed the problem. Five young men were leaning against the side of his Porsche. Instead of turning around and calling the police, he walked up to the gang. "Excuse me," he said. As he brushed by one of them, he felt a blow in the middle of his back. He turned to confront his atacker and saw the bloody knife in the thug's hand. Realizing he had been stabbed, he pulled his 9mm and shot his attacker in the throat. The rest of the gang ran off, but as he turned to seek help, he collapsed dead.

His attacker was rushed to the nearest hospital, where he recovered. He was convicted of manslaughter and given probation. The recovered slug weighed 109 grains and had a diameter of .43 caliber.

• • • • •

He looked like any other uniformed police officer in his department. He did, in fact, have a very specialized assignment — he was an Evidence Technician. He was assigned the responsibility of responding to crime scenes and processing them for evidence.

His duty weapon was a nickel-plated S&W Model 59. Contrary to department regulation, he loaded his weapon with Federal JHP ammo instead of the department-approved ball ammo. His attitude was that his city was just too dangerous to play games with FMJ ammo.

He had received a "run" to meet a precinct narcotics crew who wanted an extremely large amount of dope and money photographed at a raid location. The officer pulled his marked van in front of the site. He didn't see any other police vehicles, but he assumed they were parked in back. He grabbed his camera and with the strobe battery unit slung over his shoulder, he exited his vehicle. He knocked on the door and it was opened by a black male with a shotgun. The man took one look at the officer and yelled, "It's the cops!" The officer attempted to jump, draw his weapon, and swear all at the same time. The shotgun discharged and the officer felt the pellets hit his leg. He responded by firing five rounds through the partially closed door. He then crawled off the porch and called for help.

Responding units rushed the house and arrested its occupants, except for the dead man behind the door holding a shotgun. One round had caught him in the left arm pit and pierced the heart. The recovered slug weighed 85 grains and had a recovered diameter of .58 caliber.

Street Results: W-W 115-grain 9mm JHP Silvertip

The tow truck didn't draw a second glance, nor did its driver. An older black male in well-worn coveralls, he worked long hours to help his kids complete their college education. People who knew him marveled at how well his children had turned out in spite of the rough inner-city neighborhood they were raised in. His philosophy was simple: hard work builds character, and honesty is the only policy worth adhering to. While the man was known far and wide for his generosity, he was not naive. Tucked in his coveralls was a Browning Hi-Power that he had liberated while serving in the Korean conflict. The chamber was empty, but thirteen Silvertip hollowpoints were in the magazine.

It was 8 P.M. and his day that started at 5 A.M. wasn't close to being over. He stopped at a local diner and the waitress asked him how his kids were. He had begun to reply in great detail when a disturbance broke out in the other end of the establishment. The waitress went over in an attempt to quiet things down when one of those involved in the dispute shoved her and told her to mind her own business. The tow truck driver was offended by this and said so. The instigator turned to him and told him to shut up before he cut him. Emphasizing the point, the young man raised a large folding knife and slashed the air with it.

Pulling the Hi-Power, the driver jacked a round into the chamber and told the young man to drop the knife. The young man laughed and told him, "Old man, I ain't afraid of your old black ass or your old rusty pistol!" He stepped toward the gun and said, "Give it to me before you shoot yourself." He then lunged, and the gun discharged twice. Dropping the knife, the young man looked puzzled, screamed, and collapsed.

At a nearby hospital, a Winchester Silvertip hollowpoint was removed from the thug's spine. It weighed 78 grains and had a recovered diameter of .54 caliber.

• • • • •

He didn't look any different from any of the other male customers at the large outdoor seafood restaurant on the dock. While his attire matched that of most of the clientele, his accessories did not. Under his sport coat was a Beretta 92 9mm semiautomatic and two spare magazines. A SWAT cop from a nearby big city, he carried the same pistol both on and off duty. While other team members opted for .38 snubs and .380 autos for off-duty use, he was convinced that trouble was just around the corner.

It was his wedding anniversary and knowing his wife's love of seafood, he had good-naturedly taken her to her favorite eating spot. They were halfway through their meal when his pager went off. His wife made an uncharitable remark about the timing of criminals in their fair city. Calling in, the officer discovered that two officers had been shot and the cop killers had taken hostages. When the officer indicated his location, the team leader said that he would try to find someone closer.

The officer returned to his dinner, keeping the information about the two dead officers to himself. They

This is the much-abused Winchester 9mm 115-grain STHP Silvertip. This one, fired from a Beretta, dropped a hostage-taker in his tracks.

This Remington 9mm 115-grain JHP fatally stopped a rapist. This shows expansion larger than normal for this load.

were finishing dessert and coffee when he was paged again. This time the conversation was short and to the point: one hostage had been killed and an assault was necessary, but they needed three full teams to execute it properly.

Twenty minutes later, the officer rolled up to the assembly point. Removing his Uzi from the trunk, he slung it and headed to the briefing. The officer was assigned his usual task as entry man and his team was placed in position to make a surreptitious entry. A television helicopter was supposed to fly over and draw the bad guy's attention while his team entered. They were to take up an ambush position, and the second and third teams would then make a crisis entry, hopefully forcing the bad guys into the trap.

Gaining entry and achieving their position, the first team signaled their readiness. Thirty seconds later, the breaching charge went off and then the stun grenades. Because of the hostages present, he had slung his Uzi and was relying on his Beretta. When they entered, there stood a white male in his thirties holding a teenaged black female. He screamed, "Let us go, pigs, or I'll waste her!" As the team leader challenged the hostage taker, the officer slowly raised his Beretta and shot the felon twice in the upper back.

The cop killer's response was sudden. He shot the hostage in the head and turned toward his attacker. Before he could kill anyone else, however, a load of 00 buckshot struck him in the upper chest.

The slugs were recovered at the morgue. Neither had hit anything vital, and both had expanded in the .60-caliber range. The hostage survived a grazing wound, while the other cop killer was fatally shot by a SWAT sniper as he tried to escape out a window.

• • • • •

He was the constant source of amusement for the other campus cops on the medium-sized rural college police department. He had bugged the chief until he got permission to carry his Glock instead of the nickel-plated S&W Model 10. He also wore a Second Chance vest and a second gun.

They were quick to remind him that a cop on this campus had never even been shot at. He just grinned good-naturedly and went about his business. He worked the graveyard shift because it usually gave him a chance to study during the four hours he had to man the desk each night. Once a week he would drive out to the outdoor range they shared with the local police department and he would fire 50 rounds of 9mm reloads.

It was a cold February night and it was almost time for him to be relieved by the officer on patrol. He glanced at the TV monitors located at a variety of spots around the campus. Most of the other officers ignored them, but he took this stuff seriously. He checked the monitor in the audio-visual lab and froze suddenly. He could see movement inside the labratory. He used the camera controls to redirect the outside

The Remington 9mm 115-grain JHP produces moderate expansion and deep penetration in actual shootings. This load is instantly effective 76 percent of the time.

This shows the Winchester 9mm 147-grain OSM Type L at its very best. This slug was fired from a Beretta 92F by a state trooper.

The Winchester 9mm 147-grain Olin Super Match JHP, or Type L, has produced good expansion but fair performance. It ranks 14 out of 17 loads in this caliber.

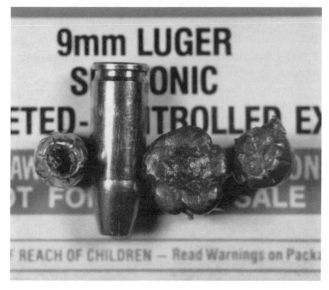

The Winchester 9mm 147-grain subsonic JHP shows varying amounts of expansion. The penetration, however, is nearly always excessively deep and the stopping power is very marginal.

camera and it zoomed in on a van parked near the back door. Two white males were taking turns placing items in it.

He called the patrol unit and informed him of the crime in progress. He then called the local police department and they indicated that backup was on the way. When he recontacted the patrol unit and reminded him to wait for backup, his partner laughed, "Ah, it's probably just some fraternity stunt. Calm down."

His concern growing, the officer put on his coat and headed toward the audio-visual building on foot. He was halfway around the building when he heard a scream and several shots. Drawing his Glock, he ran to the corner and saw one of the thugs standing over his partner, gun in hand. The officer, displaying a superior level of street sense, didn't yell "Halt!" or "Stop! Police!" Instead he simply shot the burglar. As the second thug attempted to flee on foot, he shot him too.

Responding units found the officer attempting to treat an obviously dead partner. He had been killed by his own gun. The two B&E men were dead also. One round had struck the felon in his chest, severing the spine. It weighed 45 grains and was in fragments. The other bad guy had taken three Silvertips in the back and all three had pierced the heart. The rounds weighed from 91 to 98 grains, and their recovered diameter was in the .65-caliber range.

.38 SUPER

Ballistic gelatin results for the .38 Super indicate

that the 125-grain STHP Silvertip and the Remington 115-grain JHP produce the same terminal results. Like the 9mm, the Remington load feeds in any auto pistol that will feed ball, while the Silvertip feeds in the great majority of weapons.

The Remington 115-grain JHP is the same bullet used in the 9mm JHP load. The longer 5-inch barrels on most .38 Supers and the longer cases allowing for slower-burning powders produce a muzzle velocity well over the minimum required for reliable expansion.

From a .38 Super, the 115-grain JHP has a muzzle velocity between 1,275 and 1,325 fps. This is 100 to 125 fps faster than the same bullet from the 9mm.

Muzzle energy from the 115-grain JHP is 430 foot-pounds. This is exactly the same as the 9mm +P+ Winchester Q load made for the Illinois State Police. It expands between .64 and .69 caliber and penetrates between 11.5 and 12.5 inches.

The Silvertip in .38 Super has a muzzle velocity between 1,165 and 1,225 fps for an energy level averaging 400 foot-pounds. The Silvertip expands between .62 and .65 caliber and penetrates from 9.5 to 10.5 inches.

The only other conventional load available in .38 Super is the 130-grain full-metal-jacket hardball. Even at 1,200 fps, this load produces small stretch cavities and caliber-diameter crush cavities. The penetration in gelatin exceeds 18 inches, indicating the slug will perforate in most cases.

No actual shooting results that meet the authors' criteria are available for the .38 Super.

.357 MAGNUM

Ballistic gelatin results favor the .357 Magnum 125-grain jacketed hollowpoint by a slight but clear margin over the 140- and 145-grain JHP loads. The 125-grain produces muzzle velocities betwen 1,325 and 1,425 fps and muzzle energies between 490 and 560 foot-pounds. By all accounts, the 125-grain JHP produces optimal antipersonnel terminal ballistics from a handgun.

The 125-grain JHP expands in living tissue and in ordnance gelatin with extreme reliability. In gelatin, it always expands and then fragments to produce secondary missiles or erodes the mushroom away. The recovered diameter ranges from .51 to .58 caliber, with a recovered weight rarely exceeding 65 percent of the original weight.

All 125-grain JHP loads from various manufacturers produce stretch cavities of equal volume and shape, and crush cavities of equal volume. The shape of the crush cavities does vary by manufacturer.

Speer, Hornady, Winchester and all variations of Federal expand rapidly to produce a large single crush cavity for the first third of the depth of penetration. Generally, these loads shear the mushroom to produce a .55-caliber crush cavity for the balance of the penetration.

The Remington 125-grain S-JHP expands with equal reliability. Instead of eroding the resulting mushroom, the lead from the cavity wall is spun off to become secondary missiles. This produces a .55-caliber crush cavity and multiple .10-caliber crush cavities surrounding the main bullet path for the first half of the penetration depth. The .55-caliber crush cavity completes the balance of the penetration.

The equal stretch cavity, equal penetration, and greater crush cavity that affect tissue remote from the main bullet path make the Remington the top choice, according to gelatin predictions.

The 125-grain JHP produces larger diameter stretch cavities than 110-, 140-, 145-, and 158-grain JHP loads. It produces larger crush cavities than the 110- and 158-grain JHP loads and is close to the 140- and

Table 8-5

.357 MAGNUM ACTUAL RESULTS

	Total Shootings	One-Shot Stops	Percentage	Muzzle Velocity
1. Fed 125-gr. JHP	406	390	96.05	1,563 fps
2. R-P 125-gr. S-JHP	116	109	93.96	1467 fps
3. CCI 125-gr. JHP	71	65	91.54	1,383 fps
4. Fed 110-gr. JHP	63	57	90.47	1,366 fps
5. W-W 125-gr. JHP	77	67	87.01	1,391 fps
6. R-P 110-gr. S-JHP	34	29	85.29	1,344 fps
7. W-W 110-gr. JHP	31	26	83.87	1,290 fps
8. CCI 110-gr. JHP	18	15	83.33	1,310 fps
9. W-W 145-gr. STHP	48	40	83.33	1,294 fps
10. R-P 125-gr. S-JHP (med. vel.)	12	10	83.33	1,280 fps
11. R-P 158-gr. S-JHP	27	22	81.48	1,233 fps
12. Fed 158-gr. JHP	58	47	81.03	1,217 fps
13. W-W 158-gr. JHP	72	57	79.16	1,259 fps
14. CCI 140-gr. JHP	23	17	73.91	1,330 fps
15. R-P 158-gr. JSP	23	17	73.39	1,235 fps
16. Fed 158-gr. LHP-Nyclad	11	8	72.73	1,190 fps
17. CCI 158-gr. JSP	29	21	72.41	1,178 fps
18. W-W 158-gr. SWC	89	64	71.91	1,319 fps
19. CCI 125-gr. JSP	14	10	71.43	1,410 fps
20. CCI 158-gr. JHP	20	14	70.00	1,240 fps
21. Fed 158-gr. SWC	36	25	69.44	1,152 fps
22. R-P 158-gr. SWC	71	48	67.60	1,149 fps

The Remington .357 Magnum 125-grain JHP is the second most effective of all handgun loads and calibers. It produces one-shot stops nearly 94 percent of the time.

The Remington .357 Magnum 125-grain JHP typically expands and violently spins off pieces of bullet core. It expands well even in fatty tissue and air-filled lungs.

145-grain JHP loads.

All of the 125-grain JHP loads produce an ideal penetration depth ranging from 10.5 to 12 inches in 10-percent gelatin. The 110-grain loads produce shallower levels of penetration that are more sensitive to intermediate targets and cross-torso shots. The 140-grain JHP and 145-grain STHP produce deeper, near-perforation levels of penetration. Heavier and nonexpanding loads are likely to perforate.

The Speer-Lawman 140-grain JHP, Remington 140-grain S-JHP, and Winchester 145-grain STHP Silvertip loads are close behind but second place to the 125-grain JHP. These loads produce large but more moderate stretch cavities and the largest and deepest crush cavities of any expanding .357 Magnum load. They have muzzle velocities between 1,225 and 1,345 fps and energies between 470 and 580 foot-pounds. The Remington fragments to produce secondary missiles and generally has a recovered diameter around .58 caliber, with penetration of about 15.5 inches. The Speer-Lawman expands but erodes back to a .55-caliber slug and penetrates between 15 and 15.5 inches. The Silvertip expands up to a .65-caliber mushroom and generally holds that final expansion. Sometimes the mushroom is lost passively, resulting in a .52-caliber recovered slug. The depth of penetration is more favorably moderate than the 140-grain slugs, ranging from 11.75 to 14.25 inches.

The only factor keeping these moderately heavy magnums from better ratings is their more moderate energy release and higher possibility of perforation. Again, however, the gelatin predicts these loads to

be very close to the 125-grain, especially the 145-grain Silvertip.

The only other .357 Magnum loads that meet the requirements of expansion and penetration are the 125-grain jacketed softpoint and the 158-grain jacketed hollowpoint. In general, however, these loads produce far too little expansion and far too much penetration.

The 125-grain JSP expands to between .43 and .54 caliber and penetrates 17 to 18 inches of gelatin. The 158-grain JHP expands to between .50 and .60 caliber and also penetrates 17 to 18 inches of gelatin. Both loads really need to engage a heavy bone like the sternum to produce good results.

These two loads also benefit the most from the modest increase in velocity achieved with 5- and 6-inch guns. The slightly higher velocity pushes both loads over their respective minimum expansion velocities. Conversely, they suffer the most when fired in 2.5- and 3-inch magnum snubbies.

The .357 Magnum 110-grain JHP loads are predicted to be entirely too sensitive to intermediate targets and transverse torso shots. Their large but shallow stretch cavities and shallow crush cavities are much better suited to off-duty, second gun, backup, and concealed-carry scenarios.

The 158-grain jacketed softpoint, 158-grain lead semiwadcutter, and 158-grain metal point do not expand in ballistic gelatin. They produce reasonable stretch cavities and very small crush cavities, and have profound tendencies toward perforation. As a result, all these loads are functional but produce significantly

This is the wound profile of the Federal .357 Magnum 125-grain JHP. This is the single most proven-effective hand-gun load ever used by American police officers or civilians.

less than ideal overall bullet and wound performance.

*   *   *   *   *

The .357 Magnum was introduced in the mid-1930s as a higher-powered version of the .38 Special. Although not originally developed with law enforcement in mind, it gradually found a niche in police/defensive circles.

Prior to the Super Vel line, the only "high-performance" .357 load was the Remington 158-grain jacketed softpoint. It produced only marginal expansion against human targets.

Today, of course, we have a variety of offerings in this caliber in a wide spectrum of bullet weights and styles. While some very impressive claims are made about them, most are really not very spectacular performers in actual shootings. There are a few, however, that produce stopping power results that should bring .357 carriers a feeling of real security.

Street Results: Federal .357 Magnum 125-grain JHP

The rookie officer donned his Second Chance vest, uniform shirt, and pants and reached for his Sam Browne belt. Buckling it on, he removed his S&W Model 65 duty revolver and checked to see that it was loaded with six rounds of department-issue Federal .357 Magnum 125-grain jacketed hollowpoint am-

munition. Satisfied, he reholstered his weapon and went to roll call.

Two hours later, his feet told him it was time to take a break from foot patrol and grab a cup of coffee. Approaching a nearby lunch stand, he glanced inside and froze. The cashier had both hands full of cash and was handing it to an older man leaning over the counter. The officer pulled his hand-held radio and called for help. He then drew his weapon and took up a position of cover. His original plan was to maintain cover until help arrived, but that plan evaporated when shots were fired inside. Jerking the door open, he turned to his left and was immediately fired upon.

Returning fire, he saw the holdup man stagger back and collapse. The officer remembered his lessons from the academy and took cover and waited for help. Responding officers approached the felon, but found that handcuffs were unnecessary — he was dead. The officer's slug was recovered from the bad guy's liver and weighed 101 grains and had a recovered diameter of .79 caliber.

●   ●   ●   ●   ●

It had been a frustrating eight hours. Right after roll call, an officer from a nearby department had been shot in a holdup. A witness had gotten the felon's

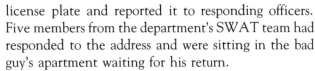

The Federal .357 Magnum 125-grain JHP is the absolute king of the hill. Its 96-percent street effectiveness is the best of any handgun load in any caliber.

Three Federal .357 Magnum 125-grain JHP bullets are shown—one each from three dead felons.

license plate and reported it to responding officers. Five members from the department's SWAT team had responded to the address and were sitting in the bad guy's apartment waiting for his return.

Unlike a lot of other specialized police teams, this unit carried the S&W L-frame .357 Magnum loaded with Federal 125-grain .357 jacketed hollowpoint ammo. Most of the team wanted high-capacity 9mms, but the Chief was a dyed-in-the-wool revolver man.

They had just called in to see if they were going to be relieved by another team when the "eye" outside reported that the wanted vehicle had just pulled into the carport below. The officers took up their positions with revolvers drawn. It was decided that, because of the thin apartment walls, four of the officers would rely on their handguns while the fifth had a mini-Uzi as backup.

They were in position when they heard footsteps in the hallway. Then they heard someone yell, "There's cops in your place! Run!" Cursing, three of the officers jerked the door open to give pursuit while two others ran to the balcony and jumped to the carport roof below.

One officer rolled off the roof to confront the suspect as he entered his Trans Am. His command to freeze was drowned out by the roar of the car's engine. The officer's response was fast and fatal. He fired two shots into the side window of the vehicle. The car sped backward, hit a cyclone fence, and stopped. Taking a covering position, the officer apprised the rest of the team of the situation and his location.

With the rest of the team present, they approached the vehicle. Looking inside, they saw that the suspect was dead. One round had missed, but the other had penetrated his arm, entered the chest cavity, and destroyed the heart. The recovered slug weighed 71 grains and had a recovered diameter of .48 caliber.

• • • • •

A reader of my column in *Combat Handguns* magazine, he had written to ask about ammo for his 4-inch Model 66 that he carried as a midnight gas station attendant in a rough neighborhood in a large western city.

Six months later I received a call from the man. He was finishing up his shift when his relief pulled up and motioned for him to open the door. As he did, two males rushed in behind him. Displaying large knives, they demanded the money. My reader's response was to pull his .357 and tell them to "get the hell out." One bad guy started to turn, but his partner stabbed the gas station attendant. He shoved his Model 66 against the holdup man's chest and pulled the trigger. As the attacker fell to the ground, he turned his attention to the second felon and shot him twice in the back. He collapsed too.

The reader's wound was superficial and only required 15 stitches to close it. Both bad guys survived, although the second has to have help with everything he does except breathing. The first one was struck in the sternum and the round nicked the heart sac. Its recovered

This Federal .357 Magnum 125-grain JHP expanded well and kept most of its mushroom. This one stopped a knife attack.

weight was 101 grains and its diameter was .78 caliber.

• • • • •

A federal agent, his S&W Model 19 was supposed to be loaded with the .38 Special + P + JHP loads. He, however, decided that the idiot who chose that round had probably never worked the street a day in his life. Instead, his weapon and HKS speed loaders (another policy violation) carried Federal 125-grain JHPs.

He was on loan to another agency to guard the wife of an organized crime figure who had agreed to testify against her husband's former friends. Several death threats had been received and it was felt they should be taken seriously. In addition to his .357, the agent had a new closed-bolt Uzi in an Adidas bag on the front seat of his car.

He was almost at the end of his shift when another agent guarding the back of the house radioed that he had movement. He described two white males coming over the back fence. Grabbing the submachine gun, the first agent racked a round and promptly jammed the weapon. He cast it aside, pulled his revolver, and ran quietly to the rear. Going prone, he peeked around the corner and saw the two suspects prying the rear door off its hinges.

Yelling "Federal agent! Freeze!" he came to a kneeling position as the first bad guy opened fire. The agent's response was rapid and deadly — he emptied his weapon, rolled behind the corner of the building, speed-loaded six rounds, and rolled back out. Noticing

that both suspects were down, he called for help on his radio and maintained his position.

Responding agents determined that both men were dead. One had taken four rounds of the .357 ammo, while the other had taken one in the stomach. Recovered slugs weighed between 82 and 94 grains, and the recovered diameter of the slug in the stomach was .66 caliber.

• • • • •

He was a sheriff's reserve deputy with one of the larger western departments. Fully trained and certified, he was allowed to patrol on his own. He had become a reserve because it would enhance his chances for full-time employment when a vacancy occurred.

He was assigned to a small town on the western end of his county. He was responsible for all police needs in this area, although in the event of a serious call the dispatcher was supposed to send another unit. It was almost 10 P.M. when he got an alarm call to the local bank. Acknowledging the run, he asked the dispatcher for backup and was informed that it was rolling but its ETA was 15 minutes.

As the reserve deputy pulled up to the bank, he noticed the lights were out, but he relaxed when he noticed that all the lights on that block were out. He assumed that a power outage had caused the alarm. Parking in front of the bank, he walked up and tugged on the front door. To his horror, it swung open. He was reaching for his belt radio when the first round struck him in the chest, spinning him around. He was reaching for his .357 when a second round struck him in the back. He fell on his face under the counter.

It took him a second to realize that he had his vest on. Becoming very angry, he pulled his .357 slowly. Suddenly, he saw movement in the back of the bank. Raising his weapon, he fired two shots. He heard a scream and the sound of someone running out the back. He maintained his position, reloaded, and called for help.

When responding units arrived, he searched the building with them. In the back hallway was a dead 63-year-old white male with a gunshot wound to the center of his chest. The Federal .357 slug had shredded his heart. It had a recovered weight of 74 grains and a recovered diameter of .69 caliber. The bank robber had a fifteen-page record and had served time for four bank holdups and the fatal shooting of a state trooper.

• • • • •

The CCI .357 Magnum 125-grain JHP ranks third overall among all calibers and loads according to actual street results. Better than nine times out of ten, this slug is effective instantly.

A veteran street cop, he relied on a S&W Model 58 .41 Magnum for his survival. Getting ready for work one afternoon, he noticed the tip of the firing pin on his weapon was broken off. Opening up his Treadlock safe, he removed a nickel-plated 4-inch S&W Model 19 with an Andy Cannon action job that had been Magna-Ported. Switching holsters and speed-loader pouches, he took 18 rounds of Federal .357 ammo out of the box and loaded for the street.

Arriving just in time for on-duty roll call, he found that his assignment had been changed and that he was to work inside as an extra clerk. Cursing his fate, he went downstairs and found that another dedicated street cop had also been drafted to work inside.

The first four hours were extremely boring, and at lunchtime he took a box of .38 wadcutters from his locker and went to the range in the basement. He was putting the empty brass back in the box when he heard someone yell, "We need help at the front desk!" Running up the stairs, he saw that a shabbily dressed male had his arm around the lieutenant's throat and was dragging him out the door.

Pulling his .357, the officer told the perpetrator to freeze. The man turned toward the officer and, displaying a large butcher knife, said "If you don't put down the gun, I'll cut this pig's throat." The officer had decided years before that he would *never* surrender a weapon! The bad guy insisted again, and the officer did the only thing he could do — he shot the felon in the throat. The thug collapsed. As the lieutenant rolled away, the officer advanced and kicked the knife

away from the downed man.

The suspect was dead on arrival at a local hospital. The recovered slug was in fragments, as it had severed the spine. The officer received a departmental citation for his prompt action, and two official reprimands: one for illegal ammunition and another for not following departmental procedure in a hostage situation!

Street Results: CCI .357 125-grain JHP

It wasn't fun anymore. He had delivered milk in this same neighborhood for almost forty years. It had been fine until two years ago, when he had been robbed at knife point. After he gave them the money, they stabbed him anyway. He had spent almost a year recovering from this attack. Now back to work, he carried a Ruger Security Six .357 Magnum in a bag next to the steering wheel.

He had made a delivery and was almost to his truck when he saw them standing on the corner. Animals, he thought, nothing but animals. When they started to approach his truck, he pulled the gun from the bag and held it behind his leg.

"Hey, old man, got change for the bus?" one asked. He told them he didn't have any change when the same teenager pulled a pocket knife and said, "That's okay, pops, cause I want it all." The sight of another knife pushed the old man over the edge and he shot the thug four times. As the other ran off, he stepped from the truck and fired one shot. The second suspect took two more steps and collapsed.

Responding officers found the old man standing over the knife-wielding youth, saying, "You stupid bastard, you stupid bastard," over and over again.

The slug weighed 71 grains and had a recovered diameter of .56 caliber. It had torn the vena cava and the 15-year-old holdup man had bled to death.

● ● ● ● ●

The widow of a state trooper killed in the line of duty, she had been given his badge, hat and S&W Model 586 .357 Magnum service revolver. Living in a remote rural area, she kept the weapon loaded in a nightstand near her bed. Her husband had taught her how to use it and the Magnum loads did not intimidate her.

Her niece and nephew had spent a week with her, and she had just returned from the bus station. As she drove into the driveway, she noticed the rear door was ajar. She couldn't remember if she had locked it or not, so she wasn't particularly worried. As she entered the house, however, her mood quickly changed. The 13-inch color TV had been moved from its regular

Two Winchester .357 Magnum 145-grain Silvertips recovered from two different robbers. Each was stopped with one shot. Textbook expansion.

location next to her sewing table.

She had just picked up the phone to call the police when she heard movement in the living room. Running to the bedroom, she removed the .357 from its hiding place. She checked to make sure it was loaded and entered the living room. What she saw shocked her beyond belief: a man and a woman were engaged in sexual intercourse on her living room rug! She yelled and they both jumped up. Asking them what the hell they thought they were doing in her house, she pointed the gun and told them to get dressed and get the hell out. They had begun to comply when the woman grabbed the fireplace poker and swung at her. The widow's response was swift and sure as she fired two rounds from the revolver. The half-dressed woman staggered and collapsed dead. The man escaped out the front door but was captured by responding officers with a tracking dog. It was later determined that they were wanted for a number of murders across the country.

One slug had pierced the aorta. It was recovered from the floor and weighed 82 grains and had a recovered diameter of .71 caliber.

• • • • •

His long hair, beard, and backpack labeled him as just another free spirit at one with nature. Actually, he was a big-city undercover narc who liked to hike. He was enjoying the clean air and solitude miles from any city. Checking his map, he verified that a small town was just around the bend. He approached the combination gas station/store, leaned his pack against the wall, and went inside.

Coming back outside, he sat down to enjoy his

yogurt. He had no sooner started when a car pulled up and three white males got out. They looked at him and exchanged amused glances. He ignored them and, finishing his yogurt, reshouldered his pack and started up the road. Ten minutes later, he heard a car pull up and someone yell, "Hey, you hippie puke. What you got in the pack?" He turned and saw the same three individuals who had been at the store. Ignoring them, he continued to walk until something hard bounced off his pack. Without looking he knew it was an empty beer bottle.

Turning, he saw one of the three exit the car with a baseball bat. He unshouldered his pack, unzipped a side pocket, and slid his hand around the grip of a .357 Magnum. The man with the bat said, "What you got in the pack, hippie? Some dope?" The officer looked at him and replied that he didn't have anything of value. Undeterred, the bat-wielding man said, "Give me the pack or I'll bash your head in!"

The officer pulled the gun and told the man to get back in the car and leave. The man laughed and advanced on the officer, saying, "I ain't afraid of no hippie even if he has got a gun!" As the bat started to swing toward him, the officer fired twice. The attacker staggered, dropped the bat, and ran back to the car. He had almost reached it when he collapsed dead.

The autopsy revealed that one slug had entered over the left nipple and damaged the spine. Its recovered weight was 89 grains and it had a recovered diameter of .42 caliber.

.41 MAGNUM

The top load for this caliber based on crush and stretch cavities is clearly the Federal 210-grain JHP. This load has a muzzle velocity of 1,325 fps and a muzzle energy of 820 foot-pounds. It expands to between .78 and .80 caliber and penetrates 14.5 inches. This results in the largest stretch and crush cavities for the caliber, with an excellent to slightly excessive level of penetration.

Close behind the Federal, and the only other .41 Magnum load to expand dependably, is the Winchester 175-grain STHP Silvertip. This load is moderate velocity and moderate recoil by design. The muzzle velocity is 1,225 fps, with a muzzle energy of 580 foot-pounds. It expands to .70 caliber in gelatin and penetrates 13.5 inches. The stretch cavities are the diameter of the best .357 Magnum hollowpoints, only longer. The .70-caliber crush cavity indicates that the Silvertip is the most effective mid-range .41 Magnum load.

Winchester also offers a non-Silvertip jacketed hollowpoint. This JHP weighs 210 grains and has a muzzle

Table 8-6

.41 MAGNUM ACTUAL RESULTS

	Total Shootings	One-shot Stops	Percentage	Muzzle Velocity
1. W-W 170-gr. STHP	44	39	88.63	1,299 fps
2. W-W 210-gr. JHP	29	24	82.75	1,260 fps
3. R-P 210-gr. JSP	25	20	80.00	1,219 fps
4. R-P 210-gr. SWC	46	35	76.08	944 fps
5. W-W 210-gr. SWC	39	29	74.35	956 fps

velocity of 1,250 fps and a muzzle energy of 725 foot-pounds. This bullet, like all non-Silvertip revolver hollowpoints, has serrations in the copper jacket. The bullet nose, however, is quite rounded and the hollow-point measures a small .07 inch in diameter.

This load may or may not expand in gelatin; when expansion does occur, the mushroom rarely exceeds .53 caliber. It produces reasonable stretch cavities (though smaller than other expanding .41 Magnum loads) and crush cavities only fractionally larger than nonexpanding loads. Penetration generally is excessive.

The 210-grain jacketed hollowpoint at 1,260 fps does not expand in gelatin, and penetration generally is excessive. Stretch cavities are still reasonable in size due to the .41-caliber hole and 1,200+ impact vel-

ocities. The crush cavity is small for the caliber.

The 210-grain load semiwadcutter was originally designed as an intermediate recoil load. At a muzzle velocity of 960 fps, it produces 430 foot-pounds of energy. The stretch cavities and the crush cavities from the SWC are the smallest for the caliber.

* * * * *

The .41 Magnum was developed in the mid-1960s as the "ultimate police cartridge." Unfortunately, a series of mishaps doomed it almost from the beginning. One department switched to the S&W Model 58 revolver in this caliber and then issued the jacketed softpoint ammo instead of the moderate-velocity lead semiwadcutter offering. The recoil difference between

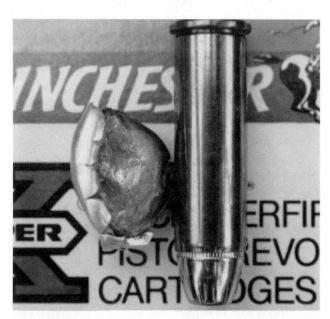

The Winchester .41 Magnum 170-grain Silvertip is the top load in this caliber. This well-expanded slug ended a sniper's shooting spree.

The Remington .41 Magnum 210-grain semiwadcutter is a medium-velocity load designed for police use. This semiwadcutter struck a rib and was deformed.

the full-power .41 and the .38 they had been carrying were dramatic. Another department carried the SWC load, but they compared qualification scores fired with .41 Mag ammo with the scores shot when they were using N-frame S&W .357s loaded with .38 wadcutters and found the latter to be much more accurate.

I first became aware of the .41 while reading an old issue of *American Rifleman* at lunchtime in the police academy. The moderate-velocity, heavy-bullet approach made a lot of sense to me, so as soon as I could find a Model 58, I bought one. I carried it for a number of years before switching to the high-capacity 9mm I carry today. It saved my life on two occasions, and I still have strong emotional ties to that caliber.

S&W's recent inclusion of the .41 Magnum in its stainless N-frame line will encourage sales, but it's got to be the most unappreciated handgun caliber. If ordered to carry a revolver, I'd certainly go back to it. Shooting data is not as extensive as with some other calibers, but impartial data has confirmed my suspicions about where it would place on the effectiveness scale.

Street Results: .41 Magnum 170-grain STHP Silvertip

An inner-city security guard, he carried a S&W Model 57 .41 Magnum revolver loaded with Winchester Silvertip ammunition. He had worked a 12-hour shift and was walking to his car when he heard screams. Moving between two rows of cars, he saw two young men leaning over an elderly woman. He yelled at the youths and one turned and ran toward him with a large knife. The teenager was on top of him before he could get his gun out and he was stabbed twice in the chest. He shoved the revolver against his attacker's stomach and fired. The youth turned, took a step, and died.

The security guard expired on the way to the hospital. The autopsy of his attacker determined that the round had traveled upward through the liver and exited. It was not recovered.

●　●　●　●　●

The minute he had seen the revolver at the gun show, he knew he had to have it. It was a S&W Model 657 stainless .41 Magnum with a 3-inch barrel and round butt. Buying two boxes of Silvertip ammo, he took his new purchase home. He took it to the range a week later and sighted it in. Returning home, he stuck it in a dresser drawer next to his bed.

A few months later, he got a call from the garage attendent in the luxury condo complex he lived in. Someone had broken into his Mercedes and attempted

The Remington .41 Magnum 210-grain lead semiwadcutter is effective instantly 76 percent of the time. This one ended a bar fight.

to steal it. He was going out the door when he quickly returned to his bedroom and slid the .41 Mag into his waistband. Chuckling silently over his own paranoia, he almost put it back. When he arrived in the garage, the attendant accompanied him to his car while he examined the damaged door.

He had returned to the elevator and was at the third level when he realized he had not checked the trunk lock. Cursing his lack of concentration, he returned to the basement garage. He walked over to his vehicle and examined the trunk. Realizing it was intact, he decided to remove the portable computer and software he had put there.

He was walking toward the elevator with both arms full when he heard footsteps. Increasing his pace, he almost made it to the elevator when he heard someone running toward him. Setting the computer down, he drew his .41 Mag and held it down by his leg. He turned and saw two shabbily dressed young men approaching him. He said, "What do you want?" The tallest of the two showed him a knife and with an ear-to-ear grin said, "Your money, dummy!"

The citizen's response was totally unexpected — he raised the pistol and shot them both. Walking to the pay phone next to the elevator, he called for the police and an ambulance. Hearing sirens, he stuck the gun back in his waistband to avoid any complications.

Both suspects were conveyed to the hospital, where they eventually recovered. Both had been shot in the stomach and currently rely on colostomy bags. One slug weighed 140 grains, while the other weighed 122 grains. The recovered diameter of the first was .57 caliber, while the second was .61 caliber.

• • • • •

A security guard in a large urban shopping center, he carried a 4-inch S&W Model 57 .41 Magnum in a shoulder holster as a concealed backup to his S&W Model 10. His area of the mall included three jewelry stores that were within 50 feet of the outside door. The other guards all laughed at his "cannon," feeling their issued .38 Specials were more than sufficient.

It was almost closing time on a Friday night just before Christmas. Unlike other agency employees, he took the threat of robbery seriously and constantly patrolled between the various stores.

He was halfway to the last one when he heard the shots. He reported shots fired and the apparent location on his walkie-talkie. Ducking behind a pillar, he saw two males backing out of the store with shotguns. Pulling his Model 57, he realized that if the bad guys got into the mall proper, there could be a massacre. Wanting to avoid such a likelihood, he quickly shot both felons in the back, killing them.

One slug severed the spine and weighed 89 grains, with a recovered diameter of .49 caliber, while the other went through the heart and was recovered from a window display. It weighed 118 grains and had a recovered diameter of .68 caliber. The security guard was arrested and charged with manslaughter. After a lengthy and expensive trial, he was acquitted. The mall and security guard company were sued for $11 million, but settled out of court for $620,000.

• • • • •

While everyone in his narcotics crew had chosen a confiscated semiautomatic pistol of one sort or another, he had decided on a well-worn S&W Model 58 .41 Magnum. The department armorer checked it out and told him that, despite a substantial loss of bluing, the weapon was functional.

Three weeks later, they teamed up with some federal agents to take down a dope dealer who was also selling stolen weapons. Our revolver-lugging narc was assigned the ram. As his partners announced themselves, he beat the door open with three enthusiastic blows. He dropped the ram and stepped aside for the shotgun man. Drawing his .41, he took a step inside the door and was immediately shot. Going to one knee, he hoped like hell the vest had done its job. He saw his attacker then, a white male with a pump shotgun.

Placing the front sight in the middle of the doper's chest, he pulled the trigger. The felon dropped the shotgun, turned, took a couple of steps, and died.

The officer had taken a load of birdshot in his vest. Except for one pellet in his elbow, he was not seriously injured. His .41 slug had shredded the bad guy's heart. The slug was recovered from a sofa behind him. It weighed 87 grains and had a recovered diameter of .47 caliber.

• • • • •

An American handgun hunter in an African country troubled by terrorism, he didn't go anywhere unarmed. Under his bush jacket was an 8.38-inch nickel-plated S&W Model 57 .41 Mag loaded with Silvertip ammo. He was going home in two days and wanted to pick up a few souvenirs for co-workers.

He was wandering through an open-air market when he heard the explosion. He quickly stepped into a darkened doorway. Suddenly, two scruffily dressed barefoot black males with AK-47s burst into the square and opened fire. Our hunter's response was fast and deadly; within seconds, one bad guy was down and the other was dragging one leg as he hobbled down an alley. Our hunter gave chase, and as the terrorist turned with his assault rifle, he took a .41 Silvertip just above the left eye.

The first terrorist had taken a bullet through the left shoulder. The round had continued on into the chest cavity, severing the aorta. It weighed 151 grains and had a recovered diameter of .79 caliber.

.44 S&W SPECIAL

The .44 Special is available in four conventional bullet designs: jacketed and lead hollowpoints and lead round-nose and semiwadcutter bullets. Tests conducted in gelatin indicate that the Winchester 200-grain STHP Silvertip will produce the best wound ballistics.

The Silvertip has a 4-inch muzzle velocity of 800 fps, giving it an energy level of 285 foot-pounds. This aluminum-jacketed bullet expands reliably to a limited amount. Recovered slugs typically measure .61 to .64 caliber, with penetration levels around 10.5 inches.

The Federal 200-grain SWC-HP only begins to expand in gelatin. It has a muzzle velocity of 850 fps and a muzzle energy of 320 foot-pounds. Recovered bullets measure .43 caliber. This load will probably have to strike bone to expand in soft tissue. Penetration depths are 14 to 16 inches, which indicates a fairly high chance of perforation.

The Remington 200-grain lead semiwadcutter, at 870 fps, and the Remington and Winchester 246-grain

Table 8-7

.44 SPECIAL ACTUAL RESULTS

	Total Shootings	One-Shot Stops	Percentage	Muzzle Velocity
1. Fed 200-gr. LHP	32	23	71.87	802 fps
2. W-W 200-gr. STHP	45	32	71.11	819 fps
3. W-W 246-gr. RNL	46	31	67.39	704 fps
4. R-P 240-gr. SWC	11	7	63.63	851 fps

lead round-noses, at 730 fps, will not expand in gelatin. These loads produce small crush and stretch cavities for the caliber, as well as excessive penetration ranging from 14 to 16 inches in gelatin.

* * * * *

Just as the .38 Special preceded the .357, the .44 Special was the forerunner of the .44 Magnum. People like Elmer Keith developed heavy handloads for this caliber that eventually generated enough interest for the .44 Magnum's birth as a commercial caliber.

Of course once the .44 Mag was a reality, interest in the Special wained. The only load available in this caliber was the 246-grain lead round-nose until Charter Arms produced the .44 Special Bull Dog. Subsequent to that, S&W reintroduced the Model 24 and only increased the demand for high-performance ammunition in this caliber. Even the hottest .44 Special loads are mild when fired in the N-frame Smith.

Street Results: Federal .44 Special 200-grain lead hollowpoints

A northwestern cop who took his job seriously, he carried a 4-inch S&W Model 29 .44 Magnum for a duty weapon and a Charter Arms .44 Special as a backup. The rural community he served had a low crime rate, but he believed in being prepared.

One of his responsibilities on the day shift was to serve as a crossing guard at the local school. He was thus engaged on a cold March morning when he saw a vehicle approaching at a high rate of speed. He moved a little girl out of the way as the driver sped past. Grabbing his portable off his belt, he gave the dispatcher the information and was informed that the car matched the description of a vehicle used in a bank robbery in a nearby community.

Finishing his traffic detail, he sped north. He drove by a local park but for some reason decided to check it out. Turning around, he parked at the entrance and

entered on foot.

Toward the back of the park he observed the same vehicle parked with three occupants. Calling for a backup, he was informed that a state patrol unit and a county deputy were responding and that their expected ETA was 15 minutes. Deciding not to wait, he approached with his Model 29 drawn.

Walking up to the vehicle, he ordered its occupants out. Their response was to accelerate suddenly in reverse and strike him a glancing blow, knocking him down and breaking his leg and separating him from his gun. The driver then jumped out, picked up his Model 29 and approached him. Grabbing the Charter Arms from under his jacket, the officer fired three times. The driver dropped the Magnum, turned, took

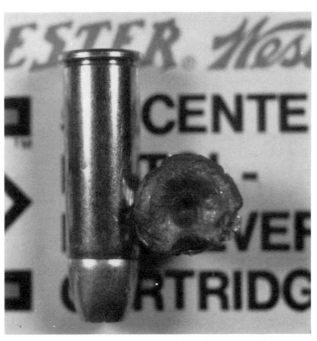

The Winchester .44 Special 200-grain Silvertip expands well even at low velocities. This one, however, failed to stop a bank robber.

three steps, and collapsed. The remaining occupants escaped in the vehicle. Unable to find his portable radio, the officer had to wait for his backup to arrive.

One Federal lead hollowpoint had entered between two ribs, traveled upward into the thoracic cavity, and was found next to the collar bone. Its recovered weight was 177 grains and it had a diameter of .52 caliber.

• • • • •

A fitness fanatic who lived in a large urban center, he looked at life realistically. His DeSantis Gunny Sack rig accompanied him on all his early morning runs. Inside it was a stainless Charter Arms Bulldog loaded with Federal lead hollowpoint ammo.

He was finishing up his daily five-mile run when he heard a car behind him. Jumping upon the curb, he continued his steady pace. "Hey faggot!" he heard someone yell. Looking to his right, he saw a beat-up station wagon occupied by five teenagers. He continued to run, ignoring them. A bottle broke near his feet and again someone made a derisive remark. He looked at them, smiled, and said, "Hey, I'm just trying to get some exercise. Leave it alone, okay?"

Their response was to jump the curb and block his path. As the occupants exited the vehicle, he opened the pouch, and pulled the gun, and assumed a Weaver Stance. "Why don't you guys just get in the car and leave?" Their verbal responses made it clear that leaving wasn't part of their agenda. The closest to him swung a beer bottle at his head, and the jogger shot him. As he went down, the rest started to flee except for one, who pulled a knife and advanced on him. Ordering him to stop, the jogger shot him when he failed to comply.

The first attacker was hit in the arm; the slug penetrated his biceps and then entered the thoracic cavity, stopping next to the heart. That slug weighed 167 grains and had a recovered diameter of .58 caliber. The second attacker was hit in the left nipple; the slug exited his back and was not recovered. The jogger was tried for felony assault but was acquitted.

• • • • •

An undercover vice officer, he carried an "off-brand" handgun because the possession of a Colt or Smith .38 snub would quickly identify him as the police. A large black male, he was posing as an out-of-town pimp looking for some new whores.

He was sitting in an illegal after-hours joint attempting to gather information about local pimps when an

obviously drunk older man staggered up and accused him of cheating him out of some money in a card game. The undercover answered that he had just come into town from Cleveland and that dice was his game, not cards. The drunk insisted and told him he wanted his money back.

What the undercover didn't understand was that he wasn't just dealing with a confused drunk. His opponent was a local hit man hired to kill him. As the officer attempted to get up and leave, the man pinned his right hand to the bar. The officer recognized the look in the man's eyes and as the hit man reached into his pocket, the officer drew his .44 Special upside down and shot him in the chest.

The officer quickly put the gun in his right hand and watched as his attacker attempted to pull a Glock 19 from his pocket. The officer was about to shoot him again when the hitman expired. The slug was recovered from the right lung, where it weighed 187 grains and had a recovered diameter of .49 caliber.

• • • • •

Tired of all her complaining, the man in the basement apartment decided to get even by killing her dog. He grabbed a baseball bat and went into the backyard. The dog, a large mutt of undetermined heritage, started to bark loudly when it saw him approach. He tried to hit it in the head, but it moved and his first blow landed on its shoulder. The dog yelped in pain and he struck it again.

He had hit it for the fourth time when he heard her yell, "Leave my dog alone!" He told her to go commit an unnatural act on herself and hit the dog again. He saw her then, standing there with a gun. Laughing, he turned on her and died. The round went through his left forearm, ranged upward through both lungs, and was recovered from his clothing at the morgue. It weighed 162 grains and had a recovered diameter of .60 caliber. It was fired from a 6.5-inch Model 24 revolver, the duty weapon of the female officer who owned the dog.

Street Results: .44 Special 200-grain STHP Silvertip
A clerk in a 24-hour convenience store, he was aware that holdup men referred to such establishments as "stop & robs." The location where he worked was just off the turnpike exit, which made him even more careful.

He had gone to a local gun shop to look for an inexpensive handgun. He had returned home with a used Charter Arms Bulldog and a box of Winchester Silvertip ammo.

Three months later, near the end of his midnight

shift, a state trooper vehicle pulled in. He was always glad to see them and was more than willing to pour them a free cup of coffee. After fifteen minutes of idle conversation, they left. A couple of minutes later, a battered green pickup pulled in. A teenaged girl came in by herself. She asked him for a cup of coffee, and as he turned to hand it to her, he found himself looking down the barrel of a .22-caliber semiautomatic pistol. Demanding money, she then ordered him into the stock room and had him lie on the floor. As the clerk went to one knee, he pulled his .44 Special and opened fire. The holdup woman fired three shots, turned, leaned against several cases of soft drinks, and died.

The clerk had taken three rounds of .22 LR in the chest and lingered in the hospital for four weeks before he died. The holdup woman took one round of .44 Special Silvertip through the left breast. The round had pierced her heart and was found resting against the spine. It had a recovered diameter of .59 caliber and weighed 182 grains.

• • • • •

A twenty-year veteran, the officer preferred the downtown foot patrol detail to any assignment available. He worked the day shift and it generally was quiet, with the serious runs given to the squad car units. The only aggravation was the street people. Generally they were no bother, but occasionally they would harass people who worked downtown and then he would have to lock a few up to keep the business people off his back.

Hearing a commotion down the block, he saw that Crazy Willie was at it again. Nobody knew Willie's real name, although he had been a permanant fixture downtown for years.

As the officer approached, he had already decided that Willie would have to go to jail for the night. He put his hand on Willie's arm and was radioing for a patrol unit when Willie started to yell, "No! no!" and reached under his jacket. The officer saw what Willie had then — a gun. As the officer spun away while attempting to draw his own weapon, the Charter Arms .44 Bulldog in Willie's hand discharged. The round struck the officer in the sternum and knocked him to the ground. Willie was standing over the downed officer with the gun when a utility worker hit him in the back of the head with a hammer, killing him.

The officer was rushed to the hospital, where the bullet was removed during emergency surgery. Its recovered weight was 178 grains and it had a recovered diameter of .63 caliber. The officer told me from his hospital bed that it felt like someone had hit him in the chest with a sledge hammer.

This Winchester .44 Special 200-grain Silvertip expanded well and quickly dropped a rapist.

• • • • •

A big-city cab driver, he had been robbed fifteen times over the last thirty years. The last time, however, was the first time he had been injured. Before returning to work he had bought a S&W Model 24 .44 Special, a Safariland shoulder holster, and a box of Winchester Silvertip ammo.

It was almost 5 A.M. when he picked up a young white male in a three-piece suit. He drove the fare to the warehouse district without giving it a second thought. The young man paid his fare, started to walk away, then turned and motioned for the cab driver to roll down his window. As he did, he looked down the muzzle of a .45 auto. "Relax man," the cabbie said, "I'll give you the money." The young man smiled and answered, "I don't want your money. I just want to know what it feels like to kill a nigger!"

The cab driver swung the door open quickly, knocking the man down. Before the thug could recover, the cabbie pulled his Model 24 and opened fire. The man jumped up and started to run. He had gone about fifteen feet when the cabbie cocked his gun and fired again. The effect was instantaneous as the bad guy went down in a heap.

The autopsy removed a Silvertip from the left lung. It had severed the aorta, causing death. The recovered slug weighed 167 grains and had a diameter of .59 caliber.

The Winchester .44 Special 200-grain Silvertip is effective 71 percent of the time. This is about as good as this low-velocity big-bore gets.

• • • • •

A cop assigned to plainclothes duties in the Major Crimes division, he had bought a customized 3-inch barreled Model 624 at a local gun show. Loaded with Silvertip ammo, it met his personal criteria for good stopping power.

He was assigned the responsibility of serving what were considered low-risk felony warrants. His approach was quite simple. He would park down the street with a uniform unit and have his office call on the phone and ask for the wanted person. If he or she answered the phone, they would go to the location and make the arrest.

They were looking for a man wanted for bad checks. When the office radioed that he was in, he and the uniform officers knocked on the front door. Identifying themselves, they were met by a barrage of rifle fire that wounded both uniform officers. The detective, who had jumped off the porch, grabbed one of the downed officers' belt radios and called for help. When he heard the door open, he slid back into the shrubbery. The wanted subject stepped onto the porch and was preparing to shoot the officers again when the detective opened fire. The felon grabbed his chest, dropped the rifle, and collapsed.

Responding units loaded the two officers and the bad guy into ambulances. Both officers were DOA, while their attacker survived to stand trial. The Silvertip had penetrated his lung and glanced off the spinal

column. It had a recovered weight of 152 grains and a diameter of .64 caliber.

• • • • •

It had been raining heavily all night. The weather frustrated the two Tac Unit officers. They were looking for serious bad guys to arrest and the inclement weather had driven them off the streets. Both officers carried S&W Model 29 .44 Magnums loaded with W-W Silvertip .44 Special ammo to match the loads they carried in their backup Bulldogs.

It was almost the end of their shift and they both cursed the quiet. They were pulling into an all-night convenience store to get a pack of cigarettes when they noticed that there wasn't anyone behind the counter. Street smart, they backed out and called for another unit. One officer went to cover the rear with the shotgun while his partner took up a position out front.

The officer out front had just gotten in position when he heard gunfire and saw three ski-masked individuals running out the front door. Realizing that yelling, "Halt police!" would probably get him killed, he opened fire. All three bad guys went down without firing a shot. The officer speed-loaded his .44 and waited for backup.

When additional officers arrived, they found three badly wounded holdup men. Rushed to the hospital, they survived to stand trial for murder and armed robbery.

Two of the bad guys had taken multiple hits while the third had taken a .44 Special Silvertip in the spine. The slug had fragmented and weighed a total of 107 grains. Its diameter was .59 caliber.

.44 MAGNUM

Ballistic gelatin results with the .44 Magnum indicate that the 180- and 200-grain jacketed hollowpoints produce the greatest wounding in this caliber.

The largest stretch volumes come from the 180-grain JHP loads from Federal and Remington. These have muzzle velocities ranging from 1,450 fps to 1,550 fps from duty-length weapons. Muzzle energy is between 840 and 960 foot-pounds.

The 180-grain JHP loads expand to between .80 and .94 caliber and produce the largest diameter and longest stretch cavity of any conventional handgun load. The penetration is deep but not always excessive at 10 to 14 inches of gelatin.

Close behind and nearly overlapping these 180-grain loads is the Speer-Lawman 200-grain JHP. This load has a muzzle velocity between 1,175 fps and 1,275 fps, with an energy level averaging 670 foot-pounds. It expands reliably to between .78 and .88 caliber and

Table 8-8

.44 MAGNUM ACTUAL RESULTS

	Total Shootings	One-Shot Stops	Percentage	Muzzle Velocity
1. W-W 210-gr. STHP	33	29	87.87	1,301 fps
2. Fed 180-gr. JHP	23	20	86.95	1,406 fps
3. R-P 240-gr. S-JHP	22	19	86.36	1,266 fps
4. W-W 240-gr. JHP	36	30	83.33	1,204 fps
5. W-W 240-gr. SWC	44	36	81.81	1,259 fps
6. Fed 240-gr. JHP	31	25	80.64	1,255 fps
7. R-P 240-gr. SWC (med. vel.)	53	39	73.58	961 fps

penetrates 12 to 14 inches of gelatin.

The Winchester 210-grain STHP Silvertip also expands reliably and produces controlled penetration. The muzzle velocity of this load is 1,225 fps, with an energy level of 700 foot-pounds. It expands to between .72 and .77 caliber and penetrates 14.5 inches of gelatin. It was designed to be an intermediate .44 Magnum hollowpoint load. The stretch and crush ballistics are just slightly behind the 200-grain Lawman.

The 240-grain jacketed hollowpoints in .44 Magnum have muzzle velocities between 1,200 and 1,275 fps, with energy levels averaging 825 foot-pounds. These loads generally expand to between .60 and .80 caliber, depending on the manufacturer.

The Remington hollowpoint has scallop serrations and a wide, cylinder-shaped hollowpoint cavity. This load expands to the largest mushroom in this bullet weight. The Federal load has a large hollowpoint cavity but no serrations in the jacket; it produces more moderate expansion. The Winchester has cut serrations but a small diameter and shallow hollowpoint cavity. This load expands the least. All of these 240-grain JHP are expected to perforate a human target.

The 240-grain lead Keith-style semiwadcutter is available from Remington and Winchester in two velocity ranges. One is the magnum-pressure 1,260 fps load while the other is the medium-velocity 950 fps load. The energy levels are 850 foot-pounds and 480 foot-pounds, repectively. Neither load will expand in gelatin.

While the high-velocity load produces a relatively large stretch cavity, both produce small crush cavities for the caliber. Both rounds are likely to perforate the target, based on 18 and 16 inches of penetration, respectively.

The 240-grain jacketed softpoint produces similar gelatin results to the SWC. It produces a muzzle velocity of 1,250 fps and an energy level of 830 footpounds. The JSP will not expand and produces a smaller stretch cavity and equal crush cavity compared to the SWC. At 16 to 18 inches of penetration, the JSP is almost certain to perforate.

*   *   *   *   *

The .44 Magnum was not given serious consideration as a law enforcement/defensive caliber until the *Dirty Harry* films. Then everyone had to have one! It didn't matter that few could control this weapon in rapid double-action fire with full-power loads; people

The Federal .44 Magnum 180-grain JHP is effective nearly 87 percent of the time. This one positively stopped a martial artist, but it did not overpenetrate.

just had to have one.

The introduction of loads like Remington's medium-velocity offering and Winchester's Silvertip (a sort of three-quarter-Magnum load) and medium-velocity SWC have made this caliber an interesting alternative for police or civilians who prefer the big-bore revolver.

Street Results: .44 Magnum 210-grain Winchester STHP Silvertip

A U.S. government employee at risk in South America, he carried a cut-down S&W Model 29 .44 Magnum revolver. His co-workers, who all carried auto pistols, laughed at him for his archaic choice of weapons. He just smiled and continued to carry his revolver loaded with Winchester Silvertip ammo.

Arriving early at work, he decided to run out for some fruit from a local market to supplement his breakfast. He had just turned down the alley he routinely used for a shortcut when he heard someone running behind him. Turning, he saw a man in his mid-30s with a machete. Pulling his Model 29, he ordered the man to halt in the local dialect. The man just smiled and swung at him. Ducking, he fired three times. Blood spurted from his attacker's mouth and he pitched forward, dead.

The autopsy determined that one round had struck just above the heart and severed the main arteries. The slug was recovered from the spine, where it weighed 172 grains and had a recovered diameter of .71 caliber.

• • • • •

The city police department that he worked for restricted its personnel to the department-issue S&W Model 10 as a duty weapon, but did not restrict second guns. This officer, like many others in the busy precinct, carried a big-bore, privately owned revolver in a shoulder holster during winter months. His backup was a 6.5-inch nickel-plated S&W Model 29 loaded with Winchester Silvertip JHP ammo.

It had been one of those quiet Sunday mornings that cops always dream of but rarely get. He and his partner had just stopped for a cup of coffee and a copy of the Sunday paper when they heard the screams. Running toward the source of distress, they found a bleeding 12-year-old girl on the sidewalk. She informed them that her dad had gone crazy and was stabbing everyone in her family.

Running to the third-floor apartment, the officer pulled his Model 29. He kicked open the apartment door and saw a scene out of his worst nightmare — there were bodies of children and adults everywhere. He heard a high-pitched laugh and was suddenly con-

This is the extremely popular .44 Magnum medium-velocity 240-grain lead semiwadcutter used by most cops who carry the big magnum. This soft lead slug expanded inside a felon and ended his career.

fronted by the knife-wielding father. "Hello, my name is God. That gun is useless against an immortal being like myself. Why don't you lay it down and I'll free you like I did the rest." Both officers backed up until they hit the wall. Their order to drop the knife was met with laughter, and the father lunged toward them. The officer fired three times and the father staggered and collapsed.

The autopsy showed that two of the three rounds had missed, but the third had entered the chest and severed the aorta. The recovered slug weighed 148 grains and had a diameter of .65 caliber.

• • • • •

A cop who was an avid hunter, he spent his vacation searching for deer with the same weapon he carried on duty — a blue-steel 6.5-inch S&W Model 29.

It was the last day before he had to head home. He had finally saved enough money to have a taxidermist mount a deer head for him. Searching for a head worthy of hanging over his mantel, he had passed up several decent bucks.

It was almost dusk when he spotted a large buck walking through the high grass. He used his binoculars to verify the massive rack on its head. He waited until the buck got within an estimated 75 yards. Cocking the Model 29, he aligned the front red insert on its shoulder and squeezed. The gun recoiled in his hand and he automatically cocked and aligned the sights.

The buck, however, was down.

The round had hit its intended mark and the deer was dead. He holstered the revolver and was getting ready to dress out the deer when he heard someone yelling. Looking up the hill, he saw a man running down with a scoped rifle in one hand. As the man got closer, he yelled angrily, "What in the hell are you doing to my deer?"

The cop told him that he had shot the deer and was going to dress it out and drag it to camp. "Like hell you are. I shot it with my 06." The rifle-armed hunter then did a very stupid thing — he pointed the rifle at the cop and told him to get away from the deer. The officer told me later, "Evan, I didn't survive sixteen years in the ghetto to be shot by this fool." The cop raised his hands, turned away, and drew his Model 29. "Freeze! Police!" he shouted. The man with the rifle, however, continued to point the .30-06 in the officer's direction. The .44 roared and the hunter dropped, dead.

The Silvertip round had pierced his left lung and exited out his back, blowing a piece out of his spine. The slug was not recovered. A coroner's inquest ruled the shooting a justifiable homicide.

• • • • •

It had been a long, hard day and the officer had only one thing on his mind — a cold beer at the local cop bar. He hung his uniform in his locker, stuck his 4-inch Model 29 into the plainclothes holster, and headed out the door. He had gotten used to the kidding about his preference for a big off-duty gun.

Three hours later he had finished his third beer when the four guys entered. One look and he knew they were trouble. His impression was confirmed when one went to the john while the other three spread out around the bar. Looking at his partner, he knew that Jim had figured it out too.

It was almost a relief when the tallest one pulled out a sawed-off shotgun and announced the holdup. The others pulled out handguns while one started to search the patrons. Jim whispered, "You, shotgun?" and our .44-equipped officer responded with a subtle nod. As the holdup man who was searching the patrons stepped in front of the shotgun-wielding bandit, the .44 appeared and fired. The shotgun man went down with two Silvertip hollowpoints in his chest.

Jim shot the searcher and turned his attention to the two handgun-toting felons. The closest one had turned and was exiting the door when a .38 hollow-point severed his spine. The last felon took a .44 Silvertip in his upper chest and went down.

The autopsy determined that the holdup man with a single Silvertip in his chest had died from massive blood loss. The slug weighed 154 grains and had a recovered diameter of .72 caliber.

• • • • •

A store owner, he had seen all of Clint Eastwood's *Dirty Harry* movies and relied on a 6.5-inch blue-steel S&W Model 29 for store protection. Hardly a conceal-ment piece, it rested on a wood dowel under the counter where it could not be seen by customers.

He had just opened and fully expected it to be a busy day, as it was the start of the Labor Day weekend. A man entered and told him that he wanted five cases of beer. The store owner sent his nephew out from behind the enclosed counter area to carry the beer to the man's car when the man forced the nephew back in and showed them a revolver.

As the owner backed up, he realized that the holdup man could not see the .44 hanging beneath the counter. Making a desperate move, he lunged for the big revolver. The holdup man shot at him but missed. The store owner's hand curled around the Model 29's grip and yanked. He pointed the gun in the felon's direction, fired, and missed. He heard the holdup man's gun go off again and heard his nephew scream. He watched in horror as the teenager collapsed, blood streaming from his head. This time the store owner took better aim and fired again. The holdup man backed up a couple of steps and collapsed.

His nephew was rushed to the hospital, where he was treated for a superficial head wound. The holdup man was conveyed to the morgue. The Silvertip round had severed the aorta, causing rapid death. The slug weighed 135 grains and had a recovered diameter of .69 caliber.

• • • • •

A female officer, she was known as "Dirty Harriet" by her co-workers. Her duty weapon was a 4-inch-barreled S&W Model 629 that had been Magna-Ported and had an Andy Cannon action job. Unlike many .44 carriers, however, she could shoot the gun quickly *and* accurately.

Assigned to a plainclothes detail one night, she had hung her .44 in a Bianchi shoulder holster and gone on patrol. They were assigned a surveillance on a gas station that had been held up on the previous four weekends.

She sat in a dark alley, a pump shotgun on the seat between her and her male partner. Five cups of coffee

This may be hard to believe. This perfectly expanded Remington .44 Magnum 240-grain S-JHP *failed* to stop a psycho armed with a chain saw. Stopping power is an illusion.

later, she had to go to the bathroom. They pulled into a gas station across the street so she could use the facilities. She had no sooner sat down when she heard her partner calling for assistance. Pulling up her pants with one hand, she drew her .44 with the other and ran across the street.

She was in the middle of the street when she heard the shots and saw a young male running toward her with a shotgun. Letting go of her stonewashed jeans, she assumed the Weaver Stance and double tapped the holdup man. He went face down in the street. She was in the process of speed-loading her .44 when the first backup unit arrived. Their first comment was

that they were in total agreement that dropping one's pants was a hell of a diversion.

The holdup man was rushed to a local trauma center, where he died in emergency surgery. One round had missed, but the other Silvertip had shattered a rib, driving bone fragments into the heart. The slug weighed 139 grains and had a recovered diameter of .56 caliber.

.45 AUTO

Ballistic gelatin tests on .45 Auto ammo indicate the same general trends as 9mm. The Remington 185-grain jacketed hollowpoint feeds and cycles in all weapons. In this case, however, it only expands perhaps 40 to 50 percent of the time.

When the Remington does expand, the mushroom measures .55 to .65 caliber and penetrates 14.5 inches. When the load does not expand, the .45-caliber bullet penetrates in excess of 18 inches like ball. It produces a muzzle velocity of 990 fps and a muzzle energy of 400 foot-pounds.

According to gelatin results, the top .45 Auto load is the Winchester 185-grain STHP Silvertip. The Silvertip feeds in most weapons and expands reliably in gelatin. The recovered mushroom measures between .75 and .84 caliber, with a penetration of just over 9 to 12 inches. The Silvertip has a velocity between 915 and 975 fps and a muzzle energy of 370 foot-pounds.

The Federal 185-grain JHP load has a velocity of 905 fps and an energy level of 335 foot-pounds. It has a pronounced semiwadcutter profile. Due to the deep, near-cylinder-shaped hollowpoint cavity, the Federal load expands reliably betwen .85 and .98 caliber. It pushes this full mushroom between 9.5 and 10.5 inches

Table 8-9

.45 AUTO AND +P ACTUAL RESULTS

	Total Shootings	One-Shot Stops	Percentage	Muzzle Velocity
1. Fed 230-gr. Hydra-Shok	43	38	88.37	819 fps
2. CCI 200-gr. JHP	62	53	85.48	928 fps
3. Fed 185-gr. JHP	91	77	84.61	1,001 fps
4. R-P 185-gr. JHP +P	24	20	83.33	1,129 fps
5. W-W 185-gr. STHP	61	49	80.32	998 fps
6. R-P 185-gr. JHP	56	44	78.57	944 fps
7. W-W 230-gr. FMJ	139	89	64.02	837 fps
8. Fed 230-gr. FMJ	166	104	62.65	868 fps
9. R-P 230-gr. FMJ	102	62	60.72	799 fps

This Federal .45 Auto 185-grain JHP was fired by a rookie cop from a S&W 4506 to stop a jailbreak. The slug shows classic expansion.

Fired from a short-barreled .45 Auto, this Federal 185-grain JHP penetrated tempered car glass before stopping a rapist. This load is effective 84.5 percent of the time.

of penetration.

The Federal JHP produces the largest wounds of any conventional .45 Auto hollowpoint. This load also produces the largest usable permanent crush cavity of any conventional police duty load.

Close behind the Federal in terms of wound ballistics is the Speer-Lawman 200-grain jacketed hollowpoint, at 930 fps. This load has an energy level of 385 foot-pounds. It expands reliably in gelatin between .76 and .91 caliber. The Lawman hollowpoint cavity is significantly wider but significantly shallower than the Federal load. Typical penetration in gelatin is 9 to 9.5 inches.

Unfortunately, the semiwadcutter profile of the Federal and the 190-grain Super Vel and the extreme hollowpoint opening on the Speer-Lawman do not permit these rounds to feed in all guns. They will feed in some guns without modifications and in others only with modifications.

Some .45 ACP pistols, however, will not tolerate the nonball profile of these loads no matter what changes are done. As such, these rounds do not meet ammo guidelines for autoloaders in terms of feed reliability. Since these loads will cycle all auto pistols, a practice used by many is to place the round with superior wound ballistics in the chamber followed by reliably feeding JHP rounds in the magazine.

The balance of the conventional ammo for the .45 Auto falls into the same category. This includes the 230-grain FMJ round nose, FMJ flat nose and jacketed hollowpoint, 185- and 200-grain FMJ semiwadcutters, and 180-grain jacketed softpoints.

All of these rounds fail to expand in ordnance gelatin and, as a result, produce identical .45-caliber crush cavities. With 16 to 18 inches of penetration in gelatin, all these loads have profound tendencies toward target perforation. Further, the stretch cavities are all quite similar, from the worst to the best in this group.

The 230-grain FMJ flat-nose load was designed to be an improvement over ball. This design effort has been attributed jointly to the U.S. Air Force and Hornady. This load feeds as well as ball, yet it produces identical crush and insignificantly different stretch cavities, and penetrates excessively like ball.

*   *   *   *   *

The big .45 auto, of course, is a very popular defensive handgun. Not seen as widely as the 9mm in law enforcement, it is nonetheless what most knowledgeable people consider a superior choice to save one's life with. I have carried one, and there is a certain emotional tie to that big old jacketed slug. The actual facts, however, do not support all the mystical qualities that have been ascribed to it.

I don't have any problem with those who prefer the .45 to other weapons, but I do object to lies, myths, and unsubstantiable anecdotal stories about it. Carriers of this round are extremely smug about the fact that none of the horror stories told about stopping-power failures with other calibers exist about the .45 ACP. Well, I hate to burst anyone's bubble, but read on.

Street Failures: .45 Auto

A southern cop, he was on midnight patrol in the downtown area. Driving past an alley, he saw two men standing in a doorway with their backs to him.

The Federal .45 Auto 230-grain Hydra-Shok shown recovered from gelatin. It has proven to be a very effective police load in actual shootings.

He called for backup but decided to investigate before his help arrived — an almost fatal error.

He yelled at the two men to turn around. They did and opened fire with the .45s they carried. The officer took five torso hits with .45 ball and collapsed. He told me from his hospital bed, "I knew I was going to die in that alley, and then I heard those bastards laughing at me." Pulling himself to one knee, he drew his duty weapon and killed them. His weapon — a S&W Model 10 loaded with a 158-grain round-nose lead ammo!

• • • • •

The rooming house residents had been arguing all day. Finally, two of them had traded blows and vowed to go get their guns. They met in the hallway. One was armed with a Government Model Colt loaded with hardball while the other had a cheap .22-caliber revolver. Our .45 lover laughed and opened fire. After he emptied his gun, he looked in amazement as the .22 carrier pointed his small revolver at his chest and fired once. The auto dropped from his hand as he died.

The .22 carrier went to his room, changed clothes, and then took two different buses to the hospital, where the doctors removed seven rounds of .45 ball from his chest.

• • • • •

A motorcycle cop, he carried a Colt Gold Cup loaded with 200-grain jacketed hollowpoint ammo. Making a traffic stop for a minor violation, he was suddenly confronted by a revolver-armed motorist. The officer fired twice and then gave chase as his attacker took off on foot. The pursuit lasted for thirteen blocks until the bad guy ran into a garage and, sticking the gun in his mouth, took his own life. The autopsy found a .38 slug in his head and two expanded .45 hollowpoints in his chest!

• • • • •

A U.S. military member with counterterrorist responsibilities, he carried a cocked-and-locked .45 everywhere he went. He and his wife were walking to their car in the theater parking lot when he was confronted by three youths. They demanded his wallet and when he told them to forget it, one pulled a knife.

The soldier's response was swift and sure. He pulled his .45 and double-tapped the kid with the knife. Turning his attention to the other youths, he suddenly heard his wife scream his name. Turning, he saw the knife sticking from her stomach. He shot the stabber again and grabbed his wife. While in the process of providing first aid for her, he heard a car start and saw the youths drive away.

His wife was rushed to the hospital, where emergency surgery saved her life. While leaving

This Federal .45 Auto 185-grain JHP was recovered from a killer. The bullet expanded to .90 caliber.

The Federal .45 Auto 230-grain Hydra-Shok is the top lad in this caliber, at 88-percent effective. This Hydra-Shok expanded past .80 caliber without hitting bone.

through the emergency exit, he saw her attacker walking in for treatment. The 16-year-old holdup man had taken four rounds of .45 ball in the chest and was still mobile four hours after the incident!

• • • • •

A citizen was in his living room when he heard sirens on his quiet residential street. Looking out the window, he saw a sheriff's deputy struggling with a man. A reserve deputy and IPSC shooter, our hero grabbed his lightweight Commander and ran outside. He had just reached his driveway when he saw that the bad guy had the deputy's magnum. The reserve quickly fired three shots from his Commander. To his horror, the bad guy shot the deputy and opened fire at the reservist. The bad guy then jumped in the deputy's vehicle and escaped. He was found three days later in a gas station by the state patrol. He had to be forcibly subdued before they could take him to the hospital, where the doctors removed three rounds of .45 ball from his back!

Street Results: Federal .45 230-grain Hydra-Shok Hollowpoint

It had rained steadily all day and the officer was tired and wet. He had responded to three automobile accidents in six hours. He had just called back into service when the dispatcher called his unit number and sent him to a residence on an unknown trouble call.

Turning the corner, he observed a large crowd of people in the street. As he exited his vehicle, he heard the screaming coming from the loaction he was responding to. He called for a backup and asked the crowd what they had seen. An older man told him that the screaming had been going on for hours and

that one of the children had come out and said that her dad was cutting her mother with a knife.

Drawing his S&W Model 4506, he walked up on the front porch. He banged on the door, announced his presence, and tried the door handle. It was locked. He banged again and the door was suddenly thrown open by a large white male covered in blood. The officer jumped back and brought his gun up as his attacker stabbed him in the arm. The officer dropped his gun and fell to his knees. He was stabbed again in the back as he picked up his pistol. Turning toward his attacker, he opened fire. The first round hit the knife, knocking it out of his attacker's grasp. The second round entered the sternum and came to rest 1 inch from the spine. The husband collapsed and was rushed to the hospital, where he survived. He was eventually convicted of his wife's murder and sentenced to death. The recovered slug weighed 196 grains and had a recovered diameter of .69 caliber.

• • • • •

A competition shooter, he kept a lightweight Commander loaded with Federal Hydra-Shok ammo in the nightstand near his bed. He had gone to sleep just before midnight and woke up just after 4 A.M. to the sound of breaking glass. Removing the gun from its resting place, he proceeded downstairs where he heard more glass breaking in the basement. He proceeded partway down the basement steps, sat down, and waited. He heard movement and the sounds of frantic whispering.

Reaching up with one hand, he flipped on the light and found himself confronted by four young men armed with baseball bats and hammers. His order to freeze went unheeded and as they advanced on him, he opened fire. Unleashing eight rounds, he managed to hit two while the other two fled back out the basement window.

The home owner went upstairs and called the police. Responding officers conveyed both youths to the hospital, where they died. One had taken a hit directly through the heart while the second's aorta had been severed. The slugs weighed 167 and 183 grains and had recovered diameters of .67 and .73 caliber.

• • • • •

He stood in line in the auto parts store with an armful of motor oil and an oil filter. Casually dressed, he looked like any other suburbanite with Saturday morning auto maintenance to perform. The difference, however, was that he was a detective assigned to the Major Case Squad, and that his college sweat shirt concealed a S&W Model 4516-1 compact auto loaded with Federal Hydra-Shok ammo.

He had no sooner placed his purchases on the counter to get out his wallet when he heard shouting to his right. He turned and saw a clerk struggling with a man who had his hand in the cash register till. She struck him with her fist, and the man said "Okay bitch!" and shot her in the chest. The lieutenant pulled his 4516 and shot the holdup man in the side. The man started to turn toward him and then dropped the gun and collapsed.

The man was rushed to the hospital, where he survived. The round was recovered from under the skin on the far side. The recovered diameter was .78 caliber and it weighed 168 grains.

• • • • •

He ran a liquor store in one of the roughest neighborhoods in his city. One of the local SWAT cops was his neighbor and he had suggested that the store owner buy a .45 auto for self-protection. The clerk at the gun shop had recommended Hydra-Shok ammo for the weapon, and that was the brand he purchased.

Three years later he was behind the counter when two local kids came in. Both were under 18, and he had sold them pop and candy for years. As he turned to face them, he found himself looking down the barrel

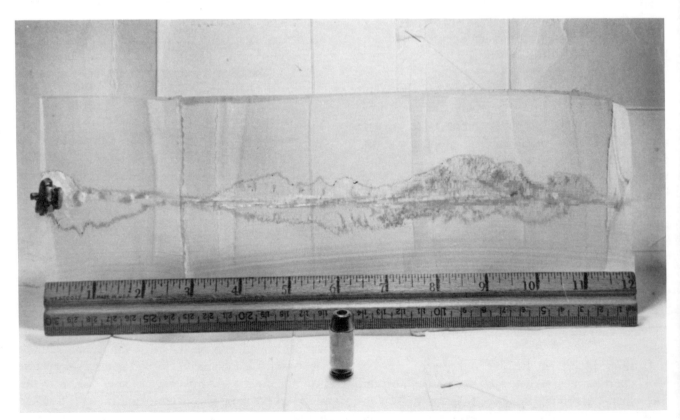

The wound profile of the Federal .45 Auto 230-grain Hydra-Shok is shown in gelatin. The stretch cavity is moderate, the penetration depth controlled, and the crush cavity one of the largest in the caliber.

of a sawed-off 20-gauge shotgun. He tried to reason with the youths but they wouldn't listen. He reminded them that he knew their parents and the smaller of the two just smiled and said, "After we kill you, nigger, you won't know anyone!"

They shot him then, and as he fell, they ran around the counter and started going through the cash register. The store owner managed to get his .45 out and before he passed out was able to fire three shots. The first two missed, but the third was removed from one of the two holdup men at the morgue. Its recovered diameter was .62 caliber and recovered weight was 179 grains.

Street Results: CCI .45 Auto 220-grain JHP

An undercover narc, he carried two .45 auto pistols. One was a Government Model Colt while the other was a stainless Officer's Model. Both, however, were loaded with CCI 200-grain JHP.

He was assigned to make a number of "buy-and-busts," where he would attempt to buy from street-corner crack sellers and then arrest them. It was considered a low-risk assignment, since the amount of money and dope was small.

They had made several such arrests when they noticed two teenaged girls sell to several passing cars in front of a liquor store. The officer exited the vehicle he was driving and approached the girls. After negotiating the deal and paying for the dope, he announced his identity. A scuffle broke out and as he and his partner were attempting to subdue their arrestees, one of the girls produced a small auto, shot his partner, and ran up the sidewalk. The officer produced his Officer's Model and opened fire. Four of his five rounds were removed from items such as parked cars and mail boxes, but the fifth was removed from her body at the morgue. The round had severed her spine and broken into several fragments, with a total weight of 122 grains.

• • • • •

An active IPSC shooter, he worked in his brother's jewelry store. The establishment was located in an exclusive neighborhood with an upper-class clientele. One could never be too careful, however, so our IPSC shooter kept his .45 compensated gun in the expensive briefcase he carried to work. Because of concerns about overpenetration, it was loaded with CCI's 200-grain JHP offering.

It had been a long and busy day. Our shooter was in the process of returning jewelry to the vault when a man entered. There was nothing about the customer's dress or demeanor to make the jeweler nervous,

but he was. Returning from the vault, he opened his briefcase and laid it on the desk just out of sight of the man.

The man told him he was looking for a ring to give his wife for her birthday. When the clerk asked him how much he was willing to spend, the man replied that he was interested in rings in the $5,000 to $10,000 range. Indicating that he would have to get that tray from the vault, he left the showroom area.

Returning from the vault, he paused to shove the .45 under his sports coat. As he placed the tray on the countertop, the "customer" produced a .38 snub-nosed revolver and told him to put his hands up. The clerk did as instructed and backed up as the holdup man came behind the counter. After emptying the trays of the best merchandise, he ordered the clerk to lie down behind the counter. He hesitated and the man told him, "Lay down and I won't hurt you." It was a lie. As he did so, the holdup man placed the gun against his back and fired twice.

Although in extreme pain, the clerk rolled over, pulled his .45, and fired two shots before dropping the gun. The holdup man turned, slumped against the counter, and died.

The clerk recovered after an extensive hospital stay due to spinal cord damage. The autopsy of the felon showed that one round had missed, while the other had entered below the waist and angled up into the heart. The recovered slug weighed 177 grains and had a diameter of .63 caliber.

• • • • •

A veteran SWAT cop, he had been in position for the last eleven hours. His team had been called out to deal with a bank holdup gone bad. Four felons had

The CCI .45 Auto 200-grain JHP ranks second in this caliber. The slug on the left came from ordnance gelatin. The slug on the right was recovered from a child molester.

The CCI .45 Auto 200-grain JHP expands with extreme reliability. This load was used to kill an off-duty police officer.

taken eighteen hostages, but skillful negotiation had convinced all but one to surrender. The last robber held five hostages, stating that he would die before going back to the penitentiary.

The hostage negotiator had reached the conclusion that the remaining hostages were at extreme risk and an entry was to be made. Three team members were going to enter the false ceiling in an attempt to gain entry to the teller's area. To facilitate movement, two would rely on their .45 autos while the third carried a supressed H&K MP5.

The officers crawled to where they believed they could safely enter the bank and started to remove the false ceiling tiles. This tactic was met by gunfire, and the lead officer took several rounds in the vest. The second threw a stun grenade and dropped to the floor below. Relying on the numbing effect of the flash bang, he found himself behind the holdup man. Not

standing on ceremony, he shot him in the back, wounding him.

The doctors indicated that the 200-grain JHP had collapsed one lung and caused massive tissue damage. It had fragmented into several pieces, with a combined recovered weight of 99 grains.

• • • • •

A federal agent, he carried a .45 auto despite agency regulations forbidding its use. Since he was already in violation, he figured that he might as well load it with hollowpoints. He chose CCI's JHP load.

His primary responsibility was surveillance of organized crime figures, and the area he sat in was run-down and dangerous. It was 3 A.M. on a rainy Sunday night and he was trying desperately to stay awake.

He noticed movement on the sidewalk outside the

The CCI .45 Auto 200-grain JHP has proven to be a reliable choice for modern double-action auto pistols. It has a street effectiveness of 85.5 percent.

social club where the target of his surveillance hung out. Getting ready for a possible move, he relaxed when he saw it was a bunch of teenagers. They passed the car and disappeared from sight. He was only half awake when a tire iron shattered the driver's side window and impacted against his temple. Stunned, he felt himself being pulled from the vehicle. As hands reached for his wallet and turned out his pockets, he pulled his .45 and opened fire.

He heard screams and swearing and then nothing. Crawling back into the car, he got on the portable radio and called for help. Responding agents found three dead teenagers. Two had taken multiple hits from the CCI 200-grain JHPs, but one had taken a round in the armpit. The slug, which had traversed his body and pierced both lungs, was recovered from his clothing. It had a recovered weight of 166 grains and a diameter of .67 caliber.

• • • • •

A female soldier, she had been assaulted twice while on security duties. On the second occasion she had shot her knife-wielding attacker with hard ball. His response was to leave her with a disfiguring scar on her neck that required plastic surgery. Learning from her mistake, she had her own .45 magazine that contained five rounds of CCI hollowpoint instead of GI ball.

It was the last holiday weekend of the summer and

traffic in and out of the base was heavy. A lone white male on foot walked up with a camera bag over his shoulder. He was defensive and belligerent when she asked for military ID. When she asked him to open the bag, he knocked her down and ran toward the barracks. Fearing a terrorist incident, she jumped up and gave pursuit with her .45 drawn. She had chased him approximately 30 yards before she remembered to chamber a round.

The man disappeared around a corner, and as she rounded the corner she was knocked off her feet. Regaining her senses, she saw her attacker approaching her with a shovel raised over his shoulder. She ordered him to freeze and when he lunged at her, she fired. He dropped the shovel, clutched his stomach, and collapsed.

Rushed to the hospital, he underwent emergency surgery to repair his wound. He survived to stand trial for narcotics violations. The camera bag had contained two pounds of pure cocaine. The recovered slug weighed 188 grains and had a recovered diameter of .64 caliber.

Street Results: Winchester .45 Auto 185-grain STHP Silvertip

A military attaché assigned to an embassy in a country plagued by terrorism, he didn't go anywhere without his Bill Wilson accurized lightweight Commander in a Milt Sparks Summer Special holster.

It was his day off and he had just dropped his daughter at a friend's when he heard the distinctive exhaust noise of a scooter. Aware that this means of transportation was often used by terrorists, he looked in the rearview mirror and was reassured by what he saw — a young girl with a very young boy on the back. Unfortunately, the "young girl" was a 27-year-old baby-faced radical whose slight build made her look 15 years younger. The boy had been rented for the occasion. Under her blouse was a Browning Hi-Power loaded with BAT (Blitz Action Trauma) rounds.

As the officer stopped for a red light, he heard the scooter again. Turning to look, he saw the girl fumbling under her blouse. His training took over and he bailed out of the car with his .45 in hand. As he ran toward the rear of his car he heard her open fire. Leaning over the trunk, he fired three rounds in her direction. He moved and when he appeared from behind cover in a different location, he saw that she was down. Approaching her, he kicked the gun away and covered her until the police arrived.

The bullet was removed at the hospital. It had deflected off a rib and collapsed one lung. It had a recovered weight of 168 grains and a recovered diameter of .58 caliber.

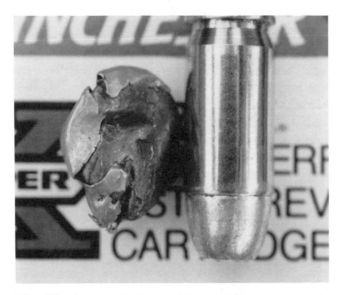

This Winchester .45 Auto 185-grain Silvertip was used by a federal agent to end a standoff. This load is effective 80 percent of the time.

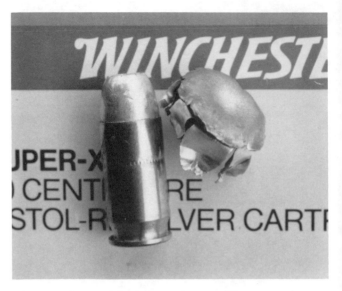

The Winchester .45 Auto 185-grain Silvertip is shown after perfect expansion. This one stopped a rape.

He had brought the .45 home from World War II. A marine who had fought on places like Iwo Jima, he had used it more than once to save his life. He took it out occasionally to shoot and clean it. Seeing the hardball that he carried in it, his cop son-in-law bought him a box of Winchester Silvertip ammo.

The pistol sat on top of a hutch in the dining room. The decorative trim around the edges hid the weapon's presence from his grandkids and other visitors.

He was in the process of painting the kitchen when he heard his wife pull into the driveway. He heard the car door close and then he heard her scream. Grabbing the .45, he chambered a round as he ran outside. A young male had her pinned against the car and they were fighting over her purse. He heard his wife scream again and saw the youth raise a bloody knife. Taking aim, he fired one shot into the attacker's back. He turned and advanced on the home owner before collapsing.

The thug died. The recovered slug weighed 161 grains and had a recovered diameter of .52 caliber.

• • • • •

A cop whose department had just approved the S&W Model 645 for on- and off-duty carry, he loaded it with Silvertip and placed it in his Bianchi holster.

Following roll call, he and his partner stopped at a coffee shop for a cup. They had no sooner sat down when a lady ran in and told the officers that a man was "acting strangely" down the street. Both officers sighed good-naturedly and walked out the front door. To their horror they were met by a man holding an AR-15 rifle.

As the officers attempted to draw their weapons, the man opened fire. One officer was killed instantly, while the other took a .223 round through his arm. Drawing his Model 645, he opened fire one-handed and missed. His attacker jumped behind a parked car. Advancing on him, the officer saw that the bad guy was inserting a full magazine into the rifle. The officer took better aim and fired again. The thug slumped down and dropped the rifle. The officer handcuffed him and called for help.

The felon was conveyed to a local hospital, where he survived despite the loss of most of his large intestine. The recovered slug weighed 118 grains and had a recovered diameter of .68 caliber.

.45 COLT

Ballistic gelatin results for the .45 Colt are similar to the .44 Special. The Winchester 225-grain STHP Silvertip expands to produce the largest crush and stretch cavities, and adequate but controlled penetration.

The Silvertip has a muzzle velocity of 800 fps and an energy of 320 foot-pounds. This load expands reliably in gelatin to between .72 and .74 caliber. The resulting penetration is 10 to 11 inches. Its overall performance is quite similar to the .45 Auto Silvertip.

The .45 Colt is available from Federal in a 225-grain lead semiwadcutter hollowpoint with a velocity of 785 fps. This load does not expand in ordnance gelatin

The Winchester .45 Auto 185-grain Silvertip produces mixed results in human tissue. Even still, this one stopped a murderer.

and can be expected to perforate the target.

The .45 Colt is also available in a 250-grain round nose, a 225-grain Keith-style semiwadcutter from Remington, and a 255-grain round nose from Winchester. These loads have a muzzle velocity ranging from 780 fps to 860 fps. Like all bullets of these designs, however, none of these loads expand. As a result, the crush and stretch cavities are not as large as other loads in this caliber.

* * * * *

The .45 Long Colt generally was neglected by those seeking a defensive handgun until two things happened. First, Smith & Wesson introduced the Model 25-5 in this caliber. It is a moderate-recoil weapon that throws a big heavy lead slug, which a lot of people find comforting. Second, Winchester and Federal gave us hollowpoint loads.

The .45 Long Colt is very popular among cops who either cannot carry a magnum or who are recoil conscious. A lot of guys and gals in my department bought and carried one.

Street Results: .45 Long Colt
Federal 225-grain SWC-LHP

They were just finishing a sandwich on an unofficial lunch break when the run came over the radio, "See the man, unknown trouble." Cursing their luck, they wolfed down their sandwiches and left the coffee shop.

Arriving upon the scene, they were flagged down by a white-haired man. "It's my son. He's always fooling around with that stuff!" When one officer asked

him what stuff, the father replied, "Explosives." Calling for backup and a supervisor, they began to gather information.

They were thus engaged when they heard a loud explosion from the backyard. Running to the rear, they saw a car partially destroyed. A young white male emerged from the garage and grinned, "Hell of an explosion, wasn't it?" One officer stepped forward to grab him when the man showed him several sticks of dynamite.

Backing off, the officers again apprised the dispatcher of their problem. The young man started to advance on the officers with the dynamite in one hand and a lighter in the other. One officer pulled his S&W Model 25-5 and told the man to drop the explosives. He just smiled and said, "Don't be silly, I just want to blow up your police car." He took one more step and the officer fired. The man went down to one knee and was trying to light the fuse when the officer snatched the explosives out of his hand.

Rushed to the hospital, the young man underwent seven hours of surgery to repair massive bleeding. The recovered Silvertip weighed 177 grains and had a recovered diameter of .54 caliber.

● ● ● ● ●

A cop's wife, she was involved in the mundane task of driving the kids to school. Returning to the house, she noticed the back door was ajar but thought nothing of it — the kids were always forgetting to close it. She was upstairs in the bathroom when she heard noises downstairs. Walking quickly but quietly to her bedroom, she unlocked the strongbox on the closet shelf and removed her husband's S&W Model 25-5. She checked to see if it was loaded and walked to the top of the stairs.

She listened for five minutes without hearing anything. Dismissing it as nerves, she was returning to the bedroom when she heard voices. She then called 911 and started downstairs. She walked quietly toward the living room, where she surprised two white males removing the VCR and color TV. She ordered them to freeze but they just laughed. "Lady, we know you ain't gonna shoot anyone, so why don't you give us that gun before someone gets hurt?"

The thugs were advancing on her with their hands outstretched when she shot them both. Running to the kitchen, she called 911 and then her husband at the precinct. She felt she had overreacted until she found out the two were wanted for several home invasions and homicides.

Both survived, and the Silvertips weighed 162 and

Table 8-10

.45 LONG COLT ACTUAL RESULTS

	Total Shootings	One-Shot Stops	Percentage	Muzzle Velocity
1. Fed 225-gr. LHP	57	44	77.19	806 fps
2. W-W 225-gr. STHP	43	32	74.41	853 fps
3. W-W 255-gr. RNL	85	59	69.41	706 fps
4. R-P 255-gr. SWC	14	9	64.28	808 fps

170 grains respectively, with recovered diameters of .49 and .57 caliber.

• • • • •

He had sent his S&W Model 25-5 to Magna-Port and they had downsized it to what he considered an ideal concealment weapon.

He had a concealed-weapon permit that allowed him to carry a gun. A pharmacist, he worked in an inner-city drugstore. There had been several attempted robberies on other shifts but so far he had been lucky.

It was almost 2 A.M. when the woman entered and handed him a prescription for a controlled substance. He examined it and noticed an erasure. Informing the woman he could not fill the order because of that, he stalled her so he could call the police. As he turned to use the phone, she demanded the prescription. When he turned to explain that he couldn't, he found himself on the wrong end of a large butcher knife.

As the woman came around the counter, the pharmacist pulled his .45 and opened fire. The first two

rounds missed, and the woman stabbed him in the chest. He fired again and she collapsed dead. The pharmacist was rushed to a nearby hospital, where he died in surgery. The recovered slug weighed 159 grains and had a diameter of .52 caliber.

• • • • •

A midwestern big-city cop, he carried a S&W Model 25-5 with a 6-inch barrel. Although departmental regulations forbade the use of hollowpoints, he carried Federal lead hollowpoint loads in his. Working the midnight shift, he had attended off-duty roll and then headed downtown for what would surely be an all-day session in court. To his surprise, the defendant had pleaded guilty and the officer had found himself on the way home to bed by 11 A.M..

He had just pulled into his driveway when the next-door neighbor approached and informed him that she had heard noises in her basement. Smiling good-naturedly, the officer said he would check it for her. Entering her house, he started downstairs and made the last mistake of his life. As he stepped off the

The Winchester .45 Long Colt 225-grain Silvertip expands well in human tissue. Despite good expansion, this big-bore load is only 74.5-percent effective.

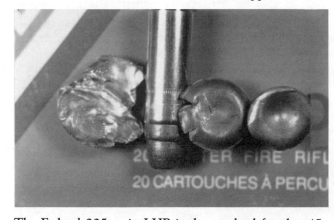

The Federal 225-grain LHP is the top load for the .45 Long Colt. The slug on the left came from a 390-pound dope dealer. The center slug came from gelatin, while the LHP on the right came from Ductseal.

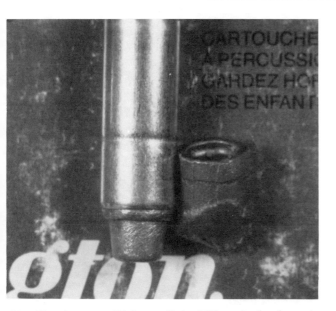

The Remington .45 Long Colt 255-grain lead semi-wadcutter only achieves a 64.5-percent rating. This one glanced off a rib and ended a domestic assault.

This Remington .45 Long Colt 255-grain SWC struck a rib bone on entry and was deformed. It went on to pierce the heart.

bottom step, he was grabbed from behind and a struggle ensued. As he attempted to draw his weapon, his attacker gained control of it and shot him in the chest. The officer staggered back and slumped against the wall. His killer was arrested several weeks later.

The slug was recovered from the officer's heart, where it had a recovered diameter of .56 caliber and a weight of 187 grains.

• • • • •

An armored car driver, he carried a S&W Model 25-5 loaded with Federal lead hollowpoints. While his co-workers were magnum or 9mm fans, he liked the big revolver and the heavy bullet it threw.

It was a Friday afternoon and their pickups at the mall were large. His partner was coming out of the last stop when a woman pushing a baby carriage ran into him. As his partner was excusing himself, a man suddenly ran up and shoved a gun in his side. Calling for help on the two-way radio, the driver exited the truck and went to his partner's aid.

The robber was turning toward him with gun in hand when the driver opened fire. He emptied his weapon without effect and ducked behind a trash can. He only had time to insert two live rounds before he heard someone running his way. Jumping up, he saw the holdup man trying to escape with the money bag. The guard fired again. The first round hit the money bag, scattering cash everywhere, but the second round was fatal.

The autopsy determined that the round had hit two inches left of the heart and caused massive bleeding. The recovered slug weighed 188 grains and had a recovered diameter of .49 caliber.

• • • • •

A public safety officer at a large university known for its carefully cultivated liberal image, he was prohibited from carrying a magnum handgun despite the fact that the campus was in one of the roughest parts of town. Fortunately, the union had gotten permission for its members to carry nonmagnum revolvers in calibers other than .38 Special. The officer had chosen a 4-inch-barreled nickel-plated Model 25-5.

He was just leaving lunch when he heard the radio call that all officers hate: "Shots fired, officer down." Only blocks away, his was the first car on the scene. A female officer from the city police department was lying in the street with a minor gunshot wound. He asked her what had happened; she indicated that she had stopped a pedestrian for jaywalking and that the citizen had snatched her 15-shot 9mm and shot her with it. She told him that her attacker had run to a nearby apartment building.

The officer stayed with her until the paramedics arrived and then ran to the building. He entered quietly. The first floor seemed okay. He climbed to the second floor and heard a loud argument. Standing on the landing, he heard a male voice say, "If you don't believe me, just look out the window. The stupid cop is still laying there."

Coming through the hallway door, he yelled "Police! Freeze!" A white male in his twenties turned and opened fire. The officer felt the impact of two rounds on his vest. Returning fire, he saw a spray of blood on the wall and watched his attacker collapse.

The thug was conveyed to a local hospital, where it was determined that he was permanently paralyzed due to spinal cord damage. The recovered slug weighed 173 grains and had a recovered diameter of .47 caliber.

● ● ● ● ●

They were a veteran narcotics raiding crew that had done this hundreds of times. They approached the building and took up their places without conversation.

Announcing their presence, they took the door down with only two blows of the ram and the shotgun man was the first in. As he ran past a bedroom, a white male exited the room and shot him in the back of the head, killing him. The second narc fired six rounds from his 6-inch S&W Model 25-5. All six missed, and he was shot. As the firefight continued, the second officer reloaded his revolver and dragged himself across the floor. Centering the front sight on the center of the doper's chest, he fired. The criminal turned, said something the officer couldn't hear, and attempted to bring his gun to bear before he collapsed.

The dope dealer survived his wound and was tried for first-degree murder. He is currently on death row. The slug was not recovered.

● ● ● ● ●

His duty weapon was a S&W Model 58 that had been rechambered for .45 Long Colt. After carrying round-nose lead ammo for several years, he had switched to Federal hollowpoints.

He had just finished the midnight shift and was on his way home when, three blocks from his house, he heard glass breaking. Pulling his car to the curb, he got out to check. He saw broken glass on the back porch. Pulling his revolver, he made his way inside. He heard a female voice from the front of the house saying, "Please, don't rape me. I'm pregnant." A male voice responded, "Bitch, I don't want to hear your excuses. Take off your clothes."

Entering the room, the officer told the man to freeze, but the rapist turned with a large butcher knife in his hand and started to advance on the officer. The officer took two steps backward and fired. The man grabbed his chest, looked at the blood, and collapsed.

The autopsy recoverd the slug under the skin just to the left of the spine. It weighed 190 grains and had a recovered diameter of .52 caliber.

CHAPTER 9

SHORT-BARREL BALLISTICS

This chapter covers results for common calibers and loads used in revolvers and auto pistols with barrels of 1.9 to 3.5 inches. These weapons are typically used by police as second or backup guns, or by civilians as concealed-carry and, sometimes, home defense guns.

These weapons typically are used from extremely close range, such as 5 feet or less, and bullet impact generally is frontal or near frontal. As such, the concern for intermediate targets such as glass, metal, and extremities is greatly reduced. Furthermore, the typically frontal shot reduces the requirement for deep penetration to cover cross-torso shots necessary for crouching and sitting felons. On a frontal or near-frontal shot, with the single exception of lower abdomen hits, vital tissue like the heart, lungs, cardiac and pulmonary vessels, liver, and spleen is relatively shallow in depth. While a police duty load needs an average penetration of 12 inches to ensure success in engaging vital tissue, the off-duty load requires only 5 to 9 inches for the same degree of success.

In this kind of scenario, it is no longer a disadvantage to tranfer energy rapidly and create a relatively large-diameter but shallow stretch cavity. In most cases, these shallow, large cavities occur at a depth where they can do the most damage. Recall that if a stretch cavity is large enough and properly placed, it can rupture blood vessels at branching points and crack bones, even at handgun velocities. A cavity placed right over a shallow-lying vital organ will maximize the damage signal to the reticular activating system.

However, most soft tissue can withstand more stretch than most handgun loads can deliver before it is actually damaged. Thus the crush cavity is still critical in pulping a hole through tissue. Also, of even greater significance than before are the fragments thrown off to become secondary missiles. These missiles are somewhat limited in their depth of penetration, but on a frontal shot, vital tissue is more commonly within their range.

The RII rating was intended to assist in the selection of police *duty* loads, but it has proven less than dependable in this task because it was based strictly on frontal shots. Ironically, the RII produces significantly better results in selecting police off-duty ammo.

While the medium-weight JHP and, in the case of the .38 Special + P, the heavy SWC-HP still produce good results in an off-duty gun, the lightest JHP loads are now predicted by gelatin results to work as well and sometimes better. The small losses in velocity put many medium-weight bullets below the velocity level necessary to expand. Often, from short-barreled guns, only the lightest and fastest loads expand. Yet regardless of the caliber, weapon, or scenario, police ammo should be expected to expand and penetrate and, in auto pistols, to feed reliably.

These lighter and lightest bullets have an additional tactical advantage. Generally they produce less recoil than heavier bullets. This means less muzzle rise and faster time between follow-up shots and engaging multiple targets. This also means that the shooter's grip

This CCI 125-grain JHP shows good expansion in human tissue from a 2.5-inch .357 Magnum.

The CCI .38 Special +P 125-grain JHP is shown recovered after two shootings. The bullet on the left was from a 2-inch gun, while the bullet on the right came from a 4-inch gun.

on the gun changes less between shots, which often occurs with guns that generally are equipped with grips designed for concealability rather than shootability. Reduced recoil from light bullets is especially significant in the .38 Special aluminum-frame snubbies from Charter, the J-frame snubbies from Smith & Wesson, and all 2.5- and 2.75-inch .357 Magnum snubbies.

Two myths surround short-barreled handguns. (For our purposes, we will define a short barrel as one measuring 3.5 inches or less. A medium barrel is 4 or 5 inches. A long barrel, for this discussion, will be 6 inches or longer.) The first myth is that short-barreled guns produce significantly less muzzle velocity than either medium- or long-barreled guns. The second is that .357 and .44 Magnums have such a velocity loss when fired from a short barrel that they are no better than .38 Special +P and .44 Special, respectively, from a longer gun. Put another way, a magnum isn't a magnum unless it is fired from a long-barreled gun.

Chronograph tests conducted on .38 Special +P and .357 Magnum ammo discounted these myths. The tests used all three barrel lengths and two bullet weights: the 110-grain JHP, which is very light for both calibers, and the 158-grain JHP, the heaviest factory bullet for each caliber. The results from the light and heavy bullets were averaged to obtain the exact scope of velocity loss from a snubbie (See Table 9-1).

The guns used for the test were a 1.9-inch S&W Model 36 .38 Special, a 2.5-inch S&W Model 66 .357 Magnum, a 4-inch S&W Model 19 .357 Magnum, and a 6-inch S&W Model 27 .357 Magnum. The rounds were all handloads made with fast-,

medium-, and slow-burning powders loaded to factory pressures.

MYTH #1: *Short-barreled handguns suffer a tremendous velocity loss compared to long-barreled handguns.*

The 4-inch magnum produced 96 percent of the 6-inch magnum's velocity. The 2.5-inch magnum produced 95 percent of the 4-inch magnum's velocity and 91 percent of the 6-inch magnum's velocity. On the average, the 2.5-inch magnum snubbie produced only 9 percent less muzzle velocity than the 6-inch magnum.

Factory ammo varies 2 to 4 percent by itself. As a general conclusion, for all practical purposes, the difference between the barrel lengths is *not* significant. It certainly takes a velocity-measuring instrument to tell the difference. If you are worried about losing muzzle velocity with a snubbie, drop the bullet weight one notch. That will more than make up for any velocity loss.

The conclusions for the .38 Special +P were similar to the .357 Magnum. The 4-inch gun produced 95 percent of the 6-inch gun's velocity. The 1.9-inch produced 91 percent of the 4-inch and 86 percent of the 6-inch. The 1.9-inch was only 14 percent behind the 6-inch weapon. Again, the actual difference between short- and long-barreled guns are greatly exaggerated.

Snubbies lose only 10 to 15 percent of the velocity of a 6-inch weapon, and 5 to 10 percent compared to the much more common 4-inch service revolver. The magnum snubbies, in particular, are accused of producing disproportionately lower velocities. The fact, however, is that between the .38 Special +P and the .357

This Remington .38 Special +P 125-grain S-JHP was recovered from the intestines of a killer. The slug shows moderate expansion from a 2-inch barrel.

The Federal .38 Special +P 125-grain JHP is especially effective from a snub-nosed gun. This bullet from an officer's off-duty gun fatally wounded a holdup man.

Magnum, the magnum is the least affected by the change from a longer to a shorter barrel.

MYTH #2: *A long-barreled gun is required to get the most out of a magnum. A .357 Magnum fired out of a short-barreled handgun is no better than a .38 Special +P out of a long-barreled handgun.*

The long-barreled, 6-inch Model 27 firing .38 Special +P produced only 74 percent of the velocity of the short-barreled, 2.5-inch Model 66 firing .357 Magnum. The 4-inch gun firing .38 Special produced only 71 percent of the 2.5-inch Model 66 firing Magnum and the .38 Special fired from the 2-inch gun produced a mere 64 percent of the .357 Magnum from the 2.5-inch gun.

The .357 Magnum *never* loses its velocity dominance over the .38 Special +P no matter how much barrel length and bullet weight are in favor of the .38 +P. For example, the heaviest factory magnum bullet, the 158-grain JHP, fired from a 2.5-inch magnum still holds over a 100-fps advantage over the light, 110-grain JHP .38 +P fired from a 6-inch barrel.

With the .357 Magnum snubbie up against the more realistic service-length .38 Special +P and the same bullet weight, the magnum outperforms the .38 by between 300 and 400 fps. This works out to *twice the muzzle energy,* even compared with the long-barreled special.

.22 LONG RIFLE AND MAGNUM

Gelatin results indicate that the .22 Long Rifle and

.22 Magnum can be far more destructive and effective than perceived by the general public. Both .22 rounds easily have the penetration necessary to be lethal. The rimfire hollowpoints have stretch cavities larger than the .38 Special 158-grain lead round nose and .380 Auto 95-grain FMJ ball, with crush cavities and penetration depths often just as large and deep.

The most damaging and disruptive of the .22 LR loads are the lightweight, so-called hypervelocity lead hollowpoints. The CCI Stinger weighs 32 grains and has a muzzle velocity of 1,100 to 1,150 fps. This load expands about half the time, with a range of recovered diameter between .22 and .38 caliber. The depth of penetration is between 8 and 10 inches in gelatin. A slightly more detructive load is the Remington Yellow Jacket using the HVTCHP bullet, which stands for High Velocity, Truncated Cone, Hollowpoint. This 33-grain bullet has a muzzle velocity of 1,175 to 1,225 fps and expands reliably to between .28 and .42 caliber, with a penetration depth ranging from 7.5 to 9.5 inches of gelatin. The 33-grain Federal and the 34-grain Winchester hypervelocity hollowpoints perform either like the Stinger or somewhere between the Stinger and the Yellow Jacket.

The heavier, high-velocity 36-grain and 38-grain lead hollowpoints from all sources peform about the same. Muzzle velocities vary from 900 to 1,000 fps from short-barreled handguns. Bullet expansion ranges from none to .38 caliber, with penetration depths from

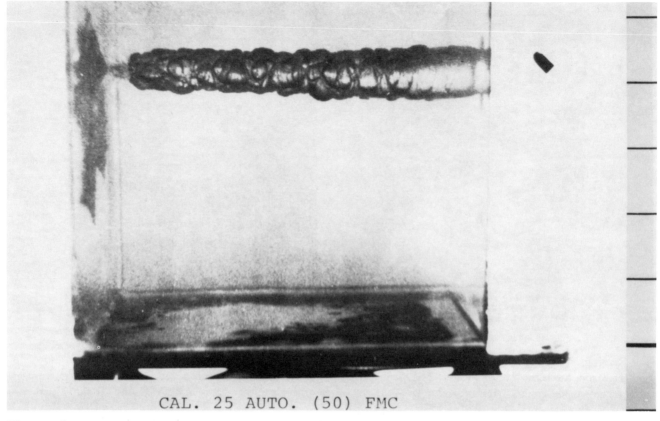

CAL. 25 AUTO. (50) FMC

The actual maximum temporary cavity for the .25 Auto 50-grain FMJ is shown. Many round-nose bullets tumble base over nose in both gelatin and soft tissue. (Photo courtesy of Winchester-Olin.)

10.5 inches to 14.5 inches.

The common 40-grain lead round-nose .22 LR generally does not expand unless it hits bone. The 40-grain round nose produces small crush and stretch cavities. However, this load penetrates from 14 to 18 inches of gelatin and is quite able to penetrate blood vessels and vital organs.

Despite its diminutive ballistics, the .22 Long Rifle is responsible for sending as many people to the morgue as any other caliber of handgun, shotgun, or rifle. The "big three" calibers on most morgue check-in sheets are the .22 Long Rifle, .38 Special, and 12-gauge. The .22 LR differs from most handgun loads only in having a smaller crush area. A .22-caliber hole in the aorta will put down an assailant as fast as a .38- or .45-caliber hole.

A recent homicide proves the point. A .22 LR round-nose bullet perforated a rib on the right side, the right lung, and the arch of the aorta and came to rest in the far side of the left lung. The victim remained active for about 20 seconds prior to collapse.

The .22 Magnum is available in a 40-grain JHP and a 40-grain FMJ. Both have a muzzle velocity of around 1,250 fps and a penetration depth ranging from 16 to 18 inches of gelatin. While the crush cavity is limited

due to expansion only up to .25 caliber with the hollowpoint, both loads produce a stretch cavity the size of a .38 Special semiwadcutter.

.25 AUTOMATIC

Gelatin tests indicate that no conventional .25 Auto load expands reliably. The only one that expands at all is the Winchester .45-grain Expanding Point. This is the so-called "pellet-nose" lead. Typical muzzle velocities are 800 to 825 fps.

The Expanding Point load has a steel number 4 birdshot pellet crimped in its hollowpoint cavity. Its function is twofold: to give the lead hollowpoint a round-nose bullet profile for feed reliability in all .25 ACP auto pistols, some of which are of poor quality, and to slow down bullet expansion, which assures deep enough penetration. The bullet expands up to .45 caliber with the pellet removed but only penetrates 5 to 6 inches of gelatin. With the pellet in place, recovered bullets measure from .25 caliber to .35 caliber, with penetration depths from 10 to 14 inches.

A 45-grain JHP is available from CCI-Speer in the Blazer line. This is a lead hollowpoint bullet with copper plating over the lead as opposed to a true copper jacket. This load has a muzzle velocity of 785 fps and has excellent feed reliability. However, it will not expand in gelatin. The resulting penetration ranges from 12 to 14 inches.

Naturally, the 50-grain FMJ load, with a velocity between 700 and 735 fps, feeds well but never expands. Its penetration ranges from 14 to 16 inches. Both the CCI 45-grain JHP and the 50-grain FMJ produce smaller stretch cavities than the rimfire hollowpoints or the rimfire magnums. Together with the 40-grain .22 Long Rifle round nose, these three loads are the least powerful of any common handgun load in terms of damage and disruption.

.32 AUTOMATIC

The .32 Automatic is also known as the 7.65mm. This caliber is available in both a 60-grain STHP Silvertip and 71-grain FMJ load. The Silvertip has a muzzle velocity of 930 fps compared to the FMJ load from various manufacturers, which has a velocity of 860 fps.

The Silvertip uses a nonserrated aluminum jacketed bullet. It produces reliable feeding, reasonable expansion, and adequate penetration. Recovered bullets measure between .42 and .44 caliber, with penetration depths ranging from 8.5 to 9.5 inches. The Silvertip's stretch and crush cavities are significantly larger than the 71-grain FMJ load. The FMJ load does not expand and produces penetration depths between 12 and 14.5 inches of gelatin.

.380 AUTOMATIC

Ballistic gelatin tests indicate the Winchester 85-grain STHP Silvertip to be the only .380 Auto hollowpoint that expands reliably. It has a muzzle velocity between 915 and 950 fps and expands in gelatin to between .51 and .62 caliber. This bullet expansion gives the Silvertip a larger crush cavity and as large a stretch cavity as any .380 Auto load. The slug penetrates between 7.25 and 7.75 inches of gelatin, which is acceptable for off-duty and concealed-carry purposes.

The Silvertip feeds and cycles reliably in most auto pistols, though even some relatively high-quality guns have trouble with it. As with all auto pistol loads, feed reliability in the particular gun must be established before carrying that load. There are numerous instances of a backup auto pistol being called into action, only to fire the round in the chamber and then jam.

The Remington 88-grain JHP is the only other .380 Auto load that expands to any degree in gelatin. This load has a velocity of 965 fps and results in bullet expansion up to .41 caliber about 40 percent of the time. It penetrates 12.5 to 13 inches in gelatin.

The Remington and the rest of the .380 Auto JHP loads need to hit bone for reliable expansion. The chances of hitting bone in the upper torso are about fifty-fifty. The Remington load is significant in that

it will feed and cycle in all weapons that will cycle FMJ ball ammo. Its rounded ogive gives it better feed reliability than all other .380 Auto expanding bullets. This includes reliability in semiauto and full-auto weapons.

The Federal 90-grain JHP and the CCI-Speer 88-grain produce muzzle velocities between 860 and 930 fps. Neither load expands to any amount in gelatin. Both produce 14 to 16 inches of penetration. The feed reliability of both loads is only fair to good due to their nonball profiles.

The FMJ ball load from various manufacturers varies from 95 to 100 grains, with muzzle velocities between 780 and 930 fps. With no expansion, these loads penetrate 16 to 18 inches of gelatin and have excellent feed reliability.

The stretch cavities of all .380 Auto STHP, JHP, and FMJ loads are quite similar in diameter and shape. The major difference between the loads is the diameter and the depth of the crush cavity. At these moderate velocities, the size of the crush cavity is the most significant component of bullet performance.

.38 SPECIAL STANDARD PRESSURE (NON +P)

Hollowpoints in standard-pressure non +P .38 Special are few in number. Yet ballistic gelatin tests show full and reliable bullet expansion is available in the non +P caliber, depending on the load.

The most significant load in this caliber is the Federal Nyclad 125-grain SWC-HP, the so-called Chief's Special load. (The Nyclad line of ammunition is discussed in detail in Chapter 12.) It has a muzzle velocity of 750 fps from a 1.9-inch S&W Model 36 Chief's Special. The latest design from Federal expands to .68 caliber in gelatin. This is genuinely impressive for any non +P load. It also penetrates between 8.5 and 9 inches of gelatin, which is perfectly acceptable for an off-duty or backup scenario. This load produces the largest stretch cavities and the largest crush cavities by far of any factory non +P load.

The only load to rival the Nyclad SWC-HP is the custom handloaded hollow-base wadcutter seated in the case with the hollow base forward. With muzzle velocities ranging from 750 to 850 fps, this load generally expands to between .56 and .76 caliber, with a penetration of 7.8 to 9.1 inches.

Most firearms and legal experts discourage the use of this kind of handloaded ammunition. This is wise advice for two reasons. First, handloaders generally have a higher opinion of the quality of their reloading than can be supported by the facts. Excessive pressures, misfires, squib loads due to improper powder selection, and poor crimps and overall seat lengths are common.

A defensive firefight calls for maximum reliability in ammo. Second, use of a handload provides fuel for the opposing attorney to create a confusing smoke screen of one's motives.

At any rate, the Federal Nyclad SWC-HP produces reliable expansion and adequate penetration in a conventional factory load at non + P pressures. But there is one catch. This excellent expansion comes only from the latest design. Federal is noted for many generations in its ammo designs. The 125-grain .357 Magnum JHP is a classic example. This Nyclad 125-grain .38 Special SWC-HP is another.

Nyclad ammo made right after Federal purchased the license from Smith & Wesson had a pronounced semiwadcutter profile. The 125-grain .38 bullet had the classic Keith, straight-sided ogive and a cone-shaped hollowpoint cavity .15-inch wide and .44-inch deep. With an impact velocity of 780 fps, this load would not expand in gelatin, water, or soft tissue unless bone was struck.

The current ammunition has a round-nose profile with a cylinder-shaped hollowpoint cavity measuring .18 inch wide and .30 inch deep. It is not known if the antimony content is different. What is known is that this bullet expands unlike any other standard-pressure non + P hollowpoint and, in fact, rivals the best high-pressure + P hollowpoints.

Gelatin tests also indicate that the non + P Winchester 110-grain STHP Silvertip will expand reliably and penetrate adequately. This serrated aluminum-jacketed load also has a rounded ogive and a large semi-cylinder-shaped hollowpoint cavity.

The muzzle velocity of the non + P Silvertip is 840 fps. It expands to .55 caliber in gelatin and penetrates 10 inches. The Silvertip produces a stretch cavity nearly as large as the Nyclad Chief's Special, but a much smaller crush cavity.

The only other common non + P hollowpoint is in the CCI-Lawman ammo line. This 110-grain JHP has a velocity of 860 fps. Due to the relatively small hollowpoint opening, it expands only about 40 percent of the time. The recovered diameter seldom exceeds .45 caliber and the depth ranges from 14 to 16 inches. This load produces smaller stretch cavities, the size of nonhollowpoint SWC bullets, and small crush cavities.

Other conventional non + P loads include the 148-grain mid-range target wadcutter at 670 fps, the 158-grain round-nose and SWC loads at 775 fps, and the 200-grain round-nose "Super Police" at 600 fps. None of these loads expands; all produce 10 to 18 inches of penetration.

The stretch cavities from these loads are similar in volume but different in shape. The wadcutter and semiwadcutter produce early, long, but small-diameter stretch cavities due to their blunt shape. The round-nose bullets produce late, short, and slightly larger-diameter stretch cavities due to the fact that the slugs tumble base over nose in tissue. The tumble gives the round-nose bullets a slightly larger crush cavity than the SWC and WC bullets.

.38 SPECIAL +P

Ballistic gelatin results show that many of the .38 Special + P JHP and SWC-HP loads that expand reliably from 4-inch guns also expand reliably from 2-inch guns. Some expand to smaller recovered diameters from the short-barreled guns, while the ones that fragment at higher velocities actually have larger recovered diameters.

Ballistic gelatin tests show the Remington 95-grain S-JHP to expand to the largest caliber of any + P hollowpoint from a 2-inch gun. At a muzzle velocity of 1,060 fps, the Remington expands to and holds a .68-caliber mushroom. It produces the largest stretch and crush cavities of any + P load from a 2-inch gun. Penetration is between 8.25 and 8.5 inches of gelatin. It should be noted that when this load is fired from longer barrels, the recovered diameter is smaller due to fragmentation, and the penetration distance is deeper.

Many other JHP and SWC-HP loads in .38 Special + P expand reliably and produce reasonable crush and stretch cavities. At 770 fps, the 158-grain lead SWC-HP expands to .52 caliber and penetrates 10.5 inches. The 110-grain JHP + P and + P +, at 905 fps and 1,050 fps, expand to between .55 and .63 caliber and penetrate 11 to 12 inches. The Winchester 95-grain STHP Silvertip, at 940 fps, expands to .53 caliber and penetrates 12 inches.

At 860 fps, the heavier 125-grain JHP and STHP loads do not expand as reliably as the lighter loads. The recovered bullets measure from .45 to .54 caliber, depending on the manufacturer. The Winchester Silvertip and the Remington scallop jacket both expand slightly more reliably and to slightly larger calibers than other manufacturers'.

None of the 140-grain and 158-grain JHP bullets nor any JSP bullets expand in gelatin when fired from 2-inch guns.

.357 MAGNUM

Ballistic gelatin tests from 2.5-inch-barrel .357 Magnums show the 125-grain JHP to produce the highest velocity, largest expansion, and largest crush and stretch cavities of any .357 Magnum load.

Most 125-grain JHPs produce between 1,250 and 1,350 fps from 2.5- and 2.75-inch magnum snubbies.

The recovered bullets generally have larger mushrooms than the same load fired from a 4- or 6-inch barrel. Most slugs measure between .62 and .69 caliber, with only small signs of erosion and fragmentation. Penetration in gelatin ranges from 12 to 13 inches.

The 110-grain loads that produced large but shallow stretch cavities are quite acceptable for backup and concealed-carry scenarios. These loads have velocities of around 1,175 fps and recovered bullets measuring

from .62 to .68 inch. Penetration in gelatin ranges from 9 to 11 inches.

The 140- and 145-grain JHP and STHP loads produce velocities between 1,200 and 1,250 fps. They typically expand in gelatin to between .50 and .60 caliber and produce 13 to 15 inches of penetration. None of the 158-grain JHP loads nor any of the JSP loads expand reliably beyond .40 caliber from the short-barrel magnums.

Table 9-1

ACTUAL BULLET EFFECTIVENESS FROM SHORT-BARRELED GUNS

	Total Shootings	One-Shot Stops	Percentage	Muzzle Velocity
.380 Auto				
1. Fed 90-gr. JHP	94	60	63.82	1,003 fps
2. PPS 54-gr. BHP (MPP)	14	8	57.14	1,142 fps
3. W-W 85-gr. STHP	59	32	54.23	985 fps
4. R-P 88-gr. JHP	31	17	54.84	1,001 fps
5. CCI 88-gr. JHP	30	16	53.33	933 fps
6. Horn 90-gr. JHP	19	10	52.63	985 fps
7. Fed 95-gr. FMJ	80	41	51.25	929 fps
.38 Special and +P (2-inch barrel)				
1. W-W 158-gr. LHP +P	57	38	66.66	789 fps
2. Fed 158-gr. LHP +P	38	25	65.78	783 fps
3. Rem 158-gr. LHP +P	35	23	65.71	781 fps
4. Fed 125-gr. JHP +P	45	28	62.22	819 fps
5. Rem 125-gr. S-JHP +P	69	42	60.86	845 fps
6. CCI 125-gr. JHP +P	35	20	57.14	822 fps
7. W-W 125-gr. JHP +P	41	23	56.09	816 fps
8. Fed 125-gr. JSP +P	68	36	52.94	878 fps
9. R-P 95-gr. S-JHP +P	83	43	51.80	1,023 fps
10. W-W 110-gr. JHP +P	73	37	50.68	924 fps
11. Fed 158-gr. SWC (not +P)	89	44	49.43	652 fps
12. Fed 158-gr. RNL (not +P)	194	95	48.96	599 fps

Table 9-2

MUZZLE VELOCITY VERSUS BARREL LENGTH

Muzzle Velocity*

Caliber and Bullet Weight	2 or 2.5 inch	4 inch	6 inch
.38 Special +P 110-gr. JHP	823 fps	919 fps	981 fps
.38 Special +P 158-gr. JHP	721 fps	788 fps	810 fps
.357 Magnum 110-gr. JHP	1,326 fps	1,420 fps	1,521 fps
.357 Magnum 158-gr. JHP	1,094 fps	1,138 fps	1,165 fps

* Averages of various manufacturers, instrumental at 5 feet.

CHAPTER 10

NONHOLLOWPOINT OPTIONS FOR POLICE

Throughout this book we have discussed the performance and failures of various handgun loads. In almost every case, the most effective offering has been some sort of hollowpoint round. Unfortunately, many police and security agencies prohibit the use of hollowpoint ammunition by their personnel. Rather than ignore this sizable group of ammo, we decided to discuss some of the options available to officers. The actual stopping-power percentages of the various nonhollowpoint options are available elsewhere in the book and will not be repeated here.

.380 AUTO

Actually, about the only nonhollowpoint option available in .380 Auto is ball ammo. PPS makes a load in this caliber that features a black nylon plug covering a hollow cavity that might satisfy or at least appear to meet the unreasonable prohibition of the use of hollowpoints. This load averages velocities in excess of 1,200 fps from a SIG P230, and expands impressively in every test medium we've tried it against. It has also done well in a small sample of actual shootings.

.38 SPECIAL

The standard police service caliber has a variety of nonhollowpoint options available. It needs to be understood that these loads offer only *slight* improvement over the traditional round-nose lead load. Yet even the slightest of improvement, of course, *may* mean the difference between life and death.

For those restricted to the round-nose lead bullet

design, it should be pointed out that +P versions of .38 Special produce markedly increased velocities. For example, the RNL standard-velocity load averages only 652 feet per second (5-shot average) when fired from my S&W Model 38. The +P version fired from the same weapon averages 789 fps. Fired from a 4-inch Ruger GP-100, the standard load averaged 734 fps, while the +P version produced a velocity of 889 fps.

The softpoint .38 Special loads do somewhat better, but again, the gains are slight. It is not widely known, but Federal offers a +P+ version of their 125-grain jacketed softpoint load. The +P JSP version averages 882 fps from a 2-inch barrel and 947 fps from a 4-inch barrel, while the +P+ version offers 929 fps from the 2-inch and 1,014 from the 4-inch. If I were going to carry a JSP load in this caliber, I would contact Federal Cartridge and obtain some of this ammo.

PPS also offers a lightweight aluminum semiwadcutter that produces velocities substantially higher than standard .38 loads. From a 2-inch barrel it averages 1,947 fps, and from a 6-inch barrel the load averages 2,822 fps. Just exactly how well this load will perform in actual shootings is open to question, but it would have to be significantly better than the round-nose lead offerings. Its high velocity and semiwadcutter shape should ensure sufficient penetration.

9MM

This caliber offers a number of nonhollowpoint options that provide serious improvements over ball ammo. Of the best, one is no longer in production

This Federal .38 Special +P 125-grain JSP only expanded slightly in a cop killer. It did not stop the felon.

This Federal .38 Special +P 125-grain JSP produced minimal expansion in an actual shooting. These loads are only 53- to 58-percent effective.

and the other is no longer being imported. The one no longer in production is a +P+ version of the Federal 95-grain jacketed softpoint. Originally loaded for the Illinois State Police, it produced an honest 1,400 fps from their Model 39s and did quite well against animated targets, producing expansion in soft human tissue. Federal, of course, is currently producing several higher-pressure loads in this caliber for law enforcement clients and I'm sure it would reproduce this load if sufficient interest existed for it.

The load no longer being imported is the MEN, an 85-grain bullet that appears to be a standard FMJ round, but actually consists of a thin copper cap over a large hollow cavity with a Hydra-Shok-like nipple. This load averages over 1,550 fps from my S&W Model 5906, and has expanded well in actual shootings. Unfortunately, the German manufacturer decided that potential sales did not justify the cost of the liability insurance necessary to market the product in this country. Before I retired from the Detroit Police Department, this was the load I carried in my 9mms.

Federal's current 9mm JSP offering is a 95-grain round that produces velocities in the 1,250 fps range. At that velocity, it does not really produce reliable expansion and its performance has been somewhat spotty. The Los Angeles Police Department initially approved this load for its officers who wanted to carry a 9mm, but it was a major disappointment. The 9mm round currently carried by LA's finest is the Remington 115-grain JHP.

CCI currently offers a 124-grain jacketed softpoint that averages 1,140 fps from my Browning Hi-Power.

Quite frankly, expansion is somewhat questionable, although if forced to choose between ball ammo and the CCI offering, I would certainly opt for the latter. Its FJM-like bullet design ensures its feeding in virtually every stock 9mm on the market.

Two other nonhollowpoint loads are the GECO Action Safety and the PPS 9mm offering. Both use plugs to cover substantial hollow cavities in the nose of the bullet. The GECO plug is separated from the bullet as it exits the barrel, while the PPS round keeps its plug in place. Both have worked well in actual shootings, but there is a lot more data on the GECO round.

.357 MAGNUM

The .357 probably offers more nonhollowpoint options than any other handgun caliber. The earliest offerings in this caliber were the lead semiwadcutter loads. Averaging over 1,100 fps, they offer substantial improvement over the traditional .38 Special Police Service loads.

There are, of course, a number of jacketed softpoints in this caliber. The best performer has proven to be the CCI 125-grain JSP. It averages 1,350 fps from a 4-inch barrel and has produced moderate expansion in soft human tissue and significantly better overall performance than other softpoint loads.

While it isn't widely known, GECO also makes an action slug in .357 Magnum. It produces velocities in excess of 1,400 fps from a 4-inch barrel and good expansion and penetration. It is, however, extremely difficult to locate and purchase in this country.

In addition, PPS offers an ultralightweight aluminum semiwadcutter load that averages 2,650 fps from a 4-inch-barreled revolver. While unproven in actual shootings it offers an interesting alternative to the 158-grain semiwadcutters.

.45 ACP

The traditional big-bore favorite of handgun carriers, the .45 ACP has long been preferred in the full-metal-jacketed version. Unfortunately, "hard ball" had not proven to be the stopper that many have imagined. Other nonhollowpoint loads in this caliber have been 230-weight FMJ offerings in other bullet configurations. Sadly, these loads have not proven to be any better stoppers than hard ball.

Samson offers a 185-grain +P semiwadcutter that is catalogued as a carbine load. It offers velocities in the 950 to 1,000 fps range, and seems to be a better choice than the heavier FMJ loads.

PPS offers a .45 ACP load that produces velocities in excess of 1,500 fps from my S&W Model 4506 and provides impressive expansion. We have a small sample of actual shootings with this load and it looks promising so far. Despite its expansion, it has penetrated deeply enough to damage vital organs and produce incapacitation.

• • • • •

While none of the loads mentioned in this chapter can equal the actual shooting performance of the best hollowpoints in their respective calibers, they *do* give increased stopping power compared to the traditional standard offerings in the various calibers.

For you police or security officers prohibited from carrying hollowpoint ammunition, these loads will go a long way toward increasing your chances for survival, which is the purpose of this book.

Table 10-1

NONHOLLOWPOINT ACTUAL RESULTS

Caliber	Total Shootings	One-Shot Stops	Percentage
.380 Auto			
1. PPS 54-gr. BHP (MPP)	14	8	57.14
2. Fed 95-gr. FMJ	80	41	51.25
.38 Special and +P			
1. Fed 125-gr. JSP +P	93	54	58.06
2. Fed 158-gr. SWC (not +P)	174	92	52.87
3. Fed 158-gr. RNL (not +P)	306	160	52.28
9mm			
1. GECO 86-gr. BHP (BAT)	85	70	82.35
2. W-W 155-gr. FMJ	148	90	60.81
.357 Magnum			
1. R-P 158-gr. JSP	23	17	73.39
2. CCI 158-gr. JSP	29	21	72.41
3. W-W 158-gr. SWC	89	64	71.91
4. CCI 125-gr. JSP	14	10	71.43
5. Fed 158-gr. SWC	36	25	69.44
6. R-P 158-gr. SWC	71	48	67.60
.45 Auto			
1. W-W 230-gr. FMJ	139	89	64.02
2. Fed 230-gr. FMJ	166	104	62.65
3. R-P 230-gr. FMJ	102	62	60.72

CHAPTER 11

SPECIALTY AMMUNITION

As long as firearms and ammunition have been around, people have tried to improve their effectiveness. One of the most famous and misused examples of this was the early work by Captain Clay at the Indian Army arsenal in Dum-Dum, India, near Calcutta. Captain Clay modified the Mark II .303 British round-nose FMJ bullet to expose one millimeter of lead core at the tip. Today we call this a jacketed softpoint bullet.

The result of this bullet alteration was seen in the Tirah campaign of 1897-1898. Although the dumdum was scandalously effective, it was never adopted by the British Army. Incredibly, the parallel but independent work at the Woolwich Arsenal resulted in the adoption of a *hollowpoint* bullet, the Mark III, in early 1897, and the Mark IV later in the year.

Nearly a hundred years later, we still have clever ammunition designers who improve on one aspect or another of a bullet's performance. Called "specialty" or "exotic" ammo, these revolutionary designs are intended to perform extremely well in some areas while giving up performance in others. Some of the ammo, like the Hydra-Shok and Nyclad, are subtle improvements over conventional ammo and achieve big gains with little or no trade-offs. Other ammunition, like the Glaser and multiple bullet loads, are very dependent on the right scenario for top performance.

GLASER SAFETY SLUG

The Glaser Safety Slug is one of the few loads whose reputation nearly always precedes it. That reputation is one of overstated stopping power and a reported 90-percent lethality rate. The carry load of choice of many lawmen, the actual ballistics don't always justify the awesome reputation. When used with certain limitations, however, the Glaser equals and often exceeds the performance of the best conventional jacketed hollowpoint loads. At the minimum, it is the most significant of all the exotic loads.

The Glaser was designed and developed by Colonel Jack Canon, and the original loads were produced under the banner of Deadeye Associates. It has gone through many subtle changes in its 15 + year history but still retains the same basic design. The Glaser bullet is a copper jacket filled with number 12 birdshot and sealed with a plastic cap. It is a single projectile until impact with a target.

Due to the low density of bird shot, the projectiles are very light and have extreme velocities compared to conventional bullets. As submitted to the NIJ/LEAA for testing, the .38 Special load weighed 96 grains, with a muzzle velocity of 1,585 from a 4-inch barrel. This is representative of Glaser velocities in all calibers.

In its original form, the Glaser had nearly a wadcutter profile, with a button-nose plastic cap. Some of the original Glasers, of which there were countless variations, even had the ironic pink nose cap.

Some of the early Glasers had the birdshot in a liquid Teflon suspension. This was supposed to increase accuracy by making a more uniformly dense projectile

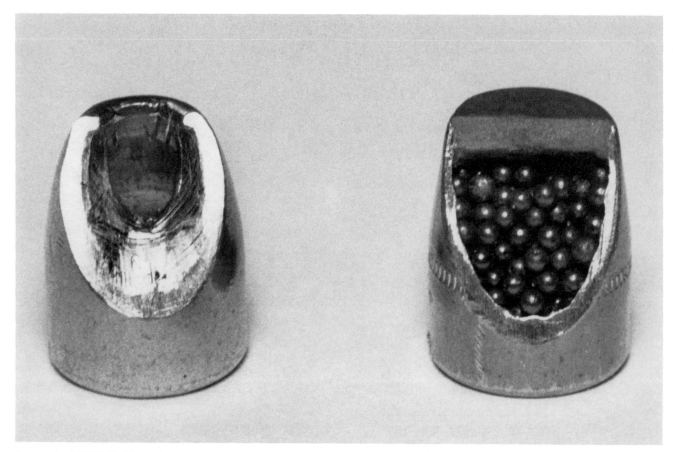

A standard JHP (left) is shown in comparison to the frangible Glaser Safety Slug (right). The Glaser prefragmented slug is a copper jacket filled with birdshot.

and allow uniform and consistent shot dispersion in the target. As manufacturing ability increased, the liquid was found to be unnecessary; in fact, it actually slowed down shot dispersion. The result was a lighter 80-grain bullet for the .38 Special. The chamber pressures were moderated and the velocity still reached 1,440 fps from a 4-inch barrel. More recently, the Glaser has had a semiwadcutter profile with a flat blue nose cap. The last of this design series had serrated copper jackets.

During this time, Glaser introduced a maximum-velocity round identified by a black nose cap. This round meets the California requirements for armor piercing. Since the round is produced in California, it is restricted to agency sales only. The MV black tip was available in 9mm and .357 Magnum but is currently only available in .357 Magnum. This is the round of choice when faced with the dual problems of felons wearing body armor and a crowded scenario mandating that the bullet not perforate the target.

The most recent Glasers have a round-nose hardball profile. This change was aimed specifically at assuring feed and cycle reliability in semiauto and full-auto weapons. The flat nose disc has been replaced with a

spherical ball. The ball displaces some of the shot, which reduces the weight of .38 Special bullets to 74 grains. There is no change in muzzle velocity.

The Glaser is available in all handgun calibers from .25 Automatic to .44 Magnum. Velocities from 3- and 4-inch guns range from 1,200 to 1,600 fps. The MV black tip is faster yet.

The projectile ruptures on impact, creating a wound resembling a scaled-down shotgun wound. The pellets saturate an area up to 3 inches in diameter and up to 6 inches deep. The mechanism of wounding is both crush and stretch. The tissue is perforated by the numerous birdshot pellets, followed by the stretch cavity. This literally dislodges pieces of tissue in the saturation area.

Like all exotic and specialty ammo, the Glaser has significant advantages and disadvantages. Its success in any shooting scenario is very predictable and depends almost entirely on how well the load is matched to the situation.

The advantages. First is massive tissue damage for as deeply as the slug penetrates. Typically, all soft tissue in a 3-inch diameter and up to 6 inches deep will be damaged by pellets and become nonfunctional.

The Glaser Safety Slug transfers energy faster than any other bullet design. It is the least likely to overpenetrate or ricochet. The wound profile for the 9mm Glaser is shown.

Even compared to the best jacketed hollowpoints, the Glaser develops a very large and shallow temporary stretch cavity that is nearly spherical. When this cavity is properly matched to the human anatomy, the Glaser deserves its reputation. The stretch cavity has fractured bones, and the crush saturation from the pellet dispersion causes enormous damage.

For reliable results, the relatively shallow penetration must be kept in mind. This shallow penetration mandates upper torso frontal, head, and neck shots, and requires that no intermediate targets of any kind interfere.

The Glaser's sensitivity to soft tissue intermediate targets is directly related to its reputation for nonperforation. It is also very sensitive to metal and glass. Both of these obstacles will rupture the slug and only spray the target with relatively harmless number 12 birdshot.

The second advantage of the Glaser is the fact that there is almost no chance of overpenetrating the primary target. The projectile ruptures in under 1 inch of penetration in soft tissue. The number 12 pellets do not have enough energy to exit the skin. With a total penetration of 6 inches, the only possibility of perforation is when the Glaser strikes an upper or lower extremity, the neck, or the very side of the torso. In those cases, only number 12 birdshot will exit. The hazard to bystanders is small to the point of being nonexistent.

Third, the Glaser has almost no downrange hazard from ricochet. The shot capsule is so fragile that it bursts upon angular impact with any hard surface. Again, the result is the tiny, low-energy, relatively harmless birdshot.

Fourth, the Glaser is less likely than any other slug to penetrate walls in a domestic scenario to endanger people in other rooms or outside the building. This especially is the case for the round-nose design but to a lesser extent is also true of the serrated semiwadcutter design. The ball in the round-nose design shoves the jacket outward, literally fragmenting the slug. No bullet can ever be considered "stray-safe," but the Glaser is the closest to that description of any ammo available.

The disadvantages. First, the Glaser produces shallow penetration, which is the exact opposite of assured penetration. The Glaser generally does not produce enough penetration on lower torso frontal shots, side-to-side shots, shots involving intermediate targets like upper arms, and others calling for deep penetration. In these shooting scenarios, the birdshot will not reach vital tissue and must rely entirely on the effects of temporary stretch for incapacitation.

Two, the Glaser is quite sensitive to car glass, car metal, and the kind of building materials a felon is likely to use for cover. In the case of glass, the Glaser will fragment and spray the occupant with number 12 birdshot. In the cases of car bodies and situations calling for barricade penetration, it will fragment and not defeat the cover. In cases of intermediate targets, the round will either be completely stopped or essentially neutralized.

Three, the Glaser cannot be used in a bullet "bouncing" or "skipping" scenario. Solid bullets can be ricocheted under car bodies to engage a felon behind the cover. The ricochet-safe Glaser will not allow this as an option, though this option has saved the life of at least one police officer.

The disadvantages seem to limit the Glaser as a general-issue police duty load, where a wide range of tactics are employed and a number of intermediate targets encountered. The advantages seem to make the Glaser an excellent police backup and second-gun load and civilian concealed-carry and home-defense load, as these scenarios typically involve frontal shots at close range where the relatively large but shallow crush and stretch cavities are the most damaging.

Unlike most exotic loads, the Glaser has been carried by enough police officers, civilians, and paramilitary personnel to be used in a number of documented gunfights. Like all gunfights, the accuracy and details vary. However, this sampling gives us typical results for the Glaser.

In the first incident, two Midwestern police officers were forced to fire at a felon in the close confines of a basement. One officer fired a .357 Magnum flat-nose Glaser while the other fired a 9mm flat-nose Glaser. The .357 slug struck the top of the forehead and glanced off the skull. It had no effect on the felon. Post-shooting debriefing indicated that any bullet with that shot placement would likewise have been ineffective.

The 9mm slug struck the lower abdomen from the front, well off center. The bullet caused a large amount of abdominal damage, including loss of a good deal of the intestines. Due to the dispersion of shot, damage was done to more tissue than from a normal, single bullet path. The result was a relatively instant dropping of the felon from an otherwise nonlethal shot placement.

Another case comes from a paramilitary instructor during a tour in El Salvador. A 9mm Safety Slug struck a running ambusher at a quartering angle in the side of the torso. The Glaser caused a large and shallow entrance hole just under the diaphragm. Whether the bullet saturated the spleen on the left side or the liver

on the right is still not certain. The reaction to the bullet is certain — the soldier rolled head over heels in mid stride and was found to be dead moments later.

Another incident involving the 9mm Glaser comes from Kentucky. A police officer shot a felon twice. A 9mm Silvertip of unknown generation struck the felon in the stomach area. The Silvertip collapsed inward on itself rather than expanding. The exact bullet path is not available.

The second shot was a Glaser flat point, which struck the felon in the groin area. This shot eviscerated the felon, putting him down immediately. At autopsy, pellets were found up in the chest cavity and down in the thighs.

The next incident comes from Florida and involved a confirmed psychotic, crack cocaine user, and prescription drug abuser. Police officers were summoned to the scene of the person's attempted suicide. The person produced a bayonet and charged one of the responding officers. From a distance of 4 feet, the 9mm Glaser struck the felon in the right shoulder under the collar bone, spinning him to the right. He dropped the knife when hit, took two steps, doubled over, and dropped to one knee with his back facing the officer. His right arm hung useless at his side. The person slowly got to his feet, picked up the knife, and stumbled 182 feet back to a residence, bleeding heavily. He was relatively mobile and dangerous for 3 minutes after the shooting.

The entrance hole was the size of a nickel. The slug did not exit. The bullet disintegrated after 2 inches, shattering the clavicle and rupturing the subclavian artery.

Another Glaser shooting comes from Texas. In this case, the Safety Slug engaged an intermediate target first and clearly failed to stop the felon due to a failure to penetrate. The details are sketchy but the important facts are known.

A .38 Special +P Glaser was fired from the side and hit the person in the upper arm. The bullet either struck a relatively large biceps or struck the biceps and the humerus bone. Regardless, the slug disintegrated in the upper arm, causing a great deal of tissue damage and disabling it. None of the bullet fragments entered the chest cavity, however. Damage to the torso was restricted to superficial wounding only. There was no damage to the rib cage or lung.

We previously have discussed the 9mm Glaser that struck the kneecap of a shotgun-wielding felon in Indiana. The patella and joint were liquefied and there was no exit. The felon fell to the ground instantly but was still dangerous. He was taken out with torso shots from a .38 Special. The consensus is that any high-velocity hollowpoint would have performed like the Glaser performed, no better and no worse, except other bullet designs would have exited.

Another case from Texas involved the .357 Magnum Glaser. A would-be cop killer was struck from behind at a slight angle. The bullet path was on a line from the spine to the heart. The slug missed the spinal bones and disintegrated instantly. Very few of the pellets actually reached the heart. The pellets did, however, saturate the pulmonary arteries and veins.

The felon collapsed instantly. At autopsy, the nature of the instant effect was discovered to be a pinched spinal cord and a chip from the vertebra blown into the spinal cord. The bullet did not physically touch the column. The shifted and chipped vertebra was attributed to a large and early temporary stretch cavity typical of the Glaser.

Yet another Glaser shooting comes from Texas. A gunfight in an office setting took place at close range. The shooter fired a mixed bag of 9mm ammunition. The round in the chamber was a 9mm Glaser flatpoint. It struck the victim in the upper right torso near the nipple at a slight frontal quartering angle. The bullet perforated and shredded the pectoral muscle and shattered two ribs. By this point the Glaser had disintegrated. Shot pellets and bone fragments continued the penetration into the right lung, creating a 5-inch-diameter defect.

The victim had been reaching for a weapon in his waistband. The bullet jerked the hand away from the waistband and spun him. The clinically lethal wounds were inflicted by the balance of the 9mm rounds fired. Some of these were Remington 115-grain JHP loads, which penetrated vital tissue but failed to expand, perforating the victim.

The following five Glaser shootings come from Gene Wolberg, senior Criminologist, San Diego Police Crime Lab. All of the rounds were of the flat-point design.

The first involved an off-duty police officer firing the .38 Special + P Glaser from a snub-nosed revolver. The range was under 10 feet in what turned out to be a classic scenario for the Glaser. The slug struck the ex-convict in the lower part of the sternum on a full frontal shot. It penetrated the sternum, saturated and almost removed the bottom of the heart, and further perforated the aorta. The attack ended almost instantly. This is an instance where the Glaser caused more damage at the ideal depth than a normal jacketed hollowpoint would have with the same shot placement.

Less detail is available on the second Glaser shooting. Again a .38 Special + P Glaser was used. Again

the scenario was ideal for the Glaser in that the bullet impacted the upper torso on a nearly frontal shot. The slug penetrated between the ribs on the right side and saturated the top of the liver. The person collapsed in under 10 seconds from a profusely bleeding wound. In fairness, any expanding, high-velocity bullet would have produced the same effect with the same placement, as the liver is so fragile.

The third shooting involved a large would-be jewelry robber and a female jeweler armed with a 2-inch Colt .38 Special. During the struggle, the woman was forced to the ground, which made her shoot upward at a high angle. The distance was less than 4 feet. The Safety Slug impacted just above the right hip on a path through the liver and to the heart. It only penetrated 3 inches of soft tissue, however, and did not even make it to the liver. Reportedly the robber yelped, ran 22 blocks, and checked himself into the hospital there. This was a clear failure to penetrate on the transverse shot and would not have stopped the aggression had the attack continued.

The fourth case involved a .38 Special + P Glaser fired from a 4-inch revolver. The range was between 8 and 9 feet. The bullet impacted the sternum at an angle between 30 and 45 degrees. However, the bullet first struck a large, heavy zipper and partly fragmented prior to impacting the sternum. Pieces of the zipper were found under the skin. As a result of this intermediate target, the shot bounced around below the skin but outside the rib cage. No pellets entered the chest cavity. The result was a bloody surface wound. The person who was shot sat down and nearly passed out. Again, the aggression stopped only because the aggressor elected to do so. This is stopping power from psychological compliance. A bullet with adequate penetration would have engaged at least one lung and either the heart or a major vessel.

The fifth case involved one of the few shootings involving the .45 Auto Glaser. Again, this was the flat-nose design. The victim was first shot in the liver with a .22 Long Rifle. She fled the house and was followed by her attacker, now armed with the .45. Catching up to the victim, the first Glaser was fired from a distance of 2 feet. The angle of impact was directly across the chest, with the round entering the right breast but not exiting. The penetration distance was 4 inches. The female stopped running and then started again.

The second Glaser also entered the right side. This time the impact was about 45 degrees in front and slightly lower. The bullet path would have been between the lungs to end up in the left shoulder blade. Instead the shot curved around the rib cage and came to rest in a fat layer. No pellets entered the chest cavity. The victim slowed down and finally collapsed. The reason for the collapse was, with near certainty, the tissue damage and blood loss associated with the .22 LR to the liver. The victim was then executed with a .45 Auto Glaser behind the ear. No pellets exited the cranium.

In this case, the first Glaser was a failure and the third a success due entirely to shot placement. All other bullets would have had a comparable effect. The second Glaser's failure to penetrate and the ease of deflection of number 12 shot caused the slug to fail where other loads would have been successful. A change to a heavier shot like number 7½, which penetrates up to 8 inches, would probably have prevented the failures in these last three accounts.

A highly successful Glaser shooting involved an off-duty sheriff's deputy in Chicago. Working as a security officer, the deputy came under fire from a man with a .22 rimfire rifle. The deputy responded with fire from his .44 Special S&W Model 24 with a 3-inch barrel.

Two of the five Glasers that were fired struck the felon, one in the upper torso, the other in an extremity. The first impacted the left nipple in the upper chest from the front at a slight angle. It fragmented after impact as designed and shredded the left lung and the left side of the heart. As is typical of the Glaser, no part of the projectile overpenetrated to endanger others. The felon collapsed backward within a second of impact and immediately lost consciousness, which was never regained.

This sampling of Glaser shootings adds valuable objectivity to a reputation that has perhaps gotten out of proportion with reality. They show that the Glaser Safety Slug can perform three ways.

One, the Glaser can produce the same result as any conventional high-velocity hollowpoint. The effectiveness on the target is not significantly different in any way.

Two, the Glaser can be partly or totally neutralized by intermediate targets. A conventional hollowpoint would not be affected, or would not be affected nearly to the extent as the Glaser. These Glaser failings mandate follow-up shots.

Three, the Glaser can perform in a way far superior to even the best jacketed hollowpoint. These cases are where the large and shallow temporary cavity takes effect or where the pellets saturate an area or an organ that would have escaped injury with the single crush cavity of most conventional hollowpoints.

As long as the odds of intermediate targets are low, such as in a home-defense or police backup scenario,

the Glaser can be expected to perform as well and possibly better than to a jacketed or lead hollowpoint. Best overall performance comes from upper-torso shots. However, some of the Glaser's superior street performance has come from mid- and side-abdomen shots not normally associated with good effectiveness from conventional hollowpoint ammo.

In January 1991, Glaser released a heavyweight Safety Slug in response to intense competition from MagSafe. The Glaser Blue is the classic design with a loose core of number 12 shot. The round-nose ball in the cap is blue in color. The heavyweight Safety Slug, available in all handgun calibers except .25 Auto and .32 Auto, is labeled as Glaser Silver.

The GSS Silver uses a core of number 6 birdshot. The shot is compressed just before the point of fusion to remove all the air space. The Silver weighs a hefty 112 grains versus 74 grains for the .38-caliber Glaser Blue. Muzzle velocity is typical of 110- to 115-grain hollowpoints in 9mm, .38 Special +P, and .357 Magnum. The bigger-bore ballistics are similar.

The news, of course, is deeper penetration from lower impact velocities and much larger pellets. Number 12 birdshot is .05 caliber versus the .11 caliber of number 6. Using the 9mm for example, the flat-point Safety Slug penetrated an average of 5.1 inches of 10-percent gelatin. The round-nose Glaser Blue extended that average penetration to 5.8 inches. The Glaser Silver punches 46 holes an average of 8.5 inches deep; some reach 9.5 inches.

Most significantly, the Glaser Silver penetrates 6 inches after first impacting plate glass. This then is its greatest advantage. The shooter now has a choice of the Glaser Blue for maximum safety against overpenetration and ricochet, or the Silver, which solves the only "problems" the original Safety Slug ever had.

MAGSAFE

As successful and effective as the Glaser Safety Slug has beome, it was inevitable that the basic concept would be imitated. Two small ammo outfits have taken the basic Safety Slug design and, at least in theory, have made some design improvements.

One firm is MagSafe Ammo, with its copper-jacketed MagSafe load. It follows the same basic design of the Glaser, with one significant and two subtle exceptions. MagSafe ammo uses a copper jacket like the Glaser, fills it with birdshot like the Glaser, and seals it with a plastic cap like the Glaser. The projectile weights are light and the muzzle velocities high, again like the Glaser.

The first subtle change is that the birdshot is potted in a hard epoxy core, as opposed to loose birdshot

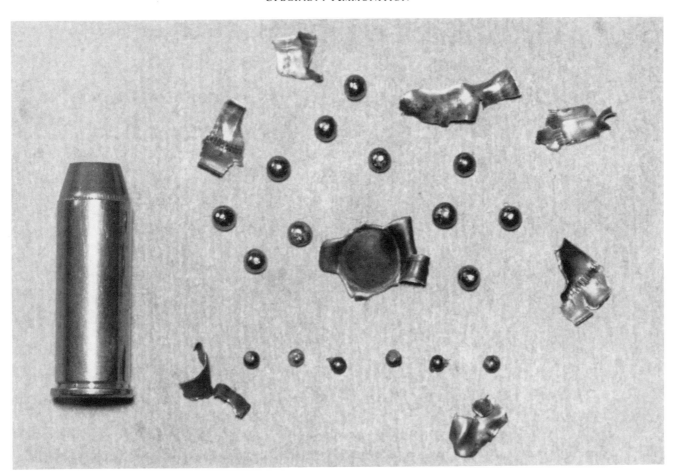

The MagSafe frangible bullet is shown recovered from gelatin. The jacket shreds on impact, releasing number 2 and number 4 birdshot inside the target.

poured into the Glaser jacket. The epoxy core must break up on impact before it can disperse into the tissue. The Glaser shot simply disperses. This one-piece core was supposed to make a more even and uniformly balanced projectile.

The second subtle change is in the plastic cap. Instead of a polymer wafer like in the flat-nose Glaser design or the polymer sphere in the round-nose Glaser design, MagSafe uses a poured epoxy cap. On loads intended to fragment early in tissue, the epoxy cap is quite thin; on loads intended for deep penetration prior to pellet release, it is thick. On some auto-pistol loads, this extra heavy cap also is intended to assist feed reliability.

The significant difference between the MagSafe and the Glaser Safety Slug is the size of birdshot. The Glaser Blue uses number 12 birdshot for all calibers. MagSafe uses number 6, 7½, or 9 for the .355 to .357 projectiles, depending on intended use, and numbers 2, 6, or 7½ for the big-bore loads.

MagSafe ammo is available in several styles in the same caliber. Some of the jackets have conical ogives with generous serrations. Others are wide-mouthed,

blunt, and semiwadcutter in profile. By changing shot size, projectile weight, jacket design, depth of the epoxy cap over the shot, type of epoxy core used to bind the shot, and muzzle velocity, MagSafe allows the shooter to pick the depth of penetration and the rate of projectile breakup desired.

Gelatin tests show that some MagSafe ammo performs to perfection and is in fact a valid ballistic improvement over the Safety Slug. Other MagSafe offerings are erratic and unreliable in breakup and saturation pattern. The earlier problem of tumbling prior to the target has been solved by a change in the manufacturing process.

Of the three loads tested, the truly excellent load was the 9mm Ultra-Velocity Green Tip. (All MagSafe loads are color-coded to indicate shot size, velocity, and other performance characteristics.) The 9mm Green Tip has a velocity of 1,673 fps using a 64-grain projectile and uses a serrated copper jacket. The core is number 7½ birdshot in an epoxy binder and epoxy cap.

Upon impact with gelatin, the Green Tip projectile shatters as fast as the Glaser and generates the spher-

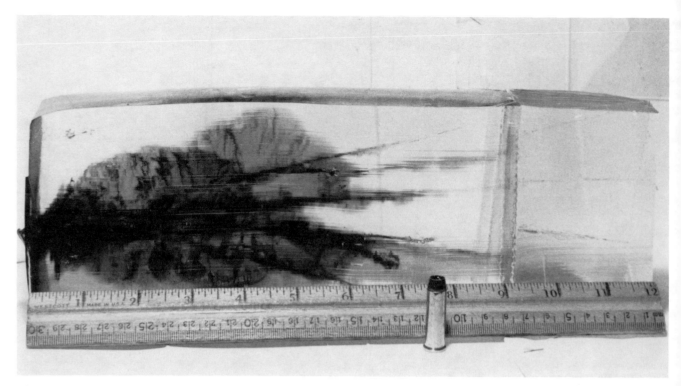

The MagSafe basically is a Glaser but designed for deep pellet penetration. This extremely large and long stretch cavity comes from the .38 Special MAX.

ical, large-diameter stretch cavity typical of the Glaser. The release of the number 7½ birdshot evenly saturates a 4-inch diameter with 20 independent pellet paths.

The MagSafe birdshot penetrates between 6 and 8 inches compared to 5 and 6 inches for the Glaser 9mm round nose. This is altogether ideal performance for a nonpolice load and overcomes the only shortcoming of the Glaser design.

The 9mm Red Tip SWAT load has a velocity of 1,722 fps with a 60-grain projectile. It uses a conventional copper jacket with no serrations and an extremely thick epoxy nose cap. The Red Tip is loaded with number 6 birdshot in an epoxy binder.

Upon impact with gelatin, the Red Tip projectile fails to fully break up. Only four of the pellets become independent projectiles, and the slug is recovered mostly intact. Penetration depth is very good with the slug at 7.5 inches and the shot between 7 and 9 inches. Target saturation, however, is poor.

The Red Tip's stretch cavity has the long football shape of most JHP slugs. However, the failure to fully break up and generate multiple secondary missiles makes this a marginal load despite its deeper projectile penetration. MagSafe is trying softer epoxy binders and other design changes in an attempt to correct this problem.

The third MagSafe load analyzed in detail was the .38 Special +P Full-House Red Tip. This load uses a serrated copper jacket with a thin epoxy cap. It is loaded with number 6 birdshot for a projectile weight of 65 grains and a muzzle velocity of 1,340 fps.

The .38 Special Red Tip fragmented completely on impact with the gelatin. The result was a spherical stretch cavity slightly smaller in maximum diameter than the Glaser counterpart. This was due to an impact velocity that is nearly 200 fps slower than the MagSafe.

The gelatin was evenly saturated with the number 6 birdshot. The birdshot was recovered at between 4 and 6 inches of penetration. The heavier but slower birdshot in this MagSafe load produced only marginally deeper penetration than a comparable Glaser.

MagSafe recently has improved its ammo enormously. Nearly all the current projectiles use number 2 copper- or nickel-plated magnum hard shot. The pellet penetration in nearly all handgun calibers is 12 to 13 inches of gelatin even after passing through common tactical obstacles. Nearly all calibers are available in a MAX load, which is at or above the maximum chamber pressures set by the Sporting Arms and Ammunition Manufacturers Institute (SAAMI). The .38 Special MAX is incredibly destructive.

MagSafe has expanded its product line to include two other specialty loads. One is the Delayed Expansion bullet. This is a conventional JHP load with epoxy placed in the hollowpoint cavity. The DX loads use the lightest and fastest JHP bullets in the caliber. The

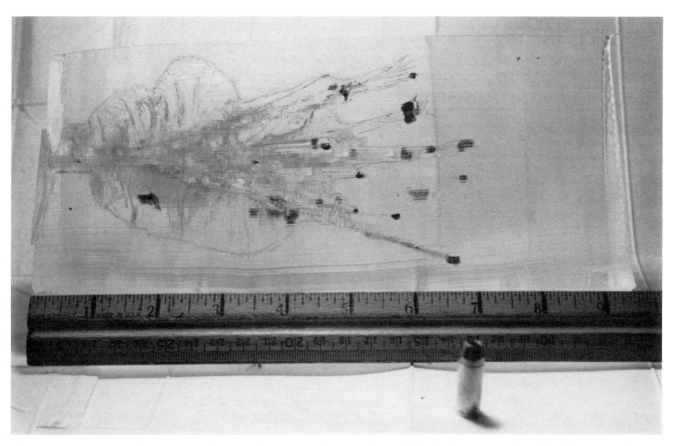

The frangible Power Plus 9mm Beehive is shown in ordnance gelatin. This load uses number 6 birdshot swaged in a copper jacket. This is the same core used in the new Glaser Silver to get a deeper penetration.

epoxy delays the violent expansion typical of these loads. The result is both large stretch cavities from high-velocity impacts and deeper penetration.

The second development is in the SWAT-labeled ammo. In the MagSafe line, SWAT means *reduced* wall or tactical penetration. Available in calibers like the .45 Auto, this load does not use lead birdshot in the bullet core at all. It is simply a copper jacket filled with epoxy and driven to speeds over 2,000 fps. Basically this is a design improvement over the Second Chance Thunder Zap.

Overall, MagSafe has the potential to be an extremely effective round. In some loads it is a clear and genuine improvement over the Glaser due to deeper pellet penetration. Like all new designs, however, bugs in some of the MagSafe rounds need to be worked out. In the final analysis, the MagSafe must serve on the street long enough for morgue and emergency room results to validate preliminary gelatin findings.

POWER PLUS BEEHIVE

The second load based on the successful Glaser Safety Slug concept is the Beehive from Power Plus. Available in all calibers, the Beehive is a lightweight, high-velocity load that uses birdshot in a copper jacket. The bullet weight for the 9mm, for example, is 85

grains. This load has a velocity of 1,503 fps from a 4-inch duty auto. All the other calibers are similar in relative projectile weights and velocities.

The Beehive differs from the Glaser in two major areas. The first, like the MagSafe, is increased shot size. The reason for the increased size is deeper penetration from the individual projectile. This is the only significant weakness with the Glaser, and both competitors have jumped on this area.

The Beehive uses a "buck-and-ball" combination of number 6 and number 2 birdshot. The number 6 shot is placed in the copper jacket with three number 2 pellets placed on top. The number 2 pellets are included in the last assembly operation essentially to seal the number 6 pellets in place.

This brings us to the other major design difference between the Beehive and Glaser. Instead of sealing the loose shot with a flat or spherical cap like the Glaser or embedding the shot in epoxy core with a poured epoxy cap like the MagSafe, the birdshot in the Beehive is crushed in place.

Once both sizes of shot are loaded into place, the bullet core is swage-formed. The end result is a jacketed hollowpoint-appearing projectile. Instead of the lead core made up of lead wire like a JHP, it is made up of birdshot crushed together.

The lightweight projectiles in a standard-length jacket result in a hollowpoint bullet that looks like a lead-lined jacket. The hollowpoint cavity is that wide and deep. The breakup after impact with gelatin is as rapid as any bullet design, generally resulting in total fragmentation in the first 1.5 to 2 inches.

The original Beehive design involved number dust birdshot crushed into a jacket and sealed with shellac. The slug had the appearance of a jacketed softpoint with a rim of the jacket exposed.

Upon impact with 10-percent gelatin, the original prefragmented and reswaged slug did indeed fully break up. Crushing the fine shot together at assembly was not enough to hold it together after impact. Significantly, however, none of the dust shot exited the main stretch cavity to create a permanent crush cavity of its own. The result was a large-diameter, shallow-depth, spherical stretch cavity. The projectile so completely disintegrated that there was no visible permanent crush cavity other than the entry hole. All of the damage came from the stretch cavity.

Fine dust lined the inner walls of what had been the temporary stretch cavity. None of the dust had penetrated, unlike the Glaser, where number 12 birdshot leaves the stretch cavity area and creates independent crush paths.

The original design had routine handling-related problems. The shellac would crack, chip, or flake off. The swaged dust core did not have enough integrity once the shellac was gone and it too would flake. This caused lead particle debris in the guns and destabilized bullets.

The dust core Beehive design was followed by a design with dust core topped off with three number 2 birdshot pellets. This solved the core integrity problem regardless of cartridge handling. During this design generation, the softpoint design was changed to a hollowpoint.

The number 2 pellets successfully broke away from the dust core to become independent wounding agents, as tested in Ductseal and modeling clay. Subsequent testing in ballistic gelatin, however, showed different results. In gelatin, dust particles still lined the inside of the temporary stretch cavity without creating independent crush cavities. Occasionally the number 2 pellets would break away from the core. The pellets would get tangled up in the dust core right behind them and fail to penetrate deeper as expected, or if they did penetrate it was only an inch deeper.

The latest generation of Beehive rounds were developed specifically for deeper penetration. The combination of numbers 6 and 2 birdshot results in independent penetration depths up to 7.5 inches. The pellet saturation diameter measures about 3.5 inches at its widest point. As such, it produces stretch and crush cavities equal to the Glaser but results in deeper penetration.

The compressed, all-lead core of the Beehive performs better than the Glaser and MagSafe in a much less significant but noteworthy area. All prefragmented rounds have a terrible time with glass. Even conventional jacketed hollowpoints and softpoints typically shed their jackets in the glass and impact as the core only. With a prefragmented bullet, the core has almost no structural integrity. The Glaser impacts targets after a .25-inch pane of glass only with number 12 birdshot pellets. The MagSafe also sheds its jacket and shatters, spraying the target with number 6 birdshot. Neither load results in more than .25-inch penetration into a plywood panel after glass penetration.

The Beehive fares slightly better. After impact, the round sheds its jacket. The compressed core sometimes remains intact but generally breaks into a dozen or so big pieces. These fragments have the ability to penetrate a layer of .25-inch plywood. This is still not up to the standard of conventional JHP, JSP, or SWC-HP bullets, but it is superior to other prefragmented loads.

The feed reliability of the Beehive auto-pistol calibers is good to very good, with the most recently submitted samples being very good to excellent. None are full-auto rated.

The bottom line with the Beehive, as well as the MagSafe, is one of finalized development. Both are relatively new products and new design departures. Both offer some inherent advantages over existing designs according to increasingly accepted guidelines using ordnance gelatin. However, neither has a street record either good or bad.

The MagSafe and Beehive have undergone subtle design improvements over the past two to three years and are still in a mode of change. The Glaser, having seen small changes and perfections over the past fifteen to twenty years, continues to improve and has a well-defined street record.

Morgue, emergency room, and police-action shooting results will be the final judge of how well the apparently superior MagSafe and Beehive loads compare to the Glaser.

ORIGINAL HYDRA-SHOK AMMO

The Hydra-Shok bullet is a design step beyond the conventional hollowpoint. Historically, the key to reliable expansion has been thinner jackets, higher velocities, larger hollowpoint cavities, and specialized jacket serrations. To this, the Hydra-Shok adds a lead post in the center of the hollowpoint cavity as an

The original Hydra-Shok for the .45 Auto was a lead hollowpoint weighing 230 grains. This bullet reliably expanded to .80 caliber.

integral part of the bullet core. This was the genius of Tom Burczynski at work.

The post is forged in the same operation that forms the cavity itself and is a solid part of the lead core. To make room for the post, the hollowpoint cavity is extremely large, giving the entire bullet nearly a wad-cutter profile.

The typical impact velocity required for a jacketed hollowpoint to expand is between 1,000 and 1,200 fps. The post in copper-jacketed Hydra-Shok ammo generates reliable expansion with secondary fragments as low as 850 fps. The post in the all-lead .38 Special Hydra-Shok ammo causes expansion to .60 caliber at as low as 675 fps.

The center post assists reliable expansion in two ways. First, it directs the hydraulic pressure away from the dead spot in the center of the cavity and toward the base of the cavity wall. The post is formed at a height to optimize the force inside the cavity. Second, it multiplies the incoming pressure. Acting as a wedge, the post amplifies the force on the cavity walls. The redirected and increased force on the inside of the hollowpoint cavity explains why the Hydra-Shok opens at a lower impact velocity and with such speed as to blow

lead fragments away from the bullet core.

The rate of expansion and, indirectly, the depth of penetration is controlled by one of two post designs. One is a conical post that is quite literally cone shaped. The other is a cylindrical post with a rounded leading edge, called the hemispherical post.

The cone post has a larger venturi area and a sharper wedge. This results in a faster rate of expansion than the hemi post. The cone post can assure reliable expansion with low-velocity loads and break up the bullet for less chance of perforation with high-velocity loads.

The hemi post has a smaller entry area and a steady rate of expansion for more moderate performance. This can be used to control the expansion to give longer crush cavities and deeper penetration.

Hydra-Shok comes in a wide variety of loads. The original load, the 148-grain Scorpion, is actually an inverted hollowpoint wadcutter with a post in the cavity seated flush with the case mouth. The velocity is mid-range only. This is the lowest performing Hydra-Shok load.

The Hydra-Shok is also available in all-lead hollowpoints and jacketed hollowpoints of various weights in various calibers. The lead hollowpoint has the low-

The original semijacketed Hydra-Shok was designed specifically to fragment. The .38 Special 125-grain Copperhead (left) spins off lead fragments as secondary missiles. The fully jacketed Federal 129-grain Hydra-Shok (right) was designed not to fragment.

est reliable opening velocity of any load known to the authors. The .38 Special non + P UPL expands to .60 caliber from a 2-inch gun, with an impact velocity of only 677 fps. A conventional lead hollowpoint generally needs + P pressures and 4-inch barrels to equal that expansion.

Most of the time, the *lead* Hydra-Shok expands to a point where the hollowpoint walls are perpendicular to the bullet path. This maximizes the crush cavity. The name "Hydra-Shok" is often associated with "hydrostatic shock," implying the temporary stretch cavity. While the Hydra-Shok loads do generate large stretch cavities, their most prominent mechanism of wounding is crush, which comes from full expansion and secondary missiles. The lead Hydra-Shok loads maximize crush.

Some of the time, the lead Hydra-Shok will expand fully and then separate into the core and the mushroomed cavity walls. The post-pointed core continues to penetrate, leaving the flat washer-appearing ring of lead in its trail. This combination of large crush followed by deep penetration is typical of the 9mm and .357 Magnum loads and others with impact velocities over 850 fps.

The copper-jacketed lead-core loads, called Cop-

perheads, are the most significant loads from Hydra-Shok. Upon expansion, the directed force from the post literally blows the cavity walls away from the core. Pieces of jacket and lead become secondary missiles that leave the main bullet path. Copperhead bullets that impact at over 850 fps generate this particle burst.

Again, this fragmentation occurs at a relatively shallow depth of penetration, saturating the first 4 inches with lead. The wounding mechanism in the first few inches is both crush and stretch in large quantities, similar to the Glaser. The resulting post-pointed core has two thirds of the original bullet weight and continues on for deeper penetration.

Compared to the better-jacketed hollowpoints, the Hydra-Shok Copperhead produces a stretch cavity of the same volume but more spherical in shape. This indicates its early and rapid energy transfer.

The Hydra-Shok crush cavity is as large in volume as the better hollowpoints, again with most of the crush action occurring early due to secondary missiles and little crush action occurring late due to the caliber-size core continuing the penetration alone. The overall level of penetration is in the 10- to 12-inch range.

The Hydra-Shok is also significant in that the re-

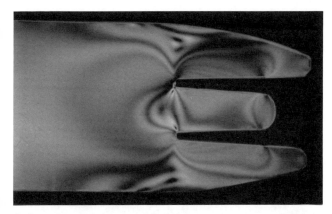

A bi-refringent image of the 9mm 147-grain Hydra-Shok made from plexiglass. Crossed-polarization produces a solid green base color common to clear elastic materials. This bullet model has been placed under the stress it undergoes immediately before expansion occurs. The flat appearance of the bullet indicates areas that are stress free. In photoelastic stress analysis, the colored lines indicate lines of stress. The more crowed the lines, the higher the stress. Areas of high stress within the cavity walls come from the pressure point in the cavity walls, forcing the hollowpoint to arch open. Note the extremely high stress areas at the base of the post, which is the fulcrum or pivot point. The high inward radial force exerted on the post by the cavity walls supports the post to keep it straight until the hollowpoint has expanded. (Photo courtesy of Tom Burczynski.)

volver loads are all moderate in pressure. The .38 Specials are all non + P and generally run 100 to 150 fps slower than + P loads of the same bullet weight. The .357 and .44 Magnum loads run 200 to 400 fps slower than conventional loads.

The street benefits of moderate-velocity loads are numerous. These include: less recoil for faster follow-up shooting in the event of a missed shot, ineffective bullet placement, or multiple felons; reduced hard-surface penetration in the event of a stray or perforating shot; less blast, which, if excessive, can cause temporary hearing loss and generate a tendency to flinch; and less flash, which, if excessive, can cause temporary night-vision loss and illuminate the shooter for return fire.

The original Hydra-Shok is still available in calibers from .380 Auto to .44 Magnum. Due to its post-in-the-cavity design, it is able to produce typical jacketed hollowpoint terminal ballistics with lower velocities and provide all the advantages that come with lower velocities.

The Hydra-Shok is not as widely distributed nor as aggressively promoted as some other specialty ammo. As a result, there are fewer civilians carrying the ammo, fewer agencies authorizing its use on or off

duty, and fewer shooting fatalities on record.

FEDERAL HYDRA-SHOK

In the mid-1980s, Federal Cartridge for many reasons felt a great deal of competitive pressure from Henry Halverson's Silvertip. The Silvertip fed well in nearly all auto pistols. Depending on the caliber, its jacket was pure aluminum, aluminum-manganese alloy, or a nickel-plated copper-zinc alloy. It also extended all the way into the hollowpoint cavity. The Silvertip expanded well due to the extremely clever "crease-fold" jacket serration design. What is more, the Silvertip had sort of gained an exotic name recognition, or "brand recognition" as the marketing types say.

Federal auto pistol ammo was, in actuality, nearly as good, and Federal revolver ammo was clearly better, yet every year Federal felt the sales pinch from the Silvertip. The company had two choices: design a semiexotic bullet to compete with the Silvertip — which would be expensive, difficult to do, and uncertain in degree of success — or purchase one of the lesser-known exotics and do some fine tuning. After all, Federal was enormously successful with the Nyclad line it picked up from Smith & Wesson.

At the same time, ammo designer Tom Burczynski and ammo maker Dick Bauman were eager to sell their production rights to the Hydra-Shok. They never did want to actually *make* ammo; all they wanted to do was design and develop it. (Since the Hydra-Shok, Burczynski has designed the Starfire, which went to PMC, and the Quick-Burst, which is under negotiation.)

Federal's decision to purchase Hydra-Shok was a natural, giving the company the semiexotic product recognition they needed. The Hydra-Shok became the first handgun loads in Federal's Premium line of ammo. The Federal Hydra-Shok was released at the 1988 SHOT Show.

While the original Hydra-Shok used exposed lead-jacketed bullets in its revolver ammo, Federal Hydra-Shok ammo is all fully jacketed like the Silvertip. Burczynski designed the cavity walls to fragment away to cause secondary wounding. (See Chapter 15 for a discussion of how secondary missiles can significantly increase wounding.)

Federal, however, adopted the same policy as Winchester — both companies have specifically stated that their bullets are designed to *avoid* fragmentation. They try to keep the mushroom that forms — fragmentation avoidance rather than fragmentation management. The pieces of lead that lie harmlessly in the bullet path are acceptable if fragmentation is unavoidable, according to both Federal and Winchester. I much

The Hydra-Shok works best at subsonic impact velocities and below. This Federal 9mm 124-grain Hydra-Shok expanded well in stopping an assassination attempt.

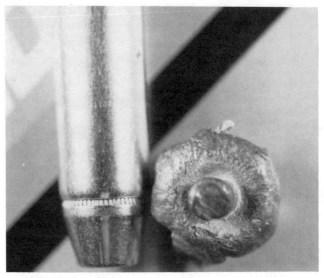

This Federal .38 Special +P 129-grain Hydra-Shok was recovered from a cop killer. The expansion is ideal.

prefer the Remington and original Hydra-Shok attempts to intentionally spin off fragments to become secondary missiles.

Despite the fragmentation theory, it is hard to argue with actual success. This is the *exact* purpose of this book. The reality on the street is that Federal Hydra-Shok ammo is extremely effective. The FBI, after extensive testing (discussed in Chapter 6), has adopted the Hydra-Shok in .38 Special +P, .45 Auto, and 9mm. In .38 Special, the 147-grain Hydra-Shok offers the exact same wounding as the legendary 158-grain SWC-HP "FBI load." As a bonus, the Hydra-Shok has much better tactical penetration.

In 9mm, Federal released a Hydra-Shok in 147 grain. Actual street results show this load to be superior to the original 147-grain OSM-JHP. Both loads produce lousy stopping power, just barely better than hard ball. However, the Hydra-Shok design works better and makes the most of this poor 9mm bullet weight.

In .45 Auto, the results are more impressive. The 230-grain Hydra-Shok is more effective in actual street fights than the 200-grain flying ashcan from CCI-Speer. Now *that* is saying something. The Speer load has always produced the most stopping power, with deep penetration and recovered diameters resembling a rifled slug. In just two years on the street, the Federal Hydra-Shok overtook it. When the Benton County,

Indiana, Sheriff's Department adopted the .45 Auto S&W Model 4506, the Federal Hydra-Shok became the duty load.

The Federal Hydra-Shok is also available in both 10mm mid-range and .40 S&W, weighing 180 grains. Other calibers include .380 Auto, .44 Magnum, .357 Magnum, and 9mm +P+. The 9mm +P+ is a good police load, and the .380 Auto is a good backup load. The two magnum loads are for hunting *only* due to deep penetration from their heavy bullets.

Some people, for one reason or another, do indeed argue with success. Despite the clear and basic physics involved with the Hydra-Shok post, people with no engineering or police background have called this design a gimmick or a sales ploy. Since the post is based on sound engineering principles, if it were removed and compared side by side with regular Hydra-Shok ammo, we should be able to see a difference.

Such a test was actually conducted by the FBI's Firearm Training Unit in 1990. The posts were removed with a milling machine for maximum precision. Posted and postless rounds in three police calibers were fired into gelatin. Tactical obstacles normally faced by police officers were then placed in front of the gelatin and all the tests repeated. The results proved that the post does indeed do something, and that what it does is always good for the shooter and bad for the shootee.

All bullets expanded with the same reliability; none were statistically erratic. Yet the Hydra-Shok expanded more with the post than without. It also penetrated deeper with the post than without; the ones without the post frequently did not achieve the 12-

The Federal .38 Special +P Hydra-Shok in the 129-grain weight has been overshadowed by the 147-grain load. These 129-grain Hydra-Shoks did reasonably well in tissue from a 2-inch revolver.

The Federal Hydra-Shok is a new addition to the .380 Auto caliber. This 90-grain load expanded to .60 caliber in a felon.

inch minimum. Overall, from an average of the 9mm, 10mm mid-range, and .45 Auto, the Hydra-Shok crushed 16 percent more tissue than the same bullet without the post. It gets better.

Due to a better balance fore to aft, the Hydra-Shok produced 22 percent tighter accuracy groups than the same ammo without a post. But the best news for police officers is the reliability of the Hydra-Shok through glass. Glass is terribly hard on all handgun bullets. The Hydra-Shok penetrated 14 percent deeper in the gelatin after the glass than the postless version.

The bottom line is that 37 percent more of the Hydra-Shok bullets in this multiobstacle battery of tests ended up in the 12- to 18-inch range than the ones with the post removed. Most of this success was due to critical improvements in the marginal area of glass penetration. In *not one* scenario was the postless bullet tied with, let alone superior to, the standard post-in-the-cavity Hydra-Shok. Thus what is considered a gimmick to some people is actually solid engineering that they simply do not understand.

From two vastly different backgrounds, both authors have become firmly convinced by hard facts that the semiexotic Hydra-Shok is a clear design improvement over the standard jacketed hollowpoint at velocities under 1,300 fps.

BRASS HOLLOWPOINTS

Three significant brass hollowpoints are available: the imported GECO Action Safety, the MEN Quick Defense, and the domestic MPP/MMC assembled by Hi-Vel, Inc. These rounds are significant for more

than just the bullet material; they are significant because each is a true hollowpoint modified for feed reliability in semiauto and full-auto weapons.

Autoloader ammo must be reliable first and high performance second. Historically, it has been a design impossibility for a conventional hollowpoint load to feed in all weapons with the same reliability as FMJ ball loads. Yet ball loads generally produce less tissue damage and disruption for the same shot placement than hollowpoints. These three designs meet the elusive goal of feeding like ball and hitting like a hollowpoint.

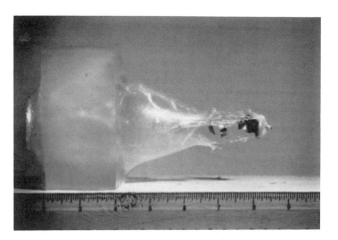

This Federal .45 Auto 230-grain Hydra-Shok is shown as fully expanded after only 2 inches of gelatin. The maximum temporary cavity formed in the wake of this successful load is visible. (Photo courtesy of Tom Burczynski.)

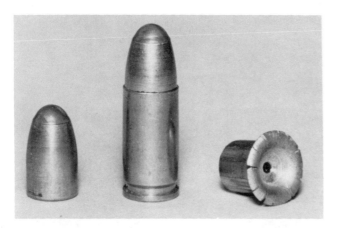

The 9mm GECO Action Safety was one of the first high-performance hollowpoints designed for full-auto feed reliability. Even with only moderate expansion, this brass hollowpoint has an actual effectiveness second only to the 9mm +P+ ammo.

The 9mm MEN Quick Defense uses a brass nose cap to cover a huge hollowpoint cavity, giving it excellent feed reliability. The QD has the largest recovered diameters of any 9mm brass hollowpoint.

The GECO Action Safety is the most popular of the three. It is made by the German company GECO-Dynamit-Nobel. The Action Safety is available in 9mm and .357 Magnum but the design significance lies only with the 9mm load. The Action Safety is also known as Blitz Action Trauma, or BAT.

This bullet is a two-part assembly made up of the main brass bullet and a plastic nose cap. The nose cap gives the Action Safety a round-nose profile, and this hard ball shape provides the excellent feed reliability.

Feed reliability is further assisted by the nose cap material. The plastic has a lower coefficient of friction than brass and is less likely to gouge, deform, or catch on the feed ramp. This keeps the slide momentum higher and the cartridge bounce more predictable.

Once in the chamber, the plastic nose cap is no longer needed and actually is a detriment, as it clogs the hollowpoint cavity. The Action Safety disposes of the nose cap by blowing it out of the bullet at the instant of ignition, exposing the hollowpoint cavity. The round accomplishes this by tiny gas ports machined all the way through the bullet from the bullet base into the hollowpoint. Upon ignition the gas pressure propelling the bullet bleeds through the port to push the nose cap out. Since the cap is so light, it exits the barrel before the bullet, and since it is molded to be counterweighted off balance, it tumbles out of the way of the oncoming bullet.

The Action Safety impacts the target as a high-velocity brass hollowpoint, causing a wide but shallow hollowpoint cavity. The 9mm round weighs 86 grains and, from a 4-inch autoloader, has a muzzle velocity of 1,395 fps. Semi and full-auto reliability is excellent.

The Quick Defense, made in Germany by Metallwerk Elisenhütte GmbH, is available only in 9mm. Like the Action Safety, the QD is a two-part bullet. The core is made from brass, and the wide and deep hollowpoint cavity contains a small center post similar to the Hydra-Shok.

The Quick Defense brass nose cap is a thin, rounded stamping crimped into the mouth of the hollowpoint to give it a round-nose profile. The QD impacts as a high-speed brass bullet with the foil-thin cap veiling the exceptionally deep cavity. Upon impact, the thin nose cap is forced into the cavity, which is large enough not to be clogged up. The foil simply disappears, forcing the hollowpoint cavity wide open.

The 9mm MEN Quick Defense weighs 86 grains and has a 4-inch muzzle velocity of 1,325 fps. Semi and full-auto reliability has proven trouble free in Walther P1 auto pistols and HK-MP5 submachine guns used by the BGS, the border patrol of West Germany.

The domestic source with the autoloader-oriented brass ammo follows the same design philosophy as the two German loads. The significant loads are available in .380 Auto and .45 Auto, although other calibers are available. The .380 Auto is called Maximum Pocket Pistol (MPP), and the .45 Auto is called Maximum Major Caliber (MMC). These are the newest of the brass hollowpoint designs, and are assembled by Hi-Vel, Inc., from components made by Buehler Precision Products under contract to PPS, Ltd.

Again, the MPP and MMC use a two-part bullet. The hollowpoint core is made from pure copper. This is in full compliance with the armor-piercing legislation S.104/H.R. 3132 "Law Enforcement Officers Protection Act of 1985." The nose cap is made from nylon 6-6. The nylon cap is heavily hollowbased to give it

The .380 Auto MPP was designed by Ed Sanow based on the 9mm Action Safety and Quick Defense. The nylon cap gives excellent feed reliability and then collapses on impact to expose the largest hollowpoint.

thin walls. The cap fills the length of the hollowpoint cavity. The bullet profile is round-nose.

Like the QD, the MPP/MMC design impacts as a cavity-protected high-speed brass hollowpoint. Like the QD, the nose cap is forced into the extra deep hollowpoint cavity upon impact. The cavity is deep enough not to be clogged by the nose cap. For its part, the nose cap shreds into ribbons of plastic, fully exposing the cavity.

The .380 Auto MPP weighs 54 grains and has a 2.75-inch velocity of 1,250 fps. The .45 Auto MMC weighs 103 grains and has a 4.25-inch muzzle velocity of 1,400 fps. Both loads cycle with full reliability in semiauto and full-auto weapons, including the Ingram/MAC/Corbray series, Thompsons, and Reisings.

Once out of the barrel, all three brass hollowpoint designs perform in a similar way. The 9mm Action Safety generally expands to between .40 and .50 caliber. Further expansion is restricted by the relatively shallow hollowpoint cavity. The 9mm Quick Defense expands to between .43 and .60 caliber. The lower velocity of the QD produces less reliable and more erratic expansion but a possible expansion much larger than the Action Safety. The .380 Auto MPP, due to razor-thin cavity walls, always expands to over .58 caliber and frequently fragments to throw off secondary missiles. The .45 Auto MMC generally expands to between .63 and .77 caliber.

The stretch cavity from all three brass designs is equal in diameter but shallower in depth compared to the best jacketed hollowpoints in each caliber. The American designs penetrate from 7.25 to 7.75 inches of gelatin. The German designs penetrate from 8.25 to 10 inches of gelatin. These are equal to or slightly

less than the best jacketed hollowpoints in each caliber. Given the relatively high muzzle velocities and relatively shallow penetration, tissue stretch is the primary mechanism of wounding.

The crush cavity from all three designs is 75 to 85 percent of the best JHP loads and on par with the average JHP and, in the case of the 9mm, light JSP loads. Some top-notch hollowpoints provide larger crush cavities, equal stretch cavities, and deeper penetration. However, no hollowpoint of any design can match the overall feed reliability of these three.

All three share the same safety aspects of light bullet weight and high velocity. They provide deeper penetration than totally fragmenting loads yet a low probability of perforating the primary target to endanger bystanders. They also demonstrate rapid velocity loss and an extremely arched trajectory, which also limits downrange bystander hazard.

In spite of these safety advantages, all three loads are as tolerant of intermediate targets as conventional jacketed hollowpoints. Upper extremities have the most effect on these light brass bullets because they absorb the large stretch cavities. Metal and glass have very little effect.

In the early 1980s, due to the limited use of the GECO Action Safety or its use by agencies unwilling to release data, actual street results were hard to come by. Massad Ayoob, the noted firearms expert and expert witness, was unable to find any Action Safety shootings prior to 1985. While teaching a Lethal Force Institute class in Caracas, Venezuela, however, Ayoob did come across the following shooting information involving GECO Action Safety ammo.

The first incident involved a hostage situation involving DISIP, the national internal security force. The elite units in DISIP carry GECO Action Safety ammo in their Browning Hi-Power pistols, Uzi and mini-Uzi weapons. The hostage was in the backseat of a car with a hostile on either side. The driver was taken out with a 7mm Remington Magnum. Two DISIP agents rushed the car, both carrying mini-Uzis.

Firing through car door metal and car glass at a distance of 5 feet, each agent emptied his 32-round magazine into each hostile. Both hostiles were hit 32 times each. The hostage was not injured. None of the GECO Action Safety bullets exited either target. Despite engaging some glass and metal in the 1.5-second burst, most of the Action Safety slugs expanded fully.

The next incident occurred during a bank robbery. One robber was double tapped in the chest with the Action Safety. One bullet impacted from the front, entering the heart. The felon jerked and spun. The second bullet entered at an angle, penetrating a lung and fracturing the thoracic spine. The felon jerked again and fell. The fight was over in under 3 seconds. Both Action Safety bullets expanded and neither perforated.

The accomplice fired a shotgun at the officer and turned to run. A GECO Action Safety bullet struck the robber in the upper leg, shattered the femur, and exited the leg. The felon fell to the ground, unconscious from the traumatic stress. This incident illustrates power and penetration not often associated with lightweight, high-velocity hollowpoints.

The final incident involved an attempted armed robbery. The officer triple-tapped the felon from the front. One bullet struck center abdomen, one struck the lower sternum, and the third struck the upper sternum. The felon rocked violently backward to the ground. All three Action Safety bullets remained in the body and all three expanded.

Even though this is a relatively small number of shootings, the Action Safety has proven successful. It is reliable in semiauto and full-auto weapons, is resistant to intermediate targets, produces sufficient penetration, expands, and generally does not perforate the target.

In the late 1980s and early 1990s, the popularity of the Action Safety tapered off in the United States but gained dramatically overseas. The 9mm Action Safety is now one of the premier antiterrorist loads. As this book went to press the GECO Action Safety has been involved in 85 shootings that meet our criteria. In 70 of these, the so-called BAT was effective instantly. This actual street performance places the Action Safety fourth overall in the 9mm caliber behind only the +P+ ammo.

The .380 Auto MPP and the .45 Auto MMC are relatively new loads but have already been involved in a number of street fights. The .380 MPP has 14 shootings that meet our criteria to include in this effectiveness study. In 8 of these shootings, the MPP was instantly effective with one torso shot. This ranks the MPP second overall in the .380 Auto caliber.

THV

THV ammunition is made in France by Société Française des Munitions (SFM). It is unique in two respects. One is its extreme muzzle velocity — the THV attains muzzle velocities between 2,300 and 2,600 fps from service-length duty weapons. These are actual chronographed velocities from carry guns, not from test barrels.

Sage International is the exclusive importer of the THV. They state that all THV loads are in compliance with the chamber pressure limits set by SAAMI. This

Armor-piercing ammo is controversial but has a definite role in police work, despite its poor wound ballistics. Shown left to right are the 9mm KTW, .357 Magnum THV, and 9mm THV.

calms fears that rifle velocities from handguns come at the expense of excessive pressures.

The second unique feature, and one of profound significance, is that THV rounds are armor piercing. They will defeat Threat Level 1, Threat Level 2A, and Threat Level 2 soft body armor. The THV is restricted to law enforcement and military sales only.

The THV is available in .38 Special +P, 9mm, .357 Magnum, and most recently in .45 Auto. It is imported as the assembled cartridge only. The bullet is made from a brass alloy. Bullet weights for the .36-caliber loads, for example, are between 42 and 44 grains.

THV revolver bullets are shaped with a concave ogive that becomes a sharp and pointed post. The autoloader rounds have the same basic shape, except the post has a rounded ball end. Both bullets resemble a short wadcutter with a protruding post, and both are machined with an exceptionally deep hollow base. The result is a surface-bearing area long enough for acceptable accuracy yet extremely light bullet weight. The hollowbase skirt does not expand significantly to fill the rifling as the lead hollowbase wadcutters are designed.

The mechanism of injury with THV bullets is almost exclusively tissue stretch. The slug does not expand or fragment. It maintains its sharp, cornered Keith profile. The concave ogive is such that the tissue in front of the bullet is wedged out of the way more. Its especially effective shape maximizes the distance away from the bullet path that tissue is thrown.

The old armor-piercing bullet, the KTW, has a

rounded semiwadcutter profile, while the Arcane and Winchester AP loads are shaped with a cone point. These loads pass through tissue with minimum disruption. Unlike these armor-piercing loads, however, the THV is designed to be inefficient in tissue. The double benefits are maximum disruption of tissue and less chance of target perforation.

At impact velocities of 2,600 fps and bullet weights of 42 grains, the THV is in the same league as the 5.56mm NATO rifle bullet when fired from the short Colt Commando.

Due to its light weight and Keith-style shoulders, the THV transfers energy very rapidly. After 5 to 6 inches of penetration, the wounding mechanism strictly is due to the crush of the .36-caliber slug. This is similar to Remington and Federal hollowpoints, which expand and then fragment or erode, respectively, back to caliber diameter. The penetration in soft tissue is 12 inches, which limits the chances of target perforation. This is less penetration than conventional fully jacketed and semiwadcutter bullets and certainly less than conventional armor-piercing bullets.

The primary wounding is from tissue stretch. The stretch cavity is nearly spherical and occurs very early. However, tissue stretch is a less efficient mechanism than tissue crush, and the THV crush cavity is relatively small. Unfortunately, the THV stretch cavity is shallow enough to fall victim to intermediate targets just like all rapid energy-transfer loads.

The THV stretch cavity is just slightly larger in diameter than the Glaser Safety Slug and the best jacketed hollowpoints of the same caliber. It is quite a bit longer in depth than the Glaser and only slightly longer than the best hollowpoints. Both the hollowpoints and Glaser have significantly larger crush cavities, giving them a stopping-power edge.

The primary advantage of the THV is guaranteed penetration against assailants wearing vests, with more tissue disruption than previous armor-piercing handgun loads. It is more likely to defeat soft and hard armor than any conventional duty load. It will defeat aluminum and steel armor that high-speed softpoint, lead semiwadcutters, and metal-pointed lead-core bullets cannot. Of course this is what you expect from AP ammo, but the THV produces a large stretch cavity not expected from AP ammo.

Like other rounds with extremely light bullets, the bullet decelerates rapidly in air. As a result, after 120 yards the THV round is going too slow to inflict a penetrating injury. It is best suited for relatively close-range exchanges.

No discussion of armor-piercing ammo is complete without a word of caution about disarms. The normal advice when selecting soft body armor or carry loads is that the officer's vest must be able to stop the officer's carry load. Of officers killed in the line of duty, 20 to 50 percent are killed with their own weapons.

The officer with THV ammo will not be able to wear enough soft armor, within reason, to stop his carry load. While all officers should be trained in disarm and retention techniques, the THV-carrying officer should be trained at instructor level. Like all techniques, they fade over time without practice. This cannot be allowed to happen with the THV AP-carrying officer.

EQUALOY SWC

The Equaloy line of ammo is significant because the bullet material is solid aluminum. Kendall International imports the aluminum bullet from England and assembles the completed round using custom loaders in the United States.

At the time of this writing, Equaloy ammo is available only in .38 Special. Kendall International has not released SAAMI chamber-pressure readings for its .38 Special load, but identifies it as standard pressure, not +P or +P+.

The .38 Special Equaloy load uses a Keith-style semiwadcutter bullet that is the same overall size as a conventional 158-grain lead bullet. Since the bullet material is aluminum instead of lead, it weighs only 38 grains. This is the lightest bullet ever loaded in .38 Special.

The entire aluminum bullet is coated with a layer of nylon similar to the Federal Nyclad. The resulting color is grey as opposed to the Nyclad blue.

The nylon coating serves a number of functions. It prevents aluminum debris from accumulating in gas ports when loaded in auto pistol or submachine gun calibers, and it prevents the bore from fouling with aluminum, which occurs at velocities over 1,00 fps. The nylon also prevents oxidation of the aluminum bullet when exposed to humid conditions.

The 38-grain bullet allows muzzle velocities in excess of 2,000 fps from 4-inch service revolvers. One particular lot of Equaloy in Laupa cases chronographed at 2,064 fps from a 4-inch Model 686.

With the exception of the police-only THV, the Equaloy has the highest velocity of any .38 Special, +P or +P+ load, at 2.5 times that of non+P conventional ammo. As a result of this extreme velocity, the muzzle energy of the .38 Special Equaloy is 360 foot-pounds. This is twice the energy of any non+P .38 Special. Only the Glaser Safety Slug +P and THV +P produce more energy.

The light bullet weight produces the least recoil of

any load in .38 Special, even with its 2,000 fps muzzle velocity. At .34 pound-seconds, the Equaloy's recoil is two-thirds of the 158-grain non + P semiwadcutter and three-fourths of the 125-grain non + P round-nose hollowpoint. This reduced recoil can be a significant street advantage, especially in small-frame and alloy-frame snub-nosed revolvers. On the other hand, the small amount of rear recoil will be a factor when Equaloy loads are developed for recoil-operated auto pistols.

In terms of wound ballistics, the solid aluminum Equaloy bullet does not expand in gelatin, water, or soft tissue. Like conventional RNL, FMJ, and SWC nonexpanding bullets, the crush cavity from the Equaloy is relatively small and is, in fact, indistinguishable from these conventional loads.

The Equaloy produces acceptable penetration depth in soft tissue. Despite its light projectile weight and early energy transfer, the Equaloy penetrates 10 to 10.5 inches of gelatin. This is deep enough to defeat intermediate targets and avoid most of the problems of transverse shots, yet not excessive to the point of assured perforation.

At 2,000 fps and nonexpanding, the primary mechanism of wounding from the Equaloy bullet, like the THV, is tissue stretch. Unlike the THV, however, the volume of tissue stretch is not as large as many conventional hollowpoints. At these elevated velocities, the flat-point profile of the Equaloy is not as effective as the concave-post design of the THV in propelling tissue away from the bullet path to form a large stretch cavity.

Compared to the Equaloy, the non + P Winchester 110-grain STHP Silvertip and the Federal 125-grain RNL-HP Nyclad both produce larger-diameter and deeper stretch cavities. Both of these top conventional loads produce a wound profile much better suited to police duty. The shallow, spherical temporary stretch cavity of the Equaloy load can be absorbed by intermediate targets and nonvital tissue on a transverse shot. This is acceptable only in an off-duty or concealed-carry scenario.

Compared to nonexpanding .38 Special non + P loads, the Equaloy produces a stretch cavity three to four times larger in diameter and roughly the same length. The exception is the .38 Special mid-range wadcutter. At less than 750 fps, the wadcutter produces a stretch cavity nearly as large as the Equaloy.

The extremely light 38-grain bullet loses muzzle velocity faster than any .38 Special load. This can be an advantage in the event of a stray shot, but it can be a disadvantage in the event of a lengthy engagement distance where the Equaloy bullet trajectory or arc will be large and the velocity at impact low enough to produce substandard wounding.

With its high-velocity and generally nondeforming bullet material, the Equaloy produces above-average penetration in building materials compared to lead and jacketed hollowpoints. It produces slightly more penetration than SWC and RNL bullets. This generally is a slight disadvantage since the Equaloy is better suited to home defense than police work.

The real penetration concern is for those who wear soft body armor and carry the Equaloy load. THV ammo is clearly armor piercing and is sold and represented as such. The Equaloy is represented as non-armor piercing against Threat Level 2A armor. However, non + P lead and lead-core bullets typically are stopped by Threat Level 1 and 1A soft armor. The person accustomed to a non + P carry load needs to know that Equaloy ammo will defeat Threat Level 1 and 1A armor.

Ballistic tests against an armor panel provided by Point Blank Armor showed an undesirable penetration compromise. On one hand, the Equaloy did not reliably defeat Threat Level 2A armor. As such, it does not have the limited advantages of an AP round like the THV. On the other hand, the Equaloy bullet defeated 11 of the 14 layers of Kevlar in the 2A panel. The backface deformation in Ductseal measured the maximum allowable at 1.7 inches.

This kind of armor penetration raises considerable concern. The Equaloy will not reliably defeat the 2A armor of your opponent but could possibly defeat your own 2A armor in the event of a disarm. Thus the Equaloy load has the disadvantages of an armor-piercing load without the advantages. Let the shooter beware.

Since the Equaloy is a relatively new load and available in only one caliber, Kendall International has no record of anyone being shot with it. Tests conducted against live animals have produced results expected from a + P semiwadcutter.

Overall, the wounding capacity of the Equaloy is certainly less than the better lead and jacketed hollowpoints in all areas of importance. The Equaloy produces greater stretch cavities than nonexpanding round-nose and semiwadcutter bullets but crush cavities equal to these lesser loads. Penetration in soft tissue is comparable to hollowpoint bullets.

Since its development in the mid-1980s, Kendall International has announced production plans for Equaloy bullets in other calibers, including 9mm, .45 Auto, .44 Magnum, 5.56x45mm, 7.62x51mm, and .30-06 Springfield. A .38 Special reduced-velocity, 1,300 fps load was also planned for use inside pres-

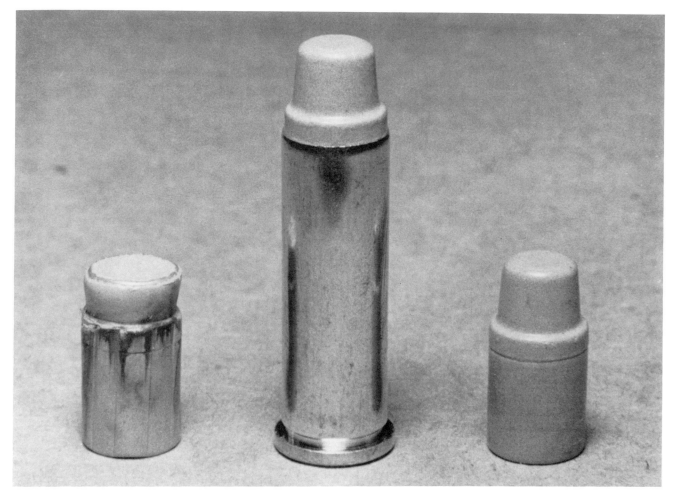

The Equaloy SWC bullet is made from an aluminum alloy and weighs 38 grains. Despite its 2,000 fps velocity, this load produces poor wound ballistics.

surized aircraft cabins, but Kendall International has announced that these are being delayed.

Recently, PPS, Ltd. released a copy of the Equaloy called the .38 Special ZC. This, too, is a 38-grain aluminum bullet with a Z-Coat finish and velocities over 2,000 fps. The ZC has all the drawbacks of the Equaloy, including the threat of armor penetration, substandard wounding, and a point of impact a couple of feet low on the target at typical combat ranges.

MULTIPLE-BULLET LOADS

Like most munitions, multiple-bullet loads are an extension of old military concepts. They have been available on and off for years. Just like inverted hollow-base wadcutters, custom handloaders have produced multiple loads, though few have been marketed nationally. This has changed recently with multiple-bullet loads now available from Silent Partner and Power Plus Enterprises in .380 Auto, .38 Special, 9mm, and .357 Magnum. These loads fire a primary projectile followed by one, two, or three secondary projectiles, depending on the caliber and manufacturer.

The primary projectile is a lightweight jacketed hol-lowpoint. In the .38 Special, for example, the JHP weighs 110 grains in the Silent Partner load and 63 grains in the Power Plus load.

The secondary projectile or projectiles are swaged lead wadcutters stacked one behind the other in the cartridge case. With some old designs, the secondary projectiles actually are nested inside one another. However, this caused failures to separate into multiple projectiles, which is clearly a drawback. The current designs all separate in the air, given enough distance to the target, or separate in tissue.

Each of the secondary projectiles engages the rifling to be spin stabilized for reasonably accurate flight. This accuracy also reduces bullet dispersion, which increases the usable range of the multiple-bullet load without jeopardizing bystanders.

The lead wadcutters from both manufacturers are relatively heavy. The Power Plus secondary wadcutters for the .38 Special weigh 50 grains each. The secondary wadcutters from Silent Partner in the same caliber weigh 70 grains each. Both loads fire one primary and two secondary bullets. Total projectile weights are 163

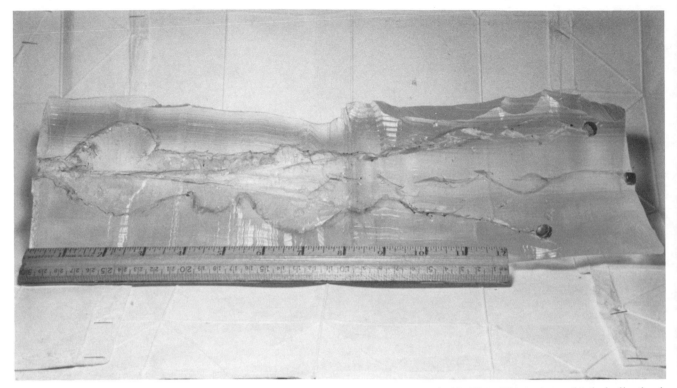

This is the wound profile of the Silent Partner MMI Multiplex in .38 Special +P. This 250-grain multiple-bullet load spreads out in tissue even if the three bullets enter through one hole.

and 250 grains, respectively.

From a 4-inch .38 Special service revolver, the Power Plus and Silent Partner loads produce muzzle velocities of 1,022 fps and 679 fps, respectively. As a comparison, the .33 caliber 00 buckshot pellet weighs 53 grains and has a muzzle velocity of 1,325 fps. The .38 Special Power Plus load produces an average projectile energy 60 percent of the 00 buckshot pellet. This places the Power Plus pellets in the acceptable energy range of number 1 buckshot. The comparable Silent Partner load has an average pellet energy 40 percent of the 00 buck pellets, placing it in the marginal pellet energy range of number 4 buckshot.

The advantage of multiple-bullet loads is the same as handgun loads generating secondary missiles after impact, buckshot loads, and submachine gun bursts — multiple and independent bullet paths. Depending on the range from the target, each of the projectiles can engage separate tissue and, in some cases, tissue in vastly different parts of the body. At their very best, multiple-bullet loads can be considered an aimed 2-, 3-, or 4-shot burst. It is possible to fire once and hit the person in the heart, liver, and one lung with one 50- to 110-grain projectile.

The effect on the person after multiple, instantaneous, and fully penetrating injuries seems to be greater than a single injury to the same organs spread over a period of time. This seems to be the case even when all projectiles strike nonvital tissue. Naturally, the odds of hitting vital tissue are higher with multiple loads.

The exact magnitude of this apparently greater effectiveness has not been documented. However, the relatively rapid effectiveness of nonexpanding, small-caliber buckshot and submachine gun bullets gives credibility to some enhanced effect. The dual-feedback loop between the central and peripheral nervous systems involving the reticular activating system arguably is involved in this higher effectiveness.

Even if this difficult-to-quantify effect does not take place, a much more reliable mechanism of collapse does. Simply put, three nonexpanding .36-caliber bullets crush three times the tissue as one nonexpanding .36-caliber bullet.

At these low-impact velocities, the primary jacketed hollowpoint does not expand unless it strikes bone. These multiple-bullet loads crush the same volume as an expanded .60-caliber bullet but spread over three different kinds of tissue.

Multiple-bullet loads can produce temporary stretch cavities as large as the better jacketed hollowpoints. The significance, however, is that the equally sized permanent crush cavities are spread out over a greater variety of tissue. Recall that of the two, the crush cavity produces more predictable and reliable wounding.

The kind of wounding from multiple-bullet loads greatly depends on the engagement distance. Depending on the caliber and manufacturer, multiple bullets produce one entrance wound at ranges under 30 feet. At ranges beyond 30 feet, they produce multiple and independent entrance wounds.

When the multiple loads impact as one, they create one crush cavity until 3 to 5 inches of penetration. Beyond this depth the bullets separate into an ever-growing pattern. This is the "billiard ball" effect, which describes the wide and uniform distribution of birdshot inside a body even though all the shot entered through one entrance wound.

By a penetration depth of 6 to 8 inches, depending on the exact tissue engaged, the multiple bullets can be 1 to 2 inches from one another. By a depth of 14 to 16 inches, the bullets can be 3 to 4 inches apart. The total penetration depth of projectiles striking together ranges from 14 to 16 inches for the Power Plus and 8 to 10 inches for the Silent Partner load.

Multiple bullets produce multiple crush cavities even when they enter the body through a single entry wound. In these cases, the multiple loads produce as large and, in some cases, larger stretch cavities than even the better jacketed hollowpoints. Further, the stretch cavity from the multiple bullet loads has, in all cases, the more desirable, longer, football-shaped profile. The permanent crush cavity is equal to or greater than the better jacketed hollowpoints.

Wounding patterns are different when the projectiles strike independently. The stretch cavity is markedly smaller. The individual stretch cavities are slightly larger in diameter than those created by round buckshot pellets and round-nose pistol bullets because the multiple bullets have a much blunter impact shape. After a very few inches, however, the stretch cavity from multiple bullets is identical to small buckshot cavities. This also applies to multiple bullets that impact as one after they separate.

The crush cavity from multiple bullets impacting separately is slightly greater than multiple bullets entering through one wound because each bullet is on its own immediately. The total penetration depth of projectiles striking independently ranges from 8 to 10 inches for the Power Plus and 5 to 7 inches for the Silent Partner.

The disadvantages of multiple-bullet loads are directly related to the advantages, unfortunately. These are the downrange pattern spread of the bullets and the heavy recoil required to launch two, three, or four sizable pieces of lead.

If the shooter is too far from the target, many if not all of the secondary projectiles will miss the target, even though they are spin stabilized. The primary projectile will strike close to the point of aim but the secondary projectiles will not.

This creates two problems. One is reduced effectiveness. The light JHP primary bullet driven at low multiple-load velocities cannot be relied on to expand. In this case, a single bullet of the same design and weight driven to normal rapid factory velocities will perform with greater effectiveness.

The second problem is the civil liability associated with one to three bullets per shot that miss the target. In both urban and rural settings, the risk of injury or damage can be quite high. This goes back to the same arguments dealing with soft-target perforation. The spin-stabilized wadcutters, with their better sectional density and ballistic coefficient, will be a hazard farther downrange than 00 buckshot.

The Power Plus load produces multiple and independent entrance wounds between 15 and 20 feet. After this distance, we see a reduction in the stretch cavities and an increase in crush cavities. Beyond 75 feet, many secondary projectiles will miss a man-size torso. The Silent Partner load produces multiple and independent entrance wounds between 30 and 40 feet. This indicates less bullet dispersion in air and a slightly longer usable range. Beyond 100 feet, these loads also produce stray shots and the problems that accompany them.

The "Officer Killed" portion of the *FBI Uniform Crime Report* documents police gunfight distances. Based on this report, 93 percent of the officers were killed at engagement distances under 50 feet. Multiple-bullet loads can produce reasonable effectiveness in about that percent of shooting scenarios.

Even within this so-called usable range, another disadvantage of multiple-bullet loads is the lack of precise and predictable placement of all the bullets at any range. The primary projectile shoots to the point of aim. The secondary projectiles impact in a pattern around that point of aim. It is rare for precise bullet placement to be required of the handgunner, but with these loads, precise bullet accountability is not possible. This is not the load of choice when firing past your partner's or spouse's ear to take out a hostage taker.

The final disadvantage of multiple-bullet loads, regardless of range to the target, is their relatively heavy recoil. An increase in projectile weight nearly always results in an increase in felt recoil. In the .38 Special, for example, both multiple-bullet loads produce 20 to 50 percent greater recoil than typical .38 Special + P loads. This is 90 percent of the impulse of some .357 Magnum and .45 Auto loads. The same guidelines apply to the other multiple-bullet calibers.

This greater recoil is not necessarily noticeable in medium-heavy and heavy-frame revolvers and steel-frame autoloaders. In other weapons, however, especially the smaller frame, short-barrel guns used for backup or concealed carry, the additional recoil is quite evident in all calibers. In a 1.9-inch Smith & Wesson J-frame, for example, either multiple bullet load would push the limits of weapon controllability. The excessive recoil increases the time between follow-up shots when facing multiple assailants or in the event of a missed or poorly placed shot.

Regardless of these disadvantages, multiple-bullet loads do have their niche in certain police and civilian scenarios. These include home defense and police raids and building searches where the engagement distances are forced by room sizes to be small.

Recently, Remington Arms has joined in the multiple-bullet market with its Multi-Ball load in .38 Special and .357 Magnum. Each is loaded with two number 000 buckshot pellets. Number 000 buck weighs 70 grains per pellet and has a diameter of .36 inch. The .38 Special version goes 830 fps, while the .357 Magnum reaches 1,155 fps. The Remington loads spread out slightly faster than the other multiple-bullet loads, which are better stabilized. However, the advantages and disadvantages of the Multi-Ball are the same as all multiple-bullet loads.

EXPLODING BULLETS

Bullets have been described as "exploding" long before Captain Clay made the .303 British jacketed softpoint at the Dum-Dum Arsenal in India in 1897. Effects described as "explosive" have appeared in medical and forensic journals for centuries. Jacketed hollowpoint and softpoint bullets have been routinely and casually identified as "dumdum" or "explosive" rounds by the ignorant general press ever since 1897.

With this kind of confusion and misnomers, it may come as a mild surprise to some that genuine exploding bullets really do exist. Plaguing exploding bullets is their reputation for unreliability, the thought that they are gimmick loads, and the pure liberal scandal of actually being a bullet that explodes.

The exploding bullets on the market today primarily are from National, though there may be some old Bingham loads still around. Exploding ammunition is or has been available in all handgun calibers, including the .22 Long Rifle. They are restricted or banned in at least four states.

The exploding bullet begins with a conventional jacketed hollowpoint. The hollowpoint cavity typically is enlarged and deepened and a small amount of explosive is placed in the cavity. The explosive usually

This is the amount of expansion the Exploder bullet gets just from the detonation of the primer in the Silvertip hollowpoint. It is an extremely controversial way to get 15 percent more wounding.

is smokeless powder, black powder, or lead-azide primer compound.

The powder is held in place with a small pistol magnum primer, which also serves as an impact detonator. The primer generally is lacquered in place to prevent it from coming loose during handling or recoil and to seal the primer and powder from moisture.

Despite fears to the contrary, most exploding loads detonate with excellent reliability. They detonate in ordnance gelatin at impact velocities as low as 800 fps. The detonator is also reliable in substances like wood, drywall, and metal.

Reports of unreliable exploding loads can be traced to aged ammunition, ammo with the primer moisture seal broken, or ammo handled roughly enough to deform or damage the primer. Actually, exploding ammo is reasonably insensitive to rough handling. The detonating primer will not go off by accident, not even with repeated drops onto a concrete floor. With reasonable care and moisture protection, the detonator will function as intended, as will the explosive charge.

The primary advantage of exploding loads is that the host hollowpoint bullet always expands or mushrooms. The function of the explosive charge is to force the hollowpoint bullet open, period. It is not to set off a bomb inside the person's body, although the technology exists to make such loads.

The explosive effect of the primer and powder does not contribute directly to wounding. It simply opens the hollowpoint more rapidly and reliably. In fact, exploding bullets generally do not throw off fragments normally associated with explosions.

An exploding bullet produces roughly a 15-percent larger stretch cavity than the host hollowpoint would alone. Its stretch cavity is slightly larger in diameter and shallower in depth due to an earlier energy transfer. This effect can be duplicated merely by increasing the impact velocity of the conventional hollowpoint by reducing its weight. There is nothing scandalous here at all.

The exploding bullet produces roughly the same to slightly smaller crush cavities than conventional hollowpoints. The detonation can blow the hollowpoint open to the point where the resulting mushroom can be eroded away as the bullet passes through tissue. The penetration depth from exploding bullets is also slightly shallower due to the early and aggressive energy dump. Therefore, a bullet that fragments to launch secondary missiles or a bullet that expands to and retains a full mushroom can exceed the crush cavity of an exploding bullet. It is also very sensitive to the upper arms as intermediate targets because so much of the stretch and crush action occurs at a relatively shallow depth. Finally, exploding rounds produce roughly 20-percent less penetration in building materials because of their enhanced expansion on impact.

Exploding bullets are best described as conventional hollowpoint bullets that always work like hollowpoints are supposed to. The explosive charge only makes bullet mushrooming more reliable and does not itself destroy tissue. Despite their reputation, the exploding bullets on the market today are quite conventional in their wound ballistics.

Documented shootings with exploding bullets are rare. Quite significantly, the attempted assassination of President Ronald Reagan involved exploding rimfire ammo. Beating the odds, the .22-caliber exploding bullet that struck President Reagan did not detonate as designed. Most of the slugs striking press secretary Jim Brady and the two police officers did detonate.

Again, a properly functioning exploding bullet works slightly better than the same bullet without a detonator and charge. An exploding bullet that fails to fire works like a softpoint bullet of the same caliber and impact velocity.

A case involving a Bingham exploding bullet comes from Texas. In this incident, the host was a Winchester 95-grain STHP Silvertip in .38 Special +P. This was a suicide where the bullet entered palatine bone in the roof of the mouth. The detonator did indeed fire. The slug did not exit. At autopsy, it was concluded that the physical damage to the bone and brain was not significantly different from similar bullet paths using the unmodified Silvertip bullet.

SABOT BULLETS

The sabot concept in small arms ammunition is another direct descendent from military munitions. Sabot bullets, like most specialty loads, were available only from small and regional custom loaders before their national acceptance.

Ballistic success with sabot loads has been mixed. The best performance comes in the rifle calibers. The Remington 55-grain .224-caliber Accelerator bullet has given the .30-30 WCF, 7.62mm NATO, and .30-06 a varmint-class velocity these .30-calibers never had before. An increase of nearly 1,000 fps makes the Accelerator shoot flatter with about the same accuracy.

Sabot shotgun loads tried to follow the same path but met with much less success. The .50-caliber projectile and its sabot typically weighed more than a conventional hollowbase or Brenneke rifled slug. As a result, the sabot slug produced less velocity and frequently produced poorer accuracy than conventional slugs. Contrary to the claims, tactical and barricade penetration from sabot rounds was often worse than conventional slugs, depending on the barricade, but especially against cars.

Sabot handgun loads have been the least successful of any sabot design. This is primarily due to the limited case capacity and limited overall cartridge lengths. Some of the problem, however, is related to sabot designs that break away with poor reliability.

The sabot is simply a sleeve or a housing. The outside diameter of the sabot is the same as the caliber of the weapon. The inside diameter is the same as the caliber of a smaller bullet. For example, most sabot loads involve the .44 Magnum case and a .38-caliber bullet.

Gas pressure forces the sabot and bullet down the bore. This pressure is exerted on either the base of the sabot or the base of the bullet and sabot together. The sabot engages the rifling as a bullet would and it and the housed bullet receive a reasonable rotational velocity and are, in theory, spin stabilized.

In theory, lighter .38-caliber bullets can be driven to higher velocities from a larger .44 Magnum case than from the .357 Magnum case. Lead bullets can also be driven well over 1,000 fps without barrel fouling because the bullet itself never touches the rifling.

The positive claims for sabot handgun loads typically are increased velocity and improved accuracy compared to conventional ammo for that caliber. Increased velocity can lead to increased stopping power if the velocity is high enough. Certainly those over 1,500 fps and especially over 2,400 fps offer increased temporary stretch cavities. At these near-rifle velocities, this can be significant. To gain in stretch cavity size, however, you may give up significant amounts of the critical crush cavity. Further, you run a great risk of reducing the overall stopping power by reducing the depth of penetration.

A 145-grain .38-caliber JHP may expand well, retain the mushroom, and penetrate deeply at a designed impact velocity of 1,300 fps. At 1,800 or 1,900 fps, however, the same bullet will expand too rapidly, blow its mushroom into pieces, and produce entirely too little penetration. Not only have you lost the difference in crush between .44 and .38 caliber, you have reduced the depth of penetration.

The .44-caliber bullets are more likely to retain the mushroom at .44 Magnum velocities than a .38 will at .44 Magnum velocities. You end up comparing a deeply penetrating .44 JHP with a recovered diameter of .75 inch to a shallowly penetrating .38 JHP with a recovered diameter of .36 inch — crush and stretch from the .44 versus stretch only from the .38.

The odds are even more against sabot handgun loads because they never actually reach the elusive rifle-velocity range. Caliber .38 bullets driven from a .44 can be faster but only marginally so at best. The rifle-size stretch cavities never materialize.

Velocity tests conducted with .44 Magnum sabot loads illustrate the point. The weapon in use was a Smith & Wesson Model 29 with an 8.375-inch barrel. A Custom Chronograph with printed screens prevented errors due to muzzle blast that skyscreens can experience.

The Remington 240-grain JHP averaged 1,302 fps. The Remington 180-grain JHP averaged 1,612 fps. The Federal 180-grain JHP averaged 1,710 fps. As a comparison, a Precision Component-loaded .38-caliber 158-grain SWC sabot load averaged 1,639 fps. One of the 158-grain handloads recommended by R&R Sabot is 24 grains of Hercules 2400; it averaged 1,635 fps.

Compared to the .44 Magnum 180-grain factory loads, the sabot loads clearly offered no increased velocity. The reason for this can be traced directly to case capacity. Once the bullet and sabot are assembled in the case, there simply is not enough room left for enough slower-burning powder. Faster-burning powders exceed the pressure limits before top velocities are reached.

Significantly, in an effort to gain powder capacity, the Precision Component loads had bullets seated to an overall cartridge length longer than SAAMI limits. In general, maximum cartridge dimensions and chamber pressures prevent the sabot load from being successful in a handgun.

Yet there are further problems. Claims of increased accuracy are generally unfounded. This is due to unpredictable and unreliable separation of some sabots from the bullet. The bullets frequently impacted the target sideways, leaving the classic "keyhole."

In addition to the S&W Model 29, a Ruger Super Blackhawk with a 7.5-inch barrel was used to evaluate accuracy. Both weapons shoot the two Remington factory loads previously discussed to under 3-inch groups at 50 yards.

From both weapons, the recommended handload using Sierra 158-grain JHP bullets grouped from 4.25 to 6.25 inches. When fired from the S&W, the sabots separated about half the time. When fired from the Ruger, all of the sabots remained attached.

For a reason perhaps related to bullet diameter, the results from the 158-grain cast and swaged lead bullets were much worse. Handloaded and factory-loaded sabot loads nearly always tumbled and keyholed. The best group was 7.5 inches. As a flip-flop, all of the sabots fired from the S&W stayed attached while most of the sabots fired from the Ruger separated.

In addition to reduced terminal ballistics and reduced accuracy, the final area of significance is the impact of the sabot load on forensics. The .38-caliber bullets of all sizes and shapes can be fired from .44 Special and Magnum handguns and leave no trace of rifling, possibly no trace of powder indentation, and possibly no trace of the sabot. Medical examiners who recover bullets with no trace of rifling should immediately suspect sabot loads in addition to revolvers with no barrels.

HANDGUN SHOTSHELLS

The handgun shotshell is an attempt to give shotgun pattern and saturation characteristics to a handgun. Handgun shotshells spread out even faster than shotgun shotshells and can strike the target with multiple pellets.

The most popular factory handgun shotshells currently in production are made by CCI-Speer, Federal Cartridge, and 3-Ten, Inc. Handgun shotshells have been or are available in .22 Long Rifle and Magnum, .38 Special, 9mm, .45 Auto, and .44 Magnum. The size of the birdshot ranges from number 6 to number 12 depending on the caliber and manufacturer.

Some people use handgun shotshells for personal defense. Depending on the caliber, design, and engagement distance, this generally is a poor selection, with the exception of the 3-Ten loads. People believe that the handgun shotshells have the same effect as a shotgun load with the same size shot, or they mistakenly confuse the shotshell with the Glaser Safety Slug. Both are potentially lethal errors.

Commercially available handgun shotshells fall into

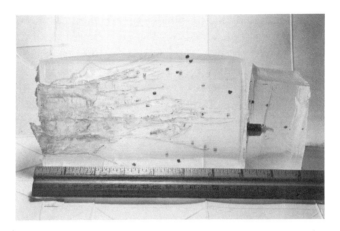

The 3-Ten .44 Magnum Bulleted shotshell is an ideal cross between a snake load and a conventional bullet. It strikes with the combination of number 6 birdshot and a 44-grain wadcutter.

two major design categories, although countless custom-loaded variations exist. These two designs are those where only the birdshot pellets are launched at the target and those where the pellets along with a copper-zinc nose cap are launched at the target.

The most popular example of the birdshot-only design is the CCI-Speer shotshell. This load fires a three-piece assembly. The projectile is made up of a plastic gas seal, a brittle plastic capsule, and the charge of birdshot. The centerfire load fires number 9 shot while the rimfire uses number 11 and number 12 shot.

The CCI-Speer projectile for the .38 Special, for example, weighs 105 grains. From a 4-inch service revolver, it produces a muzzle velocity of 925 fps. As a point of reference, this is 250 to 300 fps slower than even a shotgun skeet load with the same size shot. The handgun shotshell pellet energy is 37 percent less.

Upon firing, the rifling imparts a tremendous spin to the capsule and payload. The rifling also cuts into the plastic capsule, which weakens it. As the capsule exits the barrel, the centrifugal force of the shot shatters the weakened capsule. The shot spins radially outward into a rapidly growing pattern that is significantly larger than any shotgun load.

At the close range of 5 feet, a *shotgun* load impacts the target en masse. The entry wound measures an inch or so, with a few peripheral pellet holes. The great majority of the shotgun pellets assist each other in the penetration effort. At close range, especially near-contact, it is reasonably valid to add the individual pellet energies together to estimate their initial penetration potential.

As the pellets spread out in the air to impact on their own, however, they must be viewed as individual pellets. At a distance of 5 feet, not one single *handgun*

shotshell pellet impacts together with another pellet — the pattern spreads out that quickly and is that sparse. The wounding and penetration is what you would expect for a tiny projectile with only 1.5 foot-pounds of energy.

At 5 feet, only 10 percent of the number 9 pellets from the .44 Magnum CCI shotshell penetrate 4 inches of gelatin. At 15 feet, the maximum penetration depth is 2.5 inches. In the most favorable light, this is superficial wounding. Lack of meaningful average penetration disqualifies handgun shotshells as personal defense loads, as they can be stopped by an average winter jacket or a couple of layers of denim.

Regardless of the fact that the target can be struck multiple times, handgun shotshells do not provide deep enough penetration. The only possible meaningful injuries could be blindness or penetrating an artery in the neck. Neither of these will guarantee incapacitation on a timely basis. If these injuries are not inflicted, the handgun shotshell will quite literally produce no dependable effect.

The shot is too small, too slow, too few in number, and too spread out. Like the subcalibers, handgun shotshells can be lethal but they are not effective. They substitute intimidation for incapacitation. Loads of this design are not at all suitable for personal defense.

Shootings with handgun shotshells are relatively uncommon, but the following incident in Indiana typifies their performance.

A CCI shotshell in .22 Long Rifle was fired from a 3-inch revolver at a distance of less than 3 inches from the victim's skull. The victim was being held by the assailant. The number 12 birdshot pellets struck the skull at a 45-degree angle behind the right ear, leaving a single, nickel-sized entrance wound.

The pellets penetrated the skin and around a part of the skull but did not penetrate the skull. They did not exit. The impact caused a hairline fracture of the skull and a concussion. The victim was knocked to the ground but recovered fully. Any other load with this bullet impact would have caused a lethal injury.

An example of the birdshot and copper nose cap design is the 3-Ten Bulleted shotshell. This is an improvement over the former load from BBM called the HardCap. This design is a bridge between handgun shotshell loads and conventional ball or hollowpoint loads. It is a new release available only in .44 Magnum at the time of this writing. The shot in this payload is high-antimony, copper-plated number 6.

The BBM HardCap has been discontinued but is still available in dealer inventories and at gun shows. The BBM loads were available in 9mm and .45 Auto with either number 6 or number 9 shot. These loads have a round-nose FMJ ogive and are loaded to full pressures. As a result, they feed and cycle in semiauto and full-auto weapons.

Both the HardCap and Bulleted designs fire a four-piece projectile made up of a plastic gas seal, fiber shot collar, copper-zinc nose cap, and the birdshot payload.

As a coarse measure of performance, the conventional CCI .44 Magnum shotshell cannot stop a nine-line ground squirrel or gopher at 7 yards. The Bulleted .44 Magnum shotshell has pulled pheasants down from flight at 15 yards and quail from 20 yards. The reasons for this are larger shot sizes, larger payloads, higher impact velocities, and tighter pattern densities.

The .45 Auto HardCap and the .44 Magnum Bulleted shotshells have payloads up to 50 percent greater than the conventional .44 Magnum shotshell. The muzzle velocity from these loads is up to 100 fps faster. As such, the muzzle velocity is equal to that of normal shotgun loads. Furthermore, the higher-velocity number 6 shot has three to four times more pellet penetration energy than the number 9 shot in the conventional CCI shotshell.

The most significant part of these designs is the guiding metal nose cap. The autoloading HardCap nose cap looks exactly like an FMJ bullet without the lead. The Bulleted nose cap is in the form of a jacketed, Keith-shouldered, full wadcutter. In both cases, the nose cap gives these loads the dual effectiveness of buck and ball. The pellets provide an area saturation while the nose cap provides aimed shot accuracy. Due to the collar-restraining design and the captivating effect of the nose cap, the pattern density of the Bulleted and HardCap shotshells is 25 to 50 percent tighter than conventional shotshells.

The nose cap measures between .010 and .020 inch thick depending on the design generation. The cap engages the rifling to become spin stabilized. Both loads have the same point of impact as ball loads at 10 yards. Group sizes at this distance range from 2 inches for the Bulleted shotshell to 9 inches for the HardCap.

The major failing of the conventional CCI-style shotshells is lack of meaningful penetration. The larger shot, high velocities, tighter patterns, and copper nose cap of the Bulleted style all provide deeper penetration.

In ordnance gelatin, the HardCap and Bulleted shotshells produce up to 6.5 and 8.5 inches of penetration, respectively, from a range of 5 feet. The 44-grain nose cap from the Bulleted shotshell penetrates 7.75 inches of gelatin. On a frontal, upper-torso shot, this level of penetration can produce the kind of wounding necessary to be effective.

The Bulleted load produces a stretch cavity comparable to .38 Special +P and 9mm jacketed hollowpoints. This load also produces a shredding crush cavity two to three times larger in volume than typical big-bore hollowpoints.

Despite reasonably good close-range ballistics, both of these shotshells become dramatically less effective as the range increases, the shots become more angled, and intermediate targets are introduced. The heavier nose cap in the Bulleted load is effective at slightly greater distances than the HardCap load.

Nose cap shotshells are decidedly superior to conventional shot capsule designs in all significant areas. In perspective with other personal defense loads, however, even the superior shotshell designs are severely limited.

Perhaps the HardCap and Bulleted shotshells could be used for home defense in a house trailer or thin-walled apartment. Extreme close range, excellent chances of penetrating dwelling walls, and a high population density typify these scenarios.

Regardless of the scenario, due to limited penetration in soft tissue, even the superior shotshell designs should be restricted to use where the risks to bystanders from stray shot penetration are as high as the risk to the shooter from the attacker.

PMC ULTRAMAG BULLET

Perhaps the most revolutionary entry into the handgun ammo market of the mid-1980s was the PMC Ultramag tubular bullet. The bullet is in fact a tube — a brass semiwadcutter-profile bullet with a .67-caliber hole all the way through it. The design is based on a classified U.S. military design where the bullet material was steel.

Shortly after its introduction, the use of brass alloy in bullets was banned by federal law. PMC followed Ed Sanow's recommendation to Sales Manager Sy Wiley to make the bullet from tellurium copper (CA 145) to meet the letter of the federal armor-piercing law. The nearly pure copper tubular bullet is available in both .38 Special +P and .44 Special. The .38 Special +P bullet weighs 66 grains and leaves a 4-inch revolver at 1,435 fps. The .44 Special bullet weighs 110 grains and leaves a 4-inch revolver at 1,085 fps.

The tubular bullet is seated in a case like any other bullet. A gas wad seals the pressure behind the bullet. The wad is, of course, necessary because the bullet is hollow. Like any other bullet, the tubular bullet engages the rifling and becomes spin stabilized while the wad falls away.

The significance of the bullet rests entirely in its wounding efficiency. Throughout the book we have emphasized that the crush mechanism is a more reli-

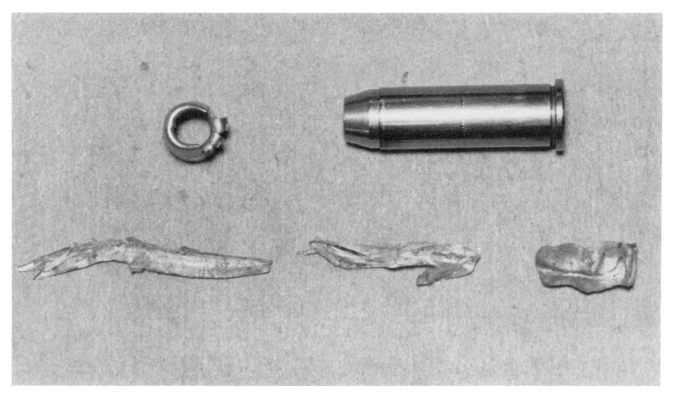

The PMC .38 Special +P 66-grain Ultramag bullet is shown recovered from ordnance gelatin. This tubular bullet acts as a cookie cutter to literally remove tissue along the bullet path.

able, positive, and efficient way to damage tissue than the stretch mechanism. Tissue can be stretched without being injured but cannot be crushed without injury.

The most efficient way to damage tissue, even beyond crushing or pulping it, is to cut it. Cut tissue bleeds much more than crushed tissue. Archers have known for centuries that sharp arrows are more effective than dull arrows. Knife fighters have known the same thing.

A cut is a more serious injury than localized blunt trauma. It is more likely to bleed and less likely to be stopped. This explains why an arrow with less than 200 foot-pounds of energy can bring down the largest game in North America. (As a comparison, a non + P .38 Special round-nose lead bullet produces 200 foot-pounds of energy.)

The mechanism of injury for the PMC tubular bullet is cutting. Tissue in the bullet path is not displaced like crush and stretch loads — it is dislodged completely. Vital organs and vessels that lie in the bullet path are removed from the body.

Muscle tissue is a good example. A passing bullet does not remove the function of muscle tissue it passes through. It is injured by displacement only. The tubular bullet, however, cuts the muscle group it contacts like a cookie cutter. The advantage is incredibly effi-

cient wounding with the ability to completely dislodge tissue for much of the bullet path.

The only other handgun load to actually dislodge tissue is the Glaser with its perforate-then-stretch mechanism. However, it does not dislodge tissue for the entire bullet path nor is the bullet path as long as the PMC tubular bullet's.

Unlike other high-velocity and exotic loads, the tubular bullet is totally unaffected by fleshy intermediate targets. It simply puts a hole in the extremity and goes in to put a hole in the torso . . . a literal hole, where tissue has been dislodged to become totally nonfunctional. The effects on human anatomy are devastating.

The tubular bullet penetrates soft tissue for a few inches, tumbles base over nose, and then penetrates base first for the balance of the bullet path. The distance prior to the tumble depends on the density and elasticity of the tissue but generally occurs between 3 and 5 inches deep. The rear-heavy bullet is prone to tumbling because the center of gravity is significantly rear of the center of rotation, just like pointed assault rifle bullets.

During the tumbling phase, the light bullet causes a good deal of tissue stretch and itself slows down rapidly. If the bullets would not tumble, the stretch and crush cavity would be smaller and the low drag through the body would certainly result in target perforation.

As it is, the Ultramag takes advantage of all three mechanisms of injury. The first 2 to 3 inches are stretch and cutting. The next 3 to 4 inches are stretch and crush as the bullet goes sideways. The remaining penetration is cutting, even though the bullet is base forward.

Maximum tissue stretch occurs in the range of 1 to 6 inches. The maximum diameter of the stretch cavity and the total stretch volume is comparable to most .38 Special hollowpoints but smaller than the best hollowpoints. The crush cavity is smaller than expanding hollowpoints. The tubular bullet does not expand. The crush cavity is enlarged over a nonexpanding bullet only during the brief period where the bullet is sideways to the bullet path.

The length of penetration is typically 9 to 12 inches. However, the bullet path has a pronounced curve to it, as the tumble action causes the bullet to veer off course. After 5 to 6 inches of penetration, the bullet continues its penetration at a 30- to 45-degree angle to the original bullet path.

It is difficult to compare this round to other loads in an attempt to predict stopping power. The primary wounding mechanism — cutting — is too different in its effect on a living target from crushing or stretching. In terms of crush, the load is poor to fair. In terms of stretch, the load is good to very good. Yet neither of these are as wound efficient as cutting. In this area, the Ultramag has no peer.

The topic of high-velocity copper or brass raises the immediate question of the Ultramag's ability to defeat soft body armor. Unfortunately, the law concerning armor penetration is not performance-oriented but instead is material-oriented. The law simply bans bullets made of certain materials like steel and brass regardless of their ability to penetrate soft armor of any specified threat level.

A much more reasonable standard would be based on performance as determined by actual firing. A maximum threat level could be established or, better yet, a maximum number of layers of a specified weave of Kevlar that a bullet would be permitted to defeat.

At the time of this writing, the PMC Ultramag is being held up pending compliance with the law. PMC is attempting to get an exemption through the law that covers sporting purposes. In this case, PMC is emphasizing the round's improved, even, match-grade accuracy, especially at extremely long range.

The ultimate question for law enforcement officers is one of performance. The .38 Special +P Ultramag, at an impact velocity of 1,437 fps, failed to defeat a

Threat Level 2A soft body armor panel provided by Point Blank Armor. In terms of tactical penetration against domestic building materials, the Ultramag penetrates as far as most conventional jacketed hollow and softpoints.

In the event of a total miss, the tubular bullet does not share the same advantages of suppressed downrange hazard as other light bullets. It has an incredibly low drag factor because it is hollow and has such a small frontal surface area. As such, it is less affected by wind drag and air density. PMC claims accuracy levels at extended ranges far superior to conventional loads. At the minimum, the retained velocity downrange is relatively high.

The PMC Ultramag is unproven in domestic law enforcement work. However, a review of general-issue ammo guidelines and priorities shows this load to have excellent law enforcement potential.

Stopping power is a top priority, especially in .38 Special +P. With average crush and stretch cavities and a potentially devastating cut mechanism, the Ultramag looks good in this area.

Low recoil is another area of emphasis. The low weight and high velocity in this case result in a load with only two thirds the felt recoil of a +P semiwadcutter. Blast and flash are average for a +P load.

Avoiding perforation is a police administration goal, while adequate penetration is a street cop goal. The Ultramag balances this with 9 to 12 inches of gelatin penetration. Further, it is less sensitive to intermediate targets like glass, steel, and tissue than most high-velocity hollowpoints.

This is one of the loads that must depend almost entirely on street results to tell us what the street performance will be. Until sufficient numbers of people are shot with tubular bullets and that information gathered and analyzed, the potential for error in commenting on the load is fairly high. A few results can give misleadingly good or poor results.

Until this data is available, we must fall back on stretch, crush, and penetration as wound predictors. In strictly these terms, the Ultramag should perform no worse than the 158-grain +P semiwadcutter, but it has the potential at least to be one of the most effective loads ever designed.

FEDERAL NYCLAD

The nylon-coated lead bullets currently made by Federal Cartridge were originally made by Smith & Wesson. The S&W Nyclad was designed specifically to reduce airborne lead accumulation in indoor shooting ranges. Independent tests indicate that Nyclad bullets produce 80 percent less airborne lead contamination. The coating on the bullet also reduces bore

Smith & Wesson designed the Nyclad (left) as a lead-free practice load with little emphasis on expansion. Federal redesigned the Nyclad Chief's Special in .38 Special non+P to produce excellent wound ballistics.

leading normally associated with swaged lead bullets at velocities over 900 fps.

As a qualifying load for indoor ranges, the Nyclad performs reasonably well, though it does not generate target- or match-grade accuracy. The nylon coating does not allow the rifling to grip the bullet as securely as a solid lead or copper-jacketed lead bullet at full chamber pressures.

When Smith & Wesson discontinued the manufacture of all handgun ammunition, Federal Cartridge picked up the rights to produce the Nyclad. Federal expanded the line and began to stress the excellent antipersonnel aspect of the Nyclad design.

The Nyclad is currently available in .357 Magnum as a 158-grain SWC and SWC-HP. The muzzle velocity of these loads is 1,200 fps. It is also available in 9mm as a 124-grain RNL-HP with a muzzle velocity of 1,100 fps.

The .38 Special and +P is available in numerous Nyclad loadings. These include the 148-grain wadcutter and 158-grain SWC and RNL at standard-pressure and +P velocities. Significantly, the Nyclad is also available as a 158-grain SWC-HP in +P and a 125-grain SWC-HP in both standard pressure and +P. The 125-grain .38 Special standard-pressure SWC-HP, called the Chief's Special, was discussed earlier.

The Nyclad SWC-HP loads expand to larger recovered diameters with a greater degree of reliability at lower impact velocities compared to conventional swaged lead bullets due to the amount of antimony used in the lead alloy. Swaged lead bullets must have a greater amount of antimony — between 1 and 3 percent — to harden the lead to reduce barrel leading and rifling stripping. Cast lead bullets, as a comparison, have between 6 and 10 percent antimony and often like amounts of tin.

Four Federal .38 Special +P 125-grain Nyclad LHP bullets recovered from four separate shootings. The bullets all expand after the Federal redesign of the Smith & Wesson concept.

The Nyclad bullets contain only traces of antimony and other alloying elements. They have roughly the antimony content used in the lead core of jacketed bullets. The low-velocity Chief's Special has the least antimony, followed by the 125- and 158-grain +P loads, with the .357 Magnum SWC-HP Nyclad containing the most alloying agents in the Nyclad line, appropriately. As a result, the soft lead Nyclad bullets expand more readily than either a SWC-HP or a JHP of the same bullet weight, cavity shape, and impact velocity.

The Federal Nyclad 125-grain .38 Special standard-pressure RNL-HP has a muzzle velocity of 750 fps from a 2-inch .38 Special snubbie. This load expands to between .66 and .70 caliber in gelatin and penetrates 8.5 to 9 inches. The same bullet profile from the +P load expands to roughly .64 caliber and penetrates 10 inches. The Nyclad 158-grain .38 Special SWC-HP has a 4-inch muzzle velocity of 890 fps, expands to 63 caliber, and penetrates 14 inches.

The Nyclad 124-grain 9mm RNL-HP penetrates 12.5 inches with a fully expanded .68-caliber slug. The Nyclad 158-grain .357 Magnum SWC-HP expands and hangs on to .62 caliber, producing a long, football-shaped stretch cavity, and penetrates a full 18 inches of gelatin.

In all cases, the Nyclad crush and stretch cavities are at least equal to the best loads of the same bullet weights in the same calibers. For example, the Nyclad SWC-HP in .38 Special +P expands and penetrates as well as any lead SWC-HP. It is a street reality that the SWC-HP load from all major manufacturers performs interchangeably.

The Nyclad line is significant because if offers lead hollowpoints in calibers and bullet weights not offered by other manufacturers. The Chief's Special Nyclad is the most significant load in the standard-pressure .38 Special. This has the non+P reduced recoil for fast follow-up shots combined with expansion and penetration formerly available only at +P pressures.

A word of caution bears repeating concerning the non+P Chief's Special Nyclad. When Federal first released the 125-grain Chief's Special load, it used the original Smith & Wesson design. With a muzzle and impact velocity of 750 fps, this load will not expand in ordnance gelatin or water, nor will it expand in soft tissue unless a bone is struck.

This nonexpanding Nyclad Chief's Special is easy to identify. The hollowpoint bullet has a pronounced semiwadcutter profile with straight ogive walls. Based on its nonexpansion or reluctant expansion tendencies, the old SWC-HP design should be used only for practice and qualifying, not carry.

This Federal .38 Special +P 125-grain Nyclad LHP worked well in a police-action shooting. It has a slightly harder core than the non+P Chief's Special load.

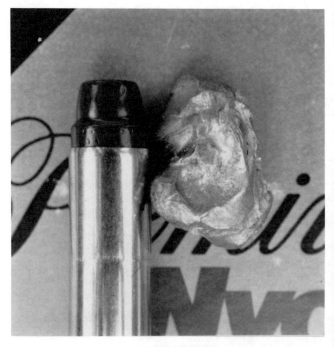

This Federal .38 Special +P 158-grain LHP was used in a holdup attempt. The Nyclad SWC-LHP has a softer lead alloy than other LHP bullets and expands readily.

To the credit of Federal Cartridge, the Nyclad Chief's Special has been redesigned. The new hollowpoint load has a gradual round-nose bullet ogive. It is no longer labeled as a SWC-HP because it no longer has a semiwadcutter profile. It is simply called an HP, but a more descriptive designation is RNL-HP. The muzzle velocity from a 2-inch S&W Model 36 Chief's Special is still 750 fps. The new round-nose loads now on the market meet the standards of performance for personal defense and antipersonnel ammo.

The 125-grain +P Nyclad SWC-HP is a reasonable alternative to the 125-grain +P JHP. Initial tests show the lead hollowpoint to open to the same recovered diameter as the jacketed hollowpoint except the lead hollowpoint opens with slightly greater reliability.

The second truly significant load in the Nyclad lineup is the N9BP 9mm. This round-nose lead hollowpoint weighs 124 grains and has a muzzle velocity of 1,100 fps from a 4-inch duty auto.

The intent of the lead hollowpoint in 9mm is clear — Federal wants to capitalize on the success of the 158-grain lead hollowpoint in .38 Special +P. The advantages of a lead hollowpoint are expansion at lower impact velocities, deeper tissue penetration, and superior performance against the intermediate targets of glass, metal, and extremities.

The 9BP has twice been changed by Federal. One was a significant change from the S&W semiwadcutter profile to the current round-nose profile. The other was a subtle change to perfect the hollowpoint cavity dimensions and bullet alloy.

Just like the .38 Special Nyclad, one should use only the round-nose 9mm load for defense. The other ammo can be used for practice. This is primarily for feed reliability reasons rather than expansion. The early S&W load expanded well in tissue when it fed. The current Federal loads will feed in full-auto weapons.

Stopping-power predictions for the Federal Nyclad 9mm will come as no surprise to the hearty advocates of the 158-grain SWC-HP in .38 Special +P. Just as the lead hollowpoint in .38 has withstood all jacketed comers, so the lead hollowpoint in 9mm is equal to and, in the authors' opinion, superior to the 115-grain JHP loads.

With the changes brought about in 1987, all the 115-grain JHP and STHP 9mm loads feed, expand, and penetrate the same or within tight range. The 115-range jacketed loads penetrate between 9.5 and 13.5 inches. The +P+ 115-grain loads penetrate between 7 and 9 inches. The Nyclad lead hollowpoint penetrates right at 12.5 inches, which is on the assured end of the ideal range.

Most 115-grain JHP loads and all +P+ 115-grain JHP loads produce relatively shallow and basketball-shaped stretch cavities peaking between 2.5 and 3 inches deep. The Nyclad 9mm produces the more moderate, football-shaped stretch cavity peaking at a full 4 inches. The volume of the Nyclad stretch cavity

This Federal 9mm 124-grain Nyclad LHP saved a female deputy sheriff in a murder attempt. It expanded and bounced off a rib before entering the heart.

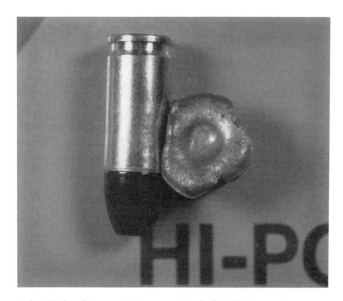

The Federal 9mm 124-grain Nyclad LHP has proven to be an effective performer in actual shootings. This one was used by a New Jersey police officer to save his partner's life.

is greater than the standard-pressure jacketed loads and second to only the +P+ loads.

The deep wound tract from the Nyclad 9mm and the .68-caliber recovered slug team up to produce the largest crush cavity of any conventional 9mm load. The Nyclad 9mm is second in crush volume only to the Glaser Safety Slug, and the Nyclad penetrates twice as deep.

Of all the changes the 9mm is undergoing, including new +P+ loads and subsonic hollowpoints, only time will tell which load will have the best street record. The Nyclad standard-pressure lead hollowpoint may prove to be one of the best, if not the best, 9mm duty load.

The most street-successful Nyclad bullet has been the 9mm 124-grain lead hollowpoint. As a total shock to those who do not trust predictions from gelatin, this Nyclad has become *more* effective than even the 115-grain JHP bullets. It ranks fifth overall in the 9mm caliber. The only 9mm loads with a better street record are the +P+ loads and the GECO Action Safety.

This makes the Nyclad the best of widely available loads. The Action Safety is hard to find. The +P+ loads generally are restricted to police use. For shooters wanting a heavy 9mm bullet, the 124-grain Nyclad is the answer.

The Nyclad has only recently been emphasized as a defensive load. As such, few people carried the load and few shooting results are available. This is especially true for the brand-new 9mm lead round-nose hollowpoint.

One shooting involving the old-style Smith & Wesson 9mm SWC-HP took place in Texas. This was the same office setting discussed earlier involving a Glaser in the chamber and rounds of various makes in the magazine. Three of those rounds were Nyclad SWC-HP rounds.

One SWC-HP entered the abdomen from a front quartering angle. The second entered the right chest nearly sideways. This bullet perforated both the right and left lungs. The exact bullet path of the third Nyclad is not available except for the fact that the bullet struck the torso.

All three Nyclad hollowpoints expanded and all three bullets remained inside the body. This compares quite favorably to the old-style Remington 115-grain JHP fired at the same time with similar bullet paths through the torso. None of the Remington loads expanded and all perforated the target.

Based on favorable gelatin tests and limited street results, the ammo in the Nyclad line seems to fully live up to expectations for both revolvers and auto pistols.

Table 11-1

SPECIALTY AMMO ACTUAL RESULTS

Caliber	Total Shootings	One-Shot Stops	Percentage
.80 Auto			
1. PPS 54-gr. BHP (MPP)	14	8	57.14
9mm			
1. GECO 86-gr. BHP (BAT)	85	70	82.35
2. Fed 124-gr. LHP-Nyclad	106	87	82.07
3. Fed 124-gr. Hydra-Shock +P+	22	18	81.81
4. Fed 124-gr. Hydra-Shok	21	16	76.19
5. Fed 147-gr. Hydra-Shok	49	35	71.42
.357 Magnum			
1. Fed 158-gr. LHP-Nyclad	11	8	72.73
.45 Auto			
1. Fed 230-gr. Hydra-Shok	43	38	88.37

CHAPTER 12

TACTICAL PENETRATION

Tactical and offensive penetration against building materials and car bodies is a two-edged sword. Just like the conflict of adequate versus excessive penetration, the opposite of good penetration against barricade materials is reduced penetration in building materials in the event of a stray shot.

Given the choice of less or more penetration, many law enforcement officers will select less penetration in the event of a missed, stray, or overpenetrating shot. This makes sense from a liability viewpoint and can still be compatible with good tactics. These officers maintain that a felon behind cover can be treated as any other barricade situation. They are reluctant to shoot into something when they cannot positively and visually identify what is behind it.

Concern over the liability associated with stray shots is well founded. The first-shot hit probability for law enforcement officers varies from 25 to 65 percent. Note that police officers are professionally trained and required to qualify with their firearms periodically. The average civilian handgun owner generally does not receive formal training nor is he required to qualify periodically. Thus, the hit probability for the average civilian is worse.

As a result, gunfights involving police officers or civilians invariably result in missed shots. Frequently, the *majority* of shots will miss the target. An incident in Illinois pitted city police officers against a runaway 4-H calf. Incredibly, the officers opened fire with their service revolvers. Not so incredibly, nearby parked cars were hit four times. The shooter is ultimately responsible and accountable for every single bullet he fires.

Occasionally, however, the shooting scenario calls for deep antibarricade penetration. Perhaps the felon is completely shielded by a door, doorframe, edgeboard, or partition made from common materials like plywood, gypsum, or hardwood. Perhaps the felon is using a car door made from sheet steel or the laminated or tempered car glass as a means of protection. One option to end the firefight at this point is to shoot through the protection to get to the felon behind it.

The term "cover" is something that can both hide the person and stop bullets. "Concealment" is something that can only hide the person but will not stop bullets. A shadow or a leafy bush can be concealment, but it is not cover.

Of course, the term cover is relative. Something that may be cover against a .380 Auto may not be against a 9mm. Something that may be cover against an exposed lead-jacketed hollowpoint may not be against a fully jacketed round-nose hardball. With the proper selection of nonexotic ammo, police *may* be able to turn cover into mere concealment. However, most common handgun loads produce quite modest levels of barricade penetration. The .38 Special will penetrate between 2 and 4 layers of half-inch plywood, for example, with most loads; the .45 Auto 4 to 6 layers. The 9mm, .357 Magnum, .41 Magnum, and .44 Magnum all produce roughly the same penetration at 5 to 7 layers.

Naturally, there are exceptions. Some steel-

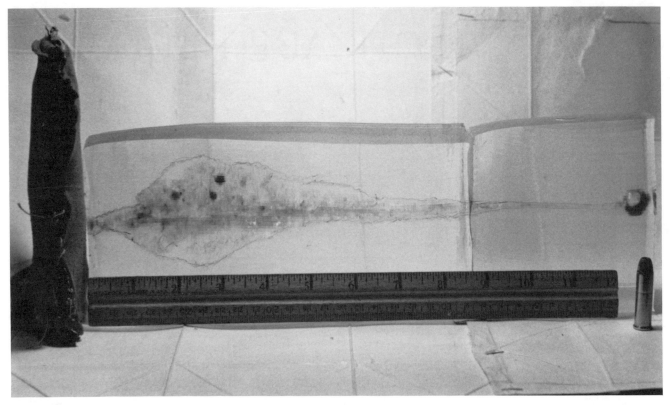

The FBI testing involved a number of tactical obstacles placed in front of the gelatin. These tough secondary targets occur in less than 20 percent of shootings, but this kind of testing is extremely valuable.

jacketed, steel-cored, or heavy copper-jacketed rounds produce significantly more penetration than common police and home-defense loads, but these generally are regulated by the Bureau of Alcohol, Tobacco, and Firearms, which has classified them as armor piercing.

While the police duty or home-defense load may penetrate a wall or door to take out an assailant, it is really a low-percentage shot. Generally, the intermediate target will decrease the bullets' wounding ability, although accidental discharges resulting in serious injuries and fatalities to innocent people in adjacent rooms prove that bullets can retain lethal power. The average penetration in building materials, however, is too little to depend on for most handgun loads to go through a door jamb, for example, and incapacitate a felon. Low expectations of tactical penetration from a handgun are in order.

Proper selection of ammo can make the most of what a caliber can offer. This starts with a basic understanding of what happens to a jacketed or lead hollowpoint bullet when it hits a hard surface. The hollowpoint cavity wall is swaged inward on itself. The lead hollowpoint becomes a reswaged lead round nose. The jacketed hollowpoint with exposed lead becomes a reswaged jacketed softpoint. The jacketed hollowpoint without exposed lead, like the Silvertip, becomes a reswaged FMJ bullet.

What the bullet becomes after impact tells how deeply it will penetrate. Fully jacketed soft-core bullets generally penetrate the deepest. Close behind and often tied are the high-antimony lead bullets. (Antimony and tin are common alloying elements that increase the hardness of the lead and increase the bullet's resistance to deformation.)

Antimony content in all lead bullets ranges from roughly 2 percent in factory swaged lead slugs up to 6 percent or higher for custom-cast lead bullets. The antimony content in the lead core of jacketed hollowpoints, jacketed softpoints, and fully jacketed ball generally is .5 percent or less.

Close behind fully jacketed bullets and antimonial lead bullets is the copper-jacketed Silvertip, as opposed to the aluminum-jacketed Silvertip. The Silvertip design has no exposed lead even in revolver bullets. The result is that the Silvertip collapses on itself to form sort of a FMJ bullet and generally penetrates deeper than JHP and JSP bullets of the same weight and impact velocity.

Jacketed hollowpoints and jacketed softpoints generally produce the least penetration. These two designs produce penetration within 5 percent of one another owing to the fact that, after impact, the hollowpoint literally becomes a softpoint.

All these differences in hard penetration can be

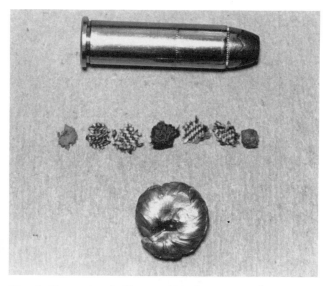

The hollowpoint bullet cavity always punches out a circle of fabric from clothing and nearly always plugs up with debris. Only calibers that expand reliably with softpoint ammo, like the .357 Magnum, will expand with a plugged hollowpoint.

traced directly to how easily the bullet is deformed on impact. Less deformation results in deeper penetration. A bullet that deforms upon impact grows in frontal area, which robs penetration energy.

This leads us to the other and quite significant factor in predicting hard penetration. Loads with greater impact energy penetrate deeper than loads with less energy, all other factors being equal. This explains why armor-piercing bullets have a hard jacket or hard core and a high velocity. Energy is velocity-dependent.

Combinations of these explanations explain why 9mm ball generally outpenetrates .45 Auto ball and why high-speed jacketed hollowpoints can outpenetrate moderate-velocity semiwadcutter loads.

The tactical area where the hangun load is really humbled is against a car. The .357 Magnum high-velocity hollowpoint has less than a fifty-fifty chance to get inside a car body. However, buckshot and even 5.56x45mm assault rifle slugs have similar problems. Veteran roadblock cops know the only reliable round for a car is a 7mm or .30-caliber rifle.

Before we discuss handgun loads versus car bodies, it is important to mention that many police officers advise against firing into a car at all. Except for some very lucky bullet placements, to quickly stop a car you must stop the driver. Except for rare circumstances, many officers are not willing to accept the liability of causing a 4,000 pound bludgeon to come to rest where it may.

The problem of shooting against car metal and car glass is twofold. In one case, the intermediate target may deflect the slug or stop it altogether. In the other,

if the slug penetrates, its wounding ability can be severely reduced.

Ammo tests against cars often are conducted by police and sheriff's departments as a part of the ammo approval process. One such car test was conducted by the Benton County, Indiana, Sheriff's Department in considering a switch from the Winchester 145-grain STHP Silvertip to the Remington 125-grain JHP in .357 Magnum.

The ten tests involved direct and angled shots through tempered glass, laminated safety glass, and car metal of all thicknesses. The Remington 125-grain STHP was successful 38 percent of the time. The slightly higher velocity of the 125-grain JHP more than made up for its exposed lead hollowpoint design. It had a slight advantage when fired through the rear windshield into the driver's seat and when fired at a 45-degree angle into the front quarter panel.

This test had two significant conclusions. First was the low overall success rate from two of the best loads in one of the most powerful law enforcement calibers in use — less than a fifty-fifty chance of success from bullets impacting between 1,300 and 1,400 fps. The second notable result was the relatively large number of shutouts, especially when impacting at an angle into metal — roughly half of the shooting scenarios where the car would be used as cover were shutouts for these magnum loads.

Going to a so-called armor-piercing round did not raise the success rate significantly. Once the slug was slightly deflected by the first layer of angled metal, defeating the second layer was rare.

A separate car penetration test involved the .357 Magnum 125-grain JHP and the .38 Special +P 158-grain SWC-HP. The four shooting scenarios were simpler, involving only door panels and glass at direct and angled shots. As a result, the success rate was higher. The 125-grain JHP Magnum was successful 100 percent of the time and the 158-grain SWC +P successful 70 percent of the time.

Although the first series of tests gave a more realistic picture, both came to the same general conclusion: the success rate against glass was considerably higher than the success rate against metal. Taking both tests together, the success rate through glass was 100 percent of the rounds fired. The success rate through metal panels was 47 percent of the rounds fired.

Significantly, the success rate through glass and metal combined was 6 percent of rounds fired. Thus, it is easy to see why Indiana State Troopers are taught to lower their side window into the door for use as cover. The glass itself can be easily defeated. Even if the bullet misses the officer, impact with the window

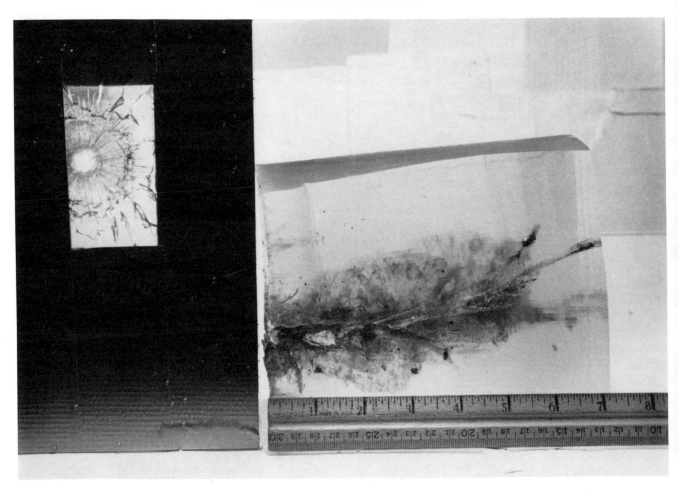

Plate, tempered, or laminated glass is extremely hard on any bullet. Glass breaks up most jacketed hollowpoints and causes them to underpenetrate, as this wound profile shows. The lead hollowpoint works best in this scenario.

can spray him or her with glass. With the glass inside the door frame, however, the door becomes nearly impossible to penetrate with the first shot.

Simply penetrating the car is hard enough, but that is only half the problem. The other is the reduced wounding ability if the bullet does manage to beat its way through. As an intermediate target, car doors and car glass take a high toll on all bullets, especially high-performance expanding loads.

Tests performed by the authors with three designs of .38 Special +P bullets in ballistic gelatin showed that bullet wounding characteristics can change dramatically after penetrating glass and metal. One test involved a piece of quarter-inch plate glass placed 4 inches ahead of a normal-size gelatin block. Another test involved two pieces of .040-inch steel placed ahead of the block.

Glass penetration actually helped the wounding performance of nonexpanding 158-grain bullets like the lead round nose and lead semiwadcutter, as well as the 130-grain fully jacketed bullet. These bullets are destabilized by the glass but generally do not lose much velocity. They begin to yaw or tumble in the air or

shortly after impact with the gelatin. The result is a larger crush cavity, a stretch cavity nearly three to four times larger, and a penetration depth in excess of 12 inches.

Impact with the metal panels also improved the performance of these nonexpanding bullets, due primarily to the fact that the lead bullets were deformed to a larger caliber prior to engaging the gelatin. These bullets did not tumble. The resulting crush cavity was significantly larger, the stretch cavity slightly larger, and the penetration depth reduced to 10 inches.

The results were mixed after firing through glass and metal with the 158-grain lead semiwadcutter hollowpoint. Compared to gelatin-only results, the crush cavity of the SWC-HP was smaller after passing through glass because the bullet was deformed slightly rather than expanded fully. The stretch cavity was larger, again due to bullet tumble.

After defeating metal, the crush cavity was slightly smaller. Since the bullet neither tumbled nor fully expanded, the stretch cavity was quite small. Penetration was again held to 10 inches.

The real toll was taken against the lightweight 95-

Table 12-1

PENETRATION IN 1/2-INCH PLYWOOD

9mm	123-gr. FMJ	8.8 layers
.357 Magnum	158-gr.-SWC	8.0 layers
.44 Magnum	180-gr. JHP	7.3 layers
12 Gauge	1 oz. Slug	7.0 layers
.41 Magnum	210-gr. JSP	6.8 layers
9mm +P+	115-gr. JHP	6.0 layers
.357 Magnum	145-gr. STHP	6.0 layers
.41 Magnum	175-gr. STHP	6.0 layers
.44 Magnum	240-gr. JHP	5.8 layers
.45 Auto	230-gr. FMJ	5.6 layers
9mm	115-gr. JHP	5.3 layers
.410 Bore	1/5 oz. slug	5.0 layers
.357 Magnum	125-gr. S-JHP	4.9 layers
9mm	115-gr. STHP	4.9 layers
.45 Auto	200-gr. JHP	4.8 layers
.45 Auto	185-gr. JHP	4.8 layers
.38 Special	158-gr. SWC	4.6 layers
9mm	124-gr. Nyclad-RN-HP	4.5 layers
.44 Magnum	233-gr. Bulleted Shot	4.5 layers
.357 Magnum	158-gr. JHP	4.3 layers
12 Gauge	00 Buck Copperplated	4.2 layers
12 Gauge	000 Buck	4.1 layers
9mm	147-gr. JHP	4.0 Layers
9mm	80-gr. Glaser RN	4.0 layers
.32 Auto	71-gr. FMJ	4.0 layers
12 Gauge	00 Buck	3.7 layers
380 Auto	95-gr. FMJ	3.6 layers
.44 Special	200-gr. SWC-HP	3.5 layers
.22 Magnum	40-gr. JHP	3.3 layers
.45 Auto	185-gr. STHP	3.3 layers
9mm	140-gr. S-JHP	3.3 layers
.38 Special +P	125-gr. JHP	3.3 layers
12 Gauge	0 Buck	3.2 layers
.38 Special +P	110-gr. S-JHP	2.8 layers
12 Gauge	1 Buck	2.8 layers
.25 Auto	50-gr. FMJ	2.7 layers
.45 Auto	135-gr. Glaser RN	2.6 layers
.38 Special +P	158-gr. SWC-HP	2.6 layers
.357 Magnum	110-gr. S-JHP	2.5 layers
.44 Special	200-gr. STHP	2.5 layers
.22 Long Rifle	Yellow Jacket	2.4 layers
12 Gauge	4 Buck	2.3 layers
.32 Auto	60-gr. STHP	2.0 layers
.22 Long Rifle	Stinger	1.9 layers
380 Auto	85-gr. STHP	1.8 layers
12 Gauge	7 1/2 Birdshot	1.0 layer
.410 Bore	7 1/2 Birdshot	1.0 layer

grain jacketed hollowpoint. Compared to gelatin-only results, the crush cavity after glass was significantly less due to less overall penetration. The light, fast bullet still expanded to .60 caliber in the gelatin but penetrated 6.5 inches versus the 9.5 inches in gelatin only. The stretch cavity was cut in half to about the size of the lead SWC-HP after glass.

After metal, the JHP produced similar results. There was a smaller crush cavity than in gelatin only due to the bullet being deformed in the metal and then not expanding in the gelatin. As a result, the bullet actually produced a deeper wound track. The stretch cavity was again significantly reduced; however, it was larger than either the SWC or SWC-HP after defeating metal.

As a summary of bullets versus cars, either tempered or laminated glass is significantly easier to penetrate than car metal. Depending on the caliber, load, angle of impact, and part of the car in question, defeating car metal averages to a fifty-fifty proposition.

Once by the glass, the bullet can produce a stretch cavity measuring half the size or three times the size, depending on the bullet. Once by metal, the stretch cavity is generally less than half the size of the gelatin-only figures.

After glass, the bullet can be expected to produce between half and two-thirds of the permanent crush cavity and more than three-quarters of the original penetration. After metal, the bullet can be expected to produce between two-thirds and three-quarters of the crush cavity and two-thirds to three-quarters of the original penetration.

After factoring the probability of defeating the car with the wound potential after car entry, these figures strongly suggest that aiming for glass holds the most promise in this difficult and ill-advised scenario.

Table 12-2

TACTICAL PENETRATION

Obstacle	.357 MAGNUM	
	Remington 125-grain S-JHP	Winchester 145-grain STHP
1/2-inch plywood	4.9 layers	6.0 layers
1/2-inch Sheetrock	6.5 layers	8.5 layers
Olds Delta 88, average	48 percent	38 percent
through windshield	4 of 4	4 of 4
hood ricochet through windshield	0 of 5	0 of 5
45 degree through glass	2 of 2	2 of 2
through glass through driver seat	1 of 3	0 of 3
through driver door	2 of 3	3 of 3
45 degree through door	5 of 8	5 of 8
45 degree front panel	6 of 9	2 of 9
45 degree rear panel	0 of 6	0 of 6
hood ricochet through fender	0 of 1	0 of 1
through steel rim	0 of 1	0 of 1

CHAPTER 13

POINT OF AIM

The classic center-of-mass hold has been taught to maximize the chance of hitting *something*. Center of mass, or the center of the torso, is right below the rib cage. The diaphragm lies as close to the visual center as anything. This is where the X ring on the B-27 police PPC target lies.

Hit distribution around this point has a better chance of engaging tissue than any other point of aim. This is important, because the average police first-shot hit probability varies between 25 and 65 percent.

As gunfight results become more documented, police training has become more sophisticated. Basic and fundamental changes have been recommended to a center-of-mass point of aim. Now there are two other worthy, optional, scenario-dependent points of aim.

We have tried to emphasize throughout this book that it is not hitting *something* that is important. It is hitting something *important* that is important. Each of these three holds focuses on something important as the point of aim.

The new general-duty hold, as recommended by the NIJ as far back as 1973, is the so-called armpit hold. The vital organ directly in line with the sights is the heart. On a frontal shot, this point of aim is 6 to 8 inches higher than the center-of-mass hold.

The significance of this hold is the vital organs in line with the sights and within a hit-distribution pattern around the heart. On the classic center-of-mass hold, the bullet penetrates the diaphragm. Shots that go 6 to 8 inches high can strike the heart, lungs, liver, spleen, and spine. Shots that go 6 to 8 inches low hit only the intestines, with a remote possibility of kidneys, major vessels, and the spine. Half of the time, the relatively insignificant intestinal organs will be struck.

The new armpit hold centers around more significant organs. With this hold the bullet strikes the heart. Shots that go 6 to 8 inches high can strike the lungs, pulmonary arteries and veins, spine, and the neck. Shots that go 6 to 8 inches low strike the spleen, liver, kidneys, major descending vessels, and the spine.

The chance of a miss to the left and right side of the head is greater with the armpit hold. However, the chance of striking a vital vascular organ is also higher. Stopping power lies in the significance of what the bullet actually hits. The armpit hold is more likely than the center-of-mass hold to strike significant tissue.

Changing to the armpit hold can increase your effective stopping power without any change in gun or ammo. The NIJ estimates that the armpit hold is fully 36 percent more effective than the center-of-mass hold based on the tissue that lies in the probable strike zone.

Not only does raising the aim point from center of mass to armpit level increase the likelihood of connecting with more significant organs and vessels, it also raises the likelihood of connecting with bone. Indeed the odds of engaging some kind of bone in the upper torso is fifty-fifty. On a perfectly placed shot, the bullet strikes mid-sternum. (This carries the slight chance of ricocheting the bullet around the rib cage, especially with angular impacts with subcaliber bullets like the

.22 LR, .25 Auto, and .32 Auto.)

The more blunt or collapsible the bullet profile, the more likely the bullet will penetrate bone rather than ricochet. Assuming a mid-thorax bullet placement, it will probably hurt the terminal effectiveness if the bullet does not continue along a relatively straight line. It will definitely reduce the effectiveness if the bullet strikes the ribs and "round-noses" around the chest cavity and out the back. Round-nose ammo should be avoided for this reason.

More likely than ricochet, bullet meeting bone produces two favorable results. One, striking bone greatly assists softpoints and heavy hollowpoints in expansion. Two, pieces of the bone can be blown into the heart and lung as secondary missiles. These sharp, bony pieces may get caught in the surrounding tissue and not do much damage. On the other hand, they may cut or puncture something significant and do a considerable amount of damage on par with the bullet itself.

Blunter and expanding bullets are more likely to generate bone fragments than rounder bullets. Faster bullets in the 1,100-to-1,400-fps range are more likely to generate bone fragments than slower bullets in the 700-to-900-fps range. Further, the faster the incoming bullet, the greater the velocity of the secondary missile fragments. Bone fragments are sharp and hard and have the potential to do a lot of area damage to tendons, nerves, blood vessels, and organs. But because they are light in weight, they lose velocity rapidly. Naturally the higher the velocity these fragments start out with, the deeper the penetration they will achieve.

The higher aim point is especially helpful when you are shooting with lower-power calibers. Small-caliber or low-power rounds that do not penetrate as deeply will benefit from the high aim point. The significant vessels and tissue are closer to the front of the body at the high aim point than they are at the low aim point, and low-power ammo has a better chance of connecting here.

The rapidly expanding hollowpoints in all calibers will also benefit from the high aim point. Bullet styles like the high-velocity, lightweight jacketed hollowpoint or Glaser Safety Slug dump their energy and destructiveness early. They do not cause as much damage at greater depths of penetration as other bullet styles like the deeper-penetrating semiwadcutter and heavy hollowpoint. This early destructiveness is better suited higher up, where the vital organs and vessels are closer to the surface on a frontal shot.

This general-purpose point-of-aim recommendation for police and civilian handgunners is exactly the same location taught to military snipers. Perfect bullet placement is anywhere inside a triangle formed by the base

of the neck and the two nipples. This kind of shot placement is the essence of handgun stopping power.

As we have discussed, even a direct shot to the heart that cuts off all blood pressure can take 10 to 12 seconds to produce unconsciousness. If the attacker can close the distance between you in that time, you are still in danger, especially if the attacker is using an impact weapon like a knife, club, or martial arts piece.

An optional point of aim for an impact-weapon scenario is on the centerline just below the belt. The vital targets in this case are the bones in the entire pelvic girdle. We want the bullet to fracture the right or left coxal or pelvic bones, the right or left femur, the sacrum, or any of the vertebrae in the lumbar or sacral region of the spine. This generally will cause mechanical collapse or mechanical dysfunction. To be effective, however, the bullet needs to penetrate further and retain more weight with this point of aim than the other two.

This pelvic point of aim has other advantages, depending on the scenario. One is sheer intimidation. Felons who are likely to laugh at an officer who points his gun at them are going to take special notice when the gun is pointed at their groin. They know you wouldn't shoot them in the chest but are not sure you won't shoot them in the perceived less lethal groin, an obvious misunderstanding of the laws concerning lethal force.

The pelvic hold has an advantage over all other points of aim in visibility. The officer has a much better field of vision, which includes the suspect's hands and waistband. These are the problem areas, not the suspect's eyes.

A final advantage is against felons suspected of wearing soft body armor, especially compared to the head hold alternative (discussed later). You probably will not discover the presence of a vest until you have fired your first shots. If armpit shots are ineffective, one should immediately trigger pelvic shots, which is an area seldom covered with soft armor.

The primary advantage of the pelvic hold lies in how slowly even well-placed torso shots take effect. Keep in mind, few bullets stop the blood pressure immediately to start the 10-second countdown. Many fatal gunshot wounds will allow the suspect to continue aggressive action for 90 seconds and longer. An officer facing a large suspect or multiple suspects is still in danger of being disarmed. The pelvic hold that "knocks down" a suspect, therefore, can be a viable option.

The other optional point of aim to use, depending on the scenario, is the head hold. This is a low-percentage shot that is very difficult to achieve. Therefore, it is the hold with the narrowest scope of use.

The term cranial *vault* should be remembered. The head is round, thick, and armored. It also is small, the most instinctively protected part of the body, and the farthest from the center of gravity, allowing it to duck and bob with great speed. Further, only a small portion of the head houses the brain and, as discussed, only a small portion of the brain gives instant results with lower-power bullets.

The advantage of the head hold is incapacitation at well under 1 second if correct placement is achieved. This hold is well suited for a hostile and hostage situation. The hostile must be given no time at all to use a knife, fire a gun, or trip a device.

The success of the head hold with most handgun loads depends on the bullet striking the brain stem. Again, the brain stem lies on a plane formed by the nose and the two ear canals. Handgun loads that do not produce significant temporary stretch cavities must be on this mark. Note that the point of aim in the head hold is not the forehead nor between the eyes. The hold producing the quickest, sometimes twinge-free result, is centered on the nose-ear plane.

Of all the action and color targets that have recently come about, one target graphically illustrates these different holds. Called the Anatomy Target, it shows the relative effects of each bullet placement. At the very minimum, it reinforces the rules of stopping power by showing the exact importance of the impact point. The purpose of shooting is amended to not just hitting but hitting something important.

By now, you should see that the search for the magic bullet and the best high-capacity handgun should be secondary to the search for effective marksmanship. Police first-shot hit probability varies from 25 to 65 percent on the average. Civilian figures are worse, as they are not required to practice or qualify. Historically, handgunners miss a lot. But even if they hit, as we have repeatedly indicated, some hits don't count at all while others take a dangerously long time to take effect. Hitting often is not enough.

Firepower and magic bullets are not the answer to stopping power. A hit with a special really is better than a miss with a magnum. One hit from a .357 is better than thirteen misses with a 9mm. And ultimately, a master with a .38 will defeat a novice with a .44.

Police and civilian handgunners will make more gains in stopping power from realistic practice than from the wickedest handgun load available. Practice against crouched or angled targets, moving and bobbing targets, multiple close-range targets, targets in low light, and partly covered targets.

Practice hitting not just the head but the nose, and not just the upper torso but the sniper triangle. Speed will come with practice.

The IPSC symbols of DVC (from the Latin: *diligentia*, meaning accuracy, *vis*, meaning power, and *celeritas*, meaning speed) should be prioritized into 1) *accuracy*, which comes from training; 2) *speed*, which comes from practice; and 3) *power*, over which you may have no control whatsoever.

The final piece of advice is to shoot high or low, depending on the situation, but break the habit of shooting center. Above all, remember that the purpose of shooting is hitting something important.

The theme of this book, and the essence of stopping power, has been captured by syndicated cartoonist Gary Larson in his comic, *The Far Side*. Two cavemen with bows and arrows are standing beside a gigantic fallen elephant with its legs straight up in the air. A single arrow, quite insignificant in size compared to the elephant, is stuck in the beast's side. Seeing the remarkable success of the little arrow, one caveman says to the other, "We should write that spot down." With this book we have tried to help you "write that spot down" in load selection, mental expectation, and point of aim.

TISSUE SIMULANTS

The best indication of future bullet performance comes from actual shooting results under varying conditions against people of varying physical sizes and mental states. However, actual shooting results in statistically valid quantities are extremely hard to come by even for law enforcement agencies. The network of communication is not very well developed between agencies and is sometimes even restricted. Ammo effectiveness gathered from clandestine operations by cloak-and-dagger organizations almost never filters down to local police or sheriff's departments.

Law enforcement agencies can be reluctant to release detailed results from actual shootings in their jurisdictions due to open court cases and other confidentiality reasons, including the privacy policies of the administration, prosecutors, and even defense attorneys. Ammo companies can be reluctant to release street results with their ammo for fear of sounding morbid or inviting lawsuits claiming excessive suffering. Further, they won't want to advertise failures to stop, whether their ammo was at fault or not. Neither will they want to release the fact that their ammo performs only the same and not better than their competition.

To make matters worse, all shooting results are anomalies, or single cases, unique to themselves. The data is strictly anecdotal. As such they blatantly defy a direct comparison to one another. Each case is filled with variables almost beyond number. Some of these variables are real. Some are only perceived.

The real, fact-based variables include but are not limited to the victim's state of mind, the presence of alcohol or other behavior-modifying chemicals such as PCP, and the physical size and stamina of the victim. Other variables include the barrel length and bullet-impact velocity, the generation and condition of ammo used, and the presence of obstacles that the bullet passed through to reach the intended target.

The largest variable in any gunfight is the exact path the bullet takes from entry until exit and the *exact* tissue the bullet engages. Two bullet paths can be identical from entry to exit. If one happens to nick something like a major artery or chip a bone in the spine, the results can be wildly different, even if the rest of the scenario is identical.

Variables in perception also exist. What appears to be real is not. Widely documented is the fact that a shooter can lose perspective of time and distance when under the stress of using lethal force. Things almost always appear larger and closer than they actually are. They also almost always appear to happen slower than they actually occur.

The shooter may recall that he emptied his gun and the guy stood unaffected for 5 to 10 seconds or that he kept coming before he finally fell. It could have happened exactly that way, or the victim could have collapsed to the ground as fast as gravity could pull him. It just seemed like the bullets took forever to produce that result.

The latter case was what actually happened in an East Coast report of ineffectiveness concerning the .357 Magnum 125-grain JHP. Officers struck the felon

These Federal .38 Special +P 125-grain Nyclads were recovered from small intestines (left), gelatin (center), and the heart after the lungs (right).

These Federal 9mm 115-grain JHP bullets were recovered from intestines (left), gelatin (center), and the lung cavity (right).

multiple times but felt the load took too long to be effective. A press camera that caught the whole incident in real time told a different story — the man was doubled over on the ground in under 3 seconds.

The most critical piece of information in the field of wound ballistics is how long the victim was able to continue hostile action. Since an error factor of 5 seconds is a large error for the time frame we are interested in, it is safe to conclude that in the majority of cases we will never reliably know how long the bullet took to have an effect. All of these variables point to the need for a large collection of shooting results.

Shooting results also are not available for many calibers. Results may be available for the .38 Special +P 158-grain SWC-HP, 9mm 115-grain STHP, and .357 Magnum 125-grain JHP because they are common police issue loads. Not so common are results from the .38 Special +P 140-grain JHP, 9mm 125-grain JSP, and .357 Magnum 158-grain SWC. These are the same calibers and familiar loads, but they have a much shorter shooting history. It is even harder to find results in less popular calibers, less popular loads, and specialty loads.

While shooting results are the ultimate prediction of a bullet's future performance, all the previously discussed problems point to the need for an artificial test medium to give preliminary results. The more relevant the test medium, the better the prediction. The more pragmatic the interpretation of results, the better the prediction.

A tissue simulant is needed to give the police officer

The Federal .38 Special +P 158-grain Nyclad LHP on the left is from ordnance gelatin. The 158-grain Nyclad LHP on the right stopped a knife attack on a police officer.

or civilian some idea of what to expect *before* that person uses the load to defend his life and the lives of others. Further, simulant allows for ammo advancements and improvements. If a large data base of actual shooting results were absolutely required before adoption of a new load, we would all still be using round-nose lead bullets. (No offense to those who still use them.) The ultimate reason for using a tissue simulant, however, is to evaluate bullet performance *independent* of the shooting scenario's largest variable: bullet placement or bullet path.

Since the test medium will help predict bullet performance in a life-and-death encounter, the selection of *what* to shoot is absolutely critical. Some simulants give extremely misleading results. Some give good relative results but poor correlation to reality. Some give good results only in certain parameters. Some, however, provide meaningful and relevant information and

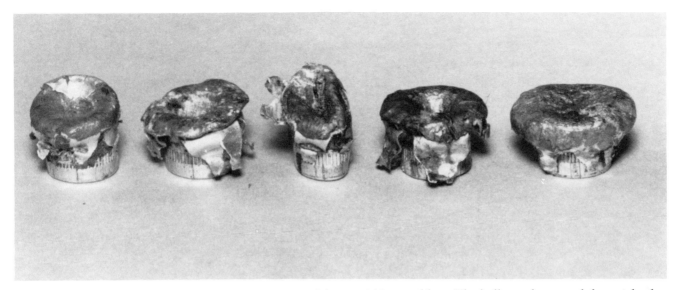

These Winchester .380 Auto Silvertips were recovered from a 140-pound hog. The bullet paths were, left to right, leg muscle, intestines, liver, lungs, and skull.

do indeed allow us to accurately predict wounding.

The best kind of test medium is a living one. Except for the cloak-and-dagger types who don't stick around for the autopsy anyway, living people are out of the question. Like police reports, reports from the military fall under the anomaly problem, yet they include even fewer loads and fewer calibers.

Living animals, especially hogs, are socially acceptable test mediums in some countries outside the United States. There was a time when tests on living pigs, cattle, sheep, and even cats were acceptable in the U.S. as long as the tests were agency conducted. Those days are gone or at least well hidden from the public.

The test medium of today's professionals in law enforcement, the ammo industry, and even the military is ballistic or ordnance gelatin. Yet many other mediums have been and continue to be used to predict effectiveness.

Although their use is limited, one of the oldest test mediums is human cadavers. More prevalent than the use of entire cadavers, as was done in the early 1900s, is the use of excised sections. Examples are the use of lower extremities, some organs and vessels due to their entry and exit significance, and layers of skin.

Unfortunately, these do not give the kind of real-world results one first may think. With a lower fluid content, excised extremities quickly lose the elasticity of living tissue. This applies to vascular tissue like arteries and veins as well. Living tissue yields and stretches, often without damage. Dead tissue tears and ruptures with the same degree of bullet contact.

The same correlation problems exist when using packaged meat as a test medium. The bullet can be deformed to a greater extent and penetrate to a lesser extent due to the greater density and lower elasticity of meat compared to living muscle tissue. Soaking meat in hot water does not improve its correlation with living tissue significantly, as meat is not hygroscopic and does not absorb water readily and thoroughly.

Evidence of significant correlation problems between living human beings and dead human cadavers has been professionally noted. According to outside sources, the recent body armor test conducted by H.P. White Labs included the use of cadavers. One of the findings was that the cadavers showed different internal damage from backface blunt trauma than is seen in actual shooting victims wearing vests.

The dissimilarity between living tissue and excised tissue or cadavers has also been observed by thoracic surgeons, among other physicians. Arteries and veins as living tissue, for example, are extremely elastic and rubbery. They can be stretched by the temporary cavity and generally escape damage. They can be pushed aside by round-nose, blunt-nose, and expanded hollowpoints short of a direct strike. Once excised, however, these vessels become unrealistically vulnerable. They tear and break open when as living tissue they often would not. They lose the elastic nature that allows the bullet to merely push them aside.

The lungs, no longer air-filled, sustain slightly more crush damage in cadavers than in living beings. The spleen and kidneys, once fluid-filled, sustain slightly less damage. Overall, with the density and elasticity of living tissue so different from nonliving tissue, the correlation of bullet expansion, total penetration, and crush and stretch cavities is too poor to be of legitimate use.

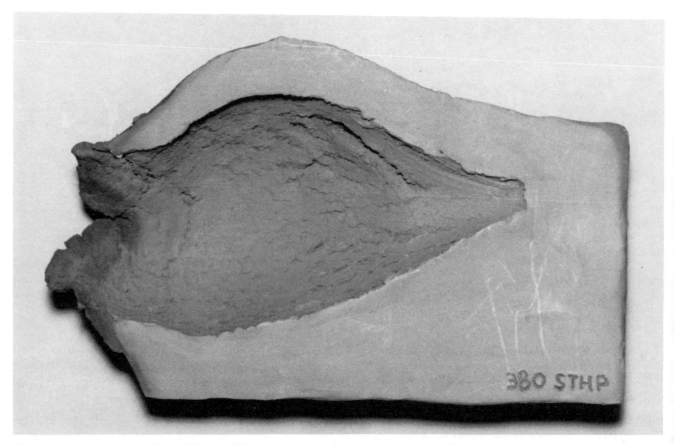

This is the stretch cavity formed by the Winchester .380 Auto Silvertip in modeling clay. The volume of the cavity is incorrect by three times, penetration depth is too shallow, and bullet expansion is far too much compared with living tissue.

Excised tissue and cadavers are as different from living tissue as all the other artificial and nonliving test mediums and should be so considered. Some artificial test mediums are significantly easier to obtain and, in some cases, can provide more information on bullet impact characteristics than even living tissue.

To evaluate and compare various kinds of artificial mediums, we fired the .380 Auto 85-grain STHP Silvertip into the five popular choices: water, soaked newspaper, electrical Ductseal, modeling clay, and ordnance gelatin. Silvertip bullets were also fired into a 140-pound hog within one minute of death in five locations to compare artificial test mediums with living soft tissue of five different densities and elasticities.

All of the .380 Auto STHP Silvertip ammo was from the same lot. The impact velocity in all cases was 885 fps.

The .380 Auto Silvertip was chosen for two reasons. This load always expands in gelatin between .51 to .63 caliber, and it produces the depth of penetration that is likely to stay inside an animal of those dimensions. A more powerful load would perforate the target and not allow a depth-of-penetration correlation.

The expansion of the bullets in the hog depended on the exact bullet path. The permanent crush cavities

were calculated, while the temporary stretch cavities were not. The degree of stretch and the real damage caused by the stretch depended on the density and elasticity of the exact tissue engaged.

Temporary stretch cavity changes in diameter and shape as it passes from one kind of tissue to another. This is the reason stretch cavities can only be compared accurately in uniform test mediums, even though the technology exists to trace the cavity as it progresses through living soft tissue.

The overall depth of penetration in the hog was measured, but these are relatively misleading figures. Most bullets were recovered under the skin on the far side of the animal due to the elastic nature of the skin. Some were just under the skin while others had just begun to engage the skin layers. The ability to penetrate skin layers on the far side can translate into many inches of penetration in soft organ tissue.

The primary significance of the hog was to provide recovered bullets that had passed through tissue of different densities. We can compare these recovered diameters of these bullets to bullets from an artificial medium but would not be able to compare wound cavities.

The first Silvertip entered the skull from the side

The Winchester .380 Auto Silvertip recovered from a variety of common bullet test materials. These are, from left to right, 10-percent gelatin, water, wet newspaper, modeling clay, and Ductseal.

at a location where the hog skull and a mature human skull are roughly the same thickness. The slug produced roughly a .75-caliber entrance hole, with cracks radiating out from the hole measuring a diameter of 1.5 inches. The slug expanded to .60 caliber and did not exit.

The second Silvertip entered from the side of the hog. It engaged the near-side ribs, shattering one, and perforated the near-side lung, missed the heart, and perforated the far-side lung. The Silvertip then perforated the far-side ribs without engaging bone and came to rest under the skin on the far side. This path represents the twin extremes of elastic lungs and dense bone, although the bone was fairly thin. The Silvertip expanded to .54 caliber and penetrated between 9.5 and 11.5 inches.

The third Silvertip engaged the near ribs, perforated the liver, and engaged a rib bone on the far side. The bullet was recovered base forward under the far-side skin. It apparently had either been deflected by the near ribs or tumbled in transition from one kind of soft tissue to another. The slug hit the far-side ribs going sideways, which somewhat flattened its expansion. The recovered slug measured .54 caliber and penetrated 9 inches. The diameter of the cracks generated in the liver measured 1.5 inches.

The fourth Silvertip engaged the intestines only. The bullet expanded to .54 caliber and penetrated 10 inches of tissue.

The fifth Silvertip engaged the skin and muscle in both hind legs while avoiding the leg bones. The combined muscle thickness at the point of entry was 6 inches. The Silvertip expanded to .44 caliber and perforated the muscle tissue in both legs. The bullet

was recovered but a penetration depth was not obtained. This can be resolved by placing a gelatin block on the far side of the far leg, but we wanted to isolate the bullet's expansion in muscle from any additional expansion that might occur in gelatin.

These five different bullet paths and tissue resistances provide a reasonable picture of the expansion and penetration of the .380 Auto Silvertip in living tissue. From the data available, the Silvertip expanded to an average of .53 caliber and penetrated an average of 9.8 inches. This figures to an average crush cavity of 2.16 cubic inches (see Table 14-1).

We were now able to evaluate various artificial test mediums to see how they compared to this standard.

The first artificial medium is electrical Ductseal, in this case made by Blackburn. This sticky putty-like compound is available from wholesale electrical supply houses. The Ductseal used in this evaluation was asbestos-free. The block temperature at bullet impact was 65°F.

The Silvertip penetrated 1.25 inches, which is significantly different from the hog average of 9.8 inches. The bullet did not expand as such. Instead, the hollow-point cavity collapsed inward on itself just as it would if it had impacted a hard surface such as plywood or gypsum. The bullet was then swaged backward and deformed outward.

The recovered bullet measured .58 caliber. This diameter was not achieved by classic expansion from internal cavity pressure. Visually, the bullet was markedly different from the bullets recovered from tissue, gelatin, and water. It was deformed in a manner similar to being struck on the nose with a concave mallet. Experience with other loads in Ductseal have produced

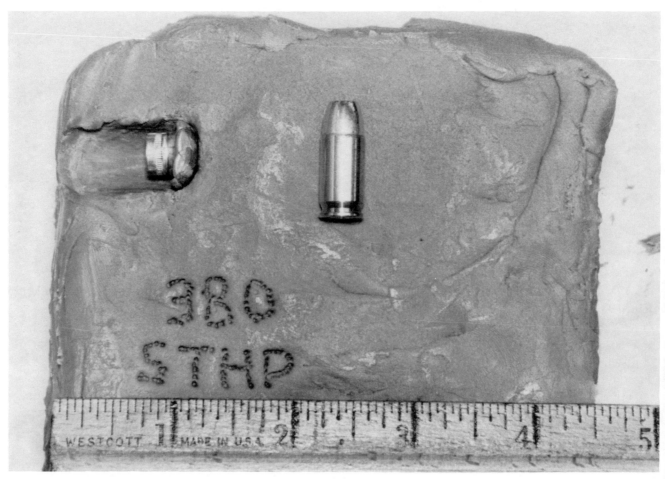

Ductseal is one of the worst mediums in which to test bullet performance. This penetration of 1.5 inches is meaningless compared to an average of 9.8 inches in living tissue.

equally misleading results.

The use of Ductseal is especially invalid in predicting whether or not a bullet will expand in tissue. Again, while the recovered diameter from Ductseal may be dimensionally similar to bullets from tissue, that diameter was achieved by deformation rather than expansion. The medium is well noted for increasing the diameter of bullets that will not expand in tissue. Equally misleading, it will actually limit the expansion of bullets that do expand reliably in tissue.

In addition to an extremely short crush cavity and a totally different effect on the bullet, the use of Ductseal suppresses the formation of a stretch cavity. Plainly, the bullet did not produce a stretch cavity in Ductseal. As such, one of the important parameters of bullet effectiveness is not available.

Overall, Ductseal is an extremely poor test medium on which to base bullet performance. The crush and stretch cavities in Ductseal are entirely unrepresentative of that produced in soft tissue. Bullets recovered from Ductseal generally bear no resemblance whatsoever to bullets recovered from live tissue.

The second artificial medium is artist's modeling clay. Although clay comes moisture sealed in blocks ready to be formed, the moisture content and texture of all clay vary widely. The block used in the test, labeled Mexican pottery clay, had a temperature of 65°F.

Upon impact, the Silvertip expanded outward and backward so far that the slightly hollowbased core resulted in a hole in the center of the recovered bullet. The recovered diameter was .76 inch. This kind of expansion was not evident even when the Silvertip struck the hog skull and bone, which always assist expansion. The penetration distance measured 5.6 inches. Again, this is significantly different from the average penetration of 9.8 inches in the hog.

The underpenetration and overexpansion team up to produce a stretch cavity that is close to that of 10 percent gelatin, 2.54 cubic inches versus 2.11 cubic inches. However, the penetration depth and recovered diameter are so unrealistic as to make this figure invalid.

The popularity of modeling clay can be directly

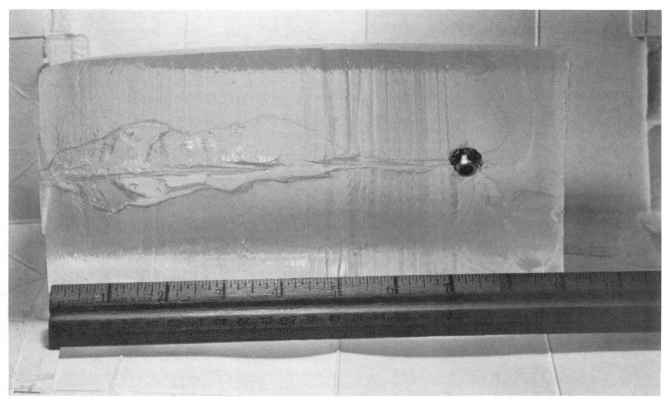

This is the wound profile made by the Winchester .380 Auto Silvertip in 10-percent ordnance gelatin. Dr. Martin Fackler developed this gelatin ration, which is the closest match for living tissue. He also validated the "2-radius" method of estimating the size of the actual temporary stretch cavity.

The hollowpoint bullet does not react the same way at all in Ductseal as it does in gelatin and tissue. The Federal .45 Auto Hydra-Shok on the left was fired into gelatin, while the same load on the right was fired into Ductseal.

traced to magazine editors who insist on splashy photos, often to the exclusion of content validity. Modeling clay is extremely photogenic to the point of being on the cover of the 1987 *Federal Law Enforcement Ammunition* catalog. Some people who use gelatin or water validly to test expansion cannot resist the temptation to use modeling clay invalidly to illustrate the effects on the target.

Modeling clay is shoved outward in the wake of the passing bullet just like tissue. A genuine temporary stretch cavity is formed in the clay. The clay has absolutely no elasticity, so the maximum diameter and the shape of the temporary cavity are permanently formed in modeling clay.

The photo of the sectioned block shows a strong resemblance to the temporary stretch cavity formed in tissue and gelatin, which is available only with expensive photographic techniques. The shape of the cavity and the depth of the maximum diameter are reasonably accurate reproductions of the stretch cavity formed in tissue.

One very significant component of modeling clay, however, is not at all realistic — the scale or real dimensions are grossly exaggerated. The diameter of the stretch cavity at any given depth is fully two to five times that of reality. (An inch-by-inch measurement of the stretch cavity formed in 10-percent gelatin, modeling clay, and soaking newspaper is in Table 14-2.) As a result, the volume of the cavity is incorrect by geometric proportions. The stretch cavity formed in modeling clay by the .380 Auto Silvertip is 2.75 times greater than the cavity formed by the same bullet in gelatin.

Modeling clay does provide a visual picture of one component of bullet performance that is not easily attainable in any other test medium. It captures, in a tangible and stop-action way, a segment of bullet and tissue interaction that only exists in reality for less than a half second.

Overall, however, oil- and water-based clay is still a poor test medium on which to base bullet performance. The recovered bullets are greatly overexpanded, bearing no resemblance to reality. The stretch cavity is also greatly overstated, giving the misleading impression of the volume of tissue affected. The depth of the permanent cavity is greatly undersized compared to reality.

The result is a patently simplistic and naive impression of wounding power, one that leads us to expect great bullet expansion and awesome effect on the target. With modeling clay, a thousand words are far superior to the misleading picture. Its use is a clear mark of a ballistics amateur or one intent on deception.

The third artificial test medium is soaking newspaper. This also includes water-soaked phone books, corrugated cardboard, and other paper products.

The important part of this test medium is not the exact paper product in use. It is that the paper product must be uniform and hygroscopic, as some paper is neither. Soaking the paper in warm water for 4 to 6 hours assures even moisture absorption. This avoids misleading results when the outer portion of the medium is wet while the inner portion is only damp or even dry.

Dry paper is extremely difficult to penetrate. It collapses hollowpoint cavities inward and deforms all types of bullets as if the bullet had struck a hard substance like plywood. The use of corrugated cardboard with hollow flutes allows a total wetting and provides a higher water-to-paper ratio than any other medium in this category.

Higher water-to-paper ratios give more realistic expansion results. The paper medium should be shot in an absolutely soaking condition. If pulled from a container, it should be shot with water still flowing off the paper.

The average expansion of the Silvertip bullet in soaking newspaper is .54 inch. The average expansion in the hog was .53 inch, with a range of .44 to .60 inch. When thoroughly wet, paper products give realistic expansion results.

The total penetration in the soaking newspaper was 7 inches. This is still quite a bit short of the 9.4-inch average for the hog, yet much closer than the more popular modeling clay and Ductseal. The permanent crush cavity volume for the Silvertip bullet in wet paper is 1.60 cubic inches. This again is shy of the 2.16-cubic-inch cavity in the hog.

The diameter of the stretch cavity in wet paper by 1-inch increments is shown in Table 14-2. Compared to gelatin, the maximum diameter of the stretch cavity is 1 inch deeper and only 55 percent of the diameter. The reduced diameter of the stretch cavity is evident at every depth. As a result, the volume of the stretch cavity in wet paper is only one third that of the stretch cavity in gelatin.

Overall, soaking paper products give a reasonable idea of bullet expansion. Neither the stretch nor the crush cavity correlates well with reality in either depth or diameter. However, if the person strictly is looking for whether or not the bullet will expand and the degree of expansion when properly used, soaking paper gives reasonably valid results.

The fourth artificial medium used to simulate tissue and test bullet performance is water. Water is noted for its simplicity, convenience, and economy. There

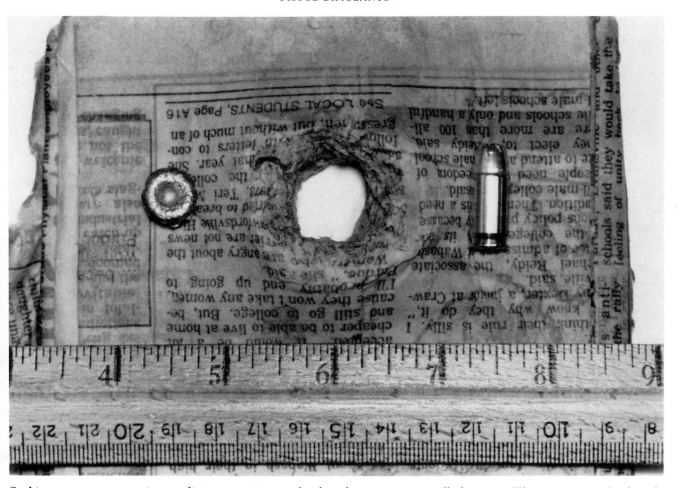

Soaking wet newspaper gives realistic expansion results, but the paper must really be soggy. The penetration depth and size of the wound cavity are *not* realistic

are no involved mixing and storage directions as with gelatin, and none of the inconsistencies found with modeling clay of different densities and moisture content or paper with varying degrees of water saturation. No sectioning or detailed analysis of medium is required, and there is no expense in medium or medium evaluation equipment.

The .380 Auto Silvertip expanded to .56 inch in water. Like expansion in wet paper, expansion in water gives excellent correlation with expansion in living soft tissue. Even the larger agencies that use sophisticated gelatin techniques frequently use plain water as a double check of the results.

In simple and direct terms, if the bullet expands in water it will expand to some degree no matter what living tissue is involved. If the bullet does not expand in water, the bullet will need to strike bone to expand to any significant degree.

The depth of penetration in water can be obtained by firing the bullet into water with calibrated baffles or by firing into small containers of water lined up behind one another. In the latter case, the containers should be easy to penetrate, such as paper milk cartons.

Regardless of the technique, the depth of penetration will only be an estimate at best.

Using partitioned paper containers, the Silvertip bullet penetrated between 11 and 13 inches of water. This is somewhat deeper than the average penetration of 9.8 inches in the hog but quite close to the depth of penetration when the bullet path was through the ribs and lungs. As such, water gives a good indication of the deepest penetration likely in a torso shot.

Since the penetration distance in water is longer than the average distance in the hog and the recovered bullet is slightly larger than the hog average, the crush cavity volume in water is overstated.

A temporary stretch cavity is not easily attainable nor measurable with water. Sophisticated photography can catch the stretch cavity, but it is grossly overstated. What most people will observe is the degree of splash. This obviously is subjective and not very meaningful.

Overall, water as a test medium gives excellent results on the probability and degree of expansion. It gives very good results in predicting penetration through some kinds of tissue, specifically lungs. It is a poor medium when the shape and diameter of the

Table 14-1

.380 AUTO SILVERTIP

Permanent Crush Cavity

	Total Penetration	Recovered Diameter	Total Volume
20% 50°F gelatin	5.8 inches	.60 inches	1.64 inches^3
10% 39°F gelatin	8 inches	.58 inches	2.11 inches^3
Modeling clay at 65°F	5.6 inches	.76 inches	2.54 inches^3
Soaking wet newspaper at 65°F	7 inches	.54 inches	1.6 inches^3
Ductseal at 65°F	1.25 inches	.58 inches *	.33 inches^3
Water at 65°F	11-13 inches	.56 inches	2.96 inches^3

140-pound domestic hog

a) skin and intestines	10 inches	.54 inches	2.29 inches^3
b) skin and hind leg muscles	6+ inches **	.44 inches	NA
c) skull and brain	NA	.60 inches	NA
d) ribs, liver, and ribs	9 inches	.54 inches	2.06 inches^3
e) ribs, lungs, and ribs	9 1/2-11 1/2 inches	.54 inches	2.40 inches^3

* The Silvertip hollowpoint cavity collapsed inward on itself then deformed outward as opposed to expanded upon impact. See the text.
**The bullet performated both hind legs.

Table 14-2

.380 AUTO SILVERTIP

Temporary Stretch Cavity Diameter

	10% Gelatin	Modeling Clay	Wet Paper
after 1 inch	1.70 inches	3.12 inches	.75 inches
after 2 inches	1.80 inches	3.25 inches	.88 inches
after 3 inches	1.55 inches	2.88 inches	1.00 inches
after 4 inches	1.40 inches	1.88 inches	.88 inches
after 5 inches	.60 inches	.88 inches	.50 inches
after 6 inches	.60 inches	-	.50 inches
after 7 inches	.60 inches	-	-
after 8 inches	.60 inches	-	-
total volume using 2r method	9.37 inches^3	25.8 inches^3	2.84 inches^3

temporary stretch cavity are required.

The fifth artificial test medium used to duplicate tissue response to the bullet is ordnance or ballistic gelatin. Detailed directions for the formulation, storage, firing, and measurement of gelatin are found in Chapter 15.

Generally, gelatin is used in two different formulations. Since the 1940s, the gelatin-to-water ratio has been 1 to 5, or 20 percent. With 20-percent gelatin, the block temperature at firing historically has been 10°C, or 50°F.

Recently, after research with living hogs and freshly excised hog muscle, a 10-percent gelatin was developed by Dr. Martin Fackler, then with the U.S. Army's Wound Ballistic Lab, now president of the International Wound Ballistics Association. Significantly, the block temperature of 10-percent gelatin must be 4°C, or 39°F.

Most agencies still use 20-percent gelatin because the bulk of their previous work is based on it, and it allows good correlation between the work done at various agencies across the country. Using the argument that everything is relative, these agencies are extremely reluctant to update to the 10-percent formula. Yet our results show good reason for doing just that.

In 20-percent gelatin, the Silvertip bullet expanded to an average of .60 inch, with a range of .58 inch to .63 inch. The Silvertip bullet in 10-percent gelatin expanded to an average of .58 inch, with a range of .55 to .60 inch. The Silvertip bullet in the hog averaged .53 inch, with a range of .44 to .60 inch.

Ballistic gelatin of both formulations slightly overstates bullet expansion at normal handgun velocities. The 20-percent gelatin overstates the expansion by an average of 13 percent, while 10-percent gelatin does so by an average of 9 percent. Both are close, but this explains why water is used as a double check.

If gelatin has a fault, it is its consistency. Gelatin has no repeatable way to put the bullet through the different densities and elasticities found in the human body. Of course, neither does any other test medium. Of the two formulations of gelatin, 10-percent gelatin gives the more realistic estimate of bullet expansion.

The two formulations of gelatin differ the most in the depth they allow the bullet to penetrate. The Silvertip penetrated 5.8 inches in 20-percent gelatin, which gives poor correlation to the penetration distances in living tissue. This shallow penetration results in an undersize crush cavity compared to all of the hog crush cavities in general and the average crush cavity in particular.

The Silvertip penetrated 8 inches in 10-percent gelatin. This is closer to the 9.8-inch average in soft tissue than any other artificial test medium. Realistic penetration distance is the most credible and street-relevant reason for the use of 10-percent over 20-percent gelatin and all other test mediums.

Like the slightly oversize expansion in 10-percent gelatin, the slightly undersize penetration compared with living soft tissue can be factored reliably into reality. Penetration distances in 10-percent gelatin consistently will be 15 to 20 percent shallower, on the average, compared to penetration in a living human being.

Most significantly, the combination of penetration distance and expanded diameter in 10-percent gelatin is the same as the average in living tissue. In this case, the crush cavity in 10-percent gelatin was 2.11 cubic inches, while the crush cavity average from the hog was 2.14 cubic inches. This is excellent overall correlation between an artificial test medium and living tissue.

Along with realistic penetration distances, the *shape* of the stretch cavity in 10-percent gelatin is realistic. The shape of the stretch cavity in 20-percent gelatin is shallow by 20 to 30 percent. As a result, 20-percent gelatin suppresses the actual depth and range of the stretch cavity. On the other hand, the shape and maximum diameter of the stretch cavity in 10-percent gelatin have a high correlation with high-speed films taken of recently excised muscle tissue.

Overall, the use of 10-percent gelatin allows the closest and most realistic estimate of the reliability and degree of bullet expansion, depth of penetration, volume of the permanent crush cavity, and diameter and shape of the temporary stretch cavity.

CHAPTER 15

ORDNANCE GELATIN

The gelatin used by the authors is the same as that used by police, military, industrial, and private agencies. It is called 250 A Ordnance Type and is available from Kind and Knox, Park 80 West, Plaza 2, Saddle Brook, NJ, 07662.

Ordnance gelatin is available in drums from 25 pounds and up for around $2.70 per pound. When properly prepared, the blocks are clear enough to permit photography of the passing bullet and the resulting fractures.

The formulation of the dry mix into a gelatin block is relatively simple, but the directions — provided by Kind and Knox — must be followed for consistent results. These call for stirring the prescribed amount of gelatin powder in cold water and heating the mixture in a double boiler to avoid direct contact of the mixture to heat. The temperature at which the mixture dissolves thoroughly is about 104°F, and the mixture will set into a gel at 50°F or below.

An alternate method of preparation that has produced consistent results involves mixing the gelatin powder in warm tap water. Most significantly, the water must not be boiled before the gelatin is mixed in. This is quite unlike the way one prepares jello.

Boiling water produces gelatin blocks that give non-repeatable responses to the bullet. The water level should be kept below 140°F/60°C. This is easily accomplished since hot tap water runs in that temperature range. You will not exceed the maximum temperature if you simply use tap water.

The proper gelatin ratio is 1 pound of gelatin to 9 pounds of water. One gallon of water weighs 8.34 pounds. Blocks can be cast in half-gallon or gallon paper milk cartons, Tupperware, or custom-built containers. In the case of milk cartons, the paper can simply be peeled off the gelatin block. Blocks in other molds can be dipped in hot water long enough to melt the gelatin in contact with the mold, allowing the block to slip out.

Following the K&K directions, the containers are to be sealed with a plastic wrap to prevent water loss due to evaporation during cooling. They should be refrigerated for a minimum of 24 hours to allow the block to set up and achieve a constant temperature throughout. With the 10-percent ratio, the block temperature should be 4°C/39°F. Again, this is convenient because most refrigerators can be set between 38° and 40°F.

The blocks should be shot immediately upon removing them from the cooler. If they must be transported to a distant shooting range, they can be kept in an ice-packed cooler. As the block warms up, the readings change drastically, so shooting them at a consistent temperature is absolutely critical.

According to K&K, the gelatin material can be reused. The block can be remelted in either a double boiler or microwave and recast. The maximum temperature guidelines still apply. Care should be exercised during remelting to minimize water loss due to evaporation, as this changes the gelatin-to-water ratio. We reuse the gelatin a maximum of two times.

The blocks can be sized according to the power

Ordnance gelatin is easier to use than most people think. It has an excellent correlation with living tissue and allows precise measurements. (Photo courtesy of Hydra-Shok Corporation.)

level of the load. As in all scientific testing, the number of variables should be kept to a minimum. Therefore, a particular load should always be fired into a particular block size. Loads of similar power levels should all be fired into blocks of the same size.

Handgun loads that produce small temporary cavities can be fired into half-gallon milk cartons, which measure 4 by 4 inches. Loads that produce large temporary cavities should be fired into 1-gallon cartons, which measure 6 by 6 inches. The cutoff is at .357 Magnum. Loads as powerful or more powerful should probably be shot into the larger block. The way to tell which block to use is to never let a stretch crack reach the outside of the block. In fact, the longest crack should not be within 1 inch of the outside.

The block or blocks should be long enough to capture the bullet. Bullets penetrate 30 percent further in 10-percent gelatin than they do in 20-percent gelatin. Blocks can be placed end to end along the proposed bullet path to get enough length. They can also be placed beside and around the main block to capture bullet fragments and bullets that veer off course.

As a point of reference, the 125-grain Remington semijacketed hollowpoint in .357 Magnum penetrates roughly 12 inches of 10-percent gelatin and throws fragments up to 6 inches from the main bullet path. The Hydra-Shok Copperhead and Glaser Safety Slug also throw fragments that must be captured in the gelatin for the most accurate wounding picture.

Blocks that are too short can produce somewhat misleading temporary wound profiles. This is especially the case with large-cavity and late energy-transfer loads. The gelatin near the next point is easier to displace because there is no surrounding gelatin to suppress the action. This is the same problem as allow-

ing the radial cracks to come too close to the outside — there simply is less resistance to the stretch. The result is a pronounced "bugle"-shaped wound profile as the cavity stretches out toward the exit more than it normally would.

Nor is it correct to shoot 5.5 inches of gelatin because the limb you are estimating only measures that distance. Gelatin equates to striated muscle and other soft organs, *not* to skin. The extreme elastic nature of the skin prevents this bugle effect at exit.

The best way to estimate temporary wounding is to capture the entire action. This also allows a precise and relevant measure of bullet penetration, which is not available when the bullet exits a short block.

Regardless of the caliber, the great majority of temporary stretch from handgun loads occurs in the first 9 inches. Since there are some losses in stretch from one block to the next, the primary block should be at least 9 inches long. A second 9-inch block placed behind the primary block will probably not see much stretch, but it will capture the bullet and allow an exact penetration measurement. This 18 inches will catch most softpoint bullets, all hollowpoint bullets, and most ball and nonmagnum semiwadcutters.

A variation on the back-to-back blocks will allow you to become even more sophisticated in your wound predictions. You can place a short 4-inch block wrapped in clothing ahead of the primary block to act as a soft-tissue intermediate target. In fact, this *must* be done at some point in the load-selection process in order to estimate realistic shooting scenarios.

When analyzing the effects of a bullet passing through the gelatin, a number of measurements must be taken to get the full wounding prediction. These include the permanent crush cavity (PCC), the temporary stretch cavity (TSC), the actual depth of bullet penetration, and the number and depth of bullet fragments that leave the main bullet path, if any.

While it remains heavily debated, we believe that the most significant (though not exclusive) measurement is the permanent crush cavity. This is the amount of tissue actually touched, crushed, or pulped by the bullet itself, and it is the dominant wound predictor at most handgun velocities. The exceptions are the highest-velocity magnum loads in the 1,400+ fps range. Other exceptions are contact-type wounds where the powder continues to burn and create pressure inside the wound.

The crush cavity is the dominant wound predictor because of its reliability. The effects of the crush cavity on tissue are predictable and repeatable from shot to shot from tissue to tissue. Simply put, if the bullet runs into a blood vessel, it will tear it or cut it in half.

If the bullet meets a lung or the liver, it will put a hole in them. At the risk of sounding too simplistic, bullets cause holes, which are real and instant damage.

This makes sense in contrast to the temporary stretch cavity. The stretch cavity can meet a blood vessel but not damage it at all. In fact, unless the maximum stretch occurs at a branching point or traps pulpy tissue, such as in the liver, or a ligament, such as the one securing the aorta, even large-size cavities generally will not produce damage.

Recall again the proven reasons why people fall: loss of oxygen from loss of blood and loss of motor control from damage to the nervous system. The most predictable way to damage something is to crush it, not stretch it. Most tissue is simply too elastic to be torn open by stretch alone — it can be stretched without damage. Most handgun loads do not exceed the limits of elasticity of most soft tissue.

The crush cavity is easily estimated. The components are the diameter of the recovered bullet, the length of the bullet track, the size of the secondary fragments, if any, and the length of their tracks. While there may be crush from incompressible fluids that flow over the bullet, this crush effect cannot be relied upon.

The formula for volume is .7854 times the diameter squared times the length of penetration. This formula must be figured for the unexpanded and recovered bullet, as well as for any fragments. For example, a .45-caliber semiwadcutter penetrating 20 inches would have a PCC of .7854 x .45 x .45 x 20, or 3.18 cubic inches. Using the same formula, a 9mm hollowpoint that expanded to .65 caliber and traveled 10 inches would have a PCC of 2.86 cubic inches. It has been proven that full expansion takes place in the first 2 inches. The crush diameter for expanding bullets in the first 2 inches is roughly the bore diameter, which in this example is .36.

A .357 Magnum hollowpoint that sends fragments off to create PCCs of their own is still relatively easy to calculate. The recovered diameter is .57 inch, with a depth of 12 inches. Six fragments measuring a .2-inch cube penetrated 5 inches on their own. The calculation is as follows. First, the unexpanded bullet at .36 x .36 x .7854 x 2. Second, the recovered bullet at .57 x .57 x .7854 x 10. Third, the fragments at .2 x .2 x 6 x 5. The PCC measures 3.36 cubic inches.

Calculating the crush cavity of a disintegrating bullet like the Glaser Safety Slug or that of a shotgun blast can be done in the same manner. The diameter of number 12 birdshot pellet is .05 inch. There are roughly 300 pellets per .36-caliber Glaser bullet. Each pellet penetrates roughly 6 inches. Therefore, .05 x .05 x .7854 x 6 x 300 = 3.53 cubic inches. This assumes each pellet creates its own crush track, which is an overstatement. However, the rapid and even dispersion of shot indicates at least 80 percent of the pellets crush individually. The net actual cavity, therefore, is estimated at 2.83 cubic inches.

Occasionally, it will be relevant to know the recovered bullet's weight and its percent of retained weight. Caution must be exercised in analyzing retained weight, however. If the weight and diameter loss is in the form of lead particles trailing behind in the wound track, that is bad. If the loss comes from genuine secondary missiles that have spun off, that is good, with exceptions to be discussed later.

The PCC is a critical part of wound-predicting analysis. The crush volume is heavily dependent upon caliber and recovered diameter. The big-bore and reliably expanding bullets produce the largest crush cavities. However, as these three examples show, the proven loads all produce roughly the same crush volume.

Even if we restrict the distance to the 12 inches of soft tissue we expect the bullet to face, the top police loads still only differ by fractions. The 9mm hollowpoint expands to .68 caliber while the .45 hollowpoint expands to .85 caliber, both penetrating the same distance and both with sub-1,500 fps velocities. Yet the street results indicate these loads to be remarkably similar despite dissimilar crush cavities.

To explain this equal street effectiveness, other wound predictors must be factored into the analysis. Of profound but secondary importance is the temporary stretch cavity, the tissue violently shoved out of the way by the passing bullet. Due to inertia, the tissue stretches radially outward away from the bullet path, forming an air cavity in the wake of the bullet.

The tissue reaches a point of maximum stretch, then collapses back to its original position. The rebounding tissue bounces off itself outward and back again in an ever decreasing amplitude until the tissue comes to rest. This entire stretch-and-collapse cycle takes place in well under half a second in most tissue.

Some tissue is stretched and actually torn open by the maximum stretch cavity, depending on its size. The liver, spleen, and kidneys are especially sensitive to stretch. Their relative density and lack of elasticity can result in actual damage 10 times greater than the diameter of the passing bullet, especially the liver. Such permanent damage is easily visible at autopsy even though the bullet did not actually touch the damaged tissue. The damage can even be quite remote from the bullet path, caused by pressure peaks carried by incompressible fluid.

If the temporary cavity occurs at the right place,

its force, even from handgun loads, can be enough to break or chip bones. A bone chip was blown into the spine of a felon in Texas, stopping him instantly even though the bullet did not strike the spine. The load was a Glaser Safety Slug, which typically produces unusually large and rapidly generated temporary stretch cavities.

In addition to permanent damage, the TSC can also generate a stress signal strong enough to overload the victim's consciousness, which is controlled by the reticular activating system (RAS) located in the brain stem. Among other functions, the RAS is a network of interrelated nerves in a double feedback loop. The nerve centers in the body send and receive signals, as does the RAS. One especially sensitive area in this system is the solar plexus, but all vital organs are also in the network.

Damage in the peripheral nervous system can relay a stress signal to the central nervous system. The message from an organ violently shoved aside in the wake of a bullet can produce the same results as if the awful injury the organ reported had actually happened. The result is unconsciousness in 1 to 2 seconds, an effect far faster than unconsciousness from blood loss.

For all the damage and effects the TSC *can* have, the problem is that absolutely nothing can also be the result. Signals to the RAS can be blocked by drugs, alcohol, and a strong mindset. Furthermore, a great deal of soft tissue in the human anatomy can be stretched significantly but not damaged. Tissue impervious to stretch includes the major blood vessels, lungs, intestines, and all muscle tissue, including the heart.

The TSC simply is localized blunt trauma. If an organ cannot be broken open by a heavy punch or baton, it is unlikely that organ will be broken open by a bullet's stretch cavity. In fact, only one organ, the liver, is absolutely intolerant of stretch. All other organs can take the blunt trauma produced by normal handgun-velocity loads.

Still, the stretch cavity is a significant factor in wound prediction. The significance has been naively estimated at 10 to 20 percent of the overall effect. The truth is, no one knows because the effects of stretch are too unpredictable, unreliable, and unrepeatable. The significance of the stretch cavity can realistically vary from 0 to 100 percent of the observed reaction.

What we do know is that the effects of the TSC are all positive in terms of stopping power. When two loads produce permanent crush cavities of nearly the same volume, the temporary stretch cavity is a valid tie breaker. This helps explain how the 9mm JHP and .45 Auto JHP can produce roughly the same street

results. The .45 produces a slightly bigger hole while the 9mm produces slightly more tissue stretch.

The exact size of the temporary stretch cavity can be determined only through high-speed photography. Photos taken at a rate of 4,000 to 8,000 frames per second are compared to a known scale to give exact volumetric readings. This involves expensive photo equipment far beyond the budgets of most police agencies and civilians. As a result, a considerable effort has been made to approximate the size of the stretch cavity from the number and length of cracks remaining after the cavity collapses.

There seems to be considerable professional disagreement in the methods used to estimate the temporary cavity from the remaining cracks in the gelatin. One method was developed by Dr. Heinz Gawlick of RWS Dynamit Nobel involving sectioning the block perpendicular to the bullet path in 1-inch increments. The lengths of all the cracks in the sections are measured and summed. Twice the sum of the radii lengths represents the circumference of the cross section of the temporary cavity. From circumference, one can calculate volume. This method is currently in use by the U.S. Secret Service and ammo companies like the German firm MEN.

Another technique currently is being promoted in the professional journals by Dr. Martin Fackler of the U.S. Army Wound Ballistics Lab at the Letterman Army Institute of Research. Dr. Fackler's method involves using only the two longest radii. These two longest cracks are added together along with a small factor to compensate for gelatin elasticity to establish the diameter.

These two measurement techniques can produce significantly different estimates of the temporary cavity. An independent source, Dr. Bruce D. Ragsdale of Georgetown University School of Medicine, tested techniques against a high-speed calibrated movie of the temporary cavity. The results were mixed and debatable but seemed to favor the two-radii method.

Use of the all-radii method seems to overstate the cavity size and show great differences between loads which do not actually exist. The authors have recently adopted the two-radii methodology.

After firing, the gelatin block must be sectioned to measure the cracks. These radial fissures are caused by the stretch exceeding the elastic limits of the gelatin.

For a detailed analysis, the block can be sectioned in 1-inch slices perpendicular to the bullet path. This will show a great number of cracks with varying lengths by the inch and assure measuring the longest crack in 1-inch increments of depth.

For a coarser analysis, the block can be split in two

along the bullet path. An effort should be made to split the block right down the largest crack. This will show the overall shape or profile of the stretch cavity and is actually the preferred technique.

From the wound profile, we can record relevant information with dial calipers. First, we can determine where the stretch cavity begins. The length after entry but before a significant stretch cavity forms is called the "neck." This is especially significant in rifle bullet analysis where the bullet may travel 2 to 5 inches before yawing. With nearly all handgun loads, the stretch cavity begins immediately.

The neck is an area of almost no stretch. This explains how a 7.62mm NATO bullet with a late yaw can leave a crush and stretch wound track identical to a .45 ACP round nose in a limb measuring only 4 to 6 inches thick.

The second important dimension to measure is the diameter of the maximum stretch cavity. Simply measure the distance of the largest crack above and below the bullet path and record the maximum diameter.

Third, record the depth at which that maximum diameter occurred. This will give us a peak pressure point. A cavity that peaks at exactly the same depth as a vital organ can be damaging.

The fourth measurment is how deep the stretch cavity extends into the block. This will give us a range of maximum stretch disruption. A stretch cavity that ends at 4 inches will not significantly damage vital organs 5 inches deep.

Knowing the stretch diameter every inch along the wound profile allows us to calculate the temporary stretch cavity volume. Again, use the equation .7854 times the diameter squared times the depth. Since the depth will always be in 1-inch segments, simply add all of the .7854 diameter squared readings for the entire bullet path.

With this information we have an excellent estimate of the actual stretch cavity otherwise available only with high-speed, 8,000-frames-per-second photography. A small allowance can be made for the elasticity of the gelatin, which keeps the crack diameter from exactly equaling the real stretch diameter prior to collapse. However, the relative significance of the TSC makes this allowance unnecessary.

We can compare various loads producing equal crush and stretch volumes by analyzing the exact profile of the stretch cavity. An early, basketball-shaped stretch cavity would be ideal for upper-torso frontal shots. A late, football-shaped cavity of exactly the same volume would be ideal for an abdominal, cross-torso, or angled shot, or one involving an intermediate target.

Quite frequently, many loads from many calibers will produce the same crush volume, stretch volume, and wound profile. Before we are willing to say these loads will give equal street results, there are two more ways to distinguish one from another.

Of profound significance is the actual depth of penetration. This separates a police-duty load from an off-duty and backup load and from loads that are best suited for hunting only. Of secondary significance is the presence of secondary missiles. This becomes a tie breaker only when the caliber and bullet weight have already been selected and you are simply deciding between manufacturers.

Underpenetration was one of the problems not addressed by the RII study. Yet failures associated with loads with high RII values have been due to underpenetration. These have taken the form of shallow energy release or just the sheer lack of getting in deep enough.

We know from the first chapter that the most reliable stopping-power results come when the bullet causes damage to a major blood vessel, nerve center, or vital organ. This tissue can be at different depths, depending on the size of the person and the exact path of the bullet.

The ideal amount of soft-tissue penetration is a heavily debated issue. One group favors enough penetration to cover all scenarios, including angled shots, which place vital tissue deeper, and intermediate targets, which rob penetration energy. The other group wants to strictly avoid overpenetration or perforation of the target, which can create a bystander hazard.

Clearly these are conflicting goals and almost mutually exclusive. Adequate but not excessive penetration is almost entirely dependent upon the path of the bullet through the body.

In law enforcement, the target frequently is at a quarter angle or sideways to the shooter. Vital tissue lies much deeper on a transverse shot than on a frontal shot. For example, the distance to the heart increases from 2 to 4 inches for a frontal shot to 8 to 10 inches on a transverse shot. Same for the large cardiac and pulmonary arteries and veins and for the very significant liver. Vital tissue also lies relatively deep on an abdominal shot, where the bullet must pass through a great deal of relatively insignificant intestines to reach the thoracic or abdominal aorta and inferior vena cava.

Police-action shootings include a higher incidence of engaging intermediate targets than civilian shootings. Common intermediate targets are upper and lower extremities, car glass, and car doors.

Intermediate targets reduce bullet effectiveness in four ways. First, they reduce the overall penetration of the bullet. A bullet that will penetrate 8 inches of soft tissue will only penetrate 4 inches of torso tissue after perforating a 4-inch-thick biceps muscle. This remaining penetration often is not enough.

Second, the intermediate target can be hard enough to physically break up the bullet or deflect it off course. It can be as obvious as a steel guard beam in a car door or as subtle as a 1-inch thick humerus bone in the upper arm. It is entirely possible for the intermediate target to stop bullet penetration.

Third, the intermediate target can absorb a great deal or, in some cases, all of the bullet's shock. Many high-velocity loads depend heavily on the effects of tissue stretch, yet they produce a temporary stretch cavity that can be completely absorbed by an upper arm, leaving crush as the only mechanism of injury inside the torso.

Fourth, the intermediate target can absorb secondary missiles thrown off by the bullet itself. Both conventional and specialty ammo are capable of spinning off these independent wounding agents. However, due to their light weight, these fragments penetrate no more than 5 inches, typically only 3 inches. An upper arm can easily absorb all these fragments and thus protect the torso.

The possible benefits of engaging a secondary target prior to the torso include expanding the bullet prior to impact and spraying the target with fragments. Both are relatively unreliable in their effect and both reduce the velocity of the primary projectile.

Transverse shots, intermediate targets, and abdominal shots demand penetration deep enough to reach vital tissue. However, loads with this deeper penetration potential also have a greater potential for target perforation. Again, this depends on the bullet path.

A load that produces ideal penetration on a transverse shot will probably exit on an upper-torso frontal shot that misses the rib cage and engages only skin, muscle, and lung tissue. Same with a misplaced shot that only engages an upper or lower extremity, the neck, or only a portion of the upper or lower torso.

One problem of perforation is that the overpenetrating bullet carries with it the energy to stretch tissue. The bullet's effectiveness is reduced when the tissue is stretched less than it would be from a bullet that does not exit.

The other problem, and in actuality the big problem, is the civil liability associated with an overpenetrating bullet. Depending on its retained weight and its exit velocity, the perforating bullet can have the ability to cause serious bodily injury and death to bystanders downrange.

Preventing target perforation is at least as significant an argument to police administrations and city councils considering hollowpoint bullets as the argument of improved bullet effectiveness. In this day and age, avoiding civil liability is given a great deal of emphasis, and it isn't limited to big-city police departments. Small sheriff's departments in sparsely populated rural counties use high-velocity, lightweight hollowpoint bullets to avoid perforation. (Population records do not accurately reflect the probability of bystanders at a police-action shooting. The only convenience store in an entire town of 1,000 people can still have 20 citizens standing around.)

Penetration distances in ordnance gelatin will show us in advance the generic penetration we can expect from the load. Again, at handgun velocities, penetration distances in 10-percent gelatin at 4°C will be 15 to 20 percent shallow compared to average depths in soft tissue. Yet it is as realistic a view available of penetration in soft tissue, including muscle and all soft organs, with the exception of the lungs. This is the major advantage of this formulation.

You or your department can decide what is underpenetration, overpenetration, and ideal penetration, depending on your situation. A couple of guidelines may put this into perspective.

First, penetration requirements are often specified in old-style 20-percent gelatin by government agencies in their purchasing contract or ammo specifications. One agency, which cannot be disclosed, requires a minimum penetration of 5.5 inches and a maximum of 7.5 inches. This specification is for antipersonnel ammo to be used in crowded urban environments worldwide. In 10-percent gelatin, this equates to a minimum of 7.25 inches and a maximum of 9.75 inches. Actually, this is a fairly tight range of penetration. However, it still leaves the door open for failures. A load capable of 7.25-inch penetration can still underpenetrate, while a 9.75-inch load can still perforate.

Much depends on the anticipated shooting scenario. Police officers using their backup guns and civilians using concealed-carry or home-defense guns *share* certain shooting characteristics. These shootings typically are face-to-face, producing frontal shots that demand less penetration. Intermediate targets like glass and steel also are rare. Due to typical ranges under 5 feet, the probability of extremities as intermediate targets is lower. The only requirement for deeper penetration would be in the event of an abdominal shot.

Penetration depths as low as 6 inches have proven to be adequate in these situations. Yet this would be viewed as severe underpenetration in other shooting scenarios. Therefore issue ammo intended for primary police duty weapons needs to penetrate deeper. The risk of perforation increases but so does the presence of effectiveness-reducing obstacles in the way.

For a law enforcement round, 10 inches is about the minimum amount of penetration required, while 15 inches is the maximum. This gives enough penetration to handle angled shots and intermediate targets, yet the controlled penetration of these loads does not have the downrange penetration ability of a slug capable of defeating 16 to 20 inches of tissue.

A law enforcement round must balance intermediate targets, angled shots, and poor placement with civil liability. The most acceptable compromise is 12 inches of penetration in 10-percent gelatin. Both authors are police officers who naturally favor the tactical edge of deeper penetration in deciding upon this ideal.

Regardless of perspective, it is absolutely critical for duty ammo selection that gelatin performance be factored to account for intermediate targets and angled shots. Recall that this is the major shortcoming of the NIJ/LEAA analysis resulting in the RII. When gelatin is analyzed with these exceptions in mind, results are as identical to actual street results as anything in terminal ballistics can be.

The methodology is relatively simple. Completely disregard any terminal effect that occurs in the first 4 inches of gelatin. The best way to do this is to shoot each load two different ways. First, fire the bullet into a block of gelatin of the normal dimensions and record all the data. Second, fire the bullet into two blocks of gelatin, the first 4 inches thick followed by a second, normal-sized block. Disregard the first block and take measurements from the second only.

Analysis of both sets of information will show possible underpenetration, loss of the temporary stretch cavity, and loss of meaningful secondary missiles. This helps indicate the wounding potential of a bullet after perforating increasing amounts of soft tissue.

Anyone recommending duty loads to police officers should perform this double analysis. This will avoid the RII mistake of recommending loads that do great damage to extremities and little damage to the torso behind the extremity.

Many loads in many calibers produce similar stretch and crush cavities and similar depths of penetration in the ideal range. As such, all these loads produce roughly the same street results. With equal stopping power, the issues of flash, blast, recoil, tactical and stray shot penetration, and economics can decide which ammo to select.

A strong case can be made for simply putting the ammo in the guns and ignoring small design differences between loads. Instead, time and effort should be spent developing shooting skills so the shooter always hits what he aims at under all shooting cicumstances. And tactics and awareness should be developed so shooting is not required at all.

Of all the small design differences between jacketed hollowpoint ammo, however, one factor stands out as relatively significant and noteworthy. That factor is fragmentation of the bullet after expansion.

Fragmentation is significant for two reasons. First, a bullet that expands and sheds all or part of its mushroomed hollowpoint obviously weighs less than the original bullet. The lighter bullet core with the same velocity has less penetration energy and less chance of target perforation.

Depending on the design and impact velocity, it is possible for recovered jacketed hollowpoint bullets to weigh as little as 50 percent of their original weight. Recovered weights of 65 to 75 percent are quite common. This means the recovered slug has only 65 to 75 percent of the penetration energy it would have if it did not fragment.

Remington and Federal JHP loads typically fragment, while some jacketed hollowpoints are specifically designed not to fragment. The Winchester Silvertip line of hollowpoints is one such example. These bullets typically have the highest retained weight of any JHP. As such, they possess greater retained penetration energy.

A fragmenting bullet has less chance of target perforation. A full mushroom-retained bullet produces deeper penetration and a larger crush cavity in the event of striking a soft intermediate target first.

In addition to the retained weight, fragmentation is significant for a second reason. Some JHP bullets spin off pieces of the hollowpoint cavity wall to become secondary missiles. Secondary missiles, in this context, are lead and copper fragments that leave the main bullet path to engage tissue separate from the bullet core. Fragments that leave the main bullet path increase the chances of hitting a vital organ, vessel, or structure. This significantly increases the realistic effectiveness of the load.

These secondary missiles are not the lead that erodes or shears off the mushroom to remain behind the bullet in the main wound canal. Secondary missiles, by definition, create their own crush cavities, their own permanent wound tracks. Pieces of lead that trail behind the main bullet and engage only the tissue touched by the bullet core do not increase wounding.

Remington scallop-serrated revolver bullets generally fragment and produce active and destructive secondary missiles. Federal and Winchester non-Silvertip bullets generally fragment and produce inactive and passive pieces that trail behind the main bullet.

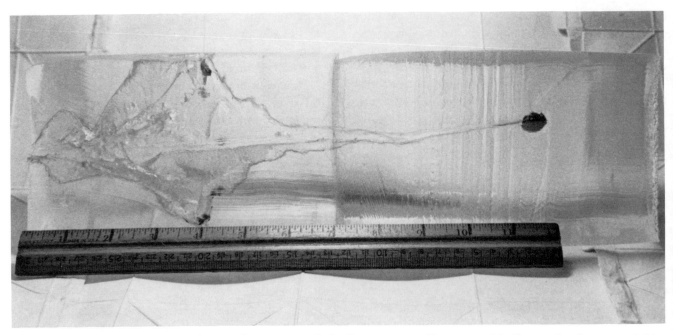

Fragmentation is a major cause of tissue disruption, and the Remington scallop-serrated bullets make the most of this. Bullet fragments that leave the main bullet path increase stopping power.

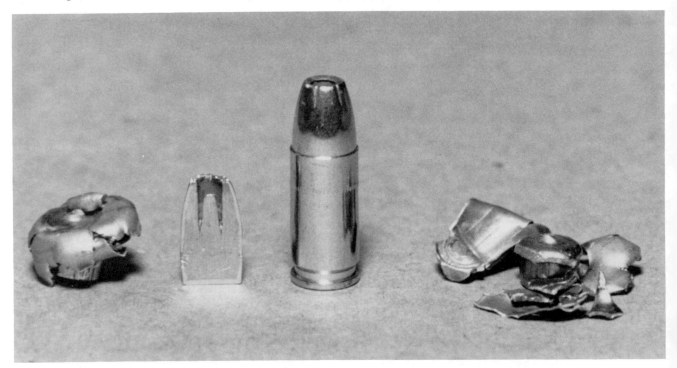

The 147-grain Hydra-Shok in 9mm sometimes will expand and other times fragment inside gelatin. A bullet that fragments in gelatin is likely to at least expand in living tissue.

As an example, the Remington .357 Magnum 125-grain S-JHP produces a lead snowstorm inside the body. This load typically launches six to seven 5-grain missiles that spin off at a 45-degree angle from the main bullet path after about 3 inches of penetration. Each missile engages 3 to 5 inches of tissue. Slower and heavier scallop-jacketed Remington bullets produce a similar effect with fewer missiles and shallower missile depths.

The overall result with secondary missiles is a smaller crush cavity for the main bullet but additional crush cavities from the fragments. The total crush cavity is often identical to bullets that penetrate deeper with a full mushroom. Yet stopping-power logic tells us that loads with secondary missiles produce a greater chance of incapacitation.

Again, the key to stopping power is hitting something important like major arteries and veins, nerve centers, and major organs like the liver, spleen, heart, and kidneys. The success of the bullet depends on putting a hole in this tissue. With more projectiles penetrating independent tissue, the chances are greater of hitting the right vital target. If a bullet misses a main artery but one of six secondary missiles hits it, we have significantly greater stopping power than was available from the bullet only.

Compared to a mushroom-retaining bullet, the missile-producing load has the advantage of upper-torso frontal shots. With these shots, the vital tissue lies within the 5-inch penetration range of the small fragments. The fully mushroomed bullet has the advantage on abdominal shots, transverse shots, and shots involving soft intermediate targets. With these shots, less significant tissue will absorb the missiles of a fragmenting load.

CHAPTER 16

IDEAL BULLET PERFORMANCE

Police officers and civilians alike expect far too much from a tiny piece of lead and copper. We discussed the elements of stopping power and what to expect of a person who has been shot. We know the victim may fall to the ground as fast as humanly possible or continue his assault totally unaffected for many minutes. With this background, we can now discuss what we can expect from the bullet.

Again, there is no such thing as a one-shot stopper, a magic bullet, a manstopper, or any other such overrated title. A survival-oriented expectation of the ammo you carry should be moderate and humble.

A bullet can produce ideal performance and still fail miserably to stop the assailant. By now the reasons for this should be clear: either the bullet placement was poor enough not to damage anything important or the mental state of the attacker was such that his body was being driven despite lethal injuries.

With this in mind, we will describe ideal bullet performance. You should not be surprised by our relatively low expectations of the bullet and the number of bullets that can produce ideal performances. It is an error to overstate differences between calibers and loads that do not exist in reality.

From a wound-mechanism point of view, we want a relatively large-diameter temporary stretch cavity that peaks between 3 and 6 inches deep. The stretch cavity should be relatively long and football-shaped, which indicates moderate energy release. This is opposed to a short, spherical stretch cavity, which transfers its energy early enough to be absorbed by soft intermediate targets or torso tissue engaged before vital tissue.

Most profoundly, we want as large a permanent crush cavity as we can generate. This can be in the form of either an expanded bullet with a retained mushroom, or an expanding bullet that fragments to produce secondary missiles and a bullet core that continues the penetration. Bullets that expand but lose the mushroom through erosion and bullets that do not expand produce smaller crush cavities. Larger-caliber bullets produce larger crush cavities than smaller-caliber bullets.

Depending on the scenario, we want the bullet to penetrate an average of 12 inches. Generally, penetration of less than 10 inches and more than 15 inches should be avoided.

These goals are all met with moderate-weight, jacketed hollowpoint bullets and lead semiwadcutter hollowpoint bullets. Nonhollowpoint options will be discussed later.

The ideal bullet should have a relatively high velocity. This assures that it will expand upon impact regardless of the barrel length. An expanding bullet will produce a larger crush cavity. High-impact velocity alone will produce a large-diameter stretch cavity. However, it is the moderate expansion of the bullet that produces a long stretch cavity.

An expanding bullet will also produce a more controlled and limited penetration depth. In fact, by selecting expanding bullets of different weights, we can produce 10, 12, 15, or 19 inches of penetration depending on which of four bullets we select.

Use of the word "expanding" does not refer to the design of the bullet. It refers to what happens to the bullet after impacting a living human being. Importantly, not all bullets designed to expand do indeed expand. Jacketed softpoint bullets rarely expand unless they strike bone or impact at velocities in the 1,400-fps range. Jacketed hollowpoints that are relatively heavy for their caliber share the same fate. Lead round-nose, semiwadcutter, and wadcutter bullets are less likely to expand. Hard-cast bullets and fully jacketed bullets are even less likely to expand. Nonexpanding or poorly expanding bullets nearly always perforate the target and produce smaller crush and stretch cavities.

In a nutshell, the bullet will have produced ideal performance and totally fulfilled our expectations if it does two things. (This is totally regardless of how the person who is shot reacts.) One, the bullet must expand to a minumum of 1.67 calibers. Expansion beyond that is better yet. Fragmentation is even better in most cases as long as active secondary missiles are produced.

Using this guideline, .38 Special, 9mm, and .357 Magnum bullets must expand to at least .60 caliber. The .44 Special and .45 Auto must expand to .73 caliber. Street results show that the smaller stretch cavity and larger crush cavity of the large-caliber bullets equals the larger stretch cavity and smaller crush cavity of the medium-caliber bullets.

Two, the bullet must penetrate deeply enough. While adequate penetration can produce acceptable results without perfect expansion, perfect expansion is absolutely worthless without adequate penetration. If the ammo fails to penetrate due to an intermediate target, that is still the fault of the ammo. Same for underpenetration on a bullet path that places vital tissue quite deep.

The slug may perforate in its attempt to produce adequate penetration. Strict avoidance of overpenetration should be enforced only when the threat to a bystander is as certain and high as the threat to the shooter.

We can instruct our people to shoot multiple times to get around problems of underpenetration, but consider this: more shots fired increase the hazard to bystanders due to low hit probability on the intended target. First-shot hit probability with trained police officers varies from 25 to 65 percent.

An average of 40 percent of officer-involved shootings involve multiple assailants. Most firefights occur under low-light conditions and against moving targets. They may not be able to hit the person with more than one bullet. That bullet, independent of any mitigating circumstances, must penetrate, hence our guideline of 12 inches in 10-percent ordnance gelatin.

A third requirement unrelated to terminal ballistics applies to ammo intended for autoloaders. This requirement is significant to the point of being a first and overriding priority. Ammo used in autoloading pistols must feed and cycle with *absolute* reliability. It must do so in both recoil-operated and gas-action designs and in stock and modified guns.

The ammo must have an ogive shape to feed in autos of general-issue condition. If the duty auto pistol is issued in a totally stock condition, the ammo must feed in totally stock weapons. If the pistol is modified by polishing or ramping by the department armorer or factory custom shop, the feed requirements can be relaxed down to that point.

Unfortunately, this widely acknowledged requirement sets the stage for the great feed-reliability versus stopping-power controversy. It is easy to see why specialty rounds like the GECO Action Safety and MEN Quick Defense are so successful despite their expense — they have the exact bullet profile of hardball yet strike the target as high-speed hollow points.

Hollowpoint bullets with wide cavity openings produce reliable expansion, large stretch and crush cavities, and controlled penetration. However, their ogive and cavity designs often produce feed failures. Hollowpoints with more rounded ogives and narrower cavity openings often feed with hard ball reliability. This is not surprising since the bullet profile is similar to that of FMJ round-nose ball. This bullet design bounces off the feed ramp and hood with the same force and angle of deflection as ball. However, these designs often produce expansion failures.

Of the two, expansion and reliability, reliability must be the first priority. As a result, auto pistol owners often give up terminal performance to gain weapon reliability. However, the difference between JHP loads of similar velocities and bullet weights are frequently overstated. Auto pistol owners do not give up as much real stopping power going to less aggressive bullet designs as one may first think.

A good example is the Remington 115-grain JHP versus the Winchester 115-grain STHP Silvertip in 9mm. The Remington load has a bullet profile and feed performance quite similar to ball. The Silvertip has a wider cavity opening and feeds well but not as well as the Remington and not in as many weapons.

The Winchester design expands reliably in soft tissue up to double its caliber. The Remington expands only about half the time, which is about the probability of hitting bone. Expansion is only moderate and penetration is often excessive.

In gelatin, the Silvertip is far and away the winner. Yet actual street results indicate only a few percentage points difference between these two loads. The Remington feeds slightly better. For auto pistols fully compatible with the Silvertip, the Silvertip hits slightly harder.

Feed reliability is only half the issue. Cycle reliability is the other half. The time-pressure curve generated by the burning powder must match the port pressure needed by gas-operated pistols like the HK-P7. If the time pressure curve does not overlap the required port pressure, the gas-operated auto will not cycle.

On recoil-operated pistols like the Smith & Wesson Model 659 and Colt Commander, the impulse momentum generated by the bullet weight and muzzle velocity of the load must unlock the slide and move it all the way to the rear. If the combination of bullet weight and muzzle velocity does not move the slide to the rear, the pistol will fail to eject or feed.

This lack of slide impulse can occur two ways. One is the use of heavy bullets at lower subsonic velocities for sound suppressor applications. The other is the use of light bullets driven at higher velocities for personal defense use. Either way, the bullet weight in grains times the muzzle velocity in feet per second must be close to the same impulse from the ball load the gun's spring rates were originally designed around. The only option, which is questionable, is to change spring rates.

Feed and cycle reliability aside, as you review the actual street results you will see that all bullets that do two things — expand and penetrate — produce nearly the same results regardless of caliber. You will also see that bullets which fail to expand and small-caliber bullets of relatively low velocity perform relatively close to loads with better performance in gelatin. This should remind us that bullet placement, not bullet performance, is the key to stopping power.

CHAPTER 17

PREDICTING STOPPING POWER USING STREET RESULTS

Contrary to what some so-called experts claim, it is entirely possible to accurately predict stopping power by testing bullets in ordnance gelatin. The first key to correct conclusions is to use *all* of the information the gelatin gives. The second key is to analyze gelatin results in a way that correlates with actual street results.

Street results with full documentation on who, what, when, where, and why are the *right* answers. These are the actual facts, how bullets really perform. Ordnance gelatin results are prediction only. In practice versus theory, results from gelatin are always theory.

As in all uses of the scientific method, the theory should be modified based on feedback from reality. The problem is, with few exceptions, no one is doing this most basic step. Many people have an opinion on how to use gelatin to predict effectiveness and are not willing to change. Not surprisingly, most people are not able to interpret the results correctly. This is even true for battlefield surgeons and medical examiners.

Oddly, none of these seekers of truth, with impressive but sterile titles, have bothered to follow the scientific method to see if their pet theories hold water or, importantly, if their exclusion of certain data is really correct. One notable exception is the Southwestern Institute for Forensic Sciences discussed in Chapter 5. Its thinking was bold and aggressive in addition to being the correct scientific procedure. However, the SIFS was limited by a somewhat small shooting data base. At that time, no one had formally documented and tabulated actual street effectiveness.

When you examine 406 actual shootings from the same load and barrel length, like the Federal .357 Magnum 125-grain JHP, you have an excellent idea of the realistic performance from that load. This then is the right answer. It is up to those who test in gelatin to tailor interpretations so the predictions match reality. In other words, we need to be able to use gelatin to predict these same answers. Those who do not use actual street results as a feedback in gelatin testing clearly are wrong. A lot of this is done even by elite agencies, and it is continuing to occur in bold defiance of actual results.

To define what is important to look for when using ordnance gelatin, we ran some correlation and linear-regression studies. Those are five-dollar words for saying how well the information from gelatin can be used to predict stopping power. In each of the popular defensive calibers, we selected the top loads, loads with so-so performance, and loads with proven-poor street records for a total of 24 loads. The actual street results we used in this statistical study came from over 1,800 shootings.

To get a set of numbers from gelatin, we fired these 24 loads into 10-percent ordnance gelatin using exactly the same makes, styles, and barrel lengths from the actual data. Naturally, the bullet and all the pieces were recovered and measured. The total depth of penetration was recorded. From this we calculated the crush cavity volume for the entire bullet path, even though some bullets were excessive and overpenetrated. We also measured the size, shape, and volume of the stretch cavity in great detail.

First, with this raw data, we can now see how well penetration depth *alone* predicts actual effectiveness. Some experts have arbitrarily picked a minimum depth of penetration and have disqualified or ignored ammo that does not meet this minimum. No matter how well the bullet performs and how good its street reputation among cops, these people demand that the bullet produce this minimum depth. It has been stated by a top member of the FBI that "although penetration and wound size govern handgun wounding effectiveness, penetration is the more critical element." Remember that dogmatic viewpoint as we review the actual results. The correlation between penetration depth and street results showed whether arbitrary minimums are correct.

Second, we can now see how well the recovered bullet diameter *alone* predicts actual effectiveness. Some people feel you must start out with a big caliber to reliably get a big-caliber wound. What about bullets that expand and then erode the mushroom or even fragment in the target? How well do these bullets, with their small recovered diameters, predict effectiveness?

Third, we can now see how well the permanent cavity *alone* predicts actual effectiveness. This is the current thinking by the FBI and is in stark contrast to the NIJ/LEAA method of just 15 years ago. The FBI bullet predictions totally ignore temporary stretch, just like the LEAA bullet predictions totally ignore permanent crush. Which is better?

Finally, we can now see how well the temporary stretch cavity *alone* predicts actual effectiveness. This is what the much-abused NIJ/LEAA study in the 1970s did. Their Relative Incapacitation Index based stopping power only on temporary cavitation. With actual street results now accumulated by Marshall, we can see how accurate the RII is or is not.

We plotted all of the known data for all 24 loads and plugged it in to a statistical calculator. This is not the prediction part — this is the *known* part. We know, for example, that a Winchester .38 Special +P 158-grain SWC-LHP penetrates 15.2 inches in gelatin and expands to .60 caliber. We know the crush cavity measures 4.3 cubic inches and the stretch cavity measures 11.9 cubic inches. And, thanks to Marshall, we know it is effective in one-shot stops based on actual shootings 71.62 percent of the time.

These become four separate sets of data. For example, .60-caliber expansion equals 71.62 percent effectiveness and 4.3 cubic inches of crush equals 71.62 percent effectiveness. We simply plug all this in for all 24 calibers. The result is a slope, intercept, corre-

lation coefficient, and confidence level. The slope and intercept give us a straight line that best fits through all the data. The correlation tells us how tightly grouped the data points are around the line. The confidence level tells us the accuracy of the whole equation, or our degree of certainty. A correlation coefficient close to +1.00 indicates a high positive relationship. As the value gets closer to zero, the two sets of data become less related.

The penetration results will be shocking to those people who talk about stopping power but do not delve into dead bodies like the rest of us. The correlation between penetration distance and street effectiveness is *negative*. That means it is inversely related, or opposite — as the depth of the recovered bullet increases, the actual stopping power *decreases*. The confidence level of that statement is between 90 and 95 percent based on actual shootings.

Bullets of SWC, RNL, and FMJ design produce deep penetration but poor street results. Bullets like the light JHPs and most SWC-HPs produce much less penetration but excellent street results. Many people outside of the elite police agencies already know this.

Instead of worrying about creating deep penetration, we ought to worry about coming to a stop with just enough penetration. We seem to have forgotten this. The 9mm hard ball load penetrates 22.1 inches and has a terrible street record. The 9mm +P+ JHP from Federal penetrates 12.7 inches and has the best street results in the caliber. The lackluster street performance from the heavy 9mm 147-grain bullets can be traced directly to too much penetration and too little expansion.

The plotted results show penetration beyond 17.1 inches to be too much. Actually, the best loads stop by 15.5 inches. With stopping power dropping off as the bullet goes deeper, we really need to be in the 10- to 14-inch range and no deeper. Don't worry about penetrating heavy clothing. Hollowpoint bullets penetrate *deeper* in tissue after striking heavy clothing first than they do in lightly clothed bodies because the cavity plugs up with debris and the bullet stops acting like a hollowpoint; instead, it penetrates like the softpoint or FMJ that it now resembles.

Is 12 inches a realistic minimum, as some experts claim? No, not according to actual results. The three loads that do not meet the 12-inch minimum on the average are extremely interesting. Most significant is the Winchester 9mm +P+ 115-grain JHP Q4174 used by the Illinois State Police (ISP). The +P+ bullet penetrates as little as 7.9 inches of gelatin, yet produces one-shot stops 88.23 percent of the time. This is an extremely effective round.

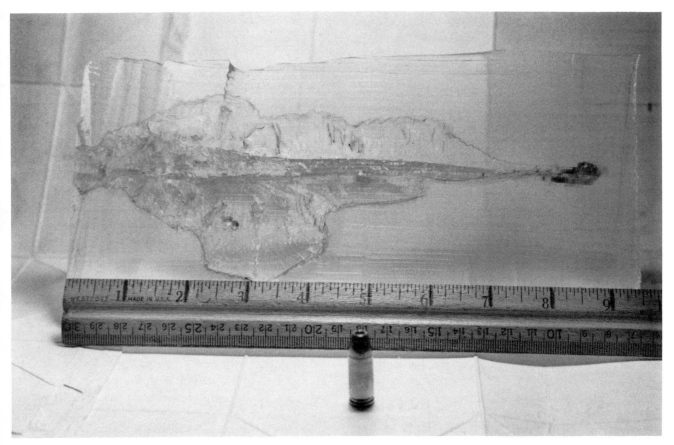

This is the wound profile of the Winchester 9mm +P+ 115-grain JHP Q4174. It is a police-only load and has proven on the street to be one of the best in the caliber, despite what some call shallow penetration.

Obviously, this 9mm +P+ round stands in defiance to those who claim 12 inches of penetration is the minimum. They claim less penetration is okay for civilians who normally make frontal shots but not okay for police who make cross-torso shots. Yet the ISP load is *for police only*, and its extreme effectiveness comes from dozens of police-action shootings. Clearly, the statement that "penetration is the more critical element" is wrong.

The second load that does not meet the FBI minimum of 12 inches — the Remington .38 Special +P 125-grain S-JHP — is also an extremely effective police load. This ammo is used by the Los Angeles Police Department. Behind only the 158-grain SWC-HP, this load has the best street record in the caliber.

The third load is the Winchester .44 Special Silvertip. This ammo is carried by many Chicago cops, where a second duty gun is allowed on the same Sam Browne as the mandatory .38 Special. It has a great street reputation in Chicago.

The most telling evidence for how deeply the police or defensive bullet should penetrate is in the average distance the top, so-so, and poor bullets actually penetrate. The average penetration distance for the best street loads is only 13.0 inches. The average depth of

the so-so loads is 15.3 inches. The average depth of the poor loads is 23.9 inches. Those who insist on penetration depths greater than 13 to 15 inches in 10-percent gelatin are dead wrong.

Next is the correlation between recovered bullet diameter and stopping power. As street results show, as recovered bullet diameter increases so does the stopping power. The two are directly related. The correlation is moderately strong, with a coefficient of .683 and a confidence level of 99.9 percent.

The only problem in using the recovered bullet size comes in the +P+ and magnum calibers. Bullets with muzzle velocities over 1,300 fps typically fragment or shed their mushroom, yet their stopping power is much higher than the size of the recovered bullet would predict.

We took out the data from all loads with velocities over 1,300 fps and ran the results again. The slope was the same, which confirms that as the recovered bullet's size increases, so does its effectiveness. However, the correlation took a giant leap up to .823 with the same confidence level. A correlation this close to +1.00 means the figures are *strongly* related.

The bottom line is that if muzzle velocity is under 1,300 fps, bigger recovered bullets positively stop people better than smaller recovered bullets. Above 1,300 fps, the formula for the size of the recovered bullet must be factored by 1.15 to equate with reality.

Now we get to the tough part. How well does the size of the permanent crush cavity predict stopping power? The FBI thinks it is the only measure of stopping power except for penetration distance. And we know penetration distance is not helpful and can even be counterproductive.

The analysis tells us that as the crush cavity increases, so does stopping power. However, the correlation coefficient is only .597. This leaves a lot of room for error. For example, a .38 Special +P 158-grain SWC-LHP has a crush cavity of 4.3 cubic inches and an effectiveness of 71.62 percent. The .357 Magnum 125-grain JHP has a crush cavity of 3.2 cubic inches but an effectiveness of 95.81 percent.

Once again, we plotted the results from ammo under 1,300 fps. Once again, for lower-velocity loads the correlation was strong, with a coefficient of .865. The current FBI test methodology is correct, but only for ammo below 1,300 fps. When evaluating ammo with velocities over 1,300 fps, the crush cavity must be factored by 1.15 for reliable predictions of stopping power. The crush cavity is one factor but not the *only* factor, as some would have you believe.

The other piece of the puzzle is the size of the stretch cavity. In spite of the bad press the Relative Incapacitation Index received from so-called experts, the study was in reality *correct* with regard to stretch cavity, despite some faulty assumptions.

Like it or not, as the size of the stretch cavity increases so does stopping power. In fact the two are strongly related. At .795, this gave the best correlation when *all* handgun ammo data was used. The size of the crush cavity is only a good predictor below 1,300 fps. Not so for the stretch cavity. It is accurate across all handgun velocity levels. And it gives more accurate predictions as speeds pick up. By the time rifle velocities are reached, stretch cavity is the *only* measurement used to predict stopping power.

The size of the stretch cavity as a measure of stopping power has been a whipping boy for armchair experts for years. And as so often happens, the experts were wrong. The NIJ/LEAA was right. This should not be the only way used to predict performance, but it is statistically valid and should be a part of the total evaluation.

Now that these four measurements from gelatin have been statistically tied to actual results, we can use their formulas to predict stopping power. The intercept, slope, and correlation coefficient for penetration, expansion, crush, and stretch are in Table 17-1. The process to come up with a reliable estimate of stopping power is simple. Again, this is based on *actual* results; it is *not* a theory. For loads above 1,300 fps, we need to add 15 percent.

To test the formulas we selected loads for which we

At bullet impacts above 1,300 fps, most JHP bullets expand then shed their mushroom, to be recovered at a smaller diameter. The proven stopping power from these loads must be factored in when predicting bullet performance based on recovered diameters.

have lots of actual shootings. Since the crush volume is built from the penetration distance and recovered diameter, we really only need to average the crush prediction and the stretch prediction for the final prediction. However, the penetration and expansion predictions should be figured so there are no nasty surprises.

The Federal 9mm 124-grain Nyclad hollowpoint crush cavity of 4.5 cubic inches figures out to a 73.4 percent effectiveness. The stretch cavity of 18.3 inches works out to 72.8 percent, for an average prediction of 73.1 percent. The street average is 81.25 percent, so the Nyclad works slightly better than predicted. The same analysis for the .38 Special +P 158-grain SWC-HP predicts 69.5 percent versus an actual of 71.62 percent.

These formulas work on the hottest loads and also on the worst loads. For a load over 1,300 fps, we used the .357 Magnum 125-grain JHP. The prediction is 95.9 percent versus an actual of 95.81 percent. The Winchester 9mm 115-grain hard ball yields a prediction in gelatin of 61.5 percent. The actual street effectiveness is 60.81 percent.

With the formulas proven on known ammo, we can now predict the effectiveness of new ammo, *which is the whole point of this study.* We want to be able to predict effectiveness *before* the lives of officers and bystanders are risked.

The Federal .38 Special +P 147-grain Hydra-Shok has been adopted as an interim load by the FBI. With a permanent crush cavity of 4.1 cubic inches and a temporary stretch cavity of 11.2 cubic inches, this new load should produce 69-percent one-shot stops. That is the same as the latest figures on the 158-grain

SWC-HP. The FBI is not giving up any stopping power from this revolver cartridge but is gaining better penetration against car bodies.

The most famous new load with no street experience is the Federal 10mm 180-grain JHP "mid-range" load. It has been adopted by the FBI and many other police departments that issue the 10mm. This unproven round has a crush cavity measuring 6.2 cubic inches and a stretch cavity measuring 17.0 cubic inches. The formulas developed from actual street fights predict a 78-percent effectiveness for this 10mm hollowpoint. Interestingly, this is right in the middle of the .45 Auto hollowpoint range.

The same analysis works on the newest police caliber, the .40 S&W. It has been adopted by the California Highway Patrol, and will probably unseat the 10mm mid-range as the cartridge of the decade. The Winchester 180-grain JHP with Silvertip serrations produces a crush cavity of 4.1 cubic inches. The stretch cavity measures 26.8 cubic inches. The expected street effectiveness based on past street effectiveness for the .40 S&W is 75.7 percent. This is just like the 10mm JHP.

That is how it all works. You build formulas from actual results. You fire the load in question into 10-percent gelatin. You record and use *all* data from the tests. You plug the penetration and expansion results in their equations to check for ringers. You plug crush and stretch results into their equations and average them.

The result is an accurate statistical prediction of stopping power based on actual shooting results. No more theories. No more guesses. No more expert opinions.

Table 17-1

HANDGUN GELATIN RESULTS

Caliber	Make & Load	Total	Recovered	Permanent	Temporary	Street Effectiveness
.380 Auto	Federal 90-gr. JHP	14.4 in.	.36 in.	1.5 in.³	8.3 in.³	63.82
	Remington 88-gr	12.8 in.	.41 in.	1.7 in.³	10.5 in.³	54.84
	Federal 95-gr. FMJ	17.0 in.	.36 in.	1.7 in.³	6.8 in.³	51.25
.38 Special & +P	Winchester 158-gr. SWC-HP	15.2 in.	.60 in	4.3 in.³	11.9 in.³	72.78
	Remington 125-gr. S-JHP	11.1 in.	.46 in.	3.6 in.³	13.43 in.³	65.11
	Federal 158-gr. RNL	28.5 in.	.36 in.	2.9 in.³	8.6 in.³	52.28
9mm, 9mm +P, 9mm + P+	Federal 115-gr. JHP +P+	12.7 in.	.53 in. (f)	2.8 in.³	20.3 in.³	89.28
	Winchester 115-gr. JHP +P+	7.9 in.	.79 in.	3.9 in.³	37.3 in.³	88.23
	Remington 115-gr. JHP	14.5 in.	.62 in.	4.4 in.³	18.7 in.³	76.42
	Federal 124-gr. Nyclad HP	12.4 in.	.68 in.	4.5 in.³	18.3 in.³	82.07
	Winchester 147-gr. JHP	15.9 in.	.57 in.	4.1 in.³	19.6 in.³	68.54
	Winchester 115-gr. FMJ	22.1 in.	.36 in.	2.2 in.³	8.8 in.³	60.81
.357 Magnum	Federal 125-gr. JHP	13.3 in.	.55 in. (f)	3.2 in.³	44.3 in.³	96.05
	Remington 125-gr. JHP-MV	15.5 in.	.75 in.	6.8 in.³	20.9 in.³	83.33
	Remington 158-gr. SWC	27.5 in.	.36 in.	2.8 in.³	12.9 in.³	67.60
.41 Magnum	Winchester 175-gr. STHP	17.0 in.	.70 in.	6.5 in.³	41.2 in.³	88.63
	Remington 210-gr. JSP	23.5 in.	.41 in.	3.1 in.³	32.5 in.³	80.00
	Winchester 210-gr. SWC	30.0 in.	.41 in.	4.0 in.³	11.3 in.³	74.35
.44 Special	Winchester 200-gr. STHP	10.4 in.	.61 in.	3.0 in.³	10.7 in.³	71.11
	Winchester 246-gr. RNL	23.0 in.	.43 in.	3.3 in.³	8.0 in.³	67.39
.45 Auto	Federal 230-gr. HS-JHP	13.3 in.	.76 in.	6.0 in.³	17.5 in.³	88.37
	Federal 185-gr. JHP	13.6 in.	.68 in.	4.9 in.³	18.1 in.³	84.61
	Remington 185-gr. JHP	17.1 in.	.59 in.	4.7 in.³	14.0 in.³	78.57
	Remington 230-gr. FMJ	27.0 in.	.45 in.	4.3 in.³	9.0 in.³	60.72

(f) denotes fragmented bullet

Table 17-2

PREDICTING STOPPING POWER (SP) USING STREET RESULTS

I. If you know the penetration distance:
   SP = (-) .733 x (distance) + 85
   correlation coefficient: *minus* .37

II. If you know the diameter of the recovered bullet:
   (under 1,300 fps)
   SP = 62.9 x (diameter) + 35.7
      correlation coefficient: .82
   (at or over 1,300 fps)
      SP = 58.7 x (diameter) + 40.6 *then* x 1.15
      correlation coefficent: .68

III. If you know the volume of the permanent crush cavity:
   (under 1,300 fps)
      SP = 6.3 x (volume) +45.0
      correlation coefficient: .87
   (at or over 1,300 fps)
      SP= 5.3 x (volume) + 53 *then* x 1.15
      correlation coefficient: .60

IV. If you know the volume of the temporary stretch cavity:
   SP = .92 x (volume) +56
   correlation coefficient: .80

Note: The closer the correlation coefficient is to +1, the more accurate the prediction.

Graph 17-1

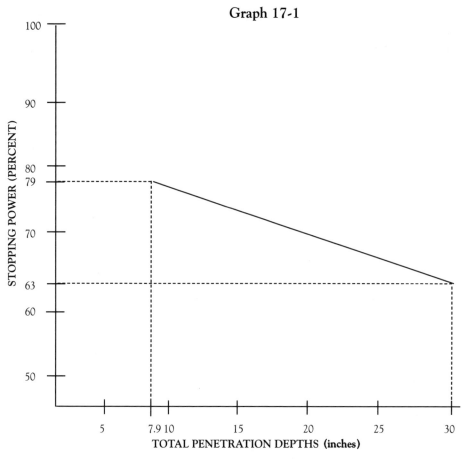

Graph 17-2

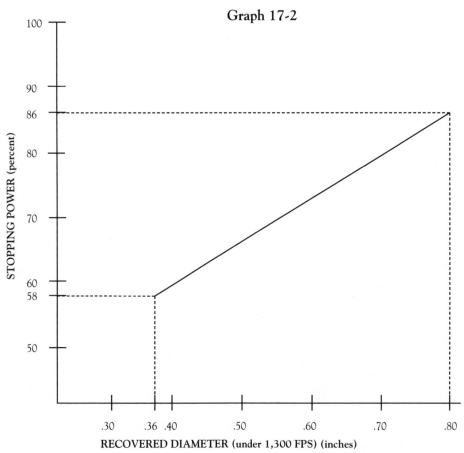

Graph 17-3

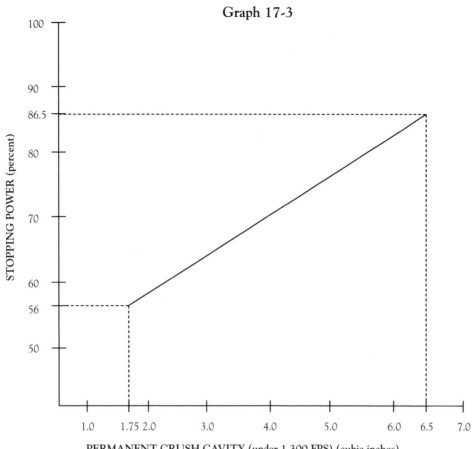

PERMANENT CRUSH CAVITY (under 1,300 FPS) (cubic inches)

Graph 17-4

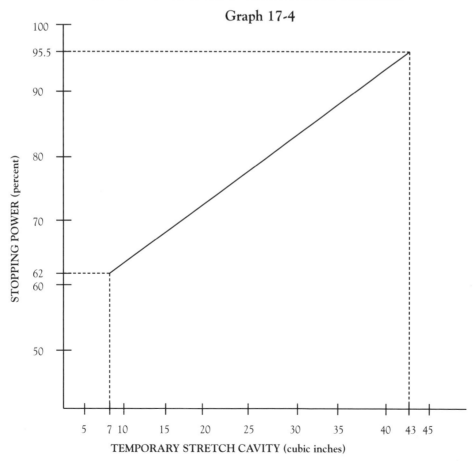

TEMPORARY STRETCH CAVITY (cubic inches)

CHAPTER 18

NEW AMMO DEVELOPMENTS

Since the FBI's Miami shootout in 1986, numerous new calibers have been released. Most are directly or indirectly related to the expensive FBI effort to find "the ideal cartridge." The "new release" with the best actual street record actually had been around for quite some time. Ironically, it was never even considered by the FBI. This cartridge is the 9mm +P+.

9MM +P+

American law enforcement is rapidly moving away from the double-action revolver. The move is away from the .38 Special +P and the mighty .357 Magnum and toward the 9mm, 9mm +P+, 10mm mid-range, .40 S&W, and .45 Auto. Of all the cartridges and calibers for the auto pistol, the one with the best street record *by far* is the 9mm +P+.

The top 9mm +P+ load is the Federal 9BP-LE 115-grain JHP, with an effectiveness of 88.46 percent. The best .45 Auto load is the Federal 230-grain Hydra-Shok, with an effectiveness of 83.33 percent. Early results on the 10mm mid-range and .40 S&W are in the 80-percent range. Technically the full-power 10mm is the most effective auto pistol load, but very few in law enforcement use it because it recoils like a .41 Magnum and produces excessive penetration.

The 9mm +P+ has a maximum average chamber pressure of 40,000 psia (pounds per square inch, absolute). As a comparison, the standard-pressure 9mm has a maximum pressure of 37,400 psia, while the 9mm NATO has a limit of 42,000 psia. The 9mm +P+ is midway between the standard 9x19mm and the mil-spec NATO cartridge.

In 1966, the Illinois State Police became the first major American police department to adopt the 9mm auto pistol. It started off with 124-grain FMJ hard ball, as the governor at that time would not allow hollowpoints. In 1969 Winchester began working with the ISP to improve the round's stopping power. They attempted to use hydrostatic shock and larger temporary stretch cavities that came from higher-velocity bullets. They tried a 100-grain FMJ, then a 100-grain JSP called the "power point." Neither showed an improvement.

In 1972, Federal joined the search for better stopping power with a 95-grain JSP "cup point" designed just for the ISP. With feed reliability problems and erratic performance in tissue, however, this was not the answer. The softpoint had been developed about as far as it could go.

In 1978, the ISP got approval for hollowpoints and adopted the ill-fated aluminum-jacketed 9mm 115-grain Silvertip. Accuracy problems, weapon fouling, and powder contaminations forced this load to be withdrawn. Winchester replaced it with a 95-grain version of its 100-grain "power point." In 1980, the ISP awarded its ammo contract to Federal, which supplied its 115-grain JHP 9BP. Even though the ISP now had the most effective load in decades, they still wanted more power. The standard-pressure 9mm was no match for the .357 Magnum against people or cars.

Since Federal had the ammo contract, it was Federal who pioneered the higher-pressure 9mm. This was not the +P+ but was the first step toward it. They powered their 115-grain JHP bullet to 1,260 fps. This was the original 9BP-Law Enforcement that today sits at

This Winchester 9mm +P+ 115-grain JHP is the issue load of the Illinois State Police. It works as well as a 110-grain .357 Magnum in actual shootings.

At 1,260 fps, this Remington 9mm +P 115-grain JHP was used by a narcotics officer to stop a cop killer. Remington also has a 9mm +P+ at 1,300 fps for police use only.

This Remington 9mm +P+ 115-grain JHP was used to stop a holdup man. These 9mm loads top the caliber with 86- to 89-percent effectiveness.

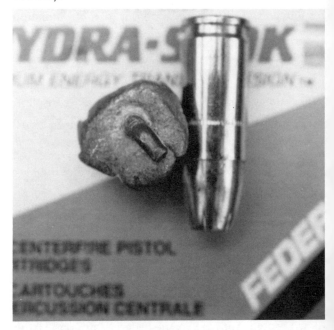

This Federal 9mm +P+ 124-grain Hydra-Shok was used by a cop to stop a car thief. This underdeveloped load is effective 82 percent of the time.

the very top of all 9x19mm loads in actual street results.

In late 1982, the ISP wrote its own specification for higher-pressure ammo, calling for a minimum of 1,300 fps. Federal was concerned about the chamber pressure — using flake powder, it was required to hit 1,300 fps with 115-grain bullets. They stayed at 1,260 fps. Using ball powder, Winchester met the 1,300 fps minimum and have supplied the ISP ever since.

The Winchester load is the Q4174, which uses a

115-grain JHP with Silvertip-style serrations and a copper jacket but no nickel plating. The load has risen to second overall in the 9mm caliber, just behind the Federal 9BP-LE.

In 1987, Federal, Remington, and Winchester announced a +P+ load for general police use. Remington makes both a +P+ and a civilian +P version of the 115-grain JHP, and IMI-Samson has a +P version available without restriction. By this time the demand from police agencies for an improved 9mm was quite heavy. Many departments had given up .357 magnums for the 9mm, but they still wanted magnum ballistics. The 9mm +P+ was the answer.

The 9mm +P+ 115-grain JHP has a street record, falling exactly midway between the standard-pressure 9mm 115-grain JHP and the .357 Magnum 125-grain JHP. The 9mm +P+ 115-grain JHP loads from Federal and Winchester exactly equal the actual stopping power of the .357 Magnum 110-grain JHP.

10MM (FULL POWER)

By bridging the gap between the 9mm and .45 Auto, the full-power 10mm cartridge was supposed to replace the .45 Auto. It was a joint effort of many people, including Whit Collins, Jeff Cooper, Dornaus & Dixon, and FFV Norma AB.

The goal was to split the difference in bore diameter between the 9mm (.355) and the .45 Auto (.451). The result was 170- and 200-grain .40-caliber bullets. That was the good news. The problem was the velocity.

The original thinking was also to split the velocity between the 9mm at 1,100 fps and .45 Auto at 900 fps to come up with a 1,000 fps load. However, this would not make the impressive ballistics on the Relative Stopping Power scale that some wanted. If a little velocity is good, a lot must be better, the early designers thought, so they jumped right over the 9mm velocity of 1,100 fps and loaded the 165-grain and then 170-grain JHP bullets at 1,250 fps.

The result was a 10mm cartridge that totally outclassed both the 9mm and .45 Auto. It even outpowered the .357 Magnum, at least on paper. Ballistically speaking, the full-power 10mm is, in fact, a .41 Magnum. That is wonderful when it comes to the effect on the target, but not so neat in its effect on the gun and the shooter.

The hot Norma ammo cracked the slide or frame on nearly every Bren Ten auto pistol for which it was developed. The 10mm was also hard on shooters. For those who felt that the .45 Auto hard ball kicked a lot, the full-power 10mm was intolerable. It kicked 20 percent *more* than the .45 Auto hard ball and the hot .357 magnum hollowpoints.

By all accounts, the Bren Ten project was a total disaster. The 10mm did not become the ideal defensive caliber because it kicked too much and shot-to-shot response time was too long. Early Norma JHP ammo did not expand much beyond .61 caliber, so the energy transfer was poor. The Bren Ten guns suffered mechanical problems due to both design and hot ammo. Magazines for the weapons were not available. The novelty of the full endorsement by Jeff Cooper soon wore off and Dornaus & Dixon went out of business. The full-power 10mm almost died.

Yet the round flashed onto the scene again in early 1987 when Colt released the Delta Elite 10mm. Norma teamed up with Colt in this venture but kept the same stout ballistics. The Delta Elite handgun was an immediate success with people who could not afford the earlier Bren Ten. Anyone who wanted a 10mm could now have one, including as many spare magazines as they wanted, thanks to the production might of Colt.

However, this too backfired. Now everyone knew that the full-power 10mm was too much in terms of recoil, not just those with the big bucks and patience to get a Bren Ten. The Delta Elite gave the hungry shooting public the 10mm they asked for, only to prove that it was not what most people wanted. By late 1988, the round was near death again.

The 10mm fills a very narrow niche in the firearms market. For all practical purposes, it is the most powerful auto pistol cartridge available. When viewed in that light rather than as an ideal defensive caliber, the full-power 10mm takes on a whole new meaning. While it has the ballistics of a .41 Magnum, it is better to think of it as a .44 Magnum. The 10mm works great from an auto pistol in the same kind of scenarios that the .44 Magnum works great from a revolver.

The .44 Magnum is *not* the ideal police and defensive caliber, and neither for the same reasons is the 10mm. Both have power to spare for any handgun use, both penetrate deeply enough to be legendary, and both kick enough to require that only the most dedicated handgunner try to tackle them.

The 10mm is available in about a dozen different JHP bullet weight and velocity combinations. The 150- to 155-grain JHP ammo has velocities around 1,325 fps, while the 170- to 180-grain ammo is generally loaded around 1,250 fps. Penetration in ordnance gelatin varies from 13 to 23 inches. Nearly all of the ammo expands well into the .70-caliber range and then fragments.

With 600 foot-pounds of energy to toss around, all of the full-power 10mm ammo will do the job of an autoloaded magnum, but one load stands out as especially effective. This is the Winchester 175-grain Silvertip. While the .41 and .44 Magnum Silvertips are downloaded slightly for better recoil control, Winchester did not do this with the 10mm Silvertip. It has the dubious honor of producing the most recoil of any 10mm ammo on the market. However, the 1,266-fps Silvertip also hits the hardest of any conventional 10mm JHP bullet.

The .40-caliber 10mm STHP expands to a full .81 caliber and holds it. The Silvertip penetrates an ideal 12.8 inches. The crush cavity measures 6.6 cubic inches, while the stretch cavity measures 40.5 cubic inches. This gives the 10mm Silvertip a predicted

This Winchester 10mm subsonic JHP expanded very well but did not stop the attack. These loads will be between 78- to 80-percent effective.

effectiveness of 89.9 percent, which is better than all the .41 and .44 Magnum loads. If you are going to suffer with the full-power 10mm recoil, the best load to pick is the Silvertip.

10MM FBI (REDUCED VELOCITY)

The reduced-velocity 10mm dates back to late 1988. The full-power 10mm, now widely available in the form of the Delta Elite, had turned off all but hard-core shooters due to its excessive recoil. Then reports started to surface that the FBI was interested in a "modified" 10mm. The industry was buzzing with conflicting reports, even among ammo company insiders. First, the talk was of a new 9.8mm cartridge, then of a 10mm auto that fired a shortened 10mm cartridge. Finally, the story became clear.

The FBI wanted a reduced-velocity version of the 10mm cartridge. They bought into the idea that a .40-caliber bullet may be better than a 9mm or a .45 Auto. But they wanted nothing to do with the 1,250-fps ammo because of recoil. The FBI wanted the felt recoil to match the .45 Auto exactly.

Federal Cartridge made a special run of Sierra 180-grain JHP bullets in Norma 10mm cases, loading them to the 1,035-fps level specified by the FBI (the velocity from a 6-inch test barrel). The FBI fired this reduced-velocity load against other calibers in a battery of tests. They published restricted side-by-side results in December 1988 and again in January and March 1989. The 10mm, in an altered state, caught its third wind and was off and running again.

As released by Federal, the final FBI-spec 10mm has a velocity of 980 fps from a 4.25-inch S&W Model 1076. The 180-grain JHP produces controllable recoil and excellent accuracy. It expands to an average

of .68 caliber and penetrates 15 inches of gelatin.

In a direct comparison, Federal .45 Auto 185-grain JHP and the Federal 10mm FBI 180-grain JHP produce the exact same wound ballistics not only in bare gelatin but also after the whole series of FBI obstacle tests. The 10mm FBI penetrates about 2 inches deeper on the average than the .45 Auto and that is the only real difference.

The mid-range load is clearly the way to go for the 10mm used in a defensive role and all the ammo companies know it. Federal released a 10mm reduced-velocity 180-grain Hydra-Shok at the 1990 SHOT Show. Winchester released a mid-range 180-grain 10mm JHP in its Ranger ammo line. Remington, too, released a 180-grain, 950-fps, 10mm JHP to go with its 170-grain, 1,260-fps, full-power JHP. CCI is also releasing a 180-grain JHP load at reduced velocities.

All these loads have excellent feed reliability and acceptable accuracy. They all penetrate between 13.8 and 15.5 inches of gelatin and expand to between .62 and .68 caliber. The crush and stretch cavities for all four loads are nearly identical. The estimated effectiveness varies from 76.3 percent for the Remington to 79.5 percent for the FBI-spec Federal. This places all these loads exactly in the middle of the actual results for the .45 Auto.

.41 ACTION EXPRESS

The .41x22mm Action Express started off in 1985 with great promise. The cartridge was a cross between the 9mm and 10mm. It fired a .41-caliber slug similar to the 10mm but used a 9mm case extractor rim. The 860 to 1,030 fps muzzle velocity was ideal, making the .41 AE the perfect overall combat cartridge.

But it was not to be. Winchester and Smith & Wesson had the inside track with the FBI. The .41 AE was obsolete by the 1990 release of the .40 S&W. Turn around is fair play. The .41 AE was based on a shortened .41 Magnum.

Many attempts have been made at a .40 caliber, 1,000 fps load. Prior to the .41 AE, one of the more successful wildcats was the .40 Guns & Ammo in 1971. Whit Collins, father of the high-pressure 10mm, designed the .40 G&A to fire a 180-grain bullet at 1,050 fps. Then came the full-power 10mm, then the downsized "Centimeter" wildcat.

The .41 AE was developed by Evan Whilden, formerly of Action Arms. Whilden simply shortened the .41 Magnum cartridge and made it into a rebated rim case, with the same head size as the 9mm Parabellum. This increased case capacity even though the cartridge's overall length remained at the 9mm level. The use of a rebated rim enabled weapons design for the 9mm Para-

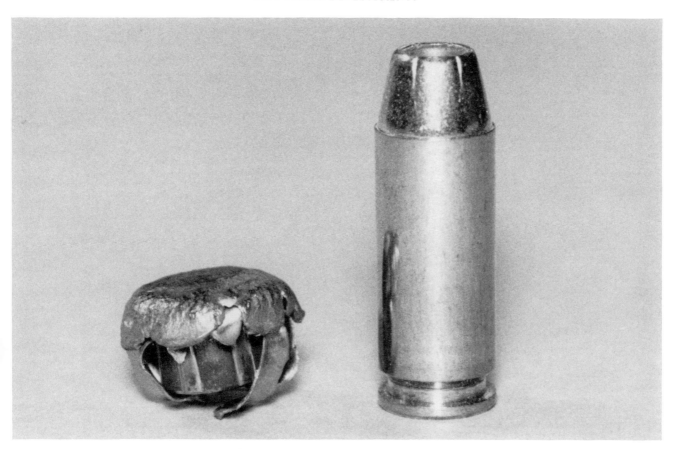

The Federal reduced-velocity 10mm was specified by the FBI to use a 180-grain Sierra bullet loaded to 1,035 fps from a 6-inch test barrel. This bullet was recovered from gelatin.

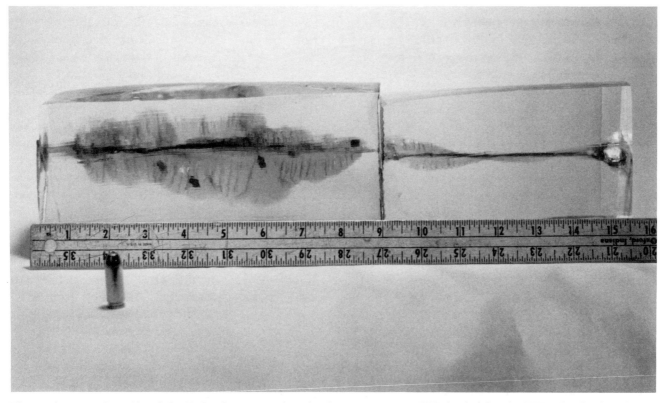

This is the wound profile of the Federal 10mm reduced-velocity 180-grain JHP loaded for the FBI. This load performs like an average .45 Auto hollowpoint and will be effective about 78 percent of the time.

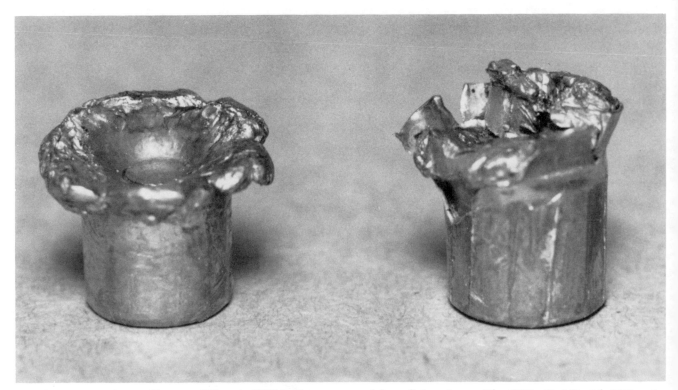

IMI-Samson .41 Action Express 170-grain JHP bullets recovered from living tissue. The CCI .41 AE with 180-grain plated hollowpoint bullets should expand to much larger diameters.

bellum to be easily modified or converted to the .41 AE.

The result was an auto pistol cartridge that fired a faster bullet than the .45 Auto and a heavier, larger-diameter bullet than the 9mm. Best of all, the big bore could be fired from a 9mm-sized pistol. No major changes needed to be made on the pistol or magazine. Even the extractor claw stayed the same.

The .41 AE is the only modern cartridge to use a rebated rim. This is an old rim design where the diameter of the extractor rim is much narrower than the diameter of the case. Cartridges like the .38 Special use a fully rimmed case where the rim is much larger than the case. The case headspaces on this rim and is both extracted and ejected by it.

The next rim style is the semirimmed case. Of the popular handgun calibers, only the .25 Auto and the .38 Super Auto use this design. The diameter of the rim is slightly greater than the case diameter to allow the auto-fed case to headspace on the rim yet work well in box magazines. As it turned out, the semirim created more accuracy problems than it solved. The .38 Super, for example, rarely chambers in a way to engage the semirim. As competitors who use the .38 Super know, the first step to accuracy in this caliber is a Bar-Sto barrel that headspaces the .38 Super on its case mouth.

The most popular rim design for semiauto and full-auto actions is the rimless case. Of course, cartridges like the .380 Auto, 9mm, 10mm, and .45 Auto still have an extractor rim. The case is called rimless because the rim is exactly the same diameter as the case — it does not stick out. This design is the easiest to feed from a box magazine, as the rim cannot interfere with the rims of other rounds in the magazine. The rimless case also lies flat in the magazine as opposed to nose down from a raised rim.

The cartridge design with the rim actually smaller than the case diameter is called the rebated rim. This makes for a most unusual-looking cartridge, but one that can be perfectly functional in semiauto and full-auto weapons. The natural question is why use this rim design when the rimless design is so proven? Due to the rebated rim, it is far easier to *convert* a 9mm-frame gun to the .41 AE than to the 10mm or the .40 S&W.

The .41 AE is a low-pressure cartridge like the .45 Auto as opposed to the higher-pressure 9mm and 10mm. As a result, the .41 AE can be fired by auto pistols of the same strength and, more importantly, of the same size as 9mm pistols. In fact, as designed by Action Arms, the same English and Italian guns can be used to fire both the 9mm and .41 AE by simply switching the barrel and recoil spring. The ejector and extractor are the same.

The goal in designing the .41 AE was to use 9mm firing and extracting hardware to cycle the round. That is why the back half of the .41 AE really is 9mm.

A larger-diameter barrel simply is needed to fire the larger-diameter bullet. The end result is a compact 9mm-sized auto pistol that fires a big-bore slug.

The only ammo popularly available for the .41 AE is made by Israel Military Industries. This Samson ammo normally has an excellent reputation for accuracy and reliability. However, the .41 AE suffered from both underdevelopment and technical problems associated with the rebated rim design.

The two IMI-Samson loads in .41 AE are the 170-grain JHP at 1,030 fps and the 200-grain FMJ-FP at 860 fps. The JHP generates 400 foot-pounds of energy. Both loads produce the exact same felt recoil as a .45 Auto 185-grain JHP, and both are extremely accurate, with 50-yard groups under 4 inches from a carbine.

The 170-grain JHP looks perfect on paper. It has a truncated cone bullet with a generous amount of exposed lead and a heavily serrated jacket. The development problem is that the bullet does not expand much in gelatin. The .41-caliber JHP opened to .46 caliber at best. After a bone was struck in living tissue, the JHP expanded to .56 caliber. Just like the Norma 10 mm JHP, the IMI .41 AE very much needed to be "Americanized" with a softer lead core and thinner, annealed copper jacket.

The other problem with the .41 AE is in the basic rim design. The diameter and the length of the cartridge versus the angle of the rebated rim as it slides under the extractor claw work against one another to hamper perfect reliability — at least that is the mechanical theory. And in practice we did see some stoppages that seemed to agree with the theory. This happened to both the English and Italian pistols and the Israeli carbine.

The .41 AE appears to be quite sensitive to the part of the feed cycle where the rim slides under the claw. Any surface roughness on the bolt face or extractor makes this worse. However, .41 AE weapons can be made quite reliable simply by polishing the bolt face, deburring the extractor, and keeping the gun clean and oiled.

The .41 AE was just slightly ahead of its time and its popularity was short-lived for such a good cartridge. The advantages it had over other auto pistol cartridges were partially lost when the medium-velocity 10mm was released. The final blow was the .40 S&W, which has all of the advantages of the .41 AE and none of the drawbacks.

.45 ACP +P

In mid-1987, Remington Arms announced improvements to its standard-pressure .45 Auto 185-grain JHP. The core was made softer by lowering the antimony content and the thickness of the copper jacket was reduced to allow it to peel back more easily. These changes were geared toward more reliable expansion and expansion to larger calibers.

During this time, Remington also experimented with a higher-pressure, higher-velocity load. The phrase "velocity is everything" refers not only to the positive effect of increased velocity on the temporary stretch cavity, but also to the ability to get through tactical obstacles such as heavy clothing and assure reliable expansion.

The most street-proven way to increase the effectiveness of any bullet in a caliber is to increase its velocity. This was dramatically proven in 9mm by pushing the same 115-grain JHP bullet to +P+ velocities. The stopping power increased. The same holds true in reverse. With the same 125-grain JHP bullet, as the velocity drops from .357 Magnum to .357 Magnum medium velocity to .38 Special +P, the stopping power goes down each time. This occurs with no other changes other than just lowering velocity. Velocity *is* everything in the context of personal defense handgun ammo.

In 1989, Remington Arms became the first major manufacturer to release a +P hollowpoint for the .45 Auto. The load uses the same 185-grain JHP as the company's standard-pressure load. The only change in the +P load is the kind and amount of powder. Larger charges of a slower-burning powder with a flatter and longer power curve were used. The maximum average chamber pressure for the standard .45 Auto is 21,000 psia. The +P ammo has a loading limit of 23,000 psia.

The change in powder burn rate and charge jumped the velocity from 940 fps to 1,128 fps. The energy jumped from 9mm levels to .357 Magnum levels and quite close to full-power 10mm levels. Of course, the recoil from the .45 Auto +P is also in the full-power 10mm range and exceeds the stiffest .357 Magnum.

The Remington .45 Auto +P 185-grain JHP expands violently on impact and then fragments to a recovered diameter of .55 caliber. This is exactly how the 9mm +P+ and .357 Magnum hollowpoints perform. A bullet that will fragment in gelatin will at least always expand in less predictable soft tissue. This bullet penetrates an ideal 12.25 inches of gelatin.

This +P load produces an average-size crush cavity for the .45 Auto caliber. However, it produces a stretch cavity much larger than any .45 Auto JHP. In fact, the wound profile is as large and violent as the best .357 Magnum and full-power 10mm.

The actual street results compiled at the time of publication do not reflect how strong this .45 Auto +P load really is. With a 2.9-cubic-inch crush cavity

This is the wound profile in ordnance gelatin of the Remington .45 Auto +P 185-grain JHP. The stretch cavity is as large as the best .357 Magnum and 10mm hollowpoints.

The new Remington .45 Auto +P 185-grain JHP has more power than any other .45 Auto load. Underrated at only 83-percent effective, this slug stopped a 400-pound man high on PCP.

The Remington .45 Auto +P load turns the .45 Auto into a full-power 10mm. This slug stopped a mob hit man with one shot.

and a 58.2-cubic-inch stretch cavity, we estimate this load to have an effectiveness of 86.4 percent. The actual effectiveness based on 24 shootings is 83.33 percent. When more shootings with the .45 Auto +P take place, the recorded effectiveness should go up. For all practical purposes, the .45 Auto +P, full-power

10mm, and .41 Magnum have the same wound ballistics.

.40 SMITH & WESSON

The FBI has been looking for the "ideal" police cartridge and bullet ever since their April 11, 1986, shootout in Miami. They quickly dropped the 9mm

The .40 S&W is certain to make 10mm reduced-velocity ammo obsolete and become the cartridge of the 1990s. These 180-grain JHP loads will be effective in the 80- to 90-percent range.

115-grain Silvertip and adopted the low-velocity 147-grain Silvertip serrated JHP. This 9mm round was *not* the "ideal" bullet. It specifically was an interim load and nothing more. It gave up a lot of wound ballistics to get greater penetration, which was exactly what the FBI wanted until they could sort everything out.

Working with Federal Cartridge, the FBI spec'd out a lower-recoil version of the hot 10mm cartridge. They called for a 180-grain Sierra "power jacket" serrated JHP at 950 fps. The full-power 10mm kicks too much for fast follow-up shooting. The FBI wanted a load that recoiled no more than a .45 Auto, and the mid-range 10mm met that requirement.

Smith & Wesson was awarded the contract for the FBI 10mm auto pistols. The result was the Model 1076 based on the large frame of the .45 Auto Model 4506. In fact, the .45 Auto Model 4506 and 10mm Model 1006 are virtually identical. The result was a large-frame auto firing a mid-range, mid-bore cartridge. That is like using an N-frame Model 27 .357 Magnum to fire a .38 Special +P — no problem with weapon control, but the piece *is* big.

Sometime during this development, S&W committed to the FBI to "optimize" its Model 1076. Since the 10mm FBI was a download, the Model 1076 would be downsized. S&W approached Winchester-Olin for a more optimal cartridge case. The company wanted a smaller case, but it insisted that the new round produce the same ballistics as the 10mm FBI.

S&W was in a perfect position to design a small .40 mid-range load. Some years before it had designed a prototype .40 caliber based on the 9mm case length

and rim design called the .40 S&W. It was never released nor was it ever even produced as a wildcat. Evan Whilden, formerly of Action Arms, later used the same principles as a starting point for his .41 Action Express.

The resulting new cartridge from the S&W and Winchester joint venture was again called the .40 Smith & Wesson. Officially, it is Smith & Wesson's cartridge and the company's first to be headstamped since the obsolete .35 S&W, introduced in 1913.

The new .40 S&W approximates a .41 AE case with a full-case-diameter "rimless" rim. The new .40 S&W was in many ways developed from the .41 AE — same case length, same overall cartridge length, same small pistol primer, nearly the same bullet diameter, just an increased rim diameter.

S&W and Winchester were concerned enough about the rebated rim design to change it on the new .40 S&W to the more conventional rimless design like the .45 Auto and 10mm. Some have said that the .40 S&W is a case-shortened 10mm. This is not true. The 10mm case is thicker to withstand higher pressures and uses a large pistol primer.

S&W, for its part, modified a 9mm-frame Model 5900-series auto pistol to accept the new .40 S&W. The result is a compact Model 4006. After nearly a half-dozen recent attempts, the shooting world had a .40/10mm-sized bullet fired from a compact 9mm-sized auto pistol.

When originally released, the .40 S&W was to have a 4-inch muzzle velocity of 990 fps. The only way Winchester could achieve this velocity was from an extremely dense load of Olin ball powder. Those who handload know that ball powder works well only within specific ranges of loading density. As early production ammo left the factory, the velocity had already dropped. As it stands now, the .40 S&W 180-grain JHP from Winchester produces 956 fps from a 4½-inch Glock 23. The early reports of 980 fps from a 4-inch S&W Model 4006 were gone. The more realistic figures of 950 fps are now being quoted.

The .40 S&W and 10mm fire the same .40-caliber projectile and have the same rim design. This means the lower-pressure .40 S&W can be fired safely from higher-pressure 10mm handguns. While both cases headspace on the cartridge mouth, the 10mm extractor will hold the .40 S&W in place, causing it to headspace on its rim. The .40 S&W bullet will have to jump a .142-inch freebore, but every .38 Special bullet ever fired from a .357 Magnum revolver jumped a .140-inch freebore before it jumped the .006-inch cylinder-to-barrel gap.

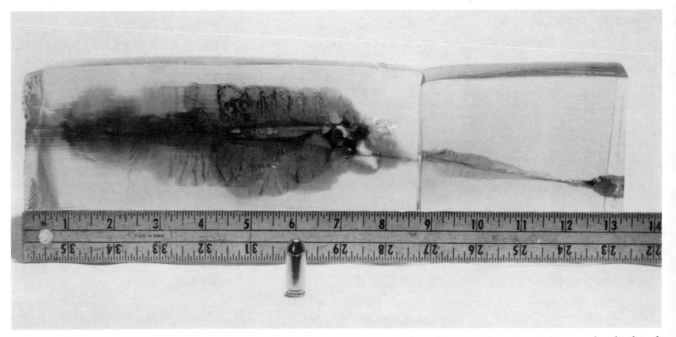

The wound profile of the Winchester .40 S&W 180-grain JHP. Note that the stretch cavity is long and cylindrical rather than short and spherical. This performance will tolerate secondary targets like arms without robbing all the bullet's stopping power.

This promising police load hits gelatin *very* hard. It produced 13.25 inches of penetration, which is just perfect. The top police load of all time, the .357 Magnum 125-grain JHP, also produces 13.25 inches of penetration. Based on actual police-action shootings, slugs that penetrate deeper than this amount produce less stopping power.

The .40 S&W expanded to between .63 and .64 caliber. It expanded to the bottom of the hollowpoint cavity and kept expanding. Any slug that expands this completely in gelatin is sure to expand to .60 caliber in an actual shooting regardless of the tissue it engages.

The shape of the stretch cavity tells how reliable the cartridge will be on the street. A more street-dependable and obstacle-tolerant load has an oblong, football-shaped stretch cavity, indicating moderate energy release. In this regard, the .40 S&W produces a long and steady stretch cavity, perfect for police and personal defense. The cavity does not start to taper off until 7 inches deep. That is quite unusual and quite good.

Using the depth of penetration, diameter of the recovered bullet, and the volumes of the stretch and crush cavities, it is possible to predict the percent of one-shot stops this new cartridge will produce. We expect the Winchester .40 S&W 180-grain JHP to be about 75.5 percent effective.

In November 1990, the California Highway Patrol became the first major agency to adopt the .40 S&W. This is, in fact, the police and personal defense big-bore cartridge that will carry us well into the next century. The .40 S&W is a near-perfect balance of recoil, stopping power, weapon size, and ammo capacity.

The debate will no longer be 9mm versus .45 Auto. Instead it will be 9mm +P+ versus .40 S&W. Right now the 9mm +P+ has a solid lead, with an actual success on the street of between 86 and 89 percent. However, the U.S. Border Patrol wants a hot 150-grain, 1,150-fps JHP for its .40 S&W auto pistols. That could give the 9mm +P+ a real run for the first time.

As we go to press, over a dozen loads for the .40 S&W are available. These vary from the fast and light 155-grain Winchester Silvertip at 1,205 fps to the conventional 180-grain JHPs to the 180-grain Federal Hydra-Shok and the 1,800-fps MagSafe. The top conventional JHP is the 150-grain Sierra JHP loaded by Master Cartridge to 1,100 fps. This velocity allows the bullet to retain a .73-caliber mushroom for a predicted effectiveness of 91.6 percent. The Hydra-Shok is close behind and the best of the 180-grain loads, with an estimated rating of 89.3 percent.

TERMS

AP: armor piercing
BAT: Blitz Action Trauma
BHP: brass hollowpoint
CCI: CCI-Speer, Division of Blount, Inc.
Fed: Federal
FMJ: full-metal jacket, same as round-nose hardball
fps: feet per second
Horn: Hornady
JHP: jacketed hollowpoint
JSP: jacketed softpoint
LHP: lead hollowpoint (same as SWC-HP
    and SWC-LHP)
LR: long rifle
med. vel.: medium or mid-range pressure and velocity
MTC: maximum temporary cavity

OSM: Olin Super Match
+P: higher pressure and velocity
+P+: highest pressure and velocity
Rem: Remington
RNL: round-nose lead
R-P: Remington-Peters
S&W: Smith & Wesson
S-JHP: semijacketed hollowpoint
STHP: Silvertip jacketed hollowpoint
SWC: semiwadcutter
SWC-HP: semiwadcutter hollowpoint
SWC-LHP semiwadcutter lead hollowpoint
WC: wadcutter
WCF: Winchester centerfire
W-W: Winchester-Western

TEST WEAPONS FOR VELOCITY

.32 ACP	Walther PPK
.380 ACP	SIG P230
.38 Special and +P (2-inch barrel)	Colt Cobra
.38 Special, +P and +P+ (4-inch barrel)	S&W Model 10
9mm, 9mm +P and 9mm +P+	S&W Model 5906
.357 Magnum	S&W Model 686 w/4-inch barrel
.41 Magnum	S&W Model 58 w/4-inch barrel
.44 Special	S&W Model 24 w/4-inch barrel
.44 Magnum	S&W Model 629 w/4-inch barrel
.45 Auto	Colt Govt w/5-inch barrel
.45 Long Colt	S&W Model 25-5 w/4-inch barrel

ACTUAL BULLET EFFECTIVENESS

Caliber	Total Shootings	One-Shot Stops	Percentage	Muzzle Velocity
A. .32 ACP				
1. W-W 60-gr. STHP	71	43	60.56	816 fps
2. W-W 71-gr. FMJ	98	49	50.00	784 fps
B. .380 ACP				
1. Fed 90-gr. JHP	106	69	65.09	1,003 fps
2. PPS 54-gr. BHP (MPP)	14	8	57.14	1,142 fps
3. W-W 85-gr. STHP	59	32	54.23	985 fps
4. R-P 88-gr. JHP	37	20	54.05	1,001 fps
5. CCI 88-gr. JHP	30	16	53.33	933 fps
6. Horn 90-gr. JHP	19	10	52.63	985 fps
7. Fed 95-gr. FMJ	87	45	51.74	929 fps
C. .38 Special and +P (2-inch barrel)				
1. W-W 158-gr. LHP +P	75	50	66.66	789 fps
2. Fed 158-gr. LHP +P	38	25	65.78	783 fps
3. Rem 158-gr. LHP +P	39	25	64.10	781 fps
4. Fed 125-gr. JHP +P	45	28	62.22	819 fps
5. Rem 125-gr. S-JHP +P	69	42	60.86	845 fps
6. CCI 125-gr. JHP +P	35	20	57.14	822 fps
7. W-W 125-gr. JHP +P	41	23	56.09	816 fps
8. Fed 125-gr. JHP +P	68	36	52.94	878 fps
9. R-P 95-gr. S-JHP +P	88	46	52.27	1,023 fps
10. W-W 110-gr. JHP +P	73	37	50.68	924 fps
11. Fed 158-gr. SWC (not +P)	89	44	49.43	652 fps
12. Fed 158-gr. RNL (not +P)	206	101	49.02	599 fps

Caliber	Total Shootings	One-Shot Stops	Percentage	Muzzle Velocity
D. .38 Special, +P and +P+ (4-inch barrel)				
1. W-W 158-gr. LHP +P	222	167	75.22	992 fps
2. Fed 158-gr. LHP +P	163	116	71.16	971 fps
3. Rem 158-gr. LHP +P	114	79	69.29	926 fps
4. W-W 110-gr. JHP +P+ (Q4070)	16	11	68.75	1,126 fps
5. Fed 125-gr. JHP +P	183	126	68.85	991 fps
6. Rem 125-gr. S-JHP +P	86	56	65.11	929 fps
7. CCI 125-gr. JHP +P	41	26	63.41	988 fps
8. W-W 125-gr. JHP +P	48	30	62.50	942 fps
9. Fed 125-gr. JSP +P	93	54	58.06	963 fps
10. R-P 95-gr. S-JHP +P	137	79	57.66	1,128 fps
11. Fed 158-gr. SWC (+P)	92	51	55.40	890 fps
12. W-W 110-gr. JHP +P	83	45	54.21	1,003 fps
13. Fed 158-gr. SWC (not +P)	174	92	52.87	767 fps
14. Fed 158-gr. RNL (not +P)	306	160	52.28	704 fps
E. 9mm, 9mm +P and 9mm +P+				
1. Fed 115-gr. JHP +P+ (9BP-LE)	76	68	89.47	1,304 fps
2. W-W 115-gr. JHP +P+ (Q4174)	63	56	88.88	1,299 fps
3. R-P 115-gr. JHP +P+	24	21	87.50	1,283 fps
4. GECO 86-gr. BHP (BAT)	89	75	84.26	1,493 fps
5. Fed 124-gr. LHP-Nyclad	185	150	81.08	1,101 fps
6. Fed 124-gr. Hydra-Shok +P+	26	21	80.76	1,264 fps
7. Fed 115-gr. JHP	147	118	80.27	1,177 fps
8. W-W 115-gr. STHP	216	173	80.09	1,204 fps
9. R-P 115-gr. JHP	106	81	76.42	1,163 fps
10. Fed 147-gr. JHP	25	19	76.00	985 fps
11. Fed 124-gr. Hydra-Shok	27	20	74.07	1,266 fps
12. CCI 115-gr. JHP	75	55	73.33	1,145 fps
13. Fed 147-gr. Hydra-Shok	57	41	71.92	988 fps
14. W-W 147-gr. JHP (OSM, Type L)	106	73	68.86	887 fps
15. Horn 90-gr. JHP	25	16	64.00	1,305 fps
16. Horn 115-gr. JHP	32	20	62.50	1,126 fps
17. W-W 115-gr. FMJ	159	99	62.26	1,149 fps
F. .357 Magnum				
1. Fed 125-gr. JHP	462	448	96.96	1,453 fps
2. R-P 125-gr S-JHP	139	130	93.52	1,467 fps
3. CCI 125-gr. JHP	84	78	92.85	1,383 fps
4. Fed 110-gr. JHP	63	57	90.47	1,366 fps
5. W-W 125-gr JHP	83	73	87.95	1,391 fps
6. R-P 110-gr. S-JHP	37	32	86.48	1,344 fps
7. W-W 145-gr. STHP	56	47	83.92	1,294 fps
8. W-W 110-gr. JHP	31	26	83.87	1,290 fps
9. CCI 110-gr. JHP	18	15	83.33	1,310 fps
10. R-P 125-gr. S-JHP (med. vel.)	12	10	83.33	1,280 fps
11. R-P 158-gr. S-JHP	27	22	81.48	1,233 fps

Caliber	Total Shootings	One-Shot Stops	Percentage	Muzzle Velocity
12. Fed 158-gr. JHP	58	47	81.03	1,217 fps
13. W-W 158-gr. JHP	72	57	79.16	1,259 fps
14. CCI 140-gr. JHP	23	17	73.91	1,330 fps
15. R-P 158-gr. JSP	23	17	73.39	1,235 fps
16. Fed 158-gr. LHP-Nyclad	11	8	72.73	1,190 fps
17. CCI 158-gr. JSP	29	21	72.41	1,178 fps
18. W-W 158-gr. SWC	89	64	71.91	1,319 fps
19. CCI 125-gr. JHP	14	10	71.43	1,410 fps
20. Fed 158-gr. SWC	45	32	71.11	1,152 fps
21. CCI 158-gr. JHP	20	14	70.00	1,240 fps
22. R-P 158-gr. SWC	71	48	67.60	1,149 fps

G. .41 Magnum

Caliber	Total Shootings	One-Shot Stops	Percentage	Muzzle Velocity
1. W-W 170-gr. STHP	50	44	88.00	1,299 fps
2. W-W 210-gr. JHP	29	24	82.75	1,260 fps
3. R-P 210-gr. JSP	28	23	82.14	1,219 fps
4. R-P 210-gr. SWC	46	35	76.08	944 fps
5. W-W 210-gr. SWC	39	29	74.35	956 fps

H. .44 Special

Caliber	Total Shootings	One-Shot Stops	Percentage	Muzzle Velocity
1. Fed 200-gr. LHP	39	28	71.79	802 fps
2. W-W 200-gr. STHP	45	32	71.11	819 fps
3. W-W 246-gr. RNL	52	36	69.23	704 fps
4. R-P 240-gr. SWC	11	7	63.63	851 fps

I. .44 Magnum

Caliber	Total Shootings	One-Shot Stops	Percentage	Muzzle Velocity
1. W-W 210-gr. STHP	38	34	89.47	1,301 fps
2. Fed 180-gr. JHP	23	20	86.95	1,406 fps
3. R-P 240-gr. S-JHP	22	19	86.36	1,266 fps
4. W-W 240-gr. JHP	39	32	82.05	1,204 fps
5. W-W 240-gr. SWC	44	36	81.81	1,259 fps
6. Fed 240-gr. JHP	35	28	80.00	1,255 fps
7. R-P 240-gr. SWC (med. vel.)	55	42	76.36	961 fps

J. .45 Auto

Caliber	Total Shootings	One-Shot Stops	Percentage	Muzzle Velocity
1. Fed 230-gr. Hydra-Shok	53	48	90.56	819 fps
2. Fed 185-gr. JHP	96	83	86.45	1,001 fps
3. R-P 185-gr. JHP +P	28	24	85.71	1,129 fps
4. CCI 200-gr. JHP	62	53	85.48	928 fps
5. W-W 185-gr. STHP	61	49	80.32	998 fps
6. R-P 185-gr. JHP	56	44	78.57	944 fps
7. W-W 230-gr. FMJ	139	89	64.02	837 fps
8. Fed 230-gr. FMJ	183	117	63.93	868 fps
9. R-P 230-gr. FMJ	102	62	60.72	799 fps

Caliber	Total Shootings	One-Shot Stops	Percentage	Muzzle Velocity
K. .45 Long Colt				
1. Fed 225-gr. LHP	57	44	77.19	806 fps
2. W-W 225-gr. STHP	46	34	73.91	853 fps
3. W-W 255-gr. RNL	85	59	69.41	706 fps
4. R-P 255-gr. SWC	14	9	64.28	808 fps

VALIDITY OF VARIOUS THEORIES OF HANDGUN STOPPING POWER

Theory	Restriction	Correlation
Thompson-LaGarde (permanent cavity)	RNL/FMJ only	.90
Cooper/Taylor-type modification to Thompson-LaGarde	all ammo & velocities	.64
Relative Incapacitation Index (temporary cavity)	all ammo & velocities	.67
Southwestern Institute of Forensic Sciences (energy loss)	all ammo & velocities	.81
FBI Multimedia Wound Value	all ammo & velocities	.53
Penetration (only)	all ammo & velocities	(-).37
Recovered Diameter (only)	below 1,300 fps	.82
Recovered Diameter (only)	above 1,300 fps	.68
Permanent Crush Cavity (only)	below 1,300 fps	.87
Permanent Crush Cavity (only)	above 1,300 fps	.60
Temporary Stretch Cavity (only)	all ammo & velocities	.80

SHOT PLACEMENT, BODY SIZE, CLOTHING

.357 Magnum-Federal 125-grain JHP (4-inch barrel)
Hits taken by adult males 180-190 lbs., between sternum and shoulders

total	*stops*	*percent*
69	67	97.10

Winter clothing - adult males 160-175 lbs., between sternum and shoulder

total	*stops*	*percent*
84	76	90.47

.38 Special W-W 158-grain lead HP +P (4-inch barrel)
Hits taken by adult males 180-190 lbs., between sternum and shoulders

total	*stops*	*percent*
53	39	73.58

Winter clothing - adult males 160-180 lbs., between sternum and shoulder

total	*stops*	*percent*
32	22	68.75

9mm-Federal 9BP (4-inch barrel) - adult males 180-200 lbs., between sternum and shoulders

total	*stops*	*percent*
34	28	82.35

9mm-Federal 9BP - adult males 160-170 lbs., winter clothing, between sternum and shoulders

total	*stop*	*percent*
26	21	80.76

.45 ACP-Winchester 230-grain FMJ - adult males 190-200 lbs., sternum to shoulder

total	*stops*	*percent*
51	35	68.62

.45ACP-Winchester 230-grain FMJ - adult males 160-170 lbs., winter clothing, sternum to shoulder

total	*stops*	*percent*
24	15	62.5

SELECT MUZZLE VELOCITIES FROM SPECIALTY AMMO

Glaser Safety Slug (fragmenting ammo)

.38 Special	80-grain	1,550 fps
.357 Magnum	80-grain	1,625 fps
9mm	80-grain	1,550 fps
.45 Auto	135-grain	1,350 fps

Brass Hollowpoints

.380 Auto MPP	54-grain	1,150 fps
9mm Action Safety	86-grain	1,493 fps
9mm Quick Defense	86-grain	1,325 fps
.45 Auto MMC	103-grain	1,400 fps

THV (brass pointed bullets)

.38 Special +P	42-grain	2,300 fps
.357 Magnum	42-grain	2,600 fps
9mm	44-grain	2,400 fps

Equaloy (aluminum semiwadcutter)

.38 Special +P	38-grain	2,070 fps

Multiple-Bullet Loads

.38 Special +P (PP)	163-grain	1,025 fps
.38 Special +P (SP)	250-grain	680 fps

Federal Nyclad (lead hollowpoint)

.38 Special	125-grain	750 fps
.38 Special +P	158-grain	890 fps
9mm	124-grain	1,100 fps
.357 Magnum	158-grain	1,200 fps

MagSafe (fragmenting ammo)

.38 Special +P	68-grain	1,490 fps
.38 Special +P+	65-grain	1,800 fps
.357 Magnum	70-grain	1,860 fps
9mm	68-grain	1,850 fps
.45 Auto	96-grain	1,760 fps
.45 Auto +P+	103-grain	1,900 fps
10mm	96-grain	1,800 fps
.40 S&W	84-grain	1,800 fps

Power Plus Beehive (fragmenting ammo)

9mm	85-grain	1,500 fps

PMC Ultramag (tubular brass bullets)

.38 Special +P	66-grain	1,435 fps
.44 Special	110-grain	1,085 fps

Handgun Shotshells

.38 Special (CCI)	105-grain	925 fps
.44 Magnum (3-Ten)	233-grain	1,220 fps

Federal Hydra-Shok (jacketed hollowpoint)

.38 Special +P	147-grain	900 fps
.357 Magnum	158-grain	1,235 fps
9mm	124-grain	1,120 fps
9mm	147-grain	990 fps
.45 Auto	230-grain	820 fps
10mm	180-grain	950 fps
.40 S&W	180-grain	950 fps

Cor-Bon Ammunition (maximum-velocity JHP ammo)

.38 Special +P+	115-grain	1,300 fps
9mm +P+	115-grain	1,350 fps
9mm +P+	125-grain	1,275 fps
9mm +P+	147-grain	1,100 fps
.45 Auto +P	185-grain	1,150 fps
.45 Auto +P	200-grain	1,050 fps
.40 S&W	150-grain	1,200 fps

ADDRESSES OF AMMUNITION MANUFACTURERS, IMPORTERS, AND DISTRIBUTORS

Action Arms, Limited
P.O. Box 9573
Philadelphia, PA 19124

Black Hills Ammunition
P.O. Box 5070
Rapid City, SD 57709

CCI-Speer/Blount Inc.
P.O. Box 856
Lewiston, ID 83501

Cor-Bon Bullets
P.O. Box 10126
Detroit, MI 48210

Federal Cartridge
900 Ehlen Drive
Anoka, MN 55303

Glaser Safety Slug
P.O. Box 8223
Foster City, CA 94404

Hi-Vel, Inc.
R2 Box 664-C
New Haven, KY 40051

Hornady Manufacturing
P.O. Box 1848
Grand Island, NE 68802

Kendall International
418 Fithian Ave.
Paris, KY 40361

MagSafe Ammo Co.
2725 Friendly Grove Rd. N.E.
Olympia, WA 98506

Master Cartridge
P.O. Box 238
Villa Rica, GA 30108

PMC-Eldorado
P.O. Box 308
Boulder City, NV 89005

Personal Protection Systems, Limited
R.D. #5, Box 5027-A
Moscow, PA 18444

Power Plus Enterprises
P.O. Box 6070
Columbus, GA 31907

Remington Arms
1007 Market Street
Wilmington, DE 19898

Sage International (police only)
630 Oakland Avenue
Pontiac, MI 48058

Sierra Bullets (bullets only)
1400 W. Henry Street
Sedalia, MO 65301

3-D Impact Ammo
112 Plum Street
Doniphan, NE 68832

3-Ten Corporation
P.O. Box 269
Feeding Hills, MA 01030

Winchester Group
Olin Corporation
Shamrock Street
East Alton, IL 62024

Zero Ammunition
P.O. Box 1188
Cullman, AL 35056

ABOUT THE AUTHORS

Evan Marshall was born on October 8, 1942, in Salt Lake City, Utah. At the time of his birth, his father was an experimental design engineer for a major ammunition firm. After attending grammar and high school in Redwood City, California, he attended Brigham Young University, Stanford University, and the University of Southern California. While at USC, he interrupted his education to spend two years as a Mormon missionary in Michigan and Indiana.

He and his wife, Maryann, were married in the Mormon Temple in Oakland, California, and then moved to Detroit, where Marshall attended Wayne State University. After graduating with a B.A. in History, he joined the Detroit Police Department.

His assignments as a police officer included: Second Precinct, Crime Lab, Crime Scene Investigation, Tactical Mobile Unit, and Court Selection. In January of 1976, he was promoted to Sergeant and assigned to the Sixteenth Precinct in northwest Detroit. Subsequent assignments included: Tactical Unit, Thirteenth Precinct, Homicide, Special Response Team, Homicide, and Eleventh Precinct Detectives. In 1982 he graduated from the University of Detroit with an M.A. in Criminal Justice. He retired in September of 1989.

He is currently the Director of Criminal Justice Studies at Kirtland Community College in Roscommon, Michigan. He has written extensively in the firearms and law enforcement press for the last 15 years and is a well-known instructor in the fields of hostage rescue and executive protection against terrorism.

He and his wife are the parents of seven children ranging in ages from 7 to 22. An Eagle Scout, he currently serves as a Scoutmaster in Midland, Michigan, where he lives. He and his family enjoy camping and hiking.

Ed Sanow was born on October 10, 1953, in Warren, Ohio. He attended Case Institute of Technology and Purdue University, earning a Bachelor of Science degree in Industrial Management with a minor in Industrial Engineering.

His law enforcement involvement began as a fire-arms instructor for road deputies prior to their academy training. He served one term as Deputy Marshal with the Boswell, Indiana, Police Department. He is a fully sworn reserve Deputy Sheriff with the Benton County, Indiana, Sheriff's Department. In addition to serving as instructor for firearms, chemical agents, and pursuit driving, he routinely performs the duties of county patrol, occasionally as the only unit on duty. He holds a Distinguished Expert firearms rating and currently holds the rank of corporal.

Sanow has toured the facilities of and held discussions with the R&D staffs at Winchester-Olin, Federal Cartridge, Hydra-Shok Corporation, and CCI-Speer. He has been a consultant to Glaser Safety Slug. He designed and developed the tellurium copper hollow-point loads currently marketed as .25 MSC, .380 MPP, and .45 MMC. He has served as an expert witness in both criminal and civil cases in Indiana and Georgia, and has authored hundreds of articles over the past 10 years on ammo and stopping power in both police and popular gun magazines.